Cradle of Gold

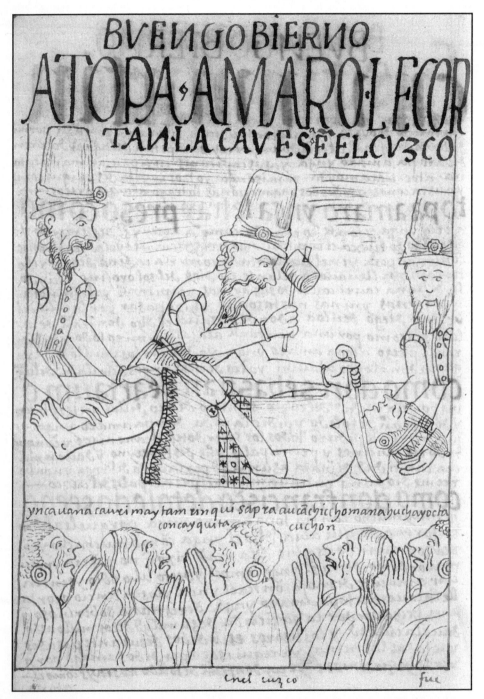

The Spaniards execute the last Inca emperor, Tupac Amaru, in Cuzco in 1572, as depicted by Guaman Poma de Ayala, an Inca noble and scribe, to appeal to the Spanish King in the early seventeenth century. Tupac Amaru's death was preceded by the loss of Vilcabamba, the Inca city that disappeared into the jungle until the twentieth century. (The Royal Library, Denmark)

Cradle of Gold

The Story of Hiram Bingham,
a Real-Life Indiana Jones,
and the Search for Machu Picchu

CHRISTOPHER HEANEY

palgrave
macmillan

Illustrations by Emily Davis Adams, in the style of the sixteenth-seventeenth–century indigenous scribe and artist Guaman Poma de Ayala

First published in 2010 by PALGRAVE MACMILLAN® in the United States–a division of St. Martin's Press LLC, 175 Fifth Avenue, New York, NY 10010.

Where this book is distributed in the UK, Europe, and the rest of the world, this is by Palgrave Macmillan, a division of Macmillan Publishers Limited, registered in England, company number 785998, of Houndmills, Basingstoke, Hampshire RG21 6XS.

Palgrave Macmillan is the global academic imprint of the above companies and has companies and representatives throughout the world.

Palgrave® and Macmillan® are registered trademarks in the United States, the United Kingdom, Europe and other countries.

ISBN-13: 978-0-230-61169-6

Library of Congress Cataloging-in-Publication Data
Heaney, Christopher.
    Cradle of gold : the story of Hiram Bingham, a real-life Indiana Jones, and the search for Machu Picchu / by Christopher Heaney.
        p.   cm.
    Includes bibliographical references and index.
    ISBN 978-0-230-61169-6 (hardback)
    1. Bingham, Hiram, 1875–1956. 2. Latin Americanists—United States—Biography. 3. Machu Picchu Site (Peru) 4. Incas—Antiquities. 5. Cultural property—Peru. 6. Incas—History. 7. Peru—History—Conquest, 1522–1548. I. Title.
F3429.B633H42 2010
974.6'04092—dc22
[B]

                                                                    2009038535

A catalogue record of the book is available from the British Library.

Design by Letra Libre, Inc.

First edition: April 2010

10 9 8 7 6 5 4 3 2 1

Printed in the United States of America.

For my parents,
and for JVD

All men dream: but not equally. Those who dream by night in the dusty recesses of their mind wake in the day to find that it was vanity: but the dreamers of the day are dangerous men, for they may act their dreams with open eyes, to make it possible.

—T. E. Lawrence, *Seven Pillars of Wisdom: A Triumph*

Contents

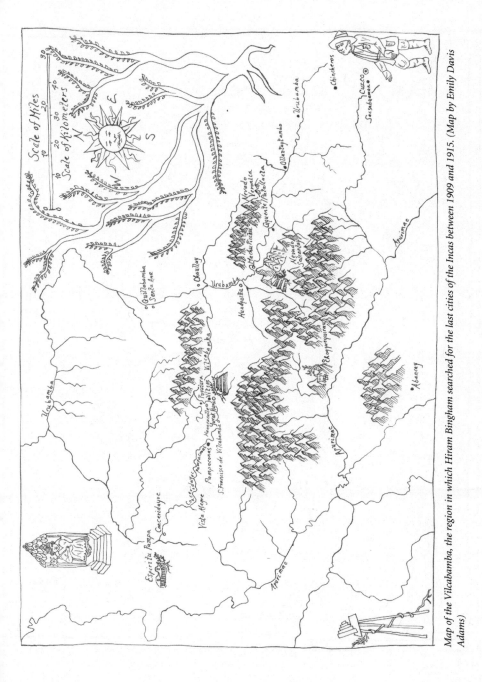

Map of the Vilcabamba, the region in which Hiram Bingham searched for the last cities of the Incas between 1909 and 1915. (Map by Emily Davis Adams)

South America, 1909, the scene of Hiram Bingham's great successes and failures. (Map by Emily Davis Adams)

Preface

Beneath the Hat

South America, 1936. A mountain looms in the distance. A small group of men carve their way through the thick jungle. A wide hat hides the face of their leader, save for his handsome, unshaven chin. His Peruvian guides are hesitant, but he is determined. He pauses, gently unfolds a disintegrating map from the pocket of his leather jacket and studies it in the dim light breaking through the canopy. A guide behind him pulls a gun, but the leader spins around and cracks his whip, knocking the weapon away. The guide runs, and our hero, an American archaeologist, steps into the light.

The party continues its march into the jungle. Behind a wall of vines they find what they've been looking for: a temple built by a people, lost long before Columbus. Bats explode from its black and forbidding entry, and the Indian porters run away in fright. The archaeologist and the remaining guide enter. There are traps to swing over and the corpse of a previous treasure hunter who failed. It is all prelude to the temple's center, where a small gold statue sits on a stone pedestal. The guide holds his breath, and the archaeologist replaces the artifact with a bag of sand. They breathe easy for a moment; but then, with a rumble and snap, the ruins come tumbling down.

This, of course, is the opening scene of the 1981 movie *Raiders of the Lost Ark,* and the debonair American archaeologist is Henry "Indiana" Jones Jr., played by Harrison Ford. Nearly three decades and three sequels later, we've seen Indy fight Nazis, Thuggee murder cults, and Communist clairvoyants for some of the most fantastic artifacts imaginable. But if there was an iconic moment to the series, then this is it: Indiana Jones running from a massive rolling boulder, walls falling around him, all without losing his hat. It is one of the most exciting introductions in movie history, and by the time Indy escapes an angry jungle tribe by swinging on a vine, he has lost the gold icon but captured our hearts.

I idolized him for most of my childhood. By the time I reached high school, I knew I wanted to become an archaeologist. I applied to Yale University, wrote my college essay on Indiana Jones, and was lucky enough to be admitted. But before I headed to New Haven, my father gave me a present that took me a little closer to reality. It was a t-shirt he had bought from Yale's Peabody Museum of Natural History, where I had spent many hours staring at dinosaurs when I was seven. The shirt featured another star from the museum's history: Machu Picchu, the beautiful "lost city of the Incas," hidden in the Andes Mountains of the South American country of Peru. And on its back was the image of the tall historian who had made it famous: Hiram Bingham III.

Born in 1875, over his 81 years he was variously a professor, writer, pilot, and U.S. senator. Hiram uncovered the ruins of Machu Picchu in 1911; in 1912, he exported its skulls, bones, beautiful ceramics, and precious metal artifacts to Yale. The cotton-and-ink face staring out at me gave no indication as to the roots of his restless ambition, but I saw something of Indy in him: the jaunty stance, the cocked hat, the sandy hair, and defiant gaze, teetering between interest and impatience. He could shout, as Ford did in *Indiana Jones and the Last Crusade,* "That belongs in a museum!" I was unsurprised when I later learned that in crafting the look of Indiana Jones, the crew of *Raiders of the Lost Ark* may have drawn from a little-known Charlton Heston movie named *Secret of the Incas,* which in turn drew from Bingham's life and work at Machu Picchu.[1] These two icons of archaeology shared the same DNA—though at the time, I thought that Indiana Jones was the exciting, full-color version and Hiram Bingham was the sepia-toned, boring reality.

At Yale I learned how wrong I was. In 2002, when I was a senior and a Latin American Studies major, I began research in Bingham's papers, archived at Yale. There, I made my own discoveries. Most accounts of Machu Picchu's revelation—a word preferable to discovery, in many ways—began with Bingham's quest to find the last cities of the Incas, the jungle-clad settlements where the most impressive pre-Columbian empire in the Americas took refuge from the Spanish in the sixteenth century. These accounts climaxed with Bingham's arrival at Machu Picchu. Only epilogues suggested what he unearthed in his excavations. Left unexplored was a full explanation of how he did it and why he quit exploring altogether in 1915. From Bingham's journals, manuscripts, and previously unexamined letters in Spanish, a far more dramatic story emerged, one full of betrayals, deaths, political intrigues, smuggling, and angry locals. It only seemed like a story of simple, heroic exploration from a distance. Beneath the hat, it was nothing less than a lost history of the Spanish conquest of Peru and its recovery through exploration; a descent into a forgotten chapter of America's often colonial, sometimes imperial relationship with the other peoples and countries of the hemisphere; and, most pressingly, a question as thorny as the vines that held Machu Picchu together: Who can own and interpret the indigenous past?

This last question is a timely one. In 2008, Peru sued Yale for the return of the artifacts and human remains that Bingham excavated from Machu Picchu. Peru claimed it had loaned Yale the collection of silver jewelry, ceramic jars, potsherds, skulls and bones and was now demanding its return. Yale called Peru's claim "stale and meritless" and asserted that now it owned the collection.[2] Peru said Yale had 46,000 pieces; Yale said it had 5,415.

Between these two distant poles, I have attempted to find the truth. After I graduated from college, I received a Fulbright Fellowship to research the story using archives and sources in Peru. In the year or so that I lived in Cuzco, the former capital of the Incas, I discussed the controversy with historians, archaeologists, tour guides, and taxi drivers of all ethnicities, who thoroughly challenged my notions of what Bingham's "discovery" meant. When I told one guide where I had gone to school, he said, "So maybe you can tell us where the gold is," echoing the legend that Bingham had stripped Machu Picchu not only of its graves but its supposed Inca treasure as well.

This book is my reply. Like the *khipu*—the Inca recording device, a long cord hanging with colorful strings whose every knot represented a different event or number—this book ties together several stories. The first is the oldest and explains why sixteenth-century Spaniards chased the heir to a once-mighty empire into the jungles of Peru and what was lost when the Spanish finished him off. The second thread explains why a twentieth-century missionary's son fell in love with an Inca ruin named the "Cradle of Gold" and then spent his career as an explorer trying to resurrect ruins whose secrets told the lost history of the Incas. His story closes with the monumental fight that ended his career as an explorer and changed how Peruvians viewed their material past and cultural heritage. The final thread pulls us to the present, asking what Hiram Bingham's revelation means today and how Machu Picchu's artifacts—and their ownership—continue to challenge the Americas' understanding of history and archaeology. When is a dig a political statement? When is a trowel a sword?

This story is also deeply personal, for reasons that will become clear. Any mistakes in the text that follow are thus my own, but I am indebted to others for almost everything else. I owe my greatest debt, however, to the two figures that fight for the heart of this story. First is the explorer Hiram Bingham, whose best self, the part that sought to understand another culture, was inextricably linked to the part of him that needed to possess. And second is a Peruvian anthropologist and public intellectual named Luis E. Valcárcel, who was first inspired by Bingham's explorations, then grew more critical of the North American's actions.

To say why—and whether his suspicions were justified—would ruin the story that follows, full of snakes, heroism, moral dilemmas, broken hearts, looting, shipwrecks, a treasure, skulls and bones, and perhaps even a curse. And unlike the adventures of Indiana Jones, it's all too true.

A NOTE ON IMAGES

In crafting this book, I was also inspired by the great Inca scribe Guaman Poma de Ayala, whose illustrated seventeenth-century manuscript *Nueva corónica y buen gobierno* has become an icon of indigenous resistance and adaptation in colonial Peru. This book begins with one of his images and I include another in the book's photo insert, but I also asked an artist and friend, Emily Davis Adams, to create images that depict Bingham's travails in a manner in keeping with Guaman Poma's aesthetic, if not his sharp political commentary. These images preface this book's four parts and, hopefully, amplify the echoes between Bingham's story and the conquest he tried to uncover.

Cradle of Gold

Introduction

The Last City of the Incas

The Sixteenth-Century Conquest

Dawn broke over South America, rolling from east to west, sliding up beaches and rivers, pushing through the treetops and vines of the Amazon jungle, until it hit the Andes, the soaring mountains that chain the continent together. Soon the sun would spill over its peaks and rush toward the beaches of the Pacific. But for a few precious minutes the light lingered on the Andes' eastern slopes, and in one steep valley, in a land called Peru, it woke two thousand Spanish and Indian nobles, soldiers, and slaves. With curses and prayers, they strapped on their armor and prepared for battle. It was June 24, 1572, the feast of St. John the Baptist, but the expedition hoped that it would soon be known as the day that the nightmarish conquest of the Incas finally ended.

It had been forty years since Francisco Pizarro and his 168 conquistadors left Central America and sailed down the western coast of the southern continent. When they landed in Peru, they faced the largest, wealthiest, most powerful indigenous empire of the Americas—the Incas. Their domain stretched from modern-day Chile to Colombia, from the Pacific to the Amazon, tied together with roads, canals, fortresses, and temples. Through force of arms and savvy alliances, the Spaniards captured and executed their emperor, Atahualpa, and conquered their capital, the gold-covered city of Cuzco.[1] But Atahualpa's successor, his fierce brother named Manco, rebelled against Spanish rule, centered in the new colonial capital of Lima, on the coast. In 1536, Manco retreated to this remote kingdom north of Cuzco. By 1539 he had built a new Inca capital—a place to worship their deity, the sun, and their ancestors in peace. Its name was Vilcabamba, "The Plain of the Sun."[2]

But it was not to be. Manco died, and his sons kept up the fight, arguing that the Spanish conquest was illegitimate and that their family had been wronged. After years of negotiations and skirmishes, the Spaniards had enough of the resistance. In April 1572, the viceroy, the Spanish king's representative, declared a "war of fire and blood." He organized an expedition led by Spaniards, but supported by indigenous allies and Inca mestizos—people born of Inca and Spanish unions, consensual or not—who sought survival and recognition within colonial Cuzco rather than independence.

The expedition had three objectives: to reach and raze Vilcabamba; to confiscate its treasure and end the Incas' sun worship; and to carry Manco's son, the Incas' eighteen-year-old emperor and leader of their religion, back to Cuzco for judgment. His name was Tupac Amaru, Quechua for "Royal Serpent," referring to the great two-headed snake that brought rain and world-shattering change. To capture him would be difficult. To get this far the Spaniards had fended off ambushes of spears, poisoned spines, and falling boulders. The landscape had grown terrifying. Here, the Andes met the Amazon: massive mountains gave way to precipitous cliffs and ravines, forest-choked valleys, and rivers that drowned the unwary. Jaguars and vipers lurked; vines and thorns ripped at clothes half-rotting from the rain and mist. The expedition had abandoned their horses and crawled along cliffs. The bravest strapped cannons to their backs, hoping for a greater share of the loot to come. The trees hid colonies of ferocious biting ants.[3] And then there were the waiting Incas and their hidden allies, the fierce jungle peoples who fought with poison arrows and, the Incas claimed, feasted on their victims. The Incas sacrificed guinea pigs to tell the future and left their disemboweled remains along the path, unnerving the Spaniards. Only through luck and an opportune defection among the Incas' captains had the expedition gotten this far. Vilcabamba would be the Incas' last stand, and the Spaniards were sure they would fight.

It was time. The sun cleared the ridge, and the men began to sweat. The general ordered the Europeans and Indians who had allied with the colonizers into columns led by captains and flag-bearers. The priests blessed the soldiers, and they began to march. The path rose, widened, and yielded a view of the river on their right. A massive Inca staircase led to an *usnu*, a ceremonial platform on which the Incas' priests paid tribute to the sun. It was midmorning, and the sun spilled over the expeditionaries' shoulders, illuminating the forbidden jungle refuge below.

But Vilcabamba was not a glittering imperial capital teeming with soldiers. It was sacked, abandoned, and burning. The Spaniards could smell the smoke.

They were shocked. Had another army beat them to the prize? They followed a long, wide staircase down into the city. Some four hundred stone houses surrounded them, eerily silent save for the last crackles of settling fires. They walked past fountains still gurgling and climbed a short staircase into the main square. After planting the royal standard and taking possession of the city for Spain, they explored, poking through the ashes of the palace and sun temple with their swords. They realized that Tupac Amaru and his Incas had destroyed the city themselves, "so effectively that if the Spaniards and their Indian allies had done it, it could not have been worse."[4] The Incas had fled into the jungle and mountains, carrying all they could, hoping that the Spaniards, deprived of their quarry, would return to Cuzco. The temple's golden icons—idols, the Spanish called them—and all of the Incas' treasures had gone with them.[5]

A few Spaniards, however, were moved by what remained. The Incas had built Vilcabamba to resemble Cuzco: a mile and a half wide but sprawling lengthwise. They had lived well in this second capital. They raised bees and gathered the honey; the warm and wet climate allowed for maize to be harvested three times a year along with sugar cane, yucca, sweet potato, and cotton. They grew the sacred coca leaf, chewed to attain strength and a mild narcotic high. "They raised parrots, hens, duck, native rabbits, turkeys, pheasants," one chronicler continued,

> curassows, macaws, and a thousand other birds of diverse, vivid colors. The houses and huts were covered in good thatch, and attractive to the eyes. There are a great number of guavas, pecans, peanuts, lucumas [a sweet, dry Andean fruit], papayas, pineapples, cherimoyas and other diverse fruit trees of the jungle. The Inca [emperor]'s house had two floors and was covered in roof tiles. The entire palace was painted with murals, all varying in style, which was quite a sight to see. There was a plaza where many people gathered to celebrate and even race horses. The palace doors were of very fragrant cedar, which there was much of in that land, and the rafters and floors were of the same material. Altogether, the Incas hardly lacked any of the gifts, greatness, and splendor of Cuzco in this distant or, better said, exiled land because whatever they wanted

of the outside, the Indians brought them. It brought them contentment
and joy, and they lived there with pleasure.[6]

Compared to the New World's still-ramshackle Spanish cities stinking with pig
manure, it was paradise.

It was a paradise now lost for good, however; the Spaniards would not return to Cuzco empty-handed. They formed parties to search for Tupac Amaru, his
heirs, and his treasure. The first party, led by mestizo nobles, returned after a week
with Tupac Amaru's nephew, who was next in line to wear the red-fringed *mascapaycha,* the symbol of the Inca's rule. The second party, mostly of Spaniards,
found the Inca's chief general and a fabulous treasure of emeralds, silver, and gold,
including the *Punchao,* the golden sun icon once worshipped in Cuzco's Temple
of the Sun. It was filled with the ground-up hearts of deceased emperors and was
the golden berth of the history and religious heritage of the Incas, their ark. Worse
yet, a third party returned with the *mallquis,* or mummies, of Manco Inca and his
eldest son, Titu Cusi Yupanqui. The Incas mummified their imperial dead and
carried and worshipped them as they had when they were alive.[7] Their capture
was a disaster: the Spanish had already burned other such "idols."

The Incas could only hope that the Spaniards' true quarry could remain at
large. If Tupac Amaru stayed free, the insurgency could limp along for years, a
thorn in the side of Spanish rule. Nevertheless, the Spaniards had a clue that he
had fled downriver, toward the Amazon, with his pregnant wife. The Spanish
commander sent forty men after them, led by an ambitious young captain named
Martín García de Loyola, whose great-uncle had founded the Jesuits, the religious
order that was converting many indigenous people in this New World.

They found and interrogated the chief of the Incas' jungle allies until he revealed that Tupac Amaru had left him only five days before, paddling by canoe to
the sea. He was delayed because his "wife was frightened and sad because she was
only a few days from giving birth. . . . Because he loved her so much, Tupac
Amaru himself was helping her carry her burden and protecting her, walking very
slowly." The chief refused the reward García de Loyola offered, "saying that it was
a great betrayal he had done to his lord."[8]

García de Loyola and his men marched for fifty miles, day and night by torchlight. They fell over waterfalls and swam for their lives. All the insects of the Amazon bit, stung, and laid eggs in their skin. Had they rested, they would have failed.
As they approached, Tupac Amaru begged his wife to flee with him by canoe. Had

she agreed, they might have escaped down the Amazon. The Spanish chroniclers claimed that she was terrified of the open water, however, and Tupac Amaru refused to abandon her. The Spaniards found the couple warming themselves at a campfire, staving off the dark. Deep in the jungle, the last emperor of the Andes surrendered, and Loyola marched him back to the city of Vilcabamba, up the grand staircase, and out of the valley. Whether the young Inca looked back at his city, his father's refuge, or whether he faced forward, girding himself for the future, is lost to history.

On September 21, the expedition returned to Cuzco. García de Loyola paraded Tupac Amaru around the plaza, leading him with a golden chain around his neck. The *mascapaycha* still lay on the young emperor's head. When they passed the window of the viceroy Francisco de Toledo, the Spanish king's colonial representative, the Inca refused to remove his royal fringe and Loyola struck him twice.[9]

The indignities continued. The viceroy wanted Tupac Amaru gone. In a sham trial, Toledo's officials charged the emperor with the murder of Spaniards in his realm and sentenced him to death. Inca and Spanish nobles alike protested the harsh punishment, but Toledo was implacable. Tupac Amaru was hoisted onto a mule and led to a black-draped scaffold in Cuzco's main square. His relatives and former subjects mobbed the streets and packed the balconies, wailing and sobbing. When the fallen emperor ascended the scaffold, he raised his hand, and the plaza went silent as he made his final declaration.

Speaking in Quechua, the Incas' imperial language, he told his people that he had converted to Christianity: "All that I and my ancestors the Incas have told you up to now—that you should worship the sun *Punchao* and the *huacas* [sacred icons], idols, stones, rivers, mountains and *vilcas* [the sacred things]—is completely false. When we told you that we were entering in to speak to the sun, this was false. It did not speak, we alone did: for it is an object of gold and cannot speak."[10] The Spaniards had broken his faith in his divinity; or perhaps he mouthed their script at the end to save his people. He laid his head on the block. An Indian executioner took his hair with one hand and with a cutlass decapitated the Inca. He raised Tupac Amaru's severed head to the sky.

The independent dynasty of Vilcabamba ended. Its treasure was divided; according to the Spanish law of the *quinto royal,* a fifth of the wealth went to the court of Philip II. The golden sun icon, the *Punchao,* disappeared into Europe. The

Spaniards built Cuzco's cathedral over one of the Incas' grandest palaces and the Dominican priory atop the Temple of the Sun. Toledo tried to break up the Incas' property and fortunes by marrying off the daughters of Inca lords to Spaniards, and he secretly burned the mummies of Manco Inca and Titu Cusi.

The Incas' subjects, now the Indian wards of the Spanish royalty, were subjected to harsh tributary laws. They died at horrific rates in mines and on haciendas. While the Spanish king got one-fifth of the Incas' wealth, by the early eighteenth century the Andean population was reduced to one-fifth of its former number, scholars estimate, by violence, disease, malnutrition, and exploitation.[11] Many Spaniards saw and lamented the abuse, but it was hard to divert the flood of policies and social assumptions that caused the disaster.

Despite these calamities, the Inca nobility survived, and in a few cases thrived, allying themselves with sympathetic Spaniards. Manco's kin claimed land and tribute and met as a body in Cuzco; the male with the greatest claim of descent from the original Incas wore the royal fringe.[12] They told their stories to chroniclers or wrote them down themselves. And as time went by, even their most resentful former subjects idealized the age of Inca rule and hoped they might return to power.[13] In 1780, that wish became flesh when José Gabriel Condorcanqui, a rural noble from the highlands south of Cuzco, took the name Tupac Amaru II and rebelled against the colonial authorities.

The reprisal was swift and terrible and had lasting consequences for the Incas' existence in Peruvian society. Condorcanqui was also executed in Cuzco's main square, but in a far more brutal manner than his predecessor. After forcing him to watch the execution of his wife and family, the Spaniards bound his arms and legs to horses, which were then driven in four directions. When he did not die, the Spaniards cut off his head, dismembered his body, and sent its parts to the towns that had supported him. "For those who viewed Tupac Amaru as an Inca, the body was not that of a prisoner," writes one historian. "Rather, it stood for the Indian nation."[14] To punish the surviving Inca nobles—even those who had supported the crown—the Spanish tried to strip them of their titles and dress. Increasingly, the only indigenous identity available for public life was as an *indio*, an Indian of low birth. When Peru won its independence from Spain in the 1820s, the Incas lost even that. Coastal elites actively scorned indigenous nobles. Inca leadership held on longer in Cuzco, but by the 1840s the coastal state so eroded the value of indigenous identities that former Incas found it preferable to intermarry with Europeans. Gradually, they lost track of the lines that linked them to one of the world's great civilizations, the most sprawling indigenous empire South America had ever known.[15]

In some quarters, however, their memory lived on. Long-suffering Indians, mestizos, and Peruvians of European descent alike found hope in the tales of their wealth and independent spirit, of what had been lost but might yet be found.

Some dreamt of their treasure. The impious traded swords for shovels and dug into the Inca temples and pre-Columbian mounds of other cultures in search of gold and silver. One of the most sadly evocative words that emerged from the Spanish colonization of Peru was *huaquear,* the transformation of the Quechua word *huaca*—a sacred site or object—into a verb meaning to dig into temples and graves in search of treasure. To some native Andeans, however, the Incas' treasure was patrimony, their inheritance. In 1802, the Prussian naturalist and explorer Alexander von Humboldt visited Cajamarca, where the Spanish killed the emperor Atahualpa. There, he met the seventeen-year-old son of a poor local *cacique* [indigenous noble] who claimed Inca descent, despite the purges of the 1780s. The son told the Prussian that the town's ruins hid a vast treasure of golden trees and litters that awaited the Incas' return; he and his parents would never dig for these treasures, which would be a sin. Humboldt was moved: "An idea generally spread and firmly believed among the natives is that it would be criminal to dig up and take possession of treasures which may have belonged to the Incas, and that such a proceeding would bring misfortune upon the whole Peruvian race. This idea is closely connected with that of the restoration of the Inca dynasty, an event which is still expected. . . . Oppressed nations always fondly hope for the day of their emancipation, and for the re-establishment of their old forms of government." The Incas' treasure, real or not, gave hope for the future.[16]

Others idealized the Incas' physical remains, hoping that their recovery might also produce a return to their rule.[17] When they executed the first Tupac Amaru, the Spaniards impaled his head on a pole in Cuzco's plazas for two days, but had to take it down when they realized that the Indians worshipped it as if it were alive. From that moment emerged a story about a hero named the *Inkarrí.* This "Inca Rey" or "Inca King" was godlike, the son of the sun, until the *viracochas*—bearded Europeans—arrived. They exterminated the *Inkarrí's* people, then captured and decapitated the lord himself. In one version of the story, the head was buried but began to regrow its body. In another version told in the jungles north of Cuzco today, the *viracochas* took his head to Lima, where it became the source of whites' wealth. The *Inkarrí's* head kept talking, however, two Indian boys told one anthropologist in the 1980s. "It does not die. The head of the Inca does not die."[18] According to the legend, the return of the *Inkarrí*'s head, or the regrowth of its body, would undo the conquest. "The promise of resurrection did exist," as one scholar notes.[19]

The third hearth of Inca spirit, however, was far more tangible: Vilcabamba itself, the remote jungle capital of the Incas' war for religious and political independence. When the Spaniards led Tupac Amaru to his death in 1572, they evacuated the city and settled its vassals closer to Cuzco. Never mapped, Vilcabamba slowly vanished. The birds came first, and then the snakes and other animals, nesting, making their homes. Vines and brush choked its plazas. Trees broke down some walls, but held others together, covering the sleeping city with a blanketing canopy of green. The last city of the Incas became the lost city of the Incas, its location known only to the Incas' former allies, the "savage" jungle peoples. By 1768 "civilized" Peru had so lost Vilcabamba's location that one geographer, Cosmé Bueno, reported that "only the memory of the retreat of the last Inca remained."[20] Nonetheless, stories emerged of hidden Inca societies, still alive but lost in the jungle.

For nearly 150 years after Bueno wrote, while Peru won its independence but further stripped its Indians of rights, the snakes of Vilcabamba slept. The city smoldered in Peruvian memory, neither dead nor alive, its meaning ever more hallucinatory. Had it been a place of imperial wealth and lost riches? Or a place of struggle, a symbol of indigenous resistance? What had happened before Tupac Amaru's execution? Why had Manco rebelled, and what brought his empire to ruin?

In 1911, a chance discovery stoked its fires once again, and answers began to emerge. The snakes awoke and a conflagration of a new sort began. This time, it would not be between Europeans and the Incas, but the peoples of two Americas, north and south. This time, the treasure was not gold and silver, but something far more potent—the physical remains of the Incas, which were claimed by one young man, who resembled the young soldier and Jesuit heir Martin García de Loyola but looked up to the rebel Incas.

His name was Hiram Bingham, and he was born in Honolulu.

Part One

The Explorer

There comes a time in every rightly constructed
boy's life when he has a raging desire to go
somewhere and dig for hidden treasure.
           Mark Twain, Tom Sawyer - 1876

Choqquequirau, the Cradle of Gold

There comes a time in every rightly constructed boy's life when he has a raging desire to go somewhere and dig for hidden treasure.

—*Mark Twain,* The Adventures of Tom Sawyer

Chapter One

The Black Temple

$\mathcal{M}$ any years later, when he hefted an Inca war club for the very first time, Hiram Bingham remembered his childhood and perhaps the familial piety that loomed over it all.[1]

In 1819, his grandfather, Hiram Bingham I, left his parents' Vermont farm, sailed around the horn of South America, and made landfall in the Sandwich Islands, as Anglos then called Hawaii. He was twenty-nine years old, tall, and darkly handsome. His name suggested potency, monuments, and service: a Biblical figure named Hiram had helped King Solomon build his temple. By his side was his wife, Sybil, a willowy, sensitive, blue-eyed schoolteacher. They had married only two weeks before leaving. Sybil would bear seven children, five of whom survived infancy.

With each child, Sybil's health grew ever more fragile, but Hiram's energies proved volcanic. He was a fierce Protestant missionary who believed his ship plowed the same waves as the *Mayflower*. But where the Pilgrims sought religious freedom, Bingham and his brethren sought conversion of the "heathen." They burned to bring native Hawaiians "the great salvation of Jesus Christ."[2]

Their timing was perfect. King Kamehameha I, who had united the islands and protected the old gods, died four months before the missionaries' arrival. His wife, Ka'ahumanu, the wealthiest woman in the islands, was in charge now, and she saw a political advantage in converting to Christianity. Before Bingham met with her, he visited an enormous, toppled temple of black lava stone named Pu'ukohola heiau, whose cornerstone had been laid by Kamehameha himself. Bingham walked its ruins with gratitude and hope.[3]

Over the next twenty years, the Binghams and their fellow missionaries converted the royal family and preached to their people. They encouraged European dress and tamped down native culture and "immoral" customs like the hula dance. Bingham designed the great religious symbol of the new regime. Its name was Kawaiaha'o, and it was Hawaii's largest building, a church built of 14,000 thick slabs of white coral, quarried underwater by King Kamehameha III's subjects.

Bingham would never see his "new Solomon's Temple" finished, however.[4] In 1840, two years before the great white church was dedicated, Sybil's health failed and the family returned to New England, where she eventually died. Bingham remarried, but the missionary board wouldn't let the domineering Vermonter go back to the islands. His piety had become a liability. While there, he had preached against the foreign merchants and sailors who had encouraged the islands' trade in alcohol and prostitution. It wasn't just Protestant prudishness; Bingham wanted the royalty to maintain their political independence. Nevertheless, his efforts won him no friends among other foreigners, and he and his fellow missionaries suffered bombardment and lynch mobs. His critics accused him of manipulating the royalty and called him King Bingham—a reputation that lasted into the twentieth century, when he served as the model for the chilly, arrogant missionary in James Michener's novel *Hawaii*.[5]

He died in New Haven, Connecticut, in 1869, but by then his legacy had passed on to the next generation. His son, Hiram Bingham Jr., married a woman named Clara Brewster, who traced her lineage back to *Mayflower* passenger William Brewster. Clara was full of an "inborn love of neatness and order," and she accompanied Hiram Jr. to a remote group of islands in the South Pacific called the Gilberts.[6] Hiram Jr.'s Christianity was as gentle as his father's was fierce, however, and their arrival in the Gilberts was as hard as his father's arrival in Hawaii was easy. Two months into their stay, Clara gave birth to a stillborn boy. Hiram Jr. buried the baby, but the Gilbertese people found the grave and spread his remains across the sand.[7] The Gilbertese saw little advantage in Christianity and wanted to make their dislike for the missionaries known. In their first seven years Hiram and Clara converted a meager four souls.

After seventeen years of struggle, they got a second chance at familial happiness. Clara was pregnant again, and although they were finally building a congregation, she decided to leave the Gilberts. Hiram Jr. was deathly ill with dysentery, and she knew that neither her husband nor baby would survive on a dry coral island. With the help of some native friends, she flagged down a passing ship and talked their way aboard even though it was going to Samoa. From there they sailed to Fiji, and from there to New Zealand, going ever farther from home. Finally, when Clara was eight months pregnant, she got them on a ship headed back to Hawaii. They arrived in Honolulu in early November, and Clara helped her husband take refuge in his sister's school, nestled in the shadow of the great white Kawaiaha'o church.[8]

Clara's contractions began six days later, and at 3:15 in the morning of November 16, 1875, she remembered, "my heart was filled with wonderful love and joy at hearing the cries of my precious darling child, a fine baby boy. Everything went well—except I had too little milk for my darling—which almost broke my heart."[9] At ten the next morning, Hiram Jr. came in to see their son, Hiram Bingham III, who had already traveled further while in the womb than most Americans would their whole lives.

For mainland American children in the nineteenth century, Hawaii was a far-off island paradise warmed by tropical breezes, filled with fabulous fruits and foreign peoples. For young Hiram Bingham III, or Hi, it was a colorful prison.

After Hi was born, the missionary community rallied around his parents, who had little save their piety and a meager stipend. When the family could not afford a home, the missionaries built them a large one in walking distance of Punahou, the school founded on land given to Hiram Bingham I by the Hawaiian royalty. The house was the religious retreat his parents needed—their life's work would be translating the Bible into Gilbertese—but for an only child, it was a cold, lonely place. There was little division between home and church. The Sabbath began Saturday evening and continued with five separate services on Sunday. Hi lived like a tropical monk, "shoved off into a sort of closet space under the slope of the roof on the second floor" where he slept under a thin mosquito netting that hung from the timbers only a few inches above.[10] Playing cards were considered diabolic, and chess and backgammon were nearly as dangerous.[11] His father kept a short, hard stick at hand for discipline.

When young tow-headed Hi wasn't being chided for not living up to his grandfather's standards at home, he was teased for them everywhere else. His father's playmates had gone into business rather than follow their parents into the church. White Americans had bought up much of the islands, shifting control away from the native royalty and disenfranchising poor Hawaiians and Asians. It was all that conversion to Christianity was supposed to prevent, and the missionaries' influence had all but disappeared. When Hi introduced himself at Punahou as "Hiram T'ird," his classmates jeered.[12]

Despite his curiosity and natural intelligence, Hi would always "[struggle] with a sense of inadequacy," one of his sons later wrote.[13] Hi was small for his age and picked on by bullies. For comfort, he escaped into books and his imagination. At first his parents only allowed illustrated Bibles and a green scrapbook containing morality tales for children, a missionary hymn written by his grandfather, and almost oracular engravings clipped from the newspaper—Roman ruins, the German geographer Mercator, an Andean condor.[14] When he grew older, however, he hid in Honolulu's library, an island on an island, where he could read everything he wanted. He loved Mark Twain's *The Adventures of Huckleberry Finn,* as much for its portrayal of America as for its story of escape. In 1887, Hi visited the United States, his "homeland," for the first time. He and his father spent the summer in California, where Hi thrilled at Gilded Age San Francisco. Brass, gold, ferries, and cable cars clanged in Hi's chest, affecting him so deeply that after returning to Hawaii, he used the money his parents had saved for his theological education to buy a steamship ticket back to the States. His father caught him at the docks before he could run away, but Hiram's sad betrayal devastated the family. "It is dreadful to think that such a boy has so deceived his parents," wrote a family friend. "I believe he got the fancy from books he has read."[15]

The family friend was right. There was something growing in Hiram that thirsted for lands less holy than Hawaii. Following his failed escape attempt, his penitent parents gave him more freedom. Hi started to hike in the mountains of Oahu with his natural history teacher, who taught him "the joys of living out-of-doors and of exploring" and how to collect zoological, biological, and antiquarian specimens for the school's small museum.[16] Under his wing, Hi might have learned that his family's belief in a 6,000-year-old biblical world now conflicted with scientific theories of evolution and geology. Christianity no longer had a monopoly on the truth.

When Hi was almost sixteen, the family returned to the United States. While his parents oversaw the publication of his father's Gilbertese Bible in New York, Hi boarded a train for Massachusetts. He enrolled in Phillips Academy, a prestigious boarding school in Andover, hoping to follow in his father's footsteps to Yale University. Andover was cruel to a boy rich in spirit, intellect, and travel, but desperately poor where it counted most. The other students made fun of his clothes, made cheaply by a Chinese tailor in Honolulu. To pay for his room and board he worked five hours a day in the dining halls. His dorm room went unheated until his father sent money for a stove that raised the room's temperature to a balmy 53 degrees in January.

The experience gave him a lifelong distaste for poverty, but it also gave him focus. A taller, more mature Hiram met his parents in the summer of 1893 at the epoch-making Columbian Exposition in Chicago. Staged in honor of Christopher Columbus's arrival in the New World four hundred years before, the Chicago World's Fair made a fittingly deep impression on young Hiram. One wonders what a boy raised by Hawaiian missionaries thought of the "White City" and its illuminated, alabaster-stucco classical architecture; what he thought of the displays of Arab alleyways and "savage" villages; and whether he was in the audience when Frederick Jackson Turner declared that because the Western frontier had been closed, American energy would need "a wider field for its exercise"—a trend that the Bingham family had observed in Hawaii for years.[17]

So much had changed since his parents and grandparents devoted themselves to saving the "heathens" of the Pacific. Science and racial theories, not religion, ruled the day. Darwin's theory of evolution had been applied to society, and with the near-total confinement of Native Americans to reservations, white America was eager, if regretful, to prematurely declare the passage of indigenous America from the national stage.[18] (Fortunately, reports of the American Indian's demise were much exaggerated.) Industry, not agrarianism, was changing the country. Dollars and adventurism, not democracy, were shaping American ambitions abroad. That January, American troops had landed in Honolulu to help American businessmen shore up a mostly white revolt against Hawaiian Queen Liliuokalani and her people.[19] Although President Grover Cleveland denounced the intervention, Hawaii was looking increasingly like America's first overseas imperial possession. Hi's grandfather had designed the great white church at Kawaiaha'o to replace the Hawaiians' black lava temples, but Anglo Hawaiians now believed that the temples' true successors were the white columns and facades like those of the fair's secular temples, alluding to European civilizations of the past and American empires of the future.

Hi entered Yale the following fall, but first he completed a sacred, filial task. Sybil Bingham, his grandmother, was buried in Massachusetts. Hiram I, who had died two decades later, was buried in New Haven, in his second wife's plot. Hiram Jr. charged Hi with exhuming his grandmother's bones, transporting them to New Haven, and reburying them alongside her husband.

Four days before starting his freshman year at Yale, Hi and a hired laborer spent a September afternoon digging through the sandy soil of her grave. Three feet down they found her. There was no trace of the box that once protected her from the dirt, save "two old fashioned brass handles."

"The bones were all together," Hi wrote his father. "The skull, leg bones and ribs were all within a few inches of each other. We looked very carefully for traces of a box but found none. . . . The gravedigger searched very thoroughly, and I believe that all of the remains that lay there were safely removed." Hiram packed his grandmother's bones in a pine box and brought it to New Haven by railroad—likely the only member of Yale's class of 1898 to arrive with his family's bones literally in his baggage.

Yet once he started classes, "Sybil's bones were not on his mind," one of Hi's sons would write. His next letter home gushed about the "fine, great, grand," university, and it wasn't until two weeks later that the young man told his father that Sybil had been reburied next to Hiram Bingham Sr. But there had been some wrangling with a family friend, a Mrs. Champion, over the headstone's epitaph.

"It seemed to me that the word 'relict' is obsolete. By the way, Mrs. C has made us a present of a very pretty sofa pillow."[20]

Perhaps Hi's chirpy transition from his grandmother's remains to physical comfort was just that—a transition, to cover the space of what may have been a truly upsetting experience. By the time he reached Yale, Hi had been so weighed down by the darkness and demands of his family legacy that perhaps there was no other way to be other than blithe and cheery, especially when burdened by the bones of his family.

If that cheeriness bothered his father, who had wept while burying and reburying his first son in foreign soils, he said nothing. He was certain Yale would keep Hi pious, as it had him, forty-five years before. Hi would respect the dead. He would be a missionary yet.

Chapter Two

The Ivory Tower

*I*t was the spring of 1898, and from the outside, Hiram's life looked perfect. He was about to graduate from Yale, one of the most prestigious academic institutions in America. He was six-feet-four and delicately handsome, a little shy but a little less stiff than he had been as a child. As for wealth, it hardly mattered where he was going. He had his life planned out for him as a missionary in China, his father wrote, as a "teacher of the Emperor of the Celestial Empire just as your grandfather was of the Kings and Queens of the Sandwich Islands."[1]

But if life was so good, then why did he confess in a letter to be "approaching insanity"?[2]

College started off well. Like his father, Hiram raced sailboats and won all cups offered in 1897. He sang, refereed football games, and, as his father hoped, found the university's religious niche. Most visibly, Hiram took a leadership role at Dwight Hall, the university's Christian public service group.

Socially, however, his time at the elite, exclusive institution was challenging. Although there were strivers like himself, Yale in the 1890s was a playground for the children of the Gilded Age, where they could search for their purpose, show off their status, and make the contacts that guaranteed them fortune and glory. Bingham's classmates included future senators, oilmen, diplomats, railroad barons, wealthy philanthropists, authors, and a Pulitzer Prize–winning composer. Some were self-made, others were heirs, and Yale filled both groups—almost all white Anglo-Saxon Protestants—with a driving ambition for worldly, not spiritual, success.

Faced with opportunity at every turn, Hiram began to relax his Puritanism. He tutored the wealthy, studying their habits. He played cards and joined the Psi

Upsilon Fraternity and Yale's Hawaiian Club, where he saw friends smoking and drinking, activities forbidden in missionary Honolulu. He read novels openly and danced with women at parties. He read the Bible as allegory, not history, and looked down his nose at evangelists. He was still Christian, he wrote his parents, but he didn't need to be a zealot to prove it.

A wave of more worldly success helped him along. At the end of freshman year, he and two other members of the Yale freshman debate team argued down Harvard's team, giving the campus "the first victory in debate which Yale can boast." The students exploded in cheers, stormed the stage, lifted the three freshmen on their shoulders, and carried them around campus, Bingham later told his sons.[3] Hiram had no illusions that he could become a railroad baron, but his intellect and rhetorical skill suggested other paths to acceptance by his peers. He presided over the senior debate society, broke the Sabbath to study, and worshipped his professors. Hi cruelly declared to his father that "no minister has one-fifth of the chance to accomplish more good and affect the world more by his influence than a teacher."[4] He took out more books than any other student, the university's librarian told him, and at the end of his junior year he was on track to graduate Phi Beta Kappa and begin a career in academia.

Instead, his dreams fell apart.

In the autumn of 1897, while gold and red leaves littered the flagstone campus like so many hopeful embers, Hiram waited for the light tap on his shoulder that welcomed seniors into one of Yale's hardly secret societies, perhaps even Skull and Bones, the most exclusive of all. The tap never came. When his fellow students began to wink at each other above scarves and tie pins, Hi knew he had been passed over. He took it badly, having accepted Yale's markers of success. He thought it was a snub of his poor and pious background. Years later, when he returned to teach at Yale, he believed that he could never be in the "inner hierarchy . . . because he was not a 'Bones man.'"[5]

He forged ahead with his secret plan to become a teacher, but his grades began to drop. That spring, while representing Yale at a religious conference, Hiram listened to a revivalist preacher who filled him with guilt at how far he had strayed from the church. His rich imagination spinning with visions of Hell, he gave the preacher all the money he had saved for his continuing education. When he came to, he was ashamed, but he agreed with his parents that it was a sign that after graduation he should steam back to Hawaii to begin his career as a missionary.

Inside, however, Hiram was in tumult, and around him, the world was at war. In February 1898, just before his epiphany, the USS *Maine* mysteriously exploded in the harbor of Havana, Cuba. The island at the time was engaged in a violent struggle for independence from Spain, which was trying to hold onto its last two New World colonies, Cuba and Puerto Rico. The newspapers of William Randolph Hearst, who would later inspire Orson Welles' *Citizen Kane,* used the *Maine* to whip the American public into a fervor, demanding that the United States intervene in the revolutionaries' fight.

To Hearst, it was high time to test the Monroe Doctrine, the unofficial U.S. policy against European meddling in the New World. Among Anglo-Americans the Black Legend of the Spanish—that they were supposedly savage, benighted, superstitious, and lazy—was infamous. (The change conveniently ignored the fact that some modicum of Spanish justice meant that its indigenous populations were not confined to barren reservations, as in the United States.) To become a world power, the United States needed a villain, and Spain served nicely.

Congress authorized President William McKinley to join Cuba's fight for independence—whether the Cubans wanted help or not—starting the Spanish-American War. Yale's campus exploded into full, riotous support for the intervention, burning effigies of Spain and its army's general, Valeriano Weyler.[6] "Every body is talking of enlistment," wrote Hi to his father. "I feel very strongly inclined to volunteer." He wanted to join the Rough Riders, the famed mounted regiment of cowboys and Ivy Leaguers led by Colonel Theodore Roosevelt.[7] Filled with patriotism and panic, Bingham wanted to escape his missionary future by proving himself with revolutionary struggle.

Fortunately, an uncle talked Hi out of enlisting. Had he followed Roosevelt in his charge up San Juan Hill, his height would have made him an easy target. Hiram tried to convince himself that it was the right decision, marveling to his parents how "few are eager and zealous to give their lives for . . . the Kingdom of God!"[8] His protests sounded hollow, however, and the many absent seats at his commencement were a silent rebuke. Even in Hawaii, the war was inescapable. On July 7, President McKinley officially annexed the islands as a U.S. territory. American troops were already leaving Honolulu for the Philippines to dismember and rearrange imperial Spain's last limbs in a way that suggested that the United States had imperial ambitions of its own. Young Hi lacked the immediate pleasure of participating, but the atmosphere of war, overseas adventure, and gilded privilege had penetrated him far deeper than thousands of hours in church.

Hiram's final days on the mainland, however, hinted at his far more fantastical future. On July 5, 1898, while visiting family in Massachusetts, Hiram climbed a tower commemorating the supposed lost civilization of Norumbega, which in the late nineteenth century was believed to be New England's El Dorado. As one archaeologist has suggested, "a youthful America, seeking its place in the world, was looking for a monumental history comparable to Schliemann's highly publicized finds at Troy and Mycenae."[9] According to legend, Norumbega was a Native American kingdom of incredible wealth, but it was more likely the mutated memory of the sprawling Native American societies that populated the Atlantic coast before the arrival of European rifles and disease. The tower's architect, however, was an eccentric, wealthy Cambridge chemist, who believed that Norumbega was actually a Norse settlement, and that North America's greatest pre-Columbian civilization was white and blonde.[10] The theory was born of speculation, the desire to put Northern Europeans in the Americas before the Spanish, and disbelief that Native Americans could have built great civilizations on their own.

Although historians and archaeologists looked down on such theories they were nonetheless prevalent in mainstream society. They were reinforced by the popular lost-race genre of late nineteenth- and early-twentieth-century novels, in which whites and Indians fought over the lost cities of the New World, filled with gold, silver, and secrets.[11] *The Young Silver Hunters or The Lost City of the Andes* told one such tale, its cover bearing four Americans with guns falling into a hole before a feather-festooned mob of "Sun Worshippers." Perhaps Hi stole away from his studies to read such dime novels, perhaps not. Nevertheless, they were as much a part of his world as the tower of Norumbega. He had gone there to get away, perhaps to understand where he was going and why. His family's mission was to supplant the native religions of the world with Christianity; Norumbega's tower did that one better by populating native history with Northern Europeans. It was just the sort of idea that Hiram one day would fight in his career as an explorer, a missionary of a different sort.

For the moment, however, he still was trapped in his family's past. "Would that the narrow-minded dwellers in the deep valleys would climb up and broaden their vision," he wrote. "What a new concept of God they would get."[12]

Hi climbed down from the tower, crossed the country by train, and took a steamship to Honolulu, where he moved back in with his parents.

Chapter Three

The Compass

O nce back in Hawaii, it took five months of sleeping under his parents' roof before Hiram Bingham abandoned the missionary life for good. He told his parents that it was because Honolulu's climate was ruining his voice, but the real reason was that Hiram had found a way out. Her name was Alfreda Mitchell.

Their upbringings could not have differed more. Alfreda's father, Alfred Mitchell, had spent his youth in Hawaii seeking his fortune in whale oil. Back on the mainland, he landed a far greater prize—the diamond-laden hand of Annie Tiffany, an heiress to the Tiffany & Co. jewelry fortune. Their daughter Alfreda grew up in a secular wonderland of wealth and finery, moving between Manhattan apartments and New England estates with ease. Although she had traveled throughout Europe and islands of the Pacific, she was sheltered, devoted to her violin, and, as Bingham later noted, "more eloquent in music than in speech."[1] As short as Bingham was tall, in her youth she had a beautifully wispy quality and had modeled for her famed artist uncle, Louis Comfort Tiffany, for his painting of "Flora," the spirit of spring.[2] Kind, gentle, and surrounded by glass and gold, she was free of the self-doubt over money and piety that had plagued Hiram's childhood but had turned him into a striver.

They were so dissimilar that Alfreda barely talked to him at their first meeting. It had been the spring of 1897, when Hiram was still a junior at Yale University. Feeling nostalgic for the islands, her father had invited Hiram and six other eligible Yale men from Hawaii to picnic at their New London home and to meet his two daughters. While his friends joked easily, Hiram sat shyly alone, looking thoroughly uncomfortable.

The triumphs and disappointments of Hiram's senior year, however, emboldened the beanpole. After graduation, a friend invited Hiram to sail up to Boston for the Harvard-Yale crew races. When they passed the Mitchells' beach, the friend rowed Hiram ashore, and the tall Hawaiian talked his way into dinner with Mrs. Mitchell and her daughters. Hiding his internal doubts, he spoke with surprising conviction of his future plans. "We enjoy Hiram immensely," Alfreda wrote in her journal.[3]

Hiram enjoyed Alfreda as well, as much taken by her as her life of gentle beauty. When the Mitchells' yacht dropped anchor in Honolulu six months later, he called at their beachfront cottage and began to woo her with leis and horseback rides on the beach. He confided in her, revealing that he was disenchanted with the missionary life and wanted to explore other careers. Alfreda's father apparently feared further entanglement with this prospectless missionary's son and took the family off to Japan. But by then it was too late—the couple was in love.

Hi understood that he had to improve his social standing to be taken seriously by this wealthy family. He quit the chapel, got a technical job in the sugar cane fields, and in four months made enough money to sail to San Francisco, the city of his childhood dreams. He moved to Berkeley and enrolled in the University of California's graduate department to study sociology. He lived it up in San Francisco society, putting on plays and dancing with debutantes at balls. He finally broke free from the guilt of his childhood. Half-apologetic, half-defensive, his letters home broke his parents' hearts.

Given his curiosity and love of knowledge, he had made the right choice. When classes began, Hiram realized that his skills as a storyteller suited him well for history. He switched from sociology and so impressed the university's president that he asked Hiram to lecture for him when he was away. His master's thesis, "The Growth of American Supremacy in Hawai'i," closed the first chapter of his life. It received high honors, but it was more of a slapdash job than his advisors knew. To get it done, Hiram had copied several long passages from other works without footnotes.[4]

Hiram had decided to try for a Ph.D. in history in a direction that, like his thesis, would link the past to America's political present. His mentor, who later sat on the U.S. commission governing the Philippines, had the answer: Spanish America. It was a radical proposal as most historians of the day limited their interest to the United States or Europe. But Bernard Moses saw an opportunity. The Spanish-American War had given the United States new heights of hemispheric influence, and the country needed new experts in Latin American culture, geography, and history.

The field fit Bingham's ambitions like a well-tailored pair of khaki jodhpurs. He could be a trailblazer, studying the revolutionary movements of the Spanish colonists who expelled the European power that had ruled them. It was a choice as political as it was pathbreaking, based on the belief that America shared a political past and future with countries like Mexico, Colombia, and Peru. Bingham would celebrate the Americas' independence and show how the United States could use that shared history for economic and political ends.[5] Just as his grandfather broke religious ground in Hawaii, Hiram could break new political ground in South America. The key difference, however, was that his grandfather was interested in native peoples. It seems that Hiram was actively not, having had his fill in Honolulu.

Flush with California sunshine, Hi rode the train East, where he was reunited with Alfreda, now his fiancée. He returned to Hawaii to spend the summer with his parents, then came back to the mainland to start a Ph.D. in history at Harvard—perhaps hoping he might be able to return to Yale afterward. He would focus on the heroes of South American independence. He dreamed of writing a biography of Simón Bolívar or, as Bingham called him, "The George Washington of South America." Sure enough, Yale's new president Arthur Hadley hinted that there might be a position teaching South American history waiting when he finished his Ph.D. Hadley predicted the path of the United States in the region and wanted Yale to blaze it. As if sealing two futures at once, on November 20, 1900, a former Yale president presided over Hiram and Alfreda's wedding.

For a few years, it seemed that Hiram had made no false moves. In September 1901, President William McKinley was assassinated, and Hi's hero, Theodore Roosevelt, was sworn in as America's new president. Under Roosevelt, the United States took an even more active role in the hemisphere. Roosevelt landed troops in Honduras and the Dominican Republic and sent warships to back a rebellion in Panama. The support guaranteed American control over the construction of the Panama Canal, passage for its warships, and, it was hoped, dominion over hemispheric trade. In a 1904 address to Congress, Roosevelt established his corollary to the Monroe Doctrine, arguing that it was the United States' duty to intervene in its neighbors' affairs when they were unstable.

To some, this seemed like poorly disguised imperialism. But Hiram, now twenty-nine, saw it as only natural—an extension of American technology and political authority. Ever topical, he wrote his dissertation on a failed Scottish colony in seventeenth-century Panama's jungle-locked Darien Gap. As he would later explain to the Carnegie Institution, his larger goal as a scholar was to prepare the descendants of "the present inhabitants of the Temperate Zone"—white Americans—"to live in the Tropics where there is more unoccupied land than in any other part of the world."[6]

The Tropics were hardly "unoccupied," but Bingham's bigger problem was that he was a decade too early. His Harvard professors did not know what to do with his interest in what they considered a historical backwater.[7] Hiram failed to reassure them. He flunked his first oral examination, struggled with Spanish, and found that there were not enough primary sources on Latin America in Harvard's library to finish his thesis. He was named Harvard's "Curator of Latin American History and Literature," but when he received his Ph.D. in 1905, the hinted-at position at Yale failed to materialize. Yale's history department was similarly skeptical of the importance of Spanish America as a field of study—and of Bingham's seriousness. The only job Bingham could find was as a personal tutor at Princeton, then headed by future President Woodrow Wilson. The job was an academic dead end.

Frustrated at work, Bingham took a sharp look at the rest of his life. At first he had enjoyed his new-found wealth. Drawing on his family's sense of moral righteousness and Alfreda's wealth and privilege, Hiram settled into the life of a true patrician. Tiffany money paid for trips to Europe, a staff of servants, and a portrait of Hiram in new riding clothes. It also paid for a nurse for his mother until she passed away in November 1903. The Mitchells bought Alfreda a three-story house in Cambridge, larger than most of his professors' homes, and built them a Japanese-style summer home in rural Salem. Their houses glowed with stained glass creations, and Tiffany & Co.'s employees did research for Hiram in Paris's National Library. Their personal life was similarly sprawling: by 1905, Alfreda had borne three sons. There were more to come. Years later, when asked whether he had a hobby, Bingham replied, "It used to be collecting books . . . but when I began to collect sons, I found that more interesting."[8]

Beneath the surface, however, Bingham struggled with his dependency on the Tiffany fortune. He "never could be sure," his son Alfred wrote years later, "how much his love for [Alfreda] was for herself and how much for her family's money."[9] He had by now realized that beneath her dreaminess she could be incurious, hamstrung by her upbringing. In photos together from those early years she was soft and out of focus, standing behind Bingham, who sat at a desk covered in books or with his sons on his lap. She encouraged Hiram's studies and devoted herself to the children. Where he seemed hawkish and sure, "she fantasized endlessly, almost brooded, with her mouth drawn into a Mona Lisa smile which later became fixed," another son, Mitchell, remembered.[10]

If Alfreda was a perfect Victorian, Bingham was something hungrier, caught between his family's missionary ideals, his own Gilded Age desires, and hours spent devouring the books of Theodore Roosevelt, Rudyard Kipling, and Joseph Conrad. He desired a "strenuous life" and envied the sense of purpose, danger, and adventure that had guided his parents and grandparents from New England into the rest of the world.[11] Bingham also wanted to write books, but he was no closer to the benchmark set by his grandfather, whose account of his twenty years in Hawaii had been a best seller, and his father, who, in the parlance of the missionaries, had "reduced" an entire spoken language to writing in order to translate the Bible. They warred with the world through words, spirit, and sweat—an energy that Hiram once possessed but had since lost. What had happened to the boy who read pulpy novels filled with lost cities and runaways, tried to escape on a ship, and collected shells in the mountains of Hawaii? Or even the Hiram Bingham of seven years before, who had tried to join the Rough Riders?

And so, not even eight months into his time at Princeton, Bingham began to plan a trip that would both satisfy his need for adventure and give him the raw materials to establish himself as an academic. He would travel to the Caribbean and visit archives in Panama, Colombia, and Venezuela, to find documents for his long-planned "great man" biography of Simón Bolívar, the hero of South American independence. To bring the Americas closer together and jump-start his career, Hiram would show the United States why Latin America's struggle for independence had been such an achievement.

He might have done so had Alfreda not been laid up at a Manhattan hospital following the birth of their fourth son. While she convalesced, Hiram stayed at the Yale Club and rubbed elbows with the sort of men who had snubbed him back at Yale. One such glad-hander was Hamilton Rice. Rice represented everything Hiram Bingham felt he gave up in marriage and academia: adventure, a free spirit, no family obligations, the ability to buy a steamship ticket without a mother-in-law's permission. Rice too had noteworthy origins—he was a grandson of the governor of Massachusetts—and like Bingham had graduated college in 1898, but from Harvard. Unlike Bingham, he was independently wealthy, and after medical school had boated from the heights of the Andes Mountains in Ecuador to the lowlands of Brazil. Along the way he had eaten monkeys, shot at wild hogs, and witnessed the tremendous cruelty of the rubber trade, which enslaved Indians to supply the stuff that cushioned American and European modernity. The adventure won Rice a coveted membership in the Royal Geographic Society. "He knew headwaters the way other society folk know headwaiters," wrote one historian. Rice would go on to found a geographical institute at Harvard—funded by his future wife, a millionaire who had been widowed by the wreck of the *Titanic*—but his colleagues were less charitable. They remembered a "scoundrel" and fierce rival of other explorers.[12]

Bingham wasn't yet that particular. Rice was the first explorer he had ever met, and the two hit it off. Rice spread out a map and suggested a new plan, one that would let Bingham be an explorer as well. Bingham had wanted to travel from Venezuela to Colombia by train and boat; but if he went overland, crossing rivers, plains, and the Andes Mountains, Rice would go with him. A light went on in Bingham's head: this was a path Bolívar and his army had marched in 1819. The route was considered impossible in the wet season, through swamps and over a miserable section of the Andes, but Bolívar's army had done it, surprising the Spanish and permanently expelling them from Colombia. Instead of hunting Bolívar through books, Hiram could follow in his footsteps, proving the accomplishment of "The Liberator" to North Americans. He could even bracket the expedition with book-buying jaunts in the capitals of Venezuela and Colombia. If all went well, he could be a historian and a husband, an explorer and an academic, all at once. Hiram had missed out on San Juan Hill with Roosevelt, but here was his chance to retrace an even more epic ascent in the annals of American victories over colonial powers.

It was a highly unorthodox decision, and one that would raise eyebrows if it failed—but if it succeeded? Filled with a sense of purpose, Bingham and Rice reckoned that the trip would take four months. If they left in December, they could be back in April. To do so, however, Hiram needed boots, a pith helmet, compasses, guns, and steamship tickets. In other words, he needed Tiffany money. Hiram went to the hospital and told Alfreda of the plan, suggesting that it was his "opportunity to accomplish a good piece of work." Her parents disapproved, but she agreed to give him what he needed. She "spent over two weeks in a hospital, while he stayed at the Yale Club and pushed ahead with his plans," their son

Alfred wrote years later.[13] Alfreda had enabled Hiram's development yet again, and she watched him steam away for a new career as an explorer.

The approval Hiram wanted most, however, was his father's. "I feel the Bingham blood stirring in my veins as I start for little known regions, as nearly all my Bingham ancestors for ten generations have done before me," he wrote to Hawaii.[14]

In some strange way, he hoped, he was going home.

Chapter Four

Into the Andes

*I*n Venezuela and Colombia, Hiram Bingham fell in love with South American exploration. He thrilled at rising among peaks and seeing an expanse of lakes and jungles stretch out before him. He relished slogging through a swamp with his rifle at the ready. He even enjoyed arguing over routes and history in a language not his own.

Yet a pith helmet, compass, and slap-leather spirit did not an explorer make. The gap between the storybook version of exploration and its reality was wide. On this first expedition, Hiram Bingham faced all the challenges of the daredevil's craft, from disagreeable guides to starvation; from getting lost to that crucial test: convincing locals that he came in peace and was not a soldier or spy.

It was a late January morning in 1907, just after dawn, and Bingham and his party were following the footsteps of Simón Bolívar's march to independence. They had been in the saddle for nearly twenty-four hours, having missed the turn for a resting place and ridden all night. As their mules splashed across the Cojedes River, a garish, screaming, and beautiful flock of macaws took flight.[1] A few turns in the path later, they got their first glimpse of the Andes Mountains, stretching the length of the continent and beyond: dry and rocky on its western slopes and wet and forested in the east; grassy in its high plains and cold and forbidding in its cloud-wrapped heights.

The Andes were still a long way off, however, and the expedition was far, far behind schedule. By Bingham and Rice's estimation, they should have been in Colombia by then, but they were not even halfway out of Venezuela. The party consisted of Bingham, Rice, a young German named Max, and two black Caribbeans—Josh Obadiah Nero and Richard Harvey. Taking up the rear were two Venezuelans, Rafael Rivas and Waldemera, responsible for a cart laden with Hiram's shopping spree at Abercrombie & Fitch: tents, blankets, pots and pans, emergency rations, brass lanterns, books, maps, surveying instruments, and the "alchemy" of Bingham's success as an explorer: a camera, tripod, and hundreds of bulky photographic plates.

Yet when they rode up to a tavern in the village of Agua Blanca that morning, all the locals could see was that the Americans were armed to the teeth. Bingham and Rice each carried a revolver and a Winchester rifle. The cart bore another revolver, a bolt-action Mauser, two repeating shotguns, and "a sufficient supply of ammunition." The guns were for hunting and protection. The Americans rode toward an area of Venezuela that had recently experienced revolutionary unrest and a stretch of Colombia where Bingham half-hoped to run into "savage" Indians.

Inside the tavern, however, the explorers learned that their guns made everyone nervous. A Venezuelan cattle owner cornered Bingham and asked him what he was doing there. He refused to believe that the Americans would spend their own money to come all the way from the United States to march over dry plains, mazelike swamps, and freezing mountains for the sake of adventure or just to prove that Simón Bolívar had done so a century before. The proposition was more than absurd; it was positively suspect. Angrily, the cattle owner demanded to know "why our Government had sent us," Hiram wrote later. "Was it contemplating taking Venezuela next after Panama?" The Venezuelan declared that no country would pay for the exploration of another unless it had conquest on the brain. "As I persisted in denying both his premises and his conclusions, he decided I must be a spy or an army officer in disguise."

Bingham enjoyed the case of mistaken identity, but the rancher's suspicions weren't as far-fetched as the American claimed. In a few years' time, the Office of Naval Intelligence would employ Harvard archaeologist Sylvanus Morley as a spy in Mexico.[2] Closer to home, ever since President Theodore Roosevelt championed his corollary to the Monroe Doctrine, Venezuela had suspected that the United States was funding insurrections to overthrow President Cipriano Castro, a dictator sometimes called the Lion of the Andes, whom President Roosevelt notoriously denigrated as an "unspeakably villainous little monkey."[3] In Caracas, Bingham had stayed at the American Legation, in a house that had belonged to a Venezuelan general who had funded the last serious revolution and whom Bingham seems to have visited in prison. Bingham had letters of introduction from the

U.S. Secretary of State and Venezuela's minister of Foreign Affairs, but they were hardly disinterested parties. Castro had recently been ill, and there were rumors of power struggles amongst his potential successors. Given that Bingham would meet with the U.S. Legation in Bogota, Colombia, on the other end, the Venezuelan cattle owner might not have been far off. Bingham may not have been in the pay of the U.S. government, but he shared information with them nonetheless. Looming before him in a khaki hunting jacket, a revolver at his waist and his pith helmet in his gloved hands, Bingham looked less like an explorer than the very personification of the colossus looming to the north, whose recent interest in Venezuela had been far from academic.

Chuckling at the man's fear of outright conquest, Bingham rounded up the rest of his group, mounted his mule, and rode on through Venezuela's western plains. By the time they reached the border with Colombia a month and a half later, however, the accusations stopped being funny. In the town of El Amparo, on the Venezuelan side of the Arauca River, they woke up to learn that they were under arrest. Locals had denounced them to the local governor, Bingham fumed, as "a party of six armed men carrying four Winchesters and two Mauser rifles, engaged in convoying a cart-load of arms and ammunition to aid the refugee revolutionists in Colombia!"

Bingham's protests were to no avail; four bedraggled Venezuelan soldiers guarded the inn. Bingham and Rice snuck out, hid the guns in the woods, and toyed with escaping by swimming the river at night. Luckily, the mayor intervened. He took Bingham to meet the "venerable" gray-bearded governor, who was waiting for Bingham on his porch in a white linen suit. He inspected the card of the Venezuelan minister of Foreign Affairs and opened a private letter addressed to the president of Colombia from his minister in Washington. He was disappointed but impressed to find that Bingham's credentials were legitimate.

Bingham drank to the governor's health and—the coup de grâce of every modern traveler—took his photograph. The next morning the expedition bid goodbye to their Venezuelan cart-drivers and loaded their gear in canoes to be ferried across to Colombia. Bingham had disliked Venezuela and was glad to put its "shiftless" people behind him; the country, he claimed, gave "the impression of rest, as though, wearied of the past, it was 'waiting for something to turn up.'" The American stepped into the ferryman's canoe, sat down, and waited to be rowed across.

Colombia was far more accommodating to Bingham's expectations of good treatment. Its officials were as warm as Venezuela's were suspicious and helped them find a guide for the next leg, one Juan de Dios. Bingham liked him because he had "Indian blood." They would later catch him stealing one of Rice's heirlooms, a golden American eagle, but even that was lucky, for the German wanderer, Max, had run off with Bingham's wallet.[4] Bingham wrote Max out of his later account and blamed the theft on de Dios instead.

Juan de Dios was an excellent guide, though, and kept the expedition from disaster when Bingham insisted that they leave the road and go through the swamps. Bingham claimed they took the detour to stay in Bolívar's footsteps, but it was also because he wanted to meet some "savages." They didn't have to wait long before a small party of partially clad Yaruros—a displaced Indian people that subsisted by hunting—approached their camp bearing spears, bows, and arrows. Nero and Harvey claimed they "were about to be eaten alive," but again the danger was more imagined than real. The worst it got was when one of the Yaruro's "vixens" almost threw two handfuls of cow dung at Bingham.

The "Indios bravos" proved friendly and helped the expedition cross the region's rivers in exchange for small trade goods. It was Bingham and Rice who were dangerous, tightly wound white men with Winchesters, raised on Frederic Remington images of noble cowboys and savage Indians. Bingham would soon have his own violent run-in, and Rice would become famous in the 1920s for turning his rifles on a tribe in Brazil. After seeing a "naked savage" running through the underbrush across a river, Rice's men would open fire, at which point 200 "Huge Cannibals" threw up a cry. Rice and his men would escape unhurt, but they did kill several of their attackers.[5]

The dangers on this trip were real but largely of the explorers' own making. Bingham's quest for historical accuracy almost got them killed. During their long detour in the swamps, they ran out of food, and Bingham had to hunt tough, gamey birds so they wouldn't starve. Rice and de Dios, the guide, were furious at the unnecessary danger and finally hauled the party out with a grueling twelve-hour march through piranha-infested waters. Hiram, however, was having a terrific time. He flashed his guns at a tavern keeper in order to get fed. Later on the trail, when four other travelers saw that Bingham was armed, they made sure their knives and revolvers were on display before riding by. "It made me feel like a brigand," Hiram wrote jauntily.

His joy only grew upon reaching the foothills of the Andes. They peered up the green valleys, rising into dark folds, topped by distant blue-white glaciers. At first, they filled Hiram with nostalgia for Hawaii, but the closer he got, the more foreign and old they seemed. The expedition arrived in one small town at the mountains' base on Good Friday. They watched as the congregation processed from the church and shuffled around the plaza, lit by small candles, wreathed in incense.

The pleasure was fleeting. On Easter Sunday, Hiram received a telegram from his in-laws, telling him that Alfreda had fallen ill with malaria while awaiting his return in Jamaica, where the Mitchells had a residence. Hiram felt awful. He had been away for nearly five months and missed his family.

Resolving never to be apart from his family for so long again, he rallied Rice, and they left the very next day, April 5, to begin their climb into the steep, rainy Andes, up rocky stairs, past orchid gatherers, and, for the first time, Andean Indians planting maize. The hardest part of the journey was a two-day traverse of the Paramo of Pisva, a section of the "cold, damp wilderness" occupying the 13,000-foot high summit of the *cordillera*. This was the route that the Spaniards thought Bolívar's army would never clear. It did not disappoint. It was bleak, absent of animal life, and covered with coarse grass, thorny plants, and "sloughs of despond." They picked their way around small freezing lakes in which their Indian guides said the Spanish hid treasure while fleeing Bolívar. The cloud-hidden hills surrounding them were actually Andean peaks 14,000 feet above sea level. Bingham and Rice made it to the grassy farmland below, but only after abandoning the Caribbean crewmen, whose mules had died. Nero and Harvey shivered through a night without fire, shelter, or food but "came limping down the valley" the next morning.

They had crossed the Andes, but it proved the expedition's breaking point. On April 21, they reached the main highway to Bogota, Colombia's capital, and Rice left Bingham behind, "owing to Bingham's conduct." To their fellow explorers, he claimed that Bingham was incompetent.[6] They never spoke to each other again, nor would either one co-lead another expedition.

Bingham rode on, hurried and tense, so eager to get to Bogota that he all but ignored one of the most interesting clues of his first expedition. On the road, a local man told Bingham that in the distance lay a "treasure lake." It was there that the "ancient kings of Tunja took their annual gold baths and threw objects of gold," said the local. A foreign company was now trying to drain the lake. Did the *gringo* want to investigate?

The *gringo* did not. It was a fascinating snippet of information, but he had heard about treasure lakes all through Colombia and thought them just another myth about the supposed civilization and lasting wealth of indigenous peoples in the Americas. He may have thought it a tall tale better left to the gullible readers of dime novels and the many sketchy early-twentieth-century newspaper reports of lost treasure in South America.[7] He noted the anecdote in his journal and rode on. For all his open-mindedness regarding Spanish American history, he still didn't think the region's indigenous people were worth studying on their own.

Of course, the hemisphere's Indians did have a rich culture and civilization, past and present. Even more ironic, in this case the legend was true. The lake was none other than Guatavita, where the revered leader of the Muisca peoples once covered himself in gold dust, swam or paddled to the lake's center, and dropped offerings into the water's depths. The legend of *El Rey Dorado,* the Golden King, became *El Dorado,* the mythical kingdom of gold sought for centuries in the jungles of South America. Hundreds, if not thousands, of wild-eyed conquistadors and explorers had ruined their reputations, gone mad, or died searching for it, from Sir Walter Raleigh to Lope de Aguirre.

Guatavita itself was no myth. In the seventeenth century, a Spaniard drained it a few feet and found gold discs and emeralds in the mud. An 1856 effort at another nearby lake recovered a "golden figure of the chief and ten attendants on a raft." The latest effort began in 1898, when an Englishman named Hartley Knowles bought out a group of Colombians. By 1907, when Bingham rode by, Knowles was cutting channels to drain it entirely. In 1912, Knowles would put 62 lots of gold ornaments, snakes, and golden masks up for auction at Sotheby's in London.[8] The following year, in a Fifth Avenue hotel, Knowles would tell a *New York Times* reporter that he had found $20,000 worth of treasure. He clutched what remained in a cigar box. "El Dorado," he said softly. "El Dorado, after centuries. The gifts of the golden man. The treasure of the sacred lake."[9]

It was almost too good to be true. Given that Knowles was looking for buyers, it might not have been. But by 1913, Hiram Bingham would be paying attention. Upon his return to the U.S. he began work on a photograph-laden book about the trip, *Journal of an Expedition Across Venezuela and Colombia.* His writing was good, if sensational—the *New York Times* teased his tendency to exaggerate their peril—and Bingham was made a fellow of the hallowed Royal Geographic Society.[10] For the rest of his life, Bingham included the prestigious "F.R.G.S." after his name in *Who's Who in America* and listed his primary occupation as "explorer."

The title was not enough, however. To be able to judge Knowles as a charlatan or a real discoverer, Bingham needed one more journey to South America. His next one would take him to Peru, where lost cities were as fantastic as El Dorado and as real as Guatavita—and where there was far more at stake than how Bolívar crossed a mountain.

Chapter Five

Cuzco, the Navel
of the World

*B*efore traveling to South America, Hiram was a tiny cog in Princeton's academic machine. When he returned in the spring of 1907, the bolts binding him fell away. Upon reaching Bogota, he had learned that Alfreda's health had improved. Now, after a tearful reunion, Alfreda handed him the letter for which he had been waiting seven years: Yale University President Arthur Hadley had finally found him a job. Because Yale's History Department remained skeptical of Bingham's qualifications, it was only a temporary appointment as a lecturer in the graduate school. It came with a meager honorarium, meaning that Hiram would have to keep living off his wife's allowance. It was unflattering, but because it was the first opportunity in U.S. academia "implying the authority to *teach* the History and Geography of South America as a specialty," Bingham took the chance. He declared "a triumph over conservative prejudice" in a letter to his father.

Hiram treated it as a calling: to prepare Yale men to take up the mantle of development and civilization in the hemisphere. "I suppose it is in my blood to wish to strike into untrod fields and take up burdens that others are not trying to lift," he wrote to his father. "*Lux et Veritas*—Yale's vaunted 'Light and Truth'—is then the proper motto for me."[1] His classes were one part history, one part geography, and one part jingoism, as his first final exam laid bare: "What Spanish American countries offer (1) excellent, (2) fair, (3) poor opportunities for (a) a Mining Engineer. (b) a Soldier of Fortune. (c) a Capitalist. (d) an average Yale graduate with good health and a capital of $5,000?"[2] Full professors whispered about their rich young colleague's gravitas, but the students liked him. One called his course "useful—which most history courses are not."[3]

Hadley had also hired Hiram to raise the university's profile in the field of exploration. Hungry for a discovery that would make him famous, Hiram was happy to oblige. When he heard that the United States would be fielding its first delegation to the next Pan-American Scientific Congress in Chile, he saw his chance. He would retrace Spanish trade routes in the southern Andes, from Argentina, land of the tango and cowboy gauchos, up to Bolivia, the indigenous peak of the continent. After breaking his journey in Chile to represent Yale at the conference, he would go on to Lima, the capital of Peru. He would be more practical this time, taking trains when it was convenient, traveling with one person at most, all the while looking for places in which his students could invest. His role model, President Roosevelt, had cooled down his militarism in his second term; there was still an empire to build, but one of business, knowledge, and culture, not military force. This time, Hiram would leave the guns at home.

In June 1908, Hiram and his fellow delegates met President Roosevelt at the White House. It pleased the thirty-three-year-old to no end to be counted among such pillars of America's international ambitions: Col. William C. Gorgas, who beat back malaria and yellow fever in Panama, permitting the construction of the canal; William Henry Holmes from the Bureau of American Ethnology, the hemisphere's leading expert on the antiquity of man; Bingham's mentor at Berkeley, Bernard Moses, back from the Philippines; and Dr. Leo S. Rowe, who would lay the foundations of the Organization of American States, the United Nations of the western hemisphere. In front of the massive globe in the corner of his hero's office, Bingham shook Roosevelt's hand, making it clear—if it wasn't already—that he explored under America's flag.

Hiram spent that summer with his family—five sons now—and his father, Hiram Bingham Jr., who had come to the mainland to recover from a stroke. For his birthday, his son made a kind gesture: they went to church together for the first time in years. Hiram Jr. fell ill afterward, and his son waited for him to leave the hospital before he boarded a steamer and weighed anchor for South America.

While Hiram was at sea, his father relapsed and died alone. Hiram would not find out for months, trailed by the letter from his wife that broke the news. "Do not form the habit of living your life without me," she underlined.[4] When he found out, however, his reaction was private and muted. He could only keep exploring. The Andes was his future, and his family seemed to plunge into the ocean behind him.

Hiram Bingham braced himself as the teeth-rattling eight-horse stagecoach left the Bolivian border town of Quiaca, picking up speed as it bounced along the high desert of the southern Andes. Hiram clutched the coach's side, praying he wouldn't be sick before the next town, but he was happy to be on his way.

He and his traveling partner, a Yale student named Huntington "Coot" Smith Jr., had taken the train from Buenos Aires up the dusty pampas to Bolivia. On the border, they traded their city clothes for riding gear but to little effect. In a wide pancake hat and a woolen Bolivian poncho, Bingham's clean boots and long frame stuck out even more. In Quiaca, two "rough-looking Anglo-Saxons" sat down with the Yale men, uninvited. Quietly, but with a note of intimidation, they began to talk about the highway robbers that haunted Bolivian roads, "driven out of the United States by the force of law and order and hounded to death all over the world by Pinkerton detectives," the private army of agents that broke strikes and guaranteed American industry's profits against theft.[5] Bingham and Coot were relieved when the stagecoach arrived.

In the next town, Hiram and Coot learned that they had literally dodged a bullet. The two roughnecks were bandits themselves, likely accomplices to two other American bandits who had robbed a cart carrying a silver mine's payroll the week before. Bolivian soldiers had cornered the latter pair—one was indeed on the run from the Pinkertons—in a lodging house. When the smoke cleared, the two bandits were buried in anonymous graves, each body a half dozen bullets heavier.

Bingham wrote the story down, not realizing its larger significance. Modern writers Anne Meadows and Daniel Buck, however, believe that the two men killed by the Bolivians were none other than the famed stick-up artists Robert LeRoy Parker and Harry Alonzo Longabaugh, also known as Butch Cassidy and the Sundance Kid.[6] The pair had been living in the area at the time, and Bingham's story corroborates several rumors of their death. And in an even stranger turn, Bingham bought one of their mules. "When his former owner had had the benefit of his fleet legs and his splendid lungs, there was no question of his being caught by the Bolivian soldiery," the lecturer later mused, not realizing his brush with yet another legend of the Americas.

Hiram soon had his own chance to test out the mule's "fleet legs." In a rural inn at 13,015 feet, a few miles outside the old silver-mining city of Potosí, Bingham had a fierce attack of *soroche*—altitude sickness—and decided to leave and seek a doctor. The Quechua Indian innkeeper refused one of Bingham's bills, saying that it was from an untrustworthy bank. The denial unnerved the American: "The idea of having a servile [Quechua] decline to receive good money was irritating, and I tried my best, notwithstanding my *soroche,* to force him to take it." Bingham tried another bill, but his hand was trembling with "chill or excitement" and he tore it. The Indian refused that one as well; Bingham rolled up the first bill, threw it, and bolted. The Indian ran after him, grabbed Bingham's bridle, and tried to halt his flight. Furious, Bingham rode the innkeeper against a wall until he let go. Bingham unrepentantly included the story in his next book. "I fully expected that he would follow us with stones or something worse, but as he was only a [Quechua] he accepted the inevitable and we saw no more of him."

Hiram continued on to the Pan-American Scientific Congress in Santiago, Chile, where he revealed what he had learned thus far about the history of South America. He declared Quechua-speaking Indians a "backward race" that made it easy to understand how the "brave, bigoted, courageous" conquistadors had defeated the Incas. By contrast, the Spaniards had achieved a "marvelously rapid conquest of America." All their modern heirs lacked was the "sense of racial unity" that made the United States possible, Bingham declared.

But Bingham's race-based understanding of history—and the direction of his life—were about to receive a stinging blow. In Bolivia, he had seen the interesting but heavily looted ruins of Tiahuanaco and inspected a copy of a very interesting book by E. G. Squier, an American diplomat who had explored the southern Andes of Peru in the 1860s. Squier was an excellent draftsman, and his drawings of the Incas' rope bridges and ruins fascinated Bingham. He had planned to take a ship straight from Santiago to Lima, Peru's capital, when the meetings and endless speeches were over. Inspired, in January 1909 he instead disembarked in the southern Peruvian port of Mollendo. With his credentials as a delegate to the congress, he talked his way into a free ticket for a train that would take him 485 miles and 14,000 feet up into the Andes. He was headed for the land of the Incas. It was the detour that defined his life.

The country outside the train window had changed much since Peru won its independence from Spain in late 1824. For the first two decades, Peruvian strongmen fought over a country bereft of capital, agriculture, and mining infrastructure. Government funds came from poorly run customs houses and "tribute" from the country's Indians.[7] Charles Darwin visited in 1835 and marveled at the state's seeming anarchy.

In the early 1840s, Peru tapped into an unorthodox gold mine: bird droppings. Peru's coastal islands were loaded with phosphate- and nitrogen-rich guano, which Europe wanted for fertilizer and gunpowder. Peru became the biggest exporter in South America, allowing it to build up its wool, sugar, copper, and saltpeter industries.

The country's stability was built on false premises, however. The government passed liberal reforms that freed the country's 20,000 slaves and eliminated indigenous tribute, but those reforms also separated many Indian peasants from their land. The money from guano concessions leached out to foreign firms and to the country's lenders.[8] When the guano boom went bust, Peru went deeper into debt, finally going bankrupt in 1870. The country reached its nadir in 1879, when British-backed Chile declared war on Peru's ally, Bolivia. Because Peru and Bolivia had a secret alliance, the Chilean army invaded Peru as well. Before Peru surrendered in 1883, ceding its own southernmost province to Chile, the invading army looted Lima.

Although the war's long-term loser was Bolivia, which lost its sea access, Peru's indigenous peoples were also hit especially hard. They were the army's first line, and many deserted to their villages, not wanting to fight in what they perceived as a white war. Some rebelled against their commanders. Still others formed their own peasant bands to fight the Chileans, but Peru's coastal elites repressed and erased them from the historical record when the war was through.[9] As one historian wrote years later: "The mixture of hatred, dismissal and fear that the great property holders—whites and coastal Peruvians—had towards the popular classes below them—Indians, Chinese and blacks—was identical to that which the Spanish conquistadors maintained towards the conquered Andean peoples."[10]

To recover from the war, Peru's elite political parties embraced a policy of near-total economic liberalization. American and British corporations received massive concessions to develop the country's infrastructure, mineral wealth, and natural resources. Peru was once again on the lips of London and New York. By 1909, Peru's economy had stabilized, and its elites were enjoying the glamour of "The Aristocratic Republic."

For the half of Peru's four to five million who were indigenous, that influx of wealth changed their status little and perhaps even worsened it.[11] American companies employed their own private police forces at their mines, ensuring that their indigenous workers did not flee. British capital helped fund a rubber-collecting boom in eastern Peru. Some jungle tribes benefited from the rapid trade in Winchesters, axes, and human lives, but other entire tribes, particularly in the northern Putumayo region, were enslaved, tortured, and killed by employees of the rubber companies.

There was some hope, however. Since the mid-nineteenth century, Indian peasants in southern Peru periodically mobilized, rebelling against government officials and landowners. Others migrated to cities to escape the countryside and improve their station. Workers in urban areas were exposed to radical politics, formed unions, and in April 1911, for the first time in Peruvian history, they would go on strike. Seeing the danger and political opportunity, Peruvian President Augusto B. Leguía in 1909 passed a series of labor laws that prohibited government authorities from demanding free work from Indians and decreed that no one was "obliged" to work in mines. Whether they were effectual or not, the country's intellectuals celebrated the country's Andean roots and its noble "Quechua race," sought to document abuses of rural Indians, and criticized the Eurocentric racism of Lima, the country's outward-looking political capital. More importantly, they idolized the Andean, pre-Columbian, still-inhabited city that Bingham's train now approached: Cuzco, or as the Inca chronicler Garcilaso de la Vega translated it, "The Navel of the World."[12]

Hiram woke up on January 28, 1909, in the town of Checcacupe. Bleary-eyed, he met his traveling partner for the last leg of this epic journey through the Andes. His name was Clarence Hay, and he was the twenty-four-year-old secretary for the U.S. delegation to Chile. His father was John Hay, the U.S. Secretary of State who died in 1905, having helped Roosevelt build America into a world power. While Clarence and Hiram talked, the train chugged down the track, entering the 11,600-foot-high Huatanay Valley. Slopes of thick cornstalks and blue-green potato plants swept by; the red earth and purple stone shone after the rains. Bingham was struck by the golden quality of the light and the apparent happiness of the people.

He was as enchanted as the Incas had been when they themselves reached the valley centuries before. According to the Incas' great origin story, their ancestors established Cuzco when the legendary Inca founder Manco Capac reached a land where he could drive his golden staff into the ground. Above the staff Manco Capac built Cuzco and its Temple of the Sun, Ccoricancha.[13] Beyond the legend, scholars in 1909 believed that a megalithic people of some great antiquity, responsible for the Andes' most massive stonework, had preceded or overlapped with the Incas at Cuzco.

Today, scholars recognize the myth-making quality of the Incas' histories and suggest that the Incas arrived in the valley from near Lake Titicaca sometime in the twelfth century. Other cultures had spread throughout the Andes before them, but the Incas were unique. Around 1440, while Spain was attempting its own reconquest of the Iberian peninsula, a nearby people named the Chancas invaded the Huatanay, nearly conquering the Incas. A leader named Pachacutec—whose name in Quechua meant 'Earthshaker' or 'World-Changer'—pushed them back, expanding Inca territory well beyond its defensive perimeter.[14]

Under Pachacutec, the Incas swept along the Andes. A master architect and state planner, he marked his conquests with new fortresses and religious structures tied together by roads and storehouses. If an ethnic group resisted, they were brutally defeated and relocated. As long as they agreed to speak Quechua and worship the sun—whose earthbound host, conveniently enough, was the emperor himself—they were treated kindly. Unlike their predecessors in Central America, the Olmec and the Maya, the Incas had not developed writing, but their braided *khipus* (or quipus) kept a tight accounting of their assets and schedules. The empire was highly stratified, but the Incas collected and allocated labor, food, and goods in a manner that would later be likened, perhaps overzealously, to agrarian socialism.

When Pachacutec died, his heirs carried on his ambitions. Inca succession was perfect for expansion: the emperor's heir inherited his title but not his lands or palaces, fueling further conquest along the Andes.[15] When the Spanish arrived, Tawantinsuyo, or the land of the four quarters, was 2,500 miles long. The northwest quarter, Chinchaysuyu, extended to modern Colombia; southwestern Cuntisuyu extended to Chile; Collasuyu extended southeast through Bolivia to northern Argentina; and to the northeast was the mysterious Antisuyu, where the eastern slopes of Andes melted into the Amazon jungle. It was a kingdom larger than any other on earth at the time—"as if a single power held sway from St. Petersburg to Cairo," journalist Charles C. Mann has suggested.[16]

While Inca power spiraled out, wealth flowed in. The Incas considered gold and silver holy and used the "sweat of the sun and tears of the moon" in Cuzco, their empire's sacred capital. Each emperor built a stone palace in which his gold-draped mummy resided after he died. They covered their plaza with seashells and tiny golden and silver llamas. Canals and channels gave the city running water. The gold-covered walls of the sun temple Ccoricancha were mounted with torches, filling the city with a warm glow at night.

Eager to see what remained, Bingham and Hay stared out the window as their train pulled into a makeshift station a quarter mile south of the city. Cuzco's prefect—the most powerful government official in this corner of the Andes—hustled the two honored delegates from the Pan-American Scientific Congress into a carriage. Rattling up an "ill-kept avenue" lined with alder trees, Bingham saw Santo Domingo, the monastery the Spaniards built atop of Ccoricancha. The gold that once covered the Sun temple, of course, was long gone. After the Spaniards landed in Peru in 1532, they were drawn to the city's wealth like bees to pollen. As John Hemming put it, "the sack of Cuzco was one of the very rare moments in world history when conquerors pillaged at will the capital of a great empire." The Indians wept as they watched the Spaniards melt down seven hundred four-and-a-half-pound plates of gold from Ccoricancha, a whole garden of silver plants and animals, and a massive gold altar. The looting shocked even the Spanish priests. "Their only concern was to collect gold and silver to make themselves all rich without thinking that they were doing wrong and were wrecking and destroying," wrote one. "For what was being destroyed was more perfect than anything they enjoyed and possessed."[17]

But there was a limit to what the Spaniards could topple. Hiram could see that the city's buildings were colonial in their exteriors—red-tiled roofs, wooden balconies, and whitewashed walls. But when their carriage stopped in the Plaza del Regocijo, he would have seen the building facing their hotel: a massive house that had belonged to the family of the Inca chronicler Garcilaso de la Vega. Its front was colonial, but its foundation, like so many of the buildings in the city center, was Inca: massive boulders still so tightly joined that not even a pin could be forced between them. When earthquakes shook the Spanish halves of buildings to pieces, these indigenous foundations remained in place.

Hiram and Hay woke the next morning to a city that only recently had shaken off the neglect of the nineteenth century, when wealth and power flowed from the provinces to Lima and Cuzco was relegated to the past. The city's population hovered at about 19,000, with a quarter identified as white, a quarter as Indian, and about half as *mestizos*.[18] Although a class of merchants and industrialists had developed in the last several decades, the city still resembled a pyramid whose tiny peak was a mostly white class of elite landowners who shuttled between their homes near the plaza and the haciendas they owned in nearby valleys. Their wealth was built on the pyramid's indigenous base, the Quechua-speaking peasants who cultivated coffee, sugar cane, cacao, pineapples, avocados, bananas, papaya, and the chewable coca leaf. In the city, they were servants, water carriers, and porters. They were earthy, hard-working, and hard-drinking people who spent long hours alongside the growing middle class in bars, drinking *chicha*, the same sacred, sour, and frothy corn beer enjoyed by the Incas. To relieve themselves, they shuffled into Cuzco's quiet, narrow cobblestone streets and used the thin canals that ran down the center of the street, just as the Incas had. Traffic moved no faster than a coach or mule train. "Barring festivals or special occasions, the streets were desolate and calm, breathing with a peaceful and lethargic atmosphere," one Cuzco son recalled. Every night, lamplighters climbed ladders and put out the gas lanterns, dissipating the city's hazy, yellow glow.[19]

For the next three days, Hiram took in as much of the place as he could. He visited the city's many Catholic churches, but then left them to run his fingers across the Incan walls across the street. He haggled with colorfully dressed indigenous market women for souvenirs for his family. He avoided the open sewers—he thought the city was filthy—and photographed fountains that supposedly had been in use since the Incas. He visited the city's central plaza where, he was told, the Spanish executed an Inca revolutionary named Tupac Amaru. Bingham was fascinated by the city's antiquity. No other city of the Americas so displayed the hemisphere's history, both ancient and modern.

Hiram visited the University of San Antonio Abad del Cuzco, which sat alongside the baroque Jesuit church on the central plaza. He thought the school "rather squalid by comparison with the church" but was impressed by its age. There had been a university in Cuzco since 1598—"thirty-eight years before Harvard College." He met with the school's rector, who was kind, if a little sleepy, and he learned that the school's goal was to prepare Cuzco's upper-middle-class sons for gentlemanly careers in law.

Bingham had visited in the midst of vacations, however. Had he waited until the students returned, he might have met a nineteen-year-old university student named Luis E. Valcárcel, who had a rather different estimation of the school and the city surrounding it. The son of merchants who moved to Cuzco in the late nineteenth century, Valcárcel's middle-class upbringing gave him the comfort to consider a career beyond business. He was passionate and impetuous enough to get himself challenged to duels twice in his youth, but he was also a scholar. Pincenez perched on his nose, beetle-black hair combed back, he read everywhere— at breakfast, in the bathroom, in the street—harboring dreams of a life of study.

If his family had enough money, they might have sent him to Lima, or even Europe, to learn from the great scientists of the day. Instead, they enrolled him at the University of Cuzco.

Yet the university was not the academic monastery Valcárcel expected. Its professors were lackadaisical, unafraid to skip their own classes. They were scholarly but "knew little about the problems of the regions and its inhabitants."[20] Valcárcel and his classmates had seen more changes in the past four years than their parents' had in their lifetime, and he and his fellow students wanted more. First had come the telegraph. Then in 1905 the city got telephone service. Around the same time a second semiregular newspaper was founded, *El Sol,* which was as radical as the older *El Comercio* was sober. In September 1908, after forty years of planning, came the greatest innovation of all: the railroad. Valcárcel would always remember how the screech of the first train—named "The Conquistador," ironically enough—cut through the city's air, echoing off the surrounding ridges.[21] He and his fellow students abandoned their classrooms to run down and join the massive crowd cheering at the tracks, where the arriving wagons, brakemen, and engineers, mostly English, seemed so strange, "something like Martians in our imaginations."

The railroad brought goods, commerce, and further advances in technology to Cuzco—in another decade an Italian aviator would be the first to fly to the Inca city from Lima—but it also brought ideas, a new sense of "modernity," and one of the greatest factors of Cuzco's twentieth-century history: tourists.[22] Increasingly aware of how outsiders viewed their city, Valcárcel and his fellow students began to grumble about their lackluster education. While Bingham met with the university's rector for tea, the students were in Cuzco's *chicha* bars, arguing over why the region was underdeveloped. Many blamed the landowners and their abuse of the Indian population. Others blamed it on elite complacency and a lack of pride in the past. Cuzco was "the only city of America where all time periods and civilizations exist," Valcárcel later declared, but his teachers were little interested in investigating their city's history using "modern" methods.[23]

What his discontent amounted to, however, was yet to be seen. Valcárcel and the fellow members of his generation were "without a doubt, not only the most brilliant that Cuzco produced in the twentieth century, but also the most influential," wrote one later historian.[24] Over the next two decades they helped shape a movement named *indigenismo,* which championed the study and protection of Indians and Incan history. Their attitudes would change the way Cuzco looked at its history, understood its present, and faced its future. But in early 1909, they were still waiting for the fight that they would make their own—one in which a certain explorer would play his part.

On their last day in the city, Hiram and Hay borrowed mules from Cuzco's prefect and rode up the steep streets into the northern quarter of the city. At the city limits, they spurred their beasts up a ravine. Higher and higher they climbed, until they made one final turn in the path and rode through a gateway twelve feet tall, made of massive boulders. Behind them, Cuzco stretched out like a careworn textile, tumbling red roofs broken by dozing streets and squares of gray and brown. And before them stretched one of the most incredible structures Bingham had ever seen: Sacsayhuaman, an Inca fortress and religious complex a third of a mile long. Three massive and zigzagging walls, stacked on each other like terraces, had once protected it from attackers. Each wall was built of "colossal boulders, some of them twelve feet in diameter." The tallest stones, as far as Bingham could see, were twenty-five feet high. He could hardly comprehend how its builders fit them in place. "There are few sights in the world more impressive than these Cyclopean walls," he wrote.

It reminded Hiram of the massive temples and beautifully jointed walls of Pacific peoples—on Easter Island, in the Carolinas, and in Hawaii. He had grown up hearing about the "heathen" complexes that his grandfather all but danced upon. But while his grandfather had felt joy in their ruin, Hiram felt something new: sadness and awe. Sadness that Cuzco's residents had pulled apart many of the site's smaller walls to build the city below. But awe at the beauty, solidity, and grandness of what remained. His parents had raised him to look at the native peoples of the world with a patronizing pity; it was only after native peoples found Jesus Christ that they would become civilized. Sacsayhuaman and Cuzco, however, told a different story: that the people of the Americas were civilized enough when Europeans arrived, and that something beautiful, not pitiable, was lost in their subjugation. As a historian, Hiram had studied the revolutionaries who struggled against Spain. Now, he wondered if he had gotten it wrong—whether the true fight for the Americas came before, when the conquistadors clashed with the Incas under this fortress's walls. Sacsayhuaman was "the most impressive spectacle of man's handiwork that I have ever seen in America," Bingham wrote. He wanted more.

Chapter Six

Choqquequirau, the Cradle of Gold

*H*iram and Hay leaned into the rain, hoping their ponchos would keep them warm on the long ride ahead. Their Cuzco hosts had implored them to avoid the dangers of the rainy season by taking the train back to the coast, where they could catch a comfortable steamship north. But after Hiram's epiphany at Sacsayhuaman, he wanted to see as much of Peru as he could. They would ride to Lima, the capital, on the old, overland road once marched by Incas, Spaniards, and revolutionaries. Hiram would learn much from the *Cuzqueños* in the near future; but at this crucial moment, he did well to follow his instincts. By traveling this final leg of the expedition by mule, Hiram exposed himself to the Inca site. That completed his transformation into an explorer of the Andes' indigenous past.

Led by a Peruvian soldier, Hiram and Hay rode to the northwest, into the high *altiplano*. The cold plains were bleak, but the next day they dropped into green forests. They braved a rocky staircase rushing with water to descend into a densely vegetated tropical region. Vines brushed their shoulders. "Beautiful yellow broom flowers were abundant. The air was filled with the fragrance of heliotrope. Parti-colored lantanas ran riot through a maze of agaves and hanging creepers. We had entered a new world."[1]

They reached the Apurimac River, one of the great, roaring sources of the Amazon. The Incas called it the Laughing Monarch or Great Speaker, the Capac Mayu, and to cross it, they built suspension bridges, whose calf-thick ropes of twisted grass cleared spans of 150 feet, swinging queasily in the midday winds.

They had long since rotted away, however, so the Americans rode their mules down a steep switchback trail to a more modest but only slightly less terrifying bridge, suspended only a few feet above the raging river. They held their breath and let their mules carry them safely across.

A dapper young Peruvian in uniform greeted them on the other side. His name was Lieutenant Cáceres, and he was there to escort them to Abancay, the next city on their route. Cáceres was bluff and friendly, and his buttons, boots, and swords gleamed in the sun. He spoke quickly in Spanish, peppering Hiram and Hay with questions as they rode past sugar plantations festooned with sprays of blue salvia and pink begonias. They rounded a bend and landed in a crowd of twenty-four smiling landowners and soldiers. They cheered and escorted the honored American *científicos* into the small city, where they met Abancay's prefect, an attentive and mustachioed man named J. J. Nuñez.

The Americans had scarcely settled into the local club when Nuñez called, sat down, and began to weave a tale of Inca kingdoms, Virgins of the Sun, fabulous treasure, and the Andes, visible from the balcony behind him.

Nuñez was new to Abancay. When he arrived, he heard of a story that had been in circulation since the late eighteenth century. A few days ride to the north, it went, there was an inaccessible mountaintop ruin that many believed was the very last city of the Incas. With the Apurimac River rushing below, this city once sheltered 15,000 people, but its most important inhabitants were the supposed Virgins of the Sun, the Inca princesses devoted to the cult of sun worship. Undiscovered by the Spanish, they died there, one by one, taking with them the secret of their empire's greatest treasure.

The site's name, said Nuñez, was Choqquequirau, Quechua for the Cradle of Gold.

Many had tried to reach it and failed, he said. A local official had organized soldiers and dragooned a legion of Indians to excavate the site systematically, but they had been unable to scale the final precipice. The few who fought through the river and the 6,000 jungle-choked feet to the ruins were so exhausted when they arrived that they could do no excavations. They returned full of tales of "'palaces, paved squares, temples, prisons, and baths,' all crumbling away beneath luxuriant tropical vegetation."

Seeing the opportunity, Nuñez organized the local landowners into a corporation of treasure hunters. Expecting profits from the sale of any Inca gold found, each landowner paid a subscription, and soon Nuñez had $3,000—more than

$70,000 today—to carry out the venture.[2] He sent Lt. Cáceres and a team of soldiers and Indians to the Apurimac, where they paid a Chinese-Peruvian peddler named Don Mariano Mendez to swim across the churning rapids with a telegraph wire. The treasure hunters used the wire to haul over a rickety bridge, and then foot by agonizing foot, they cleared a trail through the scrubby labyrinth of underbrush to the cloud-swept site.

It was as beautiful as expected, but their efforts at treasure hunting came up short. Expecting gold and silver, the soldiers had used dynamite to blow up walls, vaporizing everything but the rock and earth. They had found very little so far.

But how lucky it was that Bingham and Hay had come along, Nuñez gushed. As an American delegate to the Pan-American Scientific Congress and a historian, no less, Bingham surely knew how to excavate Choqquequirau properly, said Nuñez over Bingham's protests. Would the Americans take a further detour from their march to Lima and help Lt. Cáceres survey the Cradle of Gold?

Hiram Bingham thought for a moment, then firmly, apologetically, said no.

Despite his moment at Sacsayhuaman, he was still in a hurry. He was tired and eager to return to his family. He had never read about these particular ruins, let alone a mysterious refuge of the Incas and their princesses. It all sounded a little too much like El Dorado, a prospect Bingham had turned down before without regret.

Nuñez was taken aback. What self-proclaimed explorer could turn down such an offer? Luckily, he was a smooth negotiator and had kept some inducements until last: if Bingham and Hay visited Choqquequirau, they would be the first foreigners to do so, he claimed. Not only that, but the Peruvian president himself had telegraphed to ask that the company halt its excavations so that the Americans could see the ruins as close to their "original condition" as possible.

Flattered, Bingham relented. It would seem ungrateful to refuse such attention. If Choqquequirau was anything like Cuzco, immense prestige would come from being the first foreigner to visit it. That evening over dinner, Bingham examined an Inca mace that the landowners declared was pure gold. Bingham thought it bronze, but as he hefted it, he was reminded of Hawaii, where similar wooden clubs were used to beat *tapa*, the bark cloth of the Pacific. Had he come full circle? According to one writer, he bought it on the spot.[3]

The expedition left by mule two days later, a little hung-over but ready for adventure. Lt. Cáceres led the way, followed by Castillo, his right-hand man, and the eager Americans. A team of Indians followed on foot. Once they crossed the river, they would carry the Americans' food and supplies. Conscripted by Cáceres, they were paid a pittance and could be jailed if they refused to work. Bingham and Hay noticed the Indians' lot—the abstemious pair were particularly annoyed that the Indians had to carry the elite Peruvians' beer—but said little.

They focused on the "well-nigh impassable bogs, swollen torrents, avalanches of boulders and trees" instead. At the end of the first day, they began the descent to the Apurimac on a narrow, twisting path. An avalanche had killed a pair of mules here two weeks before. Cáceres tried to stop the party before nightfall, but Bingham and Hay were impatient to reach the river. Cáceres sighed. "All the rest was level ground," he deadpanned, then led them down the steepest section yet, hairpin turns every twenty feet. Bingham's mule lost its way in the dark. When it started trembling, Bingham realized it had wandered onto the edge of a precipice. They blindly spurred their mules over a small waterfall, Cáceres's voice their only guide.

The next morning, February 7, 1909, they crossed the river without the mules and began the hike to the ruins 6,000 feet above. The higher they got, the less the Americans needed Cáceres's bellows of *"valor!"* The climb was astounding, a switchback trail that offered ever more breathtaking views of jagged Andean peaks and the Apurimac, whose roar faded but never disappeared. The trail was so steep that at times they went on all fours. They crossed small streams beneath waterfalls, balancing on slippery logs. They clung tight to walls and pulled themselves up rickety ladders. "Most of the time we were hanging on to the side of a mountain almost by our eyelids," Bingham later told the *New York Herald*.[4]

The danger only heightened the experience. At 11,000 feet they were entranced. "Nowhere have I ever witnessed such beauty and grandeur as was here displayed," wrote Bingham. "A white torrent raged through the cañon six thousand feet below us. Where its sides were not too precipitous to admit of vegetation, the steep slopes were covered with green foliage and luxuriant flowers. From the hilltops near us other slopes rose six thousand feet beyond and above to the glaciers and snow capped summits of Mts. [Salcantay] and Soray. In the distance as far as we could see, a maze of hills, valleys, tropical jungle, and snow-capped peaks held the imagination as though by a spell. Such were our rewards as we lay panting by the side of the little path when we had reached its highest point."

Bingham and Hay pressed on ahead, eager to reach the ruins before their guides. When they spotted it, it was as if a veil had suddenly been ripped away. In the distance, about a thousand feet down in altitude, were a few cleared buildings on the saddle of a ridge. To the north, the ridge rose up into unseen glaciers and peaks. To the south, the saddle crested with a flattened hilltop, then plummeted to the Apurimac. Hiram and Hay walked faster, and the trail spat them onto a long Inca agricultural terrace, covered with scrubby trees and thick, damp undergrowth. There were terraces above and below—the ancient Andeans' ingenious method of turning steep mountains into farmland. They entered the ruins proper, and in the central plaza they waited for the rest of the party to catch up. As they did, an Andean condor, the largest flying bird of the Americas, flew down to "investigate the invaders of his domain." Its wings, Bingham claimed, stretched ten feet from tip to tip. The condor came within forty feet and then wheeled away on in its long, raggedy black feathers.

Lt. Cáceres and Castillo arrived, and the two Americans and two Peruvians together watched the sun fall behind the cloudy peaks and folds of the Andes beyond. The vine-covered Inca walls around them glowed like embers, the hearthstones of a dead empire returning to life at dusk, held together by nature—a fitting welcome to the Cradle of Gold. When the sun disappeared, the men scrambled for shelter. They were 10,000 feet above sea level and had a cold, wet night ahead. In their excitement to reach the site, the *yankís* had unwisely outpaced their Quechua porters. Their tents, blankets, food, and warm clothes would not arrive until the following morning. The Peruvians took charge, guiding the *gringos* to a small thatched hut. All four crawled inside and huddled together with only a shelter tent and dry grass for insulation.

Hiram tried to sleep, but it was too cold and damp to do anything but shiver and think of the palaces, prisons, and gardens he would explore in the daylight. Here, on the rooftop of the hemisphere, his last icicles of indifference to native history broke away.

When the porters trudged out of the clouds early the next morning, the Americans pulled on drier clothes and got to work. For the next several days they toiled and slept through near-constant rain, but their spirits were unsinkable. This was both Bingham's and Hay's first brush with archaeology, and they found its mixture of physical exertion and historical detective work intoxicating.

Bingham had with him his copy of the Royal Geographical Society's *Hints to Travelers,* which outlined what an explorer was supposed to do when confronted with ruins. Building by building, Bingham and Hay measured and photographed what Lt. Cáceres and the Peruvians uncovered on their previous visit. They started at the southernmost point of the ridge, where a parapet and two windowless buildings leaned out into space like a crow's nest. The Incas had flattened the hill-top, and Bingham speculated that they used it for signal fires to warn Cuzco of enemies approaching from the Amazon. The ridge then dropped into the leveled saddle and the site's finest buildings. There was a long high wall, a large single-story structure with many doors that was likely a meeting hall, and a block of two-story houses with gabled ends. A water channel linked a pair of well-paved tanks to what looked like a bath or fountain. The fieldstone stonework was "rude and rough" in comparison with Cuzco, but the site's trapezoidal triple-jamb doors and numerous niches, some still covered in stucco, suggested the site's ceremonial purpose; such architectural elements alluded to spiritual transitions and once housed religious icons.[5] Only a fraction of the site was uncovered, but Bingham was happy to speculate from what he saw. He wondered if one "curious little structure built with the utmost care and containing many niches and nooks . . . may possibly have been for the detention of so-called 'virgins of the sun' or have been the place in which criminals, destined to be thrown over the precipice, according to the laws of the Incas, awaited their doom."

If Nuñez thought Hiram and Hay would find treasure, he would be disappointed. It was clear that Choqquequirau had been looted long ago. Before Nuñez's men used dynamite, visitors had torn apart walls and niches with pickaxes. If there was ever anything precious at the Cradle of Gold, it was by now long gone. But Bingham's instincts as a collector—of patrons, sons, and books—found value in the humblest artifact. In one niche, he found a small stone bobbin of the sort that native Andeans still used to spin yarn. On the ground, he found a round hammerstone as big as his fist, as if a worker had just stepped off the job. Precious metals were glamorous, but these artifacts showed how Choqquequirau's people lived and worked. Both went into his bag.

Finally, in the jungle below the terraces, the Peruvians showed the Americans the Cradle of Gold's true treasure: the final resting places of the dead. The Incas mummified their emperors and carried them about as if they were still alive. The empire's more humble servants—the men and women who built and maintained Choqquequirau—were interred in small caves beneath boulders. Nuñez's workmen had already opened a dozen such tombs and had found little save bones. In one cave, however, walled up with wedge-shaped stones until Bingham's arrival, the explorer found a small earthenware jar, only an inch in diameter. It had no handles, and its opening was fitted with a perforated cap. It was empty but still upright, undisturbed for hundreds of years. It, too, went into Bingham's bag.

Bingham was more excited by the bones. Believing that evolutionary theory could be applied to concepts of race, North American and European scholars had spent the last half-century building massive collections of native skeletal remains to compare with those of whites. The origins of archaeology in the Americas were similarly unsettling. Late-nineteenth-century scholars viewed Indians as a dying race and had little compunction about paying for looted graves, much as medical students once paid "resurrectionists" to steal cadavers. During the Indian Wars the U.S. army occasionally collected the bodies of the Indians it had slaughtered, removed their flesh, and sent on their bodies to the country's east coast museums.[6] Part imperial trophies, part museum specimens, whites used the remains to ask deeply racist questions cloaked in science: Did Indian skulls prove that Europeans were superior? Other questions were more defensible, though no less political, in their implications: How long had Indians lived in the Americas before the arrival of Europeans? Two thousand years? Six thousand? Twenty-five? Scholars believed that if only the right skulls could be found, in the right context, they could pinpoint the antiquity of man in the Americas.

Bingham was no archaeologist, and the bones in Choqquequirau's graves would solve no such mystery, but he was thrilled to brush up against such questions. He sidled into the caves like a crab and began to pull out femurs, vertebrae, skulls, and bones. He turned them over in his hand and tested their solidity. He squeezed them. Some "could be crumbled with the fingers and easily broken," he noted. "Some skulls likewise were decayed and could be easily crushed with the fingers."

This was hardly science, and to the native Peruvians watching him it seemed downright sordid. "The [Quechua] Indian carriers and workmen watched our operations with interest, but they became positively frightened when we began the careful measurement and examination of the bones," an amused Bingham later wrote. "They had been in doubt as to the object of our expedition up to that point, but all doubts then vanished and they decided we had come there to commune with the spirits of the departed Incas."

The Indians had seen Peruvian soldiers dig for treasure before, but Bingham and Hay were different. These North Americans were interested in the bones themselves. Ancestral mummies, or *mallquis,* had once been objects of veneration for their descendants, the "ultimate source of food, water, and agricultural land." Disturbing them could bring grave misfortune to one's land or life. These were the last remains of a people that Andeans still identified with, who walked through their stories, whom they might one day see in the next world. The Indians perhaps felt the grief and indignation that Hiram's parents felt a half-century before, when they found their first son's bones disinterred and strewn across the ground.

Hiram, however, had broken those taboos long ago, when he disinterred his grandmother and brought her to New Haven. He consulted his trustworthy copy of the *Hints to Travelers:* "Where practicable, native skeletons, and especially skulls, should be sent home for accurate examination," it read. "How far this can be done depends much on the feeling of the people; for while some tribes do not object to the removal of bones, especially if not of their own kinfolk, in other districts it is hardly safe to risk the displeasure of the natives at the removal of the dead—a feeling which is not only due to affection or respect, but even more to terror of the vengeance of the ghosts whose relics have been disturbed."[7] He had little to worry about vengeance from ghosts or peons with Lt. Cáceres standing by, Bingham decided, and he packed the three sturdiest skulls he could find in his bag. He would bring them back to the United States with him, use them as teaching aides in his classes, and then offer them to Yale's museum, the Peabody. On his previous trip to South America, Hiram Bingham had collected books for Harvard. Yale deserved something better: skulls and bones from the lost city of the Incas.

Hiram brushed the dirt off his knees, enjoying the sensation. Before visiting Cuzco and Choqquequirau, he had never imagined studying—or collecting—the embodied history of indigenous America. That had all changed. When Hiram got back to Abancay, he wrote to his wife that this hill town where the Inca princesses had taken refuge during the conquest was "the most interesting place I have ever seen."[8] Later, in the United States, he told the *New York Herald* that he and Hay had been the first foreigners ever to visit the "lost 'City of the Incas.'" His pilgrim ancestors came to the Americas to build a "shining city on a hill"; his grandparents sailed to Hawaii to bring that city to the "heathen." Inverting that tradition, Peruvians had shown Hiram Bingham a city that shone long before Columbus even set sail. A city, Hiram imagined, untarnished by the sullying hands of the Spanish.

The only problem was that Choqquequirau was *not* the final refuge of the Incas and their Virgins of the Sun. The true last city of the Incas was still out there, and it was no place of gentle, sun-draped, dime-novel death, laden with virgins and golden treasure. It was a place of struggle, independence, and anticolonial anger. To find it, Bingham needed to learn its history.

Interlude: Manco Inca

The conquest of the Incas was not inevitable. True, the revelation of the Americas in 1492 launched ships filled with Spaniards eager for fortune and glory. When the conquistador Francisco Pizarro, 62 horsemen, and 106 foot-soldiers invaded Peru in November 1532, they did have superior weaponry on their side. As a further advantage, when they reached the Inca city of Cajamarca on November 16, they met an empire in crisis. The old emperor had died from a plague—perhaps the European smallpox that spread through the Americas like wildfire—and his sons had been fighting each other for the right to rule.[1]

Still, the Incas had the greater advantage. At Cajamarca, the Spaniards faced an army of 40,000 or more battle-hardened soldiers, well-trained in the peculiarities of Andean warfare. They were led by the thirty-one-year-old emperor Atahualpa, who had recently won the war of succession. Sneeringly majestic, he wore cloaks made from the skins of vampire bats; all that he touched was burnt as befitted a god on earth. More importantly, he was ruthless. Rightfully suspicious of the Spaniards' intentions, he planned to seize and execute them before they got any farther.

Unfortunately for Atahualpa, the Spaniards had a very similar plan. No technological, biological, or cultural advantage tipped the scales: it was simply who struck first. Atahualpa was borne on a litter into Cajamarca, followed by a retinue resplendent in feathers, silver, and gold but mostly unarmed—perhaps in the belief that the Spaniards would never be so bold as to attack them in the midst of an Inca settlement. The Spanish were hiding around the main square, and some were so terrified that they wet themselves with fear. Their Dominican friar offered Atahualpa the Bible, demanding conversion to Christianity. In some accounts, Atahualpa rejected it, giving the zealous Spaniards all the cause they needed to attack. In others, he called for their deaths, to the same effect.[2] The

Spanish soldiers swept from the wings and massacred the crowd. Pizarro himself snatched Atahualpa from the litter.

Atahualpa supplied a vast ransom—one room filled with gold and two with silver—but the Spanish executed him anyway, charging him with being an unjust ruler and plotting a rebellion. The conquistadors claimed to have liberated the empire and designated one of Atahualpa's grateful brothers as his successor. This brother quickly fell ill and died, but the Spaniards found yet another to be their figurehead, a twenty-year-old named Manco. In Cuzco, the Spaniards watched with amazement and horror as Manco's "coronation" brought forth Incas both live and dead, as the mummies of Manco's father and the other great Incas were borne about on litters behind their heir.

To the Spaniards' chagrin, their puppet had a mind of his own. Manca was a fierce warrior fresh from his own conquests in the jungle, and he quickly saw through the Spaniards' intentions. After looting the Incas' temples, Francisco Pizarro's brothers needled Manco for more silver and gold. Worse yet, Gonzalo Pizarro seized Manco's *coya*, his principal wife and sister, Cura Ocllo. By 1535, reports of conquistadors beating, decapitating, and raping Indians throughout the kingdom were trickling in. At a secret meeting of the highest officials, generals, and priests of his crumbling empire, Manco listed the many grievances against the Spaniards. "[I]f all the snow turned to gold and silver, it would not satiate them," he declared. The Spaniards had even burned Incas alive—an especially cruel deed, as the Incas believed that "souls . . . burn with the bodies and could not go to enjoy heaven." Manco threw down the gauntlet: "We should strive with full determination either to all die, or to kill these cruel enemies."[3]

With spies in their midst, it wasn't long before the Pizarros learned Manco's plan. They put Manco in irons and tortured and violated his women in front of him. The abuses only further hardened his resolve. While Indians across the empire began killing Spaniards, Manco escaped Cuzco by claiming he would bring the Pizarros a life-sized golden effigy. Instead he joined his army. By Easter of 1536, 100,000 to 200,000 Inca allies converged on Cuzco. There were so many that "by day they resembled a black carpet covering the fields for a half league surrounding the city," wrote Pedro Pizarro. "At night there were so many fires that it looked like nothing less than a serene sky full of stars."[4]

Those hundred thousand stars began to scream, terrifying the 170 Spaniards and the thousand native allies that remained in Cuzco. The great Inca rebellion had begun.

The Inca soldiers attacked, raining a holy hell of pitch-covered sling-stones upon Cuzco's roofs. The city began to burn, and the Spaniards took shelter in the chapel on the city's main square. Cut off from the recently founded capital of Lima—which was also under attack—and unable to count on reinforcements for months, the Spaniards played to their strengths: they led a desperate and audacious charge to the heart of the siege, the massive walls and towers of the sacred fortress of Sacsayhuaman. After three days of pitched fighting with axes, swords, and clubs, it was the Incas' turn to seek reinforcements.

To regroup, Manco retreated north of Cuzco and fortified a monolithic hillside site named Ollantaytambo, built by the great empire-builder Pachacutec. He enlisted archers from his jungle allies. When the Spanish approached, they rained arrows and boulders on them from the site's heights. The Spaniards hesitated and the Indians pressed the advantage, pouring out onto the plain "with such a tremendous shout that it seemed as if the mountain was crashing down."[5] Manco himself led them on horseback, then unleashed his surprise weapon: the Patacancha river, which the Inca's engineers had diverted to flood the plain. The Spaniards' horses were immobilized, and their riders fled.

Manco won the day, but the expulsion of the Spaniards from Peru was by then impossible. Manco had to make a choice. From the upper reaches of Ollantaytambo, Manco could look up the valley toward Yucay, his father's estate, filled with fertile stretches of corn. It shone golden in the sun, a beautiful reminder of the past and all that was now in jeopardy. But if he turned his back on Yucay, he could look downriver to where the Vilcanota River stopped its smooth, straight flow and began to twist and drop and rush, becoming the violent Urubamba, which cut its way northeast into the jungles of the Amazon, the *Antisuyu*.

It was a wetter, wilder land, whose tumbling rivers, sharp cliffs, and nearly impenetrable forests had challenged even the great Pachacutec. Here lay vipers and jaguars, and the Antis, the fierce lowland tribes that practiced cannibalism—or so the Incas told the Spanish. Pachacutec had pushed far enough into the region to leave several palace complexes, however, and Manco had spent the year before the Spaniards' arrival pacifying jungle tribes. In one of Pachacutec's citadels, the Incas and their jungle allies could fend off the Spanish and practice their religion as they had before the conquest.[6]

So, in 1537, as Spanish harquebusiers, cavalry, and crossbowmen closed in on their location, Manco gathered his captains and explained that they were leaving for the land of the Antis, but that they would return. His army began its exodus, and the Urubamba's canyon walls reared up around them, thick vegetation muffling their cries. After a few feints into other valleys, they crossed the Urubamba on a great rope bridge at a place named Chuquichaca.

They traveled up a tributary river into a region thick with peaks and jungle. Manco stopped at a ridgetop palace of beautiful white stone built by Pachacutec generations before. Its name was Vitcos. Here, he would make his home. In a thin green valley beside it was a sun temple containing a shrine named Yurak Rumi—a massive white granite boulder that loomed over a cold, dark spring. The Incas worshipped the sun and its personification in the Inca emperor, but Andean religion was filled with *huacas* and *apus*, shrines and spirits of water and stone. Places like Yurak Rumi, where all three elements met, were especially powerful. Twenty-five feet high, thirty feet wide, and fifty-two feet long, the shrine was covered with carved designs, channels, seats, and knobs. The sun passed overhead, casting strange shadows over the stone but not on the sheltered water below. It was Inca cosmology in miniature, "the principle shrine of those mountains."[7]

Its quiet worship did not last long. The Spaniards came in hot pursuit of the rebel Inca. Manco's men destroyed the bridge at Chuquichaca, but the Spaniards rebuilt it and charged up the river. They raided Vitcos, looted its temples, and took 20,000 of Manco's people, including his five-year-old son, Titu Cusi, back to Cuzco. Manco escaped, however, and continued his guerrilla war in the mountains, killing Spanish horsemen and collaborators. He rebuilt Vitcos, and in early 1539 he built a more remote capital—a rainy but sheltered refuge named Vilcabamba, the "Plain of the Sun." With the support of his jungle allies, Manco would shape Vilcabamba into a place to enjoy the abundance of the lower climes, to plot his war with the Spaniards, and to worship the *Punchao*, their golden sun icon. Saved from Cuzco, the icon glistened in torchlight, its interior hiding the burned hearts of the Incas.

Yet Manco was not just fortifying the Incas' past; he was adapting for the future. He amassed Spanish weapons and topped his new palace with red tiles in the style of the Spanish. He maintained the roads that led to the rest of Peru. He built terraces and homes for his future refugees from Spanish rule.

Whether they would ever come, however, remained uncertain. After Manco's flight, the Spanish consolidated their control of the Incas' former kingdom. Cuzco became a true colonial city, its burned thatched roofs replaced by red tile, the Incas' stone walls covered by plaster. The Spaniards divested Manco of the Inca's royal fringe in absentia and proclaimed his brother Paullu, their collaborator, the true Inca heir. The conquistadors tried to win over the many Incas that remained in Cuzco, guaranteeing their privileges and appealing to their comfort. Seeing how Paullu was praised, some Incas dressed in Spanish clothes; most publicly converted to Catholicism.

Others, however, looked to Vilcabamba, now home to their true emperor. One Inca who resisted Spanish overtures was Manco's son, Titu Cusi, who would always remember the speech his father gave at Ollantaytambo. Manco had commanded his people "not to forget us, my forefathers and myself, during your lives nor the lives of your descendants." He implored them not to forget their religious heritage while he was away. "Adore what we hold dear, for, as you can see, the *Willkas* [elemental deities] speak to us; and the Sun and the Moon, see them through our own eyes and what [the Spaniards] speak of do not see well. Believe that at some point, by force or deceit, [the Spaniards] will have you adore what they adore. When you cannot resist any longer, make the motions before them but never forget our own ceremonies. And if they tell you to shatter your *wakas* [icons], and do so by force, show them what you must and hide the rest. In this you will greatly please me."[8]

The Spaniards baptized the young Inca heir, Titu Cusi, but in his breast, Vilcabamba's sun shone brighter and brighter.

Part Two

The Search

When I was king and a mason — a master proven and skilled
I cleared me ground for a palace such as a king should build
I decreed and cut down to my levels, presently under the silt
I came on the wreck of a Palace such as a king had built

"The Palace," Rudyard Kipling, re-published in The Builder,
vol. 2, no. 12, early 1916. Clipped by Bingham and placed in his scrapbook.

The Ashaninkas of Espíritu Pampa

When I was King and a Mason—a master proven and skilled—
I cleared me ground for a Palace such as a King should build.
I decreed and cut down to my levels, presently, under the silt,
I came on the wreck of a Palace such as a King had built.

—Rudyard Kipling, "The Palace," republished in The Builder,
vol. 2, no. 12, early 1916, clipped by Bingham
and placed in his scrapbook

Chapter Seven

Best Laid Plans

*W*hen Hiram Bingham returned from South America in the spring of 1909, he wrote out a fifteen-year plan and titled it "The best laid plans of mice and men." He had missed his family and would spend the next three years with them, working, teaching, and writing.

He topped his short-term to-do list, however, with a task that accelerated that schedule: an article on Choqquequirau, the Cradle of Gold, which he had visited on his way to Lima.[1] Bingham remained enchanted by the ruin. According to the Peruvians, he and Hay were the first foreigners to make the trip to this last city of the Incas, the final resting place of the Virgins of the Sun, the women who attended to the emperor and the Incas' sun cult. On the promise of treasure, he had been disappointed—further hardening his belief that stories like *El Dorado* were just so much indigenous myth—but he was prepared to write up the experience as a notch on his belt as an explorer: the first foreigner to visit the last city of the Incas.

Unfortunately, when he ventured into Yale's library, the rest of the Peruvians' claims fell apart as well. To start with, Bingham was already suspicious of a slate he had seen at the ruins bearing several signatures and dates. The books of Peruvian geographers quickly confirmed that several Peruvians and a handful of foreigners, including two French explorers, had visited the ruins since they were first described in the eighteenth century.

On top of not being one of the first foreigners to the site, Bingham realized that the historical foundation for the belief that Choqquequirau was the last city of the Incas was slim. The tradition that the Cradle of Gold was the "savage asylum" of "the last survivors of the race of the sun" dated to the first half of the nineteenth century and seemed to have little to do with the Spanish chronicles, which said that the Inca's last refuge was Vilcabamba, "the town in which the Inca had his Court and his armies, and his primary temple."[2] The chronicles maintained that this Vilcabamba was two days' travel from a place named Puquiura— a town that still existed along a river named Vilcabamba, far beyond Cuzco. It seemed that past geographers had perpetuated the tradition that Choqquequirau was the Incas' refuge because it *could perhaps* be reached in two very, very long days' travel from Puquiura. That struck Bingham as "at least a very roundabout method of inference"—as if a future geographer were to declare from his armchair that Boston and Washington, DC, were one and the same simply because there could be no two places of comparable distance from New York.[3] The Cradle of Gold was wishful thinking, Bingham decided, a wonderfully florid name for what he now believed was a fortress.

Despite his disappointment, Bingham was fascinated by Vilcabamba's story. He wondered about the rebellion of Manco, whom he thought had "too much good red blood in his veins to submit to Spanish tutelage."[4] He had never been much interested in treasure, but the story of a romantic yet doomed Native American resistance against European colonizers sparked his imagination. Moreover, it seemed that no explorer to date had discovered the true last refuge of the Incas—this place named Vilcabamba. What if he did so? He could identify the very point where the Americas' greatest indigenous empire put up its last fight—an inter-American Alamo where he could fly the flag for the United States and Yale.

Finding this Vilcabamba was easier said than done, however. Just a cursory scan of the literature suggested that the area between Cuzco and this town of Puquiura was littered with Inca ruins known to locals for years. Bingham would also have competition. Andean exploration was booming, and in 1909 a young Harvard ethnologist named William C. Farabee returned from his own expedition to lands north of Cuzco, where he had collected a "rumor, pretty well authenticated, which he had got from Indians, of a big city hidden away on the mountainside above the Urubamba Valley."[5]

To add to the pile, there was a young Peruvian studying anthropology at Harvard who had his own clues. Julio C. Tello would one day be called "the New World's greatest archaeologist" for his work excavating Peru's coastal cultures. In 1910 he was a thirty-year-old of indigenous descent who had worked through medical school at Lima's most venerable university and along the way had studied pre-Columbian burials.[6] In 1909 the Peruvian government of President Augusto B. Leguía awarded him a scholarship to study archaeology and ethnology abroad, and Tello chose Harvard University, which had offered him free tuition. Tello heard about Bingham's visit to Choqquequirau, and in 1910 he sent the American explorer an article that further fueled his sense of urgency. Written by an archivist at Peru's National Library who had access to an Augustinian friar's account, the article claimed that Manco's palace was named Vitcos, not Vilcabamba, and that it was located *next* to the town of Puquiura, not two days away. The archivist had provided the information so that the director of Peru's National Museum might travel to Cuzco and find out.[7]

Bingham's head swam. He had finally found a mystery that called for his special skills in history and exploration, but the clues were out there for anyone to solve. All someone had to do was travel up the Urubamba River beyond Cuzco and look for Inca ruins near the town of Puquiura. Peru's historians were positioned to do so, and Bingham was not. The explorer spent the summer of 1910 with his steadily expanding family, finishing his manuscript on his last expedition, and wondering if he had lost the chance of a lifetime. He considered expeditions elsewhere, to Mexico or Ecuador.

In the fall, he focused on settling into his family's new home. He and Alfreda were the proud parents of six sons now, and her parents had built them a thirty-room mansion, the largest in New Haven, at the top of Prospect Hill, the city's toniest neighborhood. Hiram protested that it was ostentatiously large for a lecturer's family, but the Mitchells' only concessions were the addition of a Spanish-style red tile roof, earning it the name Casa Allegre, or Happy Home, and a tiny ladder-like staircase that connected his bedroom—he and Alfreda slept apart—to the study of his dreams. The study was spacious and airy, bound on three sides by windows. It had floor-to-ceiling bookshelves that hid a secret washroom and two roll-down maps of South America. A hand-carved desk, with Tiffany lamps and a revolving bookcase close at hand, faced the fireplace on the fourth wall. On its mantelpiece, Hiram arranged the trinity of his life so far: a small wooden idol given to his father by the Gilbertese, a wispy painting of Alfreda, and an Inca pot from Peru.[8]

He was perhaps sitting in that study on November 25, 1910, the day after Thanksgiving, when he opened a letter that suggested that all was not lost, that it was in fact the best time imaginable to return to Peru and search for Vilcabamba. It was from the University of Cuzco, which had undergone a major change since

Bingham's visit. In May 1909, the increasingly radical students—the passionate, bespectacled Luis E. Valcárcel among them—demanded a greater student voice in the university's administration, better teachers, and lower tuition. The students demanded the floor during a meeting with the faculty, the old rector refused, and an anarchist student fired a gun in the air. The faculty stampeded into the Plaza de Armas, where the market women shrieked that the male students must have come to blows over the university's three female students.[9] But it was bigger than that: the students were now on strike. Peru's president closed the university's doors, but then reopened them in early 1910 under the surprising young man now writing to Bingham, a twenty-six-year-old economist from Philadelphia named Albert Giesecke, who had impressed President Leguía by helping to reform Lima's educational system.

The university's students were wary of having an American rector at first—Cuzco was hardly immune to rumors of U.S. imperial attentions in the hemisphere. Giesecke won them over, however, with new professors, modern courses in journalism, criminal sociology, and zoology, and a likable style.[10] The students idolized him, wrote one new professor to a friend in Lima.[11]

In turn, Giesecke fell in love with the region's history, just as Bingham had. Since their revolt, the university's students had channeled their ambition into understanding the Incas and indigenous people, and they happily included Giesecke in the process. They took Giesecke to Sacsayhuaman, where Manco's men had once besieged the Spanish.[12] In the shadow of the ruins' walls, young Luis Valcárcel may have told his new mentor about the books on the Inca that he hoped to write, and for which he was already dreaming up titles.[13] Two months later, at a Fourth of July celebration in Giesecke's honor, Valcárcel regaled the audience with a speech praising the Inca empire and Peru's modern indigenous people. Giesecke returned the favor on July 26, Peru's Independence Day, by calling for the preservation of historic monuments, a new museum in Cuzco, and government support for studies of the region's ruins. He announced new courses on Inca civilization and Quechua and conferences to improve relations between local native peoples and students. Cuzco could one day be the "Mecca of South America," he declared.[14]

Yet much work remained. In October, Giesecke had tried to follow Bingham to Choqquequirau, but the rains swept away the bridge built by prefect Nuñez's treasure company. He wrote to Bingham to ask if the explorer had published yet on his visit.[15]

Bingham was thrilled. If Giesecke was still trying to visit Choqquequirau, then it was possible that no one in Cuzco yet knew that the Cradle of Gold was important in name only—and that the true last city of the Incas was still out there. Bingham rolled a piece of paper into his typewriter and promised to Giesecke that he would send copies of his article on Choqquequirau and book on the 1909 expedition when they were published. Having offered an olive branch, Bingham then pumped the potential competitor for information. "Has the Treasure Company stopped operating?" Bingham pounded out. "Has any archaeologist visited the ruins? I heard that Professor Uhle"—the National Museum's director—"was going there from Lima. Who is going to pay for rebuilding the bridge?"[16]

Giesecke's reply, when it came in mid-December 1910, was galvanizing: Nuñez's outfit was defunct. The bridge remained in disrepair. No archeologist had visited Choqquequirau or any other ruins in the region.

Bingham saw his chance: he could be in Cuzco by June 1911, searching for Vilcabamba, the city that Manco founded in the jungle and where his sons made their last stand. The only question, as ever, was how he was going to pay for it.

Tiffany money had funded Bingham's first two expeditions. For this, his third, he wanted to raise the money himself, to field a larger, multidisciplinary expedition and to prove that he was not just a wealthy dilettante. The public could dream of solitary, rich, and romantic Victorian explorers hacking their way through the jungle in search of mythical cities only to disappear without a trace. Bingham, however, wanted the sort of immortality that lay in achievement and not in eccentricity or death.

To accomplish it, Bingham developed a model that resembled polar exploration: a large, semipermanent, multidisciplinary team of experts organized like a naval expedition, whose captain won the lion's share of the credit. In April 1909, American Naval Commander Robert E. Peary snuck away from his African American associate Matthew Henson and their Inuit guides Ootah, Seegloo, Egingwah, and Ooqueah to become the first man to reach the North Pole (or so he claimed). Like Peary, Bingham would seek glory for America and himself, but in the jungles of the Andes. He would need theodolites, cameras, pickaxes, telescopes, barometers, and crates filled with dry soup and chocolate—a train of leather, brass, wood, and tinned food that could survive the jungle. As his father had piloted missionary ships in the Pacific, Hiram would helm an expedition into the Andes to collect the natural and human history of the Americas and bring it back home.

Such an expedition required a lot of money. In early 1910, Hiram had applied to the Carnegie Institution for $88,000—$1.96 million today—to establish a Department of Central and South American Research that would gather bibliographical, historical, archaeological, and geographical knowledge. Unsurprisingly, given the fact that he had yet to prove his academic bona fides, he was rejected.[17] Yale was only slightly kinder. The university agreed to lend his expedition Yale's name and opened a South American Exploration Fund to process donations, but withheld the real support of funding.

The levee finally broke when one of Bingham's former classmates—Edward Harkness, an heir to the Standard Oil fortune who had graduated from Yale in 1897—pledged $1,800 if Bingham included Yale geologist Herbert Gregory on the expedition. Bingham expanded the mission further by pitching it as a reconnaissance of the geography, geology, and archaeology of the 73rd meridian, which passed by Choqquequirau and the rumored ruins near Cuzco, an "unexplored" lake named Parinacochas, and an unclimbed mountain named Coropuna, which one archaeologist had recently suggested might be the highest in the Americas.[18]

The bigger tent attracted funding. In February 1911, Bingham attended a Yale class of 1898 dinner in New York and sat next to a classmate named Herbert Sheftel. Sheftel had barely seen Bingham since graduation, but he had a surprise for his tall friend. "When I told him about my plans and how I needed $1,800 to pay for a topographer he smiled and said '$1,800? I'll give you that!'" Bingham wrote to his wife. "I could have shouted with joy. It was such a surprise. At first I thought he must be joking. But no, he said he had been following my work for some time, and had made up his mind to help me the first chance he got. *So There!*" Bingham was still the knock-kneed young Hawaiian waiting for his peers' acceptance. Prompted by Sheftel, the sixty classmates in attendance made Hiram tell them about South America. He wrote home that they gave him "quite an ovation, very much to my surprise. I never had so many nice things said to me by my classmates. I wish you could have been present."[19]

His good fortune followed him to Washington, where he tapped U.S. president William Howard Taft for help. Besides being a Yale man, Taft appreciated what Bingham's expedition might mean for U.S. ambitions in the region. Taft shifted U.S. foreign policy from Theodore Roosevelt's active imperialism toward "dollar diplomacy," through which America could build international power by making loans to foreign countries and influencing markets. Bingham's expedition could function as an even softer, subtler sort of diplomacy: Yale could shape the study of hemispheric history while burnishing the benevolent image of America abroad. Taft got Bingham a topographer from the U.S. Coast and Geodetic Survey, a tall, shy Dane named Kai Hendrikson.

Bingham was lucky even when he got sick. His doctor was a Yale graduate named William G. Erving who had once paddled a canoe down the Nile from Cairo to Khartoum. Duly impressed, Bingham enlisted him as the expedition's surgeon. They would need him where they were going. Bingham hadn't suffered from altitude sickness on his last expedition, but they would be ascending to Cuzco quickly this time. Down in the jungle, there would be malaria, yellow fever, tetanus, snakebites, and countless stomach ailments. Erving might be in high demand.

Over the next month, the Yale Peruvian Expedition (YPE) of 1911 added four members, making it a seven-man team. Bingham enlisted his best friend Harry Foote as the expedition's "naturalist." Foote was a kind, beakish Yale chemistry professor, but he was also a collector of flora and fauna. Foote helped devise the expedition's eating system: small boxes filled with enough packaged food for two men for eight days.

A sweet-faced Yale student named Paul Baxter Lanius joined up as Bingham's assistant, his family paying his way. And to help him climb Coropuna, Bingham recruited a curious twenty-seven-year-old Harvard dropout named Herman L. Tucker, who had been a member of the expedition that had disproved Dr. Frederick Cook's claimed first ascent of Mount McKinley. Tucker would prove an earthy fellow, a socialist, and member of the Industrial Workers of the World. He would shock Bingham by drinking with the locals on the sly.

The expedition's final member was a case of keeping one's competitors close. The geologist Herbert Gregory backed out and in his place Bingham recruited Isaiah Bowman, an assistant professor in Yale's geography department. Bowman would one day help President Woodrow Wilson redraw Europe's map after World War I, direct the Council on Foreign Relations, and serve as president of Johns Hopkins University. In 1911, however, he was Bingham's chief competitor for Yale's explorer crown, having also been in Southern Peru in 1909. Built like a fireplug, Bowman believed that Bingham was privileged and lazy. Far more students took his course in South American geography, he boasted to one Harvard colleague, seeing no irony in then saying that "Bingham [was] inordinately vain and never saw the word 'modesty' in the dictionary."[20]

Bingham got Bowman to sign on to the newly christened YPE by waving a true prize below his nose: a copy of the dog-eared map that Harvard's Farabee had made during his explorations three years before.[21] With it, Bowman could go down the Urubamba River, almost to the Amazon, looking for the mounds and cities Farabee had heard about. Bowman would then continue a geographical survey westward and meet Bingham to climb Coropuna. Duly charmed, Bowman trumpeted that they were continuing "the heroic work of the first explorers and founders like Pizarro."[22]

It was a dubious accolade, to be sure, but an apt comparison nonetheless. Like the Spanish expeditions, Bingham's expedition was a privately funded venture of ambitious individuals. Bowman and Bingham would also get on almost as badly as the early conquistadors. Both had large egos, and Bingham treated Bowman as his unequal partner, so much so that years later Bowman believed that Bingham had purposefully sent him toward the Amazon to keep him away from the year's true finds.[23] As one later magazine writer described Bingham's leadership style, "Every man who obeyed him found him an able, efficient, even delightful boss; only those who had their own ideas, who resented perfection and omniscience in any man, found his leadership irksome."[24] If this expedition had a Pizarro, then Bingham was it.

The expedition's funding also hinted at its ethos. To cover everyone's food and travel expenses—each person needed $1,800—Bingham collected $11,825, partly from businesses linked to America's frontiers, literal and imaginary. The Winchester Arms Company donated a rifle and $500. Minor C. Keith—whose all-powerful United Fruit Company owned railroads and plantations throughout Central America and would involve the U.S. government in many a military imbroglio—put up $1,800 for another member and let the expedition travel on United Fruit's ships at half-fare. Finally, the Eastman Kodak Company donated cameras that Bingham promised to field test in Peru's rainy valleys.[25]

To pay his own way, Hiram promised *Harper's Magazine* four articles in exchange for $1,000. Still, he lacked $800. To raise it, Bingham cashed out one of his family's last assets from their Honolulu days—the final tract of land remaining from the grant that the Hawaiian royal family gave to Hiram I, his grandfather. Ignoring the protests of his father's missionary friends, he sold the land for $800 and with that bought a ticket to Peru.[26]

Although it injured his pride, Bingham turned to Alfreda for a final $1,800 for the expedition's surgeon. Alfreda's father had died in April, and when Mrs. Mitchell heard that Hiram was leaving again, she was as furious as Alfreda was quietly heartbroken. Alfreda couldn't say no, however, and in the midst of feelings of loss and abandonment, she gave her husband what he needed. "I shall never leave you again," he protested. "But I do believe that this next expedition will really add to Science and Truth. That will be your reward."[27]

What guilt Hiram may have felt faded in the glow of his favorite stage: promoting the expedition. He tantalized the press with the prospect of finding the "lost cities" of the Inca, then believed by the public to be the oldest, highest indigenous American civilization. "It is hardly possible that those who are interested in all that has been and may be discovered and told about the early inhabitants of America—and their number is legion—can be told [enough] about the Incas," the *Christian Science Monitor* mused. "Romance is in every page of their history so far as it is known or imagined. Uncovering their lost cities, and perhaps their lost treasures, will not detract from the charm of this romance."[28]

But when Hiram left Manhattan on the S.S. *Marta* on June 8, 1911, reporters and readers alike were foggy on what Hiram hoped to find. Was he seeking ruins? Or shining Inca gold? It was decidedly the former. Back in March, he had given the *New York Sun* his clearest answer. Given how ravaged Choqquequirau had been, he expected to find very little in the way of traditional treasure. These were conquered, looted cities, after all. On this expedition, he was solely interested in the Incas' ruins, which he hoped would further reveal the grandeur of their civilization. If they were as hidden as he hoped, most of the expedition's time would be spent clearing them of vines.

If they just happened to find any great cache of "buried treasure," however, would Yale keep it? Bingham shook his head. "Should anything be found in that line," Bingham explained, "it would become the property of the Peruvian Government."[29]

Chapter Eight

Dead Man's Gulch

$\mathcal{T}$he plan was simple. Hiram would get to Cuzco and do what no explorer had done before: gather as many leads as he could on ruins between the Incas' former capital and the Amazon to the northeast, then systematically pay Indian guides to lead him to each one. If he was right, he might find Manco Inca's lost city of Vitcos. If there was any time left over, he would attempt to climb Mt. Coropuna, or as he was calling it, the "Apex of America."

Before he could even begin, however, he had to stop in Lima, Peru's capital. When he told the *Sun* that "buried treasure" would go to the Peruvian government, he wasn't just being generous: it was Peruvian law. Peru's first legal protection of ruins and artifacts dated to 1822, after revolutionaries had declared independence from Spain but before it was won. According to that early *Decreto Supremo,* or Executive Order, pre-Columbian monuments and all they contained were the property of the nation, and the extraction of precious metal artifacts and ceramics was prohibited without prior authorization. If caught, looters would be fined 1,000 pesos and the artifacts would go to the National Museum.[1] The bedrock of all Peru's future legislation on the subject, the decree established that the Peruvian nation state was dedicated to the protection of its indigenous history, at least as a symbol. As Bingham understood it, in 1893 a Peruvian president signed an updated decree that required excavators to seek government permission, to work within a limited time frame, and to guarantee the government duplicates or photos of all artifacts found.[2] Although Hiram planned only to clear the ruins of jungle, he still needed to make sure he had the approval of the country's government and its archaeological functionaries. Laws controlling excavation had long gone unenforced, but that was changing. In 1909, for example, the government had ordered the halt of prefect Nuñez's excavation of Choqque-quirau after Bingham's visit due to Nuñez's lack of authorization.[3]

Two weeks after leaving New York, Bingham was rowed ashore by the boatmen of Callao, Lima's port. He was traveling alone, having hurried ahead while his expedition members lingered to watch the construction of the Panama Canal. It was June 23, and Lima was in the midst of its annual spell of chilly, overcast weather. A "fine drizzling mist" spattered Hiram as he breezed through customs and rode an electric streetcar to the center of Lima, a city of 150,000. Tawny young porters fought to help him with his bags as wealthy whites strolled past him, pausing in front of upscale stores showcasing the latest Parisian fashions. English and Peruvian elites alike, their women spinning parasols, rode from the city to enjoy the racetracks. Indians from the countryside hawked food and hauled loads, while engineers wired the city for electric lights. There was an "air of progressiveness and modernity about the place that makes you forget that it was built of mud," wrote one snide English visitor.[4]

Bingham checked himself into the mazelike Hotel Maury on the city's central plaza and then set out to court the country's friendship. He tellingly began not with the government but with one of the powers behind the throne: W. R. Grace & Co., an American-run trade house that had helped Peru back from bankruptcy in the nineteenth century by organizing the country's creditors into the mostly British-run Peruvian Corporation. In exchange for assuming Peru's debt, the corporation received the country's railroads, two million tons of guano, and various other tax-free concessions. Many Peruvians resented the semicolonial control that the foreign-run "Casa Grace" and Peruvian Corporation wielded over the country, but for Bingham it was the only place to start.[5]

Hat in hand, he walked through the pillars, desks, and wooden gates of W. R. Grace's massive office until he found the company's "confidential Peruvian agent," a man Bingham only ever referred to as Ballen. With Ballen at Bingham's side, the explorer walked around the block to the Presidential Palace and into the office of President Augusto B. Leguía. Hiram had met Peru's short, trim, foxlike president in 1909, and he was shocked to see how haggard he had become. Leguía had spent the last two years dealing with one crisis after another. Pistol-brandishing political opponents had kidnapped him. His own party had all but disowned him for signing decrees reforming labor practices. While Bingham explained his plans, the president was distracted. His current worry was the British government's recent threat to publish allegations that rubber companies—Peruvian-run but British-funded—in Peru's eastern jungles were enslaving, abusing, and murdering native workers.[6]

Faced with such a potential blot upon Peru's good name abroad, Leguía saw the angle in helping out a foreign scientific expedition. He gave Bingham full permission to explore, waived inspection of the expedition's luggage, and wrote Bingham a letter of introduction that guaranteed him government support and a military escort wherever he went. Leguía warned that the region Bingham was headed into—the valleys of the Urubamba and Vilcabamba Rivers—was dangerous of late. Only a few months before, Indian farmers and rubber collectors there had rebelled against the region's landowners. Across the southern highlands, Indian peasants were rising up against elites. The government in Cuzco had put down the uprising on the Urubamba, but Bingham needed to be careful. The state was only slightly more in control of the Incas' final refuge than it had been in Manco's time. By bringing Peruvian soldiers along, Bingham's expedition would actually help the Peruvian government extend its control over the country's Indians.

As Bingham saw the next morning, Peru was also struggling with its archaeology. Bingham took a hansom cab to Peru's National Museum, housed in the dusty glass Palace of the Exposition. Peru had a museum after independence, but weak funding made it impossible to monitor and protect the country's ruins. Government controls also contained a blind spot: there were no limits to buying, selling, and exporting artifacts. It was common knowledge that the shops surrounding Lima's central plaza sold fake and looted pieces to tourists.[7] The nadir came during the War of the Pacific, when Chilean soldiers looted the museum in 1881, leaving only a single carved stone slab behind, hidden in the gardens outside. The museum closed, and between 1872 and 1911, rising Western demand and Peruvian economic desperation allowed foreign collectors to buy and export more than sixty major private collections of Inca and pre-Inca artifacts to museums in Berlin, London, New York, Chicago, and Paris. Every collection that left the country meant countless tombs destroyed to satisfy increasingly cosmopolitan foreign tastes.[8]

In 1905, the president of Peru's Historical Institute had publicly challenged the country's government and people to take responsibility for their material history. "We are tired of seeing any old traveler take a gang of peons and throw themselves into digging up mummies and objects, without anyone's permission, as if they were in their own house," he told his fellow historians. "I believe that now is the time to definitively remedy this wrong, if not by absolutely prohibiting exportation, as has happened in many developed countries in Europe and in America, then at least by regulating and watching over these explorations, to curb their destructive effects."[9]

The government had yet to prohibit exportation, but it had reopened the museum that Bingham now entered. Its director was a legendary, mustachioed German archaeologist named Max Uhle. Besides authoring the first archaeological chronology of the Andes, Uhle had also exported many artifacts to foreign museums, which made him a strangely good choice to build Peru's museum. In his first few years on the job, he tripled the collection.[10] Next to him, Bingham was a novice in Peruvian archaeology; he feared that Uhle would beat him to Cuzco and turn up Manco Inca's last cities.

When Bingham actually met the "very excitable" German that morning, he stopped worrying. In recent years Uhle had made few friends after declaring that Peruvians, not foreign demand, were to blame for the country's looting. His enemies scrutinized his every move and began whispering that he was lazy—or worse, that he continued to export artifacts abroad. His funding was cut. Although the Peruvian government gave him money to go to Choqquequirau, he received nothing to fund excavation. He was "condemned to eternal inactivity" in Lima, he wrote to one colleague.[11] His famine would be Bingham's feast.

Hiram again climbed into a hansom cab. He had one final piece of business to address. On his first day in the city, he had called Carlos Romero, the archivist and author of the article that suggested a place named Vitcos, not Choqquequirau, was the last refuge of the Incas. Bingham found him a "very old man and quite feeble . . . rather deaf and somewhat cross, but quite a scholar." Romero grew up poor, but by helping rebuild the National Library after the War of the Pacific, he became one of the country's experts on pre-Independence history. He was one of the few coastal intellectuals who celebrated the rich legacy of the Inca past, perhaps because he himself appeared to have indigenous heritage.[12] He would have given "anything to be able to write with a quill, or record his thoughts with an Inca *khipu*," quipped one admirer.[13]

Romero had been pleased to see Bingham. He had written his article because he wanted to see these symbols of the Incas' anticolonial rebellion found, and Bingham seemed like a useful tool. Standing at his elbow, Romero now gave Hiram a crash course in the geography of the last Incas, as described by an Augustinian friar named Antonio de la Calancha. Bingham asked Romero for the name of Manco's last refuge. Was it Vitcos or Vilcabamba? Romero shook his head: Vilcabamba was the name of the larger kingdom, and Vitcos was Manco's capital in exile. Romero pointed out a passage that located Vitcos next to a "house of the Sun," a white stone shrine named Yurak Rumi.[14]

Yet when Romero left the American to write out clues on his own, Bingham realized that the Calancha's chronicle contradicted what Romero believed. On page 794, it read that the town of Puquiura was "two long days' journey from Vilcabamba, the town where the Inca King had his court and his army." Hadn't Romero assured him that the last capital of the Incas was Vitcos, and that it was *next* to Puquiura? Then, on page 803, Bingham found further reference to this "Vilcabamba la vieja," or Vilcabamba the Old, but here Calancha said it was *three* days from Puquiura. Vilcabamba the Old was the largest settlement of the kingdom, Calancha wrote, and it contained the Incas' "University of Idolatry, and the teachers, shamans, and masters of the abominations." It was the favored residence of Titu Cusi, Manco's eldest son, and the final home of his youngest, Tupac Amaru, before he was executed by the Spaniards.

Bingham put his pencil down, finally understanding what even Romero hadn't. Vilcabamba and Vitcos were distinct sites. Manco had moved to Vitcos, but then built Vilcabamba. Bingham wasn't searching for one lost city; he was searching for two.

The Yale Peruvian Expedition arrived in Cuzco on July 2, and Bingham immediately began collecting leads on nearby ruins. He later claimed that when he told his friends in Cuzco that he was looking for something even better than Choqquequirau, they refused to believe him, joking that he had returned to find the Cradle of Gold.

Bingham received far more help from Cuzco's residents than he let on, however. Albert Giesecke's direction of the University of Cuzco had made it a good time to proclaim one's self a friend of Cuzco and a champion of Inca ruins. Luis E. Valcárcel and the students who revolted in 1909 were studying indigenous languages and traditions, and visiting local ruins on their own. Valcárcel now helped edit the university's journal, attended meetings of the region's Pro-Indigenous Society, and wrote articles on Inca heroes for Lima newspapers.[15] Had he been in Cuzco that July, he would have been among the students who applauded Bingham when the explorer gave a short speech at the university on the Fourth of July.

Because Valcárcel only belonged to a merchant family, however, Giesecke likely did not introduce him to Bingham—not yet. Instead, Giesecke invited students whose families owned land on the Urubamba River to share their tales of ruins with the explorer. One friendly young engineer told the expedition that they would be welcomed at his father's hacienda, just below where the Vilcabamba and Urubamba rivers met. The engineer then produced another informant, José S. Pancorbo, who owned a sugar plantation along the Vilcabamba. Pancorbo confirmed one of Romero's speculations: there was indeed a group of ruins close to the town of Puquiura. "Just what I had been hoping for," Bingham wrote his wife.[16]

Bingham collected more clues, though none fit the chronicles as well as Pancorbo's. While buying machetes, pickaxes, and shovels, Hiram met an old German prospector who declared that on the river they would follow first, the Urubamba, there were ruins on a ridge above a place named Mandor Pampa, just after a hacienda named Torontoy owned by a family named Ochoa. Fifty years later, the university's rector, Albert Giesecke, would say that he too told Bingham that there were rumors of ruins at Mandor Pampa, and that he had almost visited them that January.[17] Today, Dr. Jorge Flores Ochoa, an anthropologist at the University of Cuzco, says that his family also knew of the ruins in question.[18] Giesecke and the Ochoas both lost out. When Bingham made the mystery ruins famous, he would credit the prospector for the clue and no one else.

He may have been trying to keep the glory for himself, but he also could have left out their names in distraction. The morning of July 6, he made a potentially career-making discovery of even greater importance than Inca cities. If true, he believed it would rewrite the history of the western hemisphere.[19]

Bingham was walking in the outskirts of Cuzco when he came across a *quebrada* (a gulch) that he later learned was named Ayahuacco, the *quebrada* of cadavers or, as Bingham preferred, Dead Man's Gulch. A little way in he was surprised to find what looked like human bones and a rough stone wall. The remains were unremarkable save for one surprising fact: both the bones and the wall lay in the gulch's side, embedded beneath a gravel bank almost seventy to eighty feet high. If they were buried that deep they must be old, Bingham thought. "From my knowledge of geology I should say they have been buried there for a couple of thousand years," he wrote to his wife that afternoon. "I believe they antedate the Incas by a thousand years or so."[20]

They were far older, according to Isaiah Bowman, the geographer. After pulling a human femur and several other fragments out, a "greatly excited" Bowman declared that the bones' location, their arrangement, their depth in the deposit, and the character of the gravel suggested they were *30,000 years* old. "So far as I know no bones of men of that epoch have been found before in South America," Bingham wrote to Alfreda. "This is an exciting moment for the Y.P.E. and for your husband."[21]

Exciting was one word for it. Dangerous was another. The age of native peoples in the Americas had been debated since first contact. Dismissing native claims that they had been there forever, early Europeans speculated that Indians were a Lost Tribe of Israel and had arrived from Asia by 500 BC. Biblical timelines later collapsed under nineteenth-century revelations of evolutionary theory, geological antiquity, and the presence of human skeletons and stone tools alongside extinct mammals. Humans had clearly lived in Europe during the last Ice Age, thousands and thousands of years before the days of Adam and Eve. As the archaeologist David Hurst Thomas put it, "If European history could be turned on its head by a single well-documented find, why not that of the New World? Why not an American Paleolithic?"[22]

Amateurs and scholars alike had turned up tools resembling those of Paleolithic Europe, and the American public now buzzed about the possibility that Pleistocene Indians hunted mammoths, giant bison, and saber-toothed cats 25,000 years before. With a certainty that now seems prejudiced, however, Washington's Bureau of American Ethnology and its anthropologists William Henry Holmes and Aleš Hrdlička had declared it all but impossible that Indians had been in the western hemisphere during the Ice Age. To move the history of the hemisphere back, an anthropologist and a geologist would have to find and confirm glacial-era American bones or tools in Pleistocene-age sediments. Under the bureau's regime, remembered one later anthropologist, the "question of early man in America became virtually taboo, and no anthropologist, or for that matter geologist or paleontologist, desirous of a successful career would tempt the fate of ostracism by intimating that he had discovered indications of a respectable antiquity for the Indian."[23] Hrdlička had so far dismissed any find with a claimed antiquity of more than a couple thousand years. His reach was long. Just a year before, he had traveled to South America to dismiss a colorful Argentine scientist's claim that he had found glacial skeletal materials.[24]

Taking on the bureau would be risky, but Bingham and Bowman thought their find could meet the standard of proof. The expedition mapped the gulch and excavated its walls. They found more bones, all of which they photographed, soaked in Vaseline, and packed in cotton batting for the trip back to the United States. Bingham was no anthropologist, but Bowman's geological training was sound, and he declared the gravel glacial. Bowman now suggested that the bones could be even more ancient: 40,000 years old.

Bingham was jubilant. He was only a few weeks into his archaeological exploration of the Andes, and he had already discovered bones that might make the history of human habitation in the Americas eighty times longer than the scientifically accepted date. He photographed himself standing in romantic profile on an eroded hillock near the gulch. "Is it not fortunate for the Y.P.E.?" Bingham wrote to Alfreda. As one modern historian has suggested regarding the entire expedition, if they were right, "Yale, and by extension, U.S. science, could claim to have rewritten the history of mankind."[25]

Hiram was still riding high on July 14, when he turned up one final clue for his first-priority quest that year, the search for Manco's lost cities. He and Foote, his traveling partner, had ridden north from Cuzco in search of mules. The trip over the *altiplano* was spectacular, its silvery fields mystical in the morning light. Their first glimpse of the Yucay—now known as the Sacred Valley—was equally stunning. Threaded by the slow, lovely Vilcanota River, the valley was lined with a patchwork of terraces, fields, and steep sides that exploded up to snow-covered peaks. It was the most beautiful place in Peru Hiram had seen yet. Its icy mountains were "so great and grand they absolutely satisfy one's desire for Magnificence."[26]

Hiram and Foote descended to the town of Urubamba, where they found the local subprefect Adolfo Quevedo, "genial, but drunk" and happy to help. He lined up the mules and when night fell, Quevedo and his friends regaled the Americans with stories of the land that awaited them. It was dangerous, they warned; Quevedo had been subprefect downriver until the Indians' recent revolution when he fled for his life. The government had confiscated the region's guns, but tensions remained high.

But Bingham might find what he was looking for, Quevedo acknowledged. As the temperature dropped, and the Americans tucked into a simple but hearty meal, the subprefect thought for one long drunken moment and told Bingham to follow the Urubamba River two leagues past the hacienda of Torontoy and then ask about the ruins on the mountain above.

It was the same set of directions that Bingham obtained from the German prospector in Cuzco, but this time the subprefect gave the ruins a name: Huayna Picchu.

It matched nothing Hiram had read in Lima's archives, but he wrote it in his journal anyway. "Someone here says it is better than Choqquequirau," he added.[27]

Chapter Nine

The Discoverers
of Machu Picchu

*H*iram had been in Cuzco for two-and-a-half weeks now, throwing open the windows of his room in the Hotel Central every morning to smile at the Plaza Regocijo and the house of Garcilaso de la Vega, the great Inca chronicler. He had spent his days haggling for mules, writing out itineraries for his men, and collecting rumors of ruins. He missed home, but he was increasingly convinced of the importance of his mission, especially now that it was about to begin.

On July 19, 1911 he at last began his search for the location of the Incas' last stand. Into his saddlebags went his oilskin valise, filled with all the clues he had discovered: the maps from the Harvard anthropologist Curtis Farabee and Lima's Geographical Society; the packet of notes relating to Vitcos and Vilcabamba from Carlos Romero's Spanish chronicles; and the notebook containing the names of the ruins at Huayna Picchu, supposedly even more fabulous than Choqquequirau. As Bingham buckled his saddlebags shut, he may have wondered whether the ruins at Huayna Picchu were actually the "big city hidden away on the mountainside above the Urubamba Valley" that Farabee had heard about. He tucked a picture of Alfreda into his pocket.[1]

But there was one last key he needed for his quest: the help of the local Peruvians, mostly indigenous, who lived in these valleys beyond Cuzco. To guarantee their help, he stopped at the office of Nuñez, who had introduced Bingham to Choqquequirau in 1909 and was now the prefect of Cuzco. Bingham told Nuñez where he was going: north over the *altiplano* to the Yucay Valley, so sacred to the Incas, then northwest to Ollantaytambo, and up the Urubamba River to the valley of Vilcabamba. Nuñez nodded. The route was easy enough. Bingham would be following a road blasted in the 1890s to give Cuzco's entrepreneurs access to the area's rubber and haciendas. Still, Hiram had to be careful. Many of the Indians in the area were descendants of those who fled with Manco Inca almost four hundred years before; some had participated in the recent uprising against landowners and rubber collectors. To guarantee their cooperation and translate their Quechua into Spanish, Nuñez gave Bingham an armed military escort, one Sergeant Carrasco.

Bingham's party began the ride out of the Huatanay Valley, the red-tile roofs of Cuzco shrinking beneath them. The higher they climbed, the more Hiram's spirits lifted. He was following Manco Inca's trail toward his stronghold of resistance. The silvery hills rolled beneath them and the sky glowed above, and they soon stared down at the extraordinary view of the Yucay Valley threaded by the mighty Vilcanota River. They stayed that night in Urubamba, where the tippling subprefect who had given Bingham the clue to "Huayna Picchu" agreed to lend Bingham an extra soldier to assist the expedition's topographers.

Blue clouds hugged the hills when they awoke, and they shook off the cold to ride northwest along the Vilcanota, deeper into Manco's history. Bingham was delighted to realize that the expedition was camped under wispy trees beneath the massive fort of Ollantaytambo, in the very plain where Manco diverted the river to turn back the Spaniards. The next day, July 21, Bingham climbed the ruins. He found the view breathtaking: "The greenness of the fields standing out in marked contrast to the rocky, cactus covered hillsides. The soft foliage of the willows and poplars contrasting strongly with the gray blocks of the famous fortress." Although looters had pulled apart the ruins' smaller buildings, the stronghold's carefully fitted walls and the monolithic temple above would last for years. Ollantaytambo "deserves to be a place of pilgrimage," he wrote.[2]

After Manco had fended off his pursuers, he went downriver toward the *Antisuyu*, the Incas' jungle realm. On July 22, Bingham, Harry Foote, the naturalist, William Erving, the surgeon, Carrasco, their two muleteers, and two porters started off after him—much like the Spaniards' expeditions had nearly four centuries before. After three miles, Bingham and his party faced a choice. Here, Manco had taken a road that climbed to the east, over the Panticalla Pass and into a parallel valley. Rather than follow as historically accurate a route as he had in Colombia, however, Bingham kept to the river, which here became the fast and twisting Urubamba. There were ruins above the Urubamba, he had heard in Cuzco.

He made the right choice. The river was magnificent. "[S]uch a Valley!" Bingham wrote. The elevation dropped, and the river began to roil, wind, and swerve. The vegetation grew thicker around them, and precipitous granite cliffs and snow-clad mountains hung above. The landscape was better than the Alps, the Rockies, and the Rhine, Bingham thought. From its walls hung evidence of a formerly massive population. Abandoned agricultural terraces stepped down the mountainsides like frozen waterfalls. Their Indian porters pointed out Salapunco, a small fortress, and the ruins of a large town named Q'ente (hummingbird). Bingham apologized for his enthusiasm to his later readers. "We made slow progress, but we lived in wonderland."

His reverie was shattered forty-five minutes later, however, when they came upon the rest of the expedition, which had terrible news. The day before, Kai Hendriksen and Herman Tucker had been looking for a way to cross the fast-moving Urubamba River. An Indian boy—whose name was never recorded—was with them, carrying Hendriksen's topographical equipment strapped to his back. Tucker and Hendriksen found a shallow spot and started across on their mules. They were nearly at the other side when they realized that the boy was following them on foot. Hendriksen and Tucker "both shouted for him to return, and even threw rocks at him, but he kept on crossing for a short distance," Paul Baxter Lanius, the expedition' youngest member, wrote in his journal. "Where the current was swiftest he lost his footing and in a second was swept down the stream into a more powerful current. He was never able to regain his feet again, and in a few minutes was lost to sight."[3] Tucker and Hendriksen spent several frantic hours searching for the boy. Finally, they found the alidade—Hendricken's sighting device—and the boy's poncho lodged between two rocks. The boy's body was gone, they said.

At least, this was the story they told Bingham. A half year later, a Cuzco professor retracing Bingham's path would hear a different version from the Indians of the area. They confirmed that the boy's death was an accident—the river took him like so many others—but in their version, the North Americans had sent the boy across to test the waters. After he slipped, Tucker and Hendriksen actually found the drowned boy, removed the alidade from his shoulders, and pushed the body back into the river.[4]

Was it true or just a rumor? Bingham would only write about the event weeks after the fact, crediting his men's version entirely. He blamed the young boy himself for "disobeying" orders to turn back: "An older Indian would not have crossed with a load without someone to help him. Hendriksen had been trying for two days to repair the damage to his alidade."

It is incredible to imagine that Bingham, who had children of his own, felt no sadness for the boy's death. Nevertheless, the expedition may have been damned in the local Indians eyes' for what Bingham did next: he ordered the expedition to keep exploring. Hendriksen and Tucker would continue mapping, and Isaiah Bowman, the geographer, and Lanius would explore the lower Urubamba. If anyone in the expedition notified the boy's family, which likely lived nearby, they made no record of it.

Bingham would write about this expedition for the rest of his life, but besides that single journal entry, he never mentioned—at least to the public—the only death to occur on any of his expeditions. "Perhaps he felt Indians were more expendable than surveying instruments, and the instruments, though damaged, had been saved," one of his own sons wrote years later.[5] Or perhaps Bingham later realized exactly what his expedition had lost in that moment, however mawkish it may seem: its innocence. In the days to come, he would find the ruins that would make him famous. But as he would later learn, that meant nothing to the Indians he relied upon. They already knew where the ruins were. To them, his was no holy quest; his expedition had seen a boy die, then just rode away.

Bingham and his party continued downriver. The cliffs closed in, and the green chasm of the valley rose precipitously above them. They were in "Real tropical jungle," Bingham wrote excitedly in his journal. On the evening of July 23, they reached the little sandy plain named Mandor Pampa, just after they passed the hacienda of Torontoy. Hiram had been told to ask for the ruins at Huayna Picchu when he got here.

As the muleteers made camp, Bingham and Carrasco walked over to a small house beside the road, in which they found Melchor Arteaga who sold supplies to travelers. Arteaga was drunk, but when Bingham asked him where the ruins were, he "pointed straight up to the top of the mountain," to a ridge that connected a high, thin peak to a much larger, more solid mountain. This peak was Huayna Picchu, and the ruins were on the ridge. The larger mountain's name, Arteaga slurred to Carrasco, was Machu Picchu, or "Old Peak."

Machu Picchu. Bingham thought the name was "awful" at first, not appreciating the charm of its internal rhyme.[6] He may have read it before—it was mentioned in one of the books he had consulted, and the peak was on at least one of the maps in his saddlebags—but neither it nor Huayna Picchu was among the

Inca names he had copied from the Spanish chronicles in Lima.[7] Bingham may have considered riding on: they were too close to Cuzco to have reached the ruins of Vitcos and Vilcabamba, his true goals that year.

Bingham was also diligent; he had told himself that he would investigate every ruin he heard about, no matter how unpromising. His Harvard counterpart Farabee had told Bingham the rumors of large cities above the Urubamba—if Bingham passed one by, he would never forgive himself. Bingham hired Arteaga as a guide for the next day, in exchange for two Peruvian *soles*, or one silver American dollar. The climb up to the ruins would at least be a good warm-up for future tramps through the jungle.

July 24, 1911, dawned cold and rainy, and low clouds hid the ridge from view. Bingham tried to rouse Arteaga, who waved him off until the weather and perhaps his hangover improved. Just after ten, Arteaga emerged from his house, stretched, and strode off down the road toward Ollantaytambo, Bingham and Carrasco scurrying behind. To their regret, Foote and Erving decided to work in camp. At a quarter to eleven, Arteaga left the path and cut through the brush to the river. He took off his shoes and gingerly crept over a fragile bridge, made of four logs bound together by vine, followed by Carrasco and then Bingham, on his hands and knees.

They entered the jungle, and the river's noise dropped to a dull roar. Orchids and hummingbirds broke the green darkness of liana-choked trees. The path grew steep and muddy, and leaves dripped onto their clothes. Arteaga picked his way around the rocks, using tree trunks that he had notched like ladders. Bingham tried to keep up, panting. "A good part of the distance we went on all fours, sometimes holding on by our fingernails." It was only somewhat of an exaggeration. Arteaga might have told him to be careful with his hands. Tree roots had a funny way of turning into vipers up there.

The higher they climbed, the more Hiram's earth-bound worries fell away. The sun cleared the peaks to the east, burning off the clouds. The trees grew smaller and smaller, until he could see the river twisting 2,000 feet beneath them, still in shadow. The slope began to level off; the brush gave way to waving grass. After an hour and a half of exertion, they collapsed into a peaceful clearing. And there, Bingham got a surprise: a single hut. Staring out of it, shocked at the intrusion, was a family of Indian farmers.

These were the Richartes, Arteaga explained. Twenty-four-year-old Torvis and his family had left lands closer to Cuzco four years ago to farm on the rich terraces opened up by the new Urubamba road. There were good fertile lands on this ridge, 8,000 feet above sea level; the nightly mists kept crops watered, and the daily sun helped them grow. Their ten-by-fifteen-foot home was cozy enough—guinea pigs scurried underfoot—and with two neighboring families they harvested maize, potatoes, sugar cane, beans, peppers, tomatoes, and berries. For the pleasure of living here, they hiked twelve Peruvian *soles*' (six dollars American) worth of produce a year halfway to the river to leave for Arteaga. They hoped to one day have land of their own. To the many who would follow, this ridge would seem like a window back through time, but for the Richartes, who had escaped the abuse of working for a white landlord, it was a refuge, and their home.[8]

The intrusion of the outside world that morning was thus worrisome. They knew Arteaga, but the rest of his party was threatening. It was rarely good to see a soldier like Carrasco—even half out of uniform from the hot climb. Was he searching for instigators of the recent rebellion? Or to dragoon Torvis into the army? Their nervousness increased when they saw the third and final hiker, Bingham—probably the tallest person they had ever seen, his long alien legs tucked into tall leather boots, wrapped with cloth, and ballooning into khaki jodhpurs. He was panting from the climb, and his hunting jacket and gray cardigan were likely tucked under his arm. A strange, rifle-like device was strapped to his back. Beneath a beaten and misshapen gray hat and a head of hair that was lightening in the sunshine, the gringo flashed his tight-lipped smile.

The tension melted away when Arteaga explained in Quechua that this strange foreigner simply wanted to see the ruins. The Richartes sat Bingham on a shaded wooden bench and brought him cold, refreshing water in a gourd and delicious sweet potatoes for lunch. They "laughingly . . . admitted they enjoyed being free from undesirable visitors, officials looking for army 'volunteers' or collecting taxes." Staring out at the enchanting view, Bingham understood their desire for solitude. This was a special place. To the east, the snow-capped range of dark cliffs tumbled through a cloak of green to the invisible, but still faintly audible, Urubamba River two miles below. To the north, the jungle-covered ridge seemed to continue for a mile until it exploded upward in the spiraling tooth of Huayna Picchu. And at Bingham's back, to the south, was the impassive peak of Machu Picchu.

It was as good a place for a lost city as any. Bingham stood up, ready to go. Arteaga was tired and passed the job off to Richarte and his forty-eight-year-old neighbor, Anacleto Alvarez, who had lived on the mountain for eight years. They in turn passed it off to Richarte's barefoot son, whose name may have been Pablito.[9] He was no older than eight and small. His hair was thick and black, and his skin was a rich brown, edging out from the cuffs of his rough pants and the sleeves of a thin white shirt. He wore a small, pancake-shaped hat and a woolen poncho, its thick colorful stripes meeting at the seam down his chest.

The Richarte boy began down the path toward Huayna Picchu. "Sir, come . . . I know where there are Incan houses, over there . . . I know the way," the boy supposedly told Bingham and Carrasco.[10] Bingham struggled to keep up, trying not to get his hopes up. He had been just as excited for Choqquequirau, for all the good it did him. It was impossible not to feel a small, mounting thrill, however: he was walking into ruins that his fellow historians and anthropologists likely had not visited. Perhaps no outsider had stepped foot here since the conquest.

Thorns tore at Bingham's clothes, and he stooped low to avoid the branches and vines that the boy dodged easily. Bingham saw that the trail led them onto a series of old terraces, as at Choqquequirau. The difference here was that the boy's family had reclaimed them for their own agriculture. Finally, rounding a promontory, the boy gestured and Bingham looked up. His eyes caught the peak of Huayna Picchu first, large and impressive. His gaze drifted down, and then he saw it: "a jungle-covered maze of small and large walls, the ruins of buildings made of blocks of white granite, most carefully cut and beautifully fitted together without cement. Surprise followed surprise until there came the realization that we were in the midst of as wonderful ruins as any ever found in Peru."

Covered by a foam of "trees and moss and the growth of centuries," the temples, fountains, and palaces, buildings seemed to rise and fall along the ridge until they crashed upon the base of Huayna Picchu like a wave. Bingham couldn't be sure where the ruins ended and the mountain began. In one thicket, the Richarte boy showed him the day's first architectural wonder, an incredible piece of stonework: a cave that had been shaped, carved, and lined with beautiful, interlocking stones. A stone carved with four graceful steps edged its triangular entrance. An hourglass of blocks linked the cave's outer lip to an adjacent boulder. The inside of the cave was lined with yet more carefully worked stones. Mysterious pegs protruded from the walls. Beneath them were "very large niches, the best and tallest that I have ever seen," wrote Bingham. The Incas had once placed their golden icons, and, more importantly, the *mallquis*, or mummies of their dead emperors, in niches like these. Had this been a royal tomb, where emperors sat forever in state, their leathery skin still clad in the brightly colored tunics of Inca royalty, their ears still hanging with massive gold earplugs, their brows covered with the royal red fringe?

The boy pointed above the cave, where the stone thrust up into a curved, tower-like structure. Rounded walls were rare in Inca architecture and were often features of sun temples. The most sacred point of the great Ccoricancha in Cuzco was its curved western wall, whose massive niche guarded a golden icon. By contrast, this wall had a single window facing east, which was surrounded by pegs carved gently from the rock. Had they been used to secure some other long-lost icon that blazed with the morning sun? Bingham followed the boy up a set of stairs and saw that the structure flowed into an even more stunning wall made of regular, finely grained ashlars of pure white granite.

"Clearly, it was the work of a master artist," he later wrote,

> *The interior surface of the wall was broken by niches and square stone-pegs. The exterior surface was perfectly simple and unadorned. The lower courses, of particularly large ashlars, gave it a look of solidity. The upper courses, diminishing in size towards the top, lent grace and delicacy to the structure. The flowing lines, the symmetrical arrangement of the ashlars, and the gradual gradation of the courses, combined to produce a wonderful effect, softer and more pleasing than that of the marble temples of the Old World. Owing to the absence of mortar, there were no ugly spaces between the rocks. They might have grown together. On account of the beauty of the white granite this structure surpassed in attractiveness the best Inca walls in Cuzco, which had caused visitors to marvel for four centuries. It seemed like an unbelievable dream. Dimly, I began to realize that this wall and its adjoining semicircular temple over the cave were as fine as the finest stonework in the world.*
>
> *It fairly took my breath away.*[11]

The boy pulled Bingham up a stairway, past a series of dried-up fountains, and into an open space that suggested it was the site's ceremonial heart, its sacred plaza. The boy's family had cleared it for a vegetable garden, and on its western side, the slope fell away, yielding a view of the mighty Urubamba River. The plaza's other three sides, however, bore stone buildings. The building to the south had niches and pegs that reminded Bingham of Choqquequirau; he wondered if it had been a priest's quarters. On the plaza's northern side was a "truly megalithic" temple. It lacked a southern wall, but its other three sides were made of huge blocks of white granite, quarried from the mountain itself and "fitted together as a glass stopper is fitted to a bottle." The largest block was more than fourteen feet long and was carved like an altar. Here, an Inca priest might once have lifted gifts to the sun and then stepped inside the temple to spread them upon the altar.

On the plaza's eastern edge was its most enchanting temple. Though it also lacked a wall to the plaza, a single erect stone suggested a lost beam that would have supported a roof. It was wider than the others, and its main wall had three large, beautiful windows, each three feet wide and over four feet high. The three windows overlooked a more public plaza, where the site's attendants may have worshipped, and then beyond, to the "tumbled mass of gigantic forest-clad mountains, rising to snow-capped peaks" to the east. One felt pulled to these windows like a soul leaving a dying body, as if beyond them were a better world. They jogged something in Bingham's memory—what, he couldn't yet figure out.

The only false note in this poem of stone and jungle was a "rude scrawl" on the three-windowed temple, "Lizarraga 1902." Bingham wrote it down, hoping it wasn't another explorer. He had climbed up the hill expecting little, but his imagination was already soaring, writing the story he would tell Alfreda and his readers at home. "Fine ruins—much better than Choqq," he wrote in his journal.

He set up his camera and began to take pictures—capturing the scene for his audience at home.[12] The boy motioned for Bingham to follow, and the explorer carried the tripod up a steep set of stairs to the ruins' highest point. Here was the site's last mystery, at least for that day: a large boulder carved into a two-tiered table, its smooth gray surface broken by a tall rectangular column, like the pommel on a saddle. It was an *intihuatana,* Bingham learned, a sort of religious sundial to mark the passage of seasons, harvests, and holy days. Bingham had read about them in the works of Clements Markham and E. G. Squier but had never seen one himself. There had once been an *intihuatana* at Ollantaytambo, but like so many other native objects of worship, the Spanish had destroyed it. Another *intihuatana* above Pisaac, a town along the Vilcanota, had been defaced in the last century. That this one survived was cause for celebration and a clue that the Spanish might never have sacked the site. Had they even known about it? Hiram had gone in search of the last cities of the Incas—but had he found something even older? What was this place?

Five days out of Cuzco, and Hiram had already discovered the great mystery of his life: the identity and purpose of Machu Picchu.

Bingham wanted to linger, but after five feverish hours, the sun was going down. Moreover, he had a schedule to keep: the true objects of his search—Vitcos and Vilcabamba—were supposed to be still farther along. Promising himself that he would return to uncover the site's remaining buildings, the American followed the Richarte boy and the soldier out of the ruins and back to the hut. He said good-bye to the boy's family and then descended with Carrasco and Arteaga to the river below. Over dinner, Bingham told Eaton and Foote what he had seen, and they wondered about the surprises to come. If no one had celebrated a beautiful ruin like Machu Picchu so close to Cuzco, who knew how incredible the actual last cities of the Incas might be?

The next morning, Hiram started a letter to his wife sharing the good news of his climb up "to a wonderful old Inca city called Machu Picchu."[13] There would be no breathless telegrams to the press, however, no extra editions on the streets of New York announcing the discovery of a beautiful lost city. Hiram was still a hungry explorer, looking to make his name, but he wanted to avoid the rash excitement he felt after visiting Choqquequirau. He needed to slow down his usual impatience and figure out what the site was, and what his visit *meant.* Was it something new? Or like at Choqquequirau, had he visited a previously described site? In one very loaded word, was he the "discoverer" of Machu Picchu?

While their *arriero* searched for two lost mules, Bingham questioned Melchor Arteaga about the signature he had seen on the three-windowed temple: "Lizarraga, 1902." Based on what Arteaga replied, Bingham was at first disappointed: "Agustin Lizarraga is discoverer of Machu Picchu and lives at San Miguel Bridge just before passing," he wrote in his journal. When the *arriero* returned with the mules, Hiram sought Lizarraga at the bridge. Agustín wasn't home, but the darker color of his brother Angel's face gave Bingham relief. The Lizarragas were poor, local mestizos, or, as Bingham would later refer to them, "half-castes"—neither white nor Indian, therefore untrustworthy in American racialist eyes. Although Agustín and two friends, Gabino Sanchez and Enrique Palma, visited Machu Picchu in July 1902, Hiram did not view them as competitors.

Still, Bingham refrained from firing off a triumphant telegram home. Machu Picchu was known locally, but the more difficult question was whether any other scholar had published on it. Bingham needed to go no further than the 1865 map of the geographer Raimondi in his saddlebags to see that the *mountain* of Machu Picchu had been documented for nearly half a century.[14] The mountain had appeared on many maps since, including one published in 1910 by the English Inca expert Sir Clements Markham.[15]

As for references to the ruins—they too existed. Bingham had already referred to the geography of Charles Wiener, who in 1880 reported rumors of ruins at Machu Picchu and Huayna Picchu.[16] Wiener had not visited them, but others perhaps had—even if Bingham hadn't heard of them. In 1877, a German named Herman Göhring published an account of a doomed expedition down the Urubamba, in which he noted the existence of a fortress at "Picchu."[17] In 1887, another German, Augusto R. Berns, founded the Inca Mining Company to loot Inca ruins around the hacienda of Torontoy.[18] Bingham would later receive a document in which the Peruvian government gave Berns permission to excavate the area, provided he turn over ten percent of any precious metals found.[19] Yet Berns seems not to have done any digging. The following year the company's vice president resigned, "accusing Berns of having misappropriated funds for personal use and, worse, of failing to launch a single expedition."[20] Finally, in 1904, a Peruvian named Carlos B. Cisneros published an *Atlás del Perú*, in which he noted the existence of ruins at Huayna Picchu: "The entire territory is seeded with ruined Inca populations that offer a great field for investigation by archaeologists, for the numerous objects of precious metal, and the many other things, that surround the shrines and ancient tombs."[21]

In other words, Cuzco residents and outsiders both knew the area to be dotted with ruins, and a few no doubt reached Machu Picchu itself. But no one had yet described Machu Picchu, photographed the ruins, or tried to understand them as a historical site. And that, to Bingham, was discovery, an achievement he would later defend with a lawyer's taste for nuance. In 1922, after he had sworn off exploration and gone to war, Bingham wrote: "I suppose that in the same sense of the word as it is used in the expression 'Columbus discovered America' it is fair to say that I discovered Machu Picchu. The Norsemen and the French fishermen undoubtedly visited North America long before Columbus crossed the Atlantic. On the other hand it was Columbus who made America known to the civilized world. In the same sense of the word I 'discovered' Machu Picchu—in that before my visit and report on it, it was not known to the geographical and historical societies in Peru, nor to the Peruvian government. It had been visited by a few Indians and half-castes and possibly by one European."[22] Bingham was not claiming to be the first at Machu Picchu, only the first to proclaim the site's historical importance. In that sense, he at least had the Oxford English Dictionary on his side: by 1908, the word "discover" had picked up a new definition: "To bring to public notice, to make famous or fashionable."[23] As Peruvian intellectuals admitted the following year, Bingham could be called the "scientific discoverer."

Yet the whole fight over whose pale face first peeked over the ridge first seems absurd when placed next to the simple fact that there had been three Indian families living and farming in the ruins for years; that what they called the site— scholars later learned—had come from the Incas; that they had their own theories about what the site meant, about where its most spiritual parts lay, and what happened to those who offended the Incas and their memory. Bingham had discovered the tip of the iceberg, but still remained ignorant of the bulk of belief beneath.

Bingham thus needed to be careful. While he was trying to figure out what Machu Picchu was, the indigenous people of the region were trying to understand why the explorer was there. What they came up with was worrisome. Rumors already swirled about the young boy who died. The story would be in full flower by the rainy season, when a second tragedy occurred. In February 1912, Agustín Lizarraga, the earlier "discoverer of Machu Picchu" whom Bingham never met, was crossing a fragile bridge in the ridge's shadow, when he lost his grip, slipped, and drowned. His body was never found, despite a nine-mile search downstream.[24] His wife was inconsolable, and his family, over the years, began to tell a story that suggested the resentment already gathering around the Yale expedition: Lizarraga had not lost his grip on Sunday, February 11, 1912, as was reported, but had fallen when the bridge's ropes were cut; some in his family later hinted that the crime's author was none other than Bingham.[25]

The accusation is not widespread and is improbable. On February 11, 1912, Bingham was planning his next expedition with the help of President William H. Taft. Bingham's papers show no evidence that he had any motive for or involvement in the accident. Bingham had rejected Agustín as a threat and would conduct business with his brother the following year.

The changing story of Lizarraga's death reflects a dramatic aspect of Bingham's story, however: his expedition and his arrival at Machu Picchu meant something entirely different to the Peruvians, whose help he needed.

Upon arriving in Peru that June, Bingham had announced that he was searching for the lost cities of the Incas. Doing so had put him in the company of all the foreigners who had come to Peru to grow wealthy off the country's natural and indigenous resources. On July 27, 1911, only three days after his visit to Machu Picchu, Cuzco's newspaper *El Comercio* published a fable-like story that made the link clear. Titled "The Treasure of the Inca; the Hunters of Gold," it reflected the popular belief that every every foreigner searched for shining treasure. The city had yet to hear about Bingham's visit to Machu Picchu, but its timing was far from coincidental, given that Bingham had spent weeks in Cuzco, asking for tales of Inca ruins.

"There is a country in South America, that from top to bottom is a vast mine," began the author, J. P. Paz Soldán. "Gold in its southern reaches. Silver and copper in its center. Rubber, pearls and emeralds in the north. This country is Peru."[26] Peru's greatest treasure, however, was that which the Incas hid throughout the Andes during the Spanish conquest. Tales of that treasure traveled far and wide, attracting adventurers and explorers in search of fortune and glory. Most of these explorers failed, but others left more indelible marks.

One recent day, near an American-owned mine in the Andes, wrote Paz Soldán, a Peruvian gentleman named Don Fernando de Alcántara stopped one such adventurer, an American mining engineer named Williams, from beating an elderly and impoverished Indian to death. In gratitude the Indian, whose name was Coparti, said he would tell the Peruvian gentleman a secret that the American had failed to bludgeon out of him: that Coparti's grandfather was a descendant of the Inca emperor Titu Cusi Yupanqui—the son of the rebel Manco Inca and resident of Vilcabamba. What's more, Coparti's grandfather had passed down the location of Titu Cusi's treasure.

Coparti saw that Alcántara did not believe him. "Look at my hands," demanded the Indian. "I have thrust them up to my elbows in gold. There's enough wealth there to cover you three times over." Coparti climbed a nearby mountain, commanding the Peruvian gentleman to follow. When Alcántara failed to keep up, Coparti ran on without him. Less than five minutes later, he returned with his arms full of golden chains, jars, chalices and bowls, tunics woven with emeralds, diadems, bracelets. Alcántara was astounded. Coparti swore that it represented only one one-hundredth of Titu Cusi's treasure. Tomorrow he would show Alcántara the rest.

The fable ended tragically, however. Coparti carried the treasure to Alcántara's hotel for him and said goodnight. But when Alcántara woke up the next morning, it was to screams: "He has murdered him! Poor Coparti!" Stumbling down to the door of the hotel, Alcántara found Coparti dead, shot by the American, who stood over the corpse "nakedly smiling, without showing the least repentance." Williams went unprosecuted, and the treasure of the last rebel Incas was lost forever.

It was just a story, far too fabulous to be true. But its publication in Cuzco's leading newspaper a week after Bingham left Cuzco to begin his own search for the last Incas was at best bad timing. At worst, the article was a premonition of how some Peruvians viewed Bingham, as an agent of U.S. exploitation, not exploration. As Bingham rode down the valley, his search for the palaces of Manco Inca and his family at its very brightest, Cuzco's newspaper readers were grimacing at a darker version of his tale, in which a quest for Inca secrets destroyed modern indigenous lives, and lost Peru's treasure for good.

Chapter Ten

The White Temple

On July 25, 1911, Bingham continued along the Urubamba River, looking for Manco's kingdom of the Vilcabamba. Nearly 350 years before, an expedition of Spaniards rode into the region to capture Tupac Amaru, Manco's son. In the years since, the region had passed in and out of the records like an angry ghost. The Inca mines never yielded the gold and silver the Spaniards expected, and revolts by black slaves ended attempts to turn the region into a major producer of sugar and coca. The missionaries fled soon after, leaving only a few abusive Spanish traders behind.[1] When various development schemes failed, the Peruvian government opened up the entire region in the late nineteenth century with the road Bingham now followed. Here, the peaks were slightly lower, and farmland and flowers stretched out on either side.

Beneath the region's bucolic beauty, however, it remained a hard place. The lower Urubamba was the frontier between the bright, cold Andes and the dark, hot Amazon. It was an extreme region whose temperatures pitched from near freezing at night to blistering during the day. Settlers awoke to find their cattle bleeding from the bites of vampire bats. Wealthy landowners ruled large haciendas where Indians toiled in fields of sugar cane, coffee, cacao plants (whose seeds are ground to make chocolate), and coca. The state was weak, and the landowners dominated the peasants with a mixture of paternalism and abuse; if cheap alcohol didn't release the tension, then there was always the threat of gunpowder. The Indian peasants often fought back, as had happened during the revolt earlier that year. The place was a human tinderbox.

With a military escort, however, Bingham could worry less and focus on his search for the ruins of Vitcos, Manco's palace, and Vilcabamba the Old, Manco's religious refuge. When they stopped for the evening at a massive sugar and sheep-raising hacienda named Huadquiña, Bingham could only talk about his search. Bingham showed the estate's owner, a wealthy widow, the paragraphs he had copied from the chronicles in Lima. She was no stranger to this sort of madness. Her son-in-law had also caught the Inca bug, but he tramped around the mountains in search of artifacts, not ruins. The next morning, she called her most knowledgeable workers and ordered them to tell Bingham what they knew about the area. One trusted foreman offered two names. The first, Ccollumayu, was unfamiliar, but the second, Yuray Rumi, sounded familiar. In Lima, Hiram had learned that Manco's first palace, Vitcos, could be identified by a nearby "house of the Sun," a white stone shrine named Yurak Rumi, sitting atop a spring, "from which the Devil emerged and was adored by those idolaters."[2] Had its name changed to Yuray Rumi?

Writing to Alfreda afterward, Bingham was ebullient. "I started to tell you yesterday about my new Inca City, Macchu Picchu [*sic*]," he wrote to his wife. "It is far more wonderful and interesting than Choqquequirau. The stone work is as fine as any in Cuzco! It is unknown and will make a fine story." Bingham hoped to return for a full week at Machu Picchu, he boyishly told his wife, but new discoveries beckoned. "I have learned here of some more big ruins nearby! It's most exciting."[3]

Bingham's hopes were high when they set out, but Ccollumayu proved a red herring. The Indian guides spent two days thrashing the forest searching for the promised ruins. Scraping bamboo and thorny vines ripped the Americans' clothes to shreds. On the third day their guide admitted that he had only heard about the ruins from someone else, who had seen them ten years before. Worse still, when the guides took Bingham to the promised Yuray Rumi, he saw only three or four round structures with one opening and no windows, and one square building with four small windows. Bingham was exasperated: there was no great sun shrine here. "[T]o compare it to Ollantaytambo, as the foreman had done, was to liken a cottage to a palace or a mouse to an elephant."[4] He blistered his heels stomping back to the hacienda and told his men to pack up their gear. Had Machu Picchu just been a fluke?

The expedition continued downriver to an Indian town named Chaullay, whose residents had been sympathetic to the recent rebellion against the white landowners. They glared from their doorways at the tall white stranger and his hated military escort. Their mistrust of outsiders was historic. If the chronicles were right, then Chaullay had once guarded the Incas' spectacular braided bridge of Chuquichaca, the legendary entrance to Manco's refuge kingdom. Here, the Urubamba mingled with the waters of another river—one significantly named the Vilcabamba.

Bingham, however, did not investigate Chaullay's connection to Manco's kingdom—at least not yet. First, they rode a little further down the Urubamba, to "the last corner of Peru." They rested at an estate named Santa Ana, owned by Don Pedro Duque, the white-mustachioed father of the young engineer who had helped the expedition in Cuzco. A dapper old gentleman, Duque took such interest in Bingham's search for the lost city of the Incas that he planted an exciting, if deeply flawed, idea in Bingham's mind. Thrilled by the explorer's description of Machu Picchu, Duque proposed that his "new ruins (the fine ones at Machu Picchu) must be those referred to in the chronicles by the name of Vitcos or Pitcos," Bingham wrote to his wife. "Pitcos is an easy transition from Pichu or Pitchu. Machu simply means 'old' in Quechua." And Machu Picchu, Bingham explained, fit the chronicles' descriptions of Vitcos—a palace on a ridge. "It is really most exciting, for Vitcos (or Pitcos) was the actual residence of the last three Incas who lived over here in Vilcabamba after the Spanish Conquest," Bingham explained. "In fact it was, as you know, with the hope of making this discovery that I came."[5] He dashed off another letter to the Royal Geographic Society, providing the meat for the public's first taste of his achievement.[6]

That afternoon, Bingham realized he was celebrating too soon. In the subprefect's office of the nearby town of Quillabamba, he met a "crusty old fellow" named Evaristo Mogrovejo, the *teniente* or government administrator, of a town named Lucma, a hard day's travel up the Vilcabamba River. Mogrovejo knew his local ruins. Two days beyond Lucma, there was a hilltop ruin named Rosaspata, he said. In a jungle valley beyond Rosaspata, there was a group of ruins known by two names. The first was Espiritu Pampa, which could be evocatively translated as Plain of Ghosts, but made no appearance in the chronicles; its second name, however, was promising: Vilcabamba Viejo (Vilcabamba the Old). In Lima, Bingham had found a reference to a Vilcabamba that was the largest population center in the province, home of the Inca's priests. Could this Espiritu Pampa be it? The only way to find out was to go there.

There was a catch, however. The region separating Rosaspata and Espiritu Pampa was a no-man's land, a place where "savage" Indians held sway, Mogrovejo explained. To reach Espiritu Pampa, Bingham first would have to pass through a place named Concevidayoc, where a Peruvian had been murdered a decade before. There, Bingham would meet the only non-Indian who had braved the region and lived: a mysterious individual named Saavedra, whose very mention made the white men in the subprefect's office bristle.[7] This Saavedra had supposedly gone so far off the beaten track, into the realm of the Indians, that he had become like Kurtz in Joseph Conrad's *Heart of Darkness*—a white who had "gone native" in Africa and become a tyrant. "All assured us that it was a terrible place to reach," Bingham wrote, "and that the savage Indians [there] would not let us come out alive."[8]

It was music to Bingham's ears. The explorer pulled his magic talisman from his jacket pocket: the letter from President Leguía that ordered all government officials to assist the Yale expedition in their endeavors. Mogrovejo's shoulders sunk. The crusty old official would be Bingham's guide.

Before they could leave the next morning, however, Bingham received a telegram from Cuzco that boded ill for the expedition's future. It was from Prefect Nuñez, and it tersely announced that the Yale expedition was "only empowered to study and explore [ruins], but not to excavate. There must be no excavations, as excavating is contrary to law."

Bingham was confused. He thought he had the permission of Peruvian President Leguía to carry on whatever work he needed. Bingham worried that the political support for his explorations was shifting beneath his feet. Don Pedro Duque reassured Bingham, however: Nuñez might have heard from a relative in the valley that Bingham had found Machu Picchu, and he might have "conjured up this old law" to interfere with the expedition's work and save the excavating for himself.[9]

Trusting Duque entirely, Bingham assured the local officials that they would not damage any ruins. He sent off telegrams to his business friends in Lima, asking them to explain the situation to President Leguía and confirm that the expedition had permission to at least clear vegetation from what they found.[10]

"But there was no time to wait for an answer," Bingham wrote in his journal. It was already eight o'clock, and Nuñez's telegram had destroyed their early start. If he waited any longer, the local officials could make his search for the last cities of the Incas impossible.

Bingham, Foote, Carrasco, and a very reluctant Mogrovejo rode back to the threatening village of Chaullay, crossed its bridge, and began their ride up the Vilcabamba River. It was easy to see why they and the Incas made it their home: the valley was remote, well protected, and fertile. It reminded Hiram of Hawaii.

For those very reasons, the region was similarly attractive to the whites who had built *haciendas* and lorded over the locals. Bingham's first stop was the hacienda of José Pancorbo, the landowner whom Bingham had met in Cuzco. In the city, Pancorbo had seemed like a perfect gentleman. Here, his reputation suggested otherwise. Mogrovejo rode on without them, refusing to stay with Pancorbo because the landowner had stolen his mules. Bingham learned that Pancorbo was so "dyspeptic, disagreeable, and harsh . . . that people do not work for him because they like him, but because they have to." The local Indians so hated Pancorbo that in order to eat, the landowner confiscated produce from the people "passing through his yard . . . forcing them to take whatever price he sees fit to give them."[11]

Pancorbo, of course, thought that the threat of force was necessary to fend off what he perceived as native savagery. He himself was off tending his rubber interests farther down the Urubamba, but in his absence during the recent rebellion, Bingham learned, the Indians had attacked his hacienda, set his cane fields on fire, looted his house, and pulled down his great gates. According to his employees, that had been the Indians' fault, not his own, and Bingham was risking his life by venturing into their territory. They warned him that "[n]o one had been [to Concevidayoc] recently and returned alive."[12]

Alert, Bingham, Foote, and Carrasco left early the next morning, quietly reveling in the soaring scenery. As they climbed its steep hills, the river rushed far below, and fearsome cliffs loomed opposite, dappled with blue and green lichens like lizard skin. Above the road was tropical jungle, and below were light green cane fields. If the path to Machu Picchu was ascension and mystery, then this road was sheer majesty.

They reached Mogrovejo's town that night. To cheer up the grumbling official, Bingham offered him a deal—fifty cents for every ruin he could find and a dollar if the ruins were especially fine. Duly motivated, Mogrovejo spent the next day showing Bingham the area. Lucma was older than the Spanish conquest, and the inhabitants of its stone and mud houses knew the valley well. Mogrovejo called in various locals to name ruins for Bingham, who struggled to tie down the beautiful but confusing Quechua names in his journal. One description in particular stood out. Mogrovejo had already told Bingham that there was a "fortress" on the ridge of Rosaspata. Now, one villager claimed that there was a big stone near it named Ñusta España, or Ñusta Hispanan. The folded passages from the Spanish chronicles in Bingham's pocket suggested that Manco's palace was near a stone sun shrine named Yurak Rumi. Were Ñusta España and Yurak Rumi one and the same? Was Rosaspata Vitcos? "No one has been up here," he scribbled to his wife. "We have got some long hard tramps ahead of us."[13] It was the last letter he'd write for three weeks.

Mogrovejo led them further up the Vilcabamba the next day. The valley curved and widened and the road joined the river below. They crossed the river on a sturdy bridge and followed the path as it turned south, continuing to climb but more gently now. They rounded one ridge and suddenly they could see the length of the valley before them—green farmland and dark gray peaks on either side. Straight ahead was "a truncated hill a thousand feet high, its top partly covered with a scrubby growth of trees and bushes, its sides steep and rocky."[14] Rosaspata, Mogrovejo muttered. At its top were the ruins. And below it, the Indian village named Puquiura, the key geographical point in all colonial descriptions of the Incas' last kingdom. Bingham had to suppress his excitement. Rosaspata matched the chronicles' description of Vitcos almost exactly: next to Puquiura, "on a high eminence surrounded with rugged crags and jungles, very dangerous to ascend and almost impregnable."[15] And according to the chronicles, a few days beyond Puquiura was Vilcabamba.

They tied up their mules and, after lunch, hiked up to see the Inca remains. Led by an unnamed Indian guide from the town, Bingham, Foote, and Mogrovejo recrossed the Vilcabamba River. They walked through a ruined quartz-stamping mill, a remnant of the gold rush of the late sixteenth century. They crossed another thin river and began the steep climb uphill. The guide pointed out a decrepit Inca ruin in the hill's saddle, a single long structure with six doors and rough walls that had been converted to a pasture. Bingham wondered whether it had been a fort stormed by the Spaniards.

The guide led them along the western side of the ridge and then pointed. The ridge lowered and flattened into a wide, open plaza, overgrown with grass but bounded on its north side by a long ruined building. Bingham marveled at its size—it looked larger than any Inca structure Bingham had yet seen except Sacsayhuaman, the massively-walled complex above Cuzco. Approaching it from the south, Bingham counted one, two, fifteen doors. He circled around the back side and found another fifteen. The palace was a whopping 245 feet long and 43 wide. Although not quite so polished as Machu Picchu's, the stonework was still exceptional. Three doors facing the plaza were intact and shone with white granite doorjambs and massive, two-meter-long lintels. There were three large rooms inside and three long hallways connecting them. Many of the blocks had been re-moved to make walls for pastures, and Bingham saw "a considerable amount of digging . . . in efforts at treasure hunting."[16] Enough remained to suggest the place's former grandeur, however. Machu Picchu had filled Bingham's mind with thoughts of sacrifice and sun worship, but he thought this place suitable "for the residence of a king."

The ridge beyond the building gave a perfect view back down the valley. Snow-capped mountains rose behind them to the south, and the passage of the sun could be followed over the wooded valleys east and west. Bingham could have closed his eyes and imagined Manco Inca plotting his revenge against the Spaniards.

But was it Vitcos? Bingham compared his folded copy of the Spanish chron-icles to what he was seeing. The chronicles said that Vitcos was next to a white stone shrine and water spring named Yurak Rumi. If he found the shrine, then he could be sure.

The sun began to set, and they returned to Huancacalle, the town next to Puquiura. The next morning, after measuring the palace, Bingham joined Foote in a narrow, bucolic valley east of the ruins, where a thin stream trickled past cul-tivated fields, around stone fences and trees. The valley was covered with carved granite boulders, but none matched the chronicles' description of Yurak Rumi. One was large and white, and had a carved seat on its north side, but wasn't near a spring. Another had a low, circular *intihuatana*, or sun-post, but was far too small. The scene was eerily quiet, and as the sun fell behind Rosaspata, the stones turned a shadowy blue. This thin valley seemed as sacred as Machu Picchu, but in an entirely different way. Where Machu Picchu reached grandly to the sky, this valley offered peace.

At four o'clock that afternoon, they reached a clearing like an amphitheater. Small boulders dotted the outer edges, some carved like chairs. On the clearing's western side, abutting the Rosaspata ridge, were the remains of a once-solid rec-tangular structure. In the center of the clearing, however, was a great white gran-ite boulder, bigger than a house. It was covered with carvings, and it loomed over a cold, dark spring of water and swampy grasses like some great prehistoric beast. Its north face had been flattened, and four-to-eight inch cubes—horizontal *inti-huatanas*, almost—sprouted from the rock. As the sun passed overhead, the knobs cast curious shadows and made cubist tricks of depth and perception. The rock's top bore a number of altars or seats and was dark with lichens. A single, shallow crack bisected its peak. The crack looked artificially widened, Bingham thought; he wondered whether a sun priest perched atop the rock to greet the rising sun, or more sensationally, used the crack "to drain the blood of the victim killed on top of the rock."[17]

This was Ñusta España, or Ñusta Hispanan, the guide said—the site they had heard about in Lucma. Bingham and Foote began to celebrate. They had found it: Ñusta Hispanan was surely the modern name for Yurak Rumi, Manco Inca's great sun shrine. And if this was Yurak Rumi, then the palace on the hill above was none other than Vitcos, Manco Inca's beautiful palace in exile. It was to Vitcos that Manco first fled to survive, fight off the Spanish, and worship in peace. It was not as spectacular as Machu Picchu, but the whole complex, from the palace to the sun shrine, had a quiet, pensive beauty.

Machu Picchu might make a "fine story," but identifying Vitcos and Yurak Rumi would be Bingham's clearest achievement—made possible, of course, by the archivist Carlos Romero's preliminary research in Lima. For the first time in centuries, Manco's first palace returned to the map, ending years of speculation. By marrying the historian's archival tools to the explorer's compass and his own magnificent enthusiasm, Bingham had proved that the chronicles could be trusted, and that Inca history was real, not the stuff of myth. Later scholars would deem his publications on Vitcos and other Inca sites would be "the beginning of scientific literature for the Inca heartlands"—the start of modern Inca archaeology.[18]

But as Bingham stared at the great sun shrine, its color shifting in the setting sun, he realized that this discovery raised more questions than it answered. If Rosaspata was Vitcos, Manco's first palace in exile, then what was Machu Picchu? Why did the sides of Yurak Rumi, this sun shrine, seem both blackened and cracked—as if it had been burned? And if this was Vitcos, then where was the city that Manco built as his final refuge? Where was Vilcabamba the Old?

Chapter Eleven

The Plain of Ghosts

*U*ntil now Hiram had visited Inca sites near modern settlements—places still technically on the map, even if their names had faded. But to continue his search for Vilcabamba, he would have to go beyond, into a land that whiter Peruvians feared, like the Spaniards before them. He would have to enter the jungle, past the reaches of any known settlement in Inca history, where he had heard there was a ruin with the most evocative of names—Espiritu Pampa, the Plain of Ghosts.

Espiritu Pampa was guarded by equally spectral jungle Indians, one of the few indigenous groups to have beaten back the Spanish conquest. For the first 350 years of colonization in the Americas, the Indians of the eastern Andes had slipped through European efforts to subjugate them like minnows through a fisherman's net. Once allies and enemies of the Incas, after the conquest they retook control of the region and defended it from Spanish invasion. Divided by hundreds of language groups and intermittent ritual warfare, the Asháninka, Shuar, Machiguenga, and countless other peoples organized themselves by small, polygamous households. They hunted, fished, and practiced small-scale slash-and-burn agriculture. They traded, intermarried, and exchanged gifts to establish sacred communal bonds. To sort the good spirits from the bad—and to punish the latter—they prepared and consumed a powerfully hallucinogenic vine named *ayahuasca*, or *yagé*, a substance so potent that eastern Andean people believed that it made even God bow to their superior wisdom.[1]

These jungle dwellers were also deeply independent, resistant to being converted into a religion that demanded they become submissive farmers. They peppered conquistadors and settlers with poisoned arrows. To gain metal goods, they flirted with missionaries who wavered between wanting to save their souls from European corruption and punishing them for their "savagery." When the missionaries pushed too far, the backlash was fierce. In the 1740s, the jungle Indians of the central eastern Andes—along with some crucial black allies—rallied around a Cuzco Indian named Juan Santos who proclaimed himself heir to the Inca Atahualpa. Together they threw out the Franciscans' missions.[2]

For the next hundred years Europeans left the jungle alone, until the mid-nineteenth century, when global demand for a newly important product gave Europeans a reason to return: *caucho,* or raw latex, the milky substance wept by *Hevea brasiliensis,* the Brazilian rubber tree. To collect this highly lucrative substance, rubber barons—even worse than their rubber-baron cousins in the United States—incorporated the region's previously independent indigenous groups into a system that swung between debt peonage and outright slavery, bound together by trade goods, physical coercion, torture, and murder. The death toll of the more well-known rubber regime in King Leopold II of Belgium's Congo Free State was far larger than the violence in the worst region in South America—the Putumayo of Peru, Ecuador, and Colombia—but the difference was one of scale, not savagery.[3] Foremen used punishment as an excuse to exorcise four centuries of fear of their indigenous workers, committing acts of cruelty that went well beyond the pale. While Bingham was trying to decide whether to continue on to Espiritu Pampa, an Irishman named Roger Casement was pushing the British government to publish a report that documented the death of 30,000 Indians in the Putumayo regions alone.[4]

As Bingham learned, the atmosphere in southern Peru was only slightly less charged. While preparing to leave Puquiura, the landowner Pancorbo caught up with Bingham and warned him that if he wanted to reach Espiritu Pampa, he would have to pass through Concevidayoc, the home of the settler Saavedra and his fierce indigenous minions. The landowner admitted there were ruins there, but said that if Bingham went with Peruvian soldiers in tow, the Indians would disappear, leaving no one to show them the site. And if they went unarmed, without soldiers, "they may attack us and shoot us down in our tracks."

The stakes of Bingham's search for the lost cities of the Incas were never clearer. He could turn around and ride back to Cuzco, rest on the laurels of his rediscovery of Vitcos, and spend the next month safely clearing Machu Picchu. Or, he could continue on into the jungle to search for Espiritu Pampa to investigate whether it was Vilcabamba the Old, the religious heart of Manco's rebel kingdom. By doing so he would risk becoming embroiled in a violent conflict that had been simmering since the conquest.

There was never any real doubt about the decision Bingham would make. He thanked Pancorbo for the warning but said he would not be following it. Pancorbo scowled and rode away in a huff, his armed bodyguard following behind; it was Bingham's funeral, not his.

The trail out of Puquiura was picturesque but steeply pitched, and Bingham, Foote, Mogrovejo, Carrasco, and their muleteer rose quickly above the tree line. An hour later they reached a quiet 10,000-foot-high village named San Francisco de la Victoria de Vilcabamba, or Vilcabamba the New, built by the Spanish to commemorate their victory over the Inca rebel kingdom. When the nearby gold and silver mines tapped out, the town's population plummeted. All that remained from that time was a towering, ancient church, far too large for the few muleteers, shepherds, and farmers who had stayed behind.

The town's good-natured Indian mayor, Manuel Condore, called together the town's villagers to meet the visitors. As Bingham interviewed them, clues sprouted before him like pins on a map. One villager confirmed that there was "a place way down in the jungle called Vilcabamba or Vilcapampa Vieja," about four days away. No one in Vilcabamba the New had seen it, but in the next valley over, villagers in a town named Pampaconas knew about it.[5]

Condore also introduced Bingham to the new Vilcabamba's oldest resident, Juan Quispicusi. Eighty-year-old Quispicusi had been born in a time when a few residents in Cuzco still traced Inca descent; his parents may have been alive during the indigenous rebellion of Tupac Amaru II in 1780. Humble and deferent, he doffed his hat in Bingham's presence, revealing a knitted cap and graying hair. Under a poncho of green, red, and yellow, and with his calves bare to the cold, he recited the tradition he had learned as a child: an Inca had lived at Rosaspata, or Vitcos, and then had fled south to a series of six other sites, all of which he named. The itinerary matched a route that Manco Inca's armies had once traveled to raid the Spanish settlements and convoys.[6]

Bingham was amazed. The Spaniards had tried their hardest, but 350 years after the conquest, the original Inca names still clung to the landscape, remembered by their former subjects. Bingham wondered whether this memory extended to Espiritu Pampa, or whether the Plain of Ghosts was just his own wishful think-ing: "Would the ruins turn out to be 'ghosts'? Would they vanish on the arrival of white men with cameras and steel measuring tapes?" he wondered.[7]

When they left the next morning, their party had swollen to eight: the Amer-icans Bingham and Foote; Sgt. Carrasco and the other soldier provided by the government; the cheerful mayor Condore, and the gruff *teniente* Mogrovejo from Lucma; and two Indian *arrieros* to handle the nine mules.

It was raining hard, and the trail out of "new" Vilcabamba turned to mud. By midmorning they were 12,500 feet up at the Kollpacasa Pass. Behind them were the Vilcabamba River and its valley. Beneath them was the Pampaconas River. This new valley was steep and grassy in its upper reaches, but where it turned to jungle below, it and its river had another name: the Concevidayoc, which Bing-ham had been warned about. On Bingham's map the river and its valley turned south toward the Apurimac River. In real life, it seemed to go north, toward the Urubamba. Bingham realized he was in uncharted territory. One of his topogra-phers would later show that the Apurimac and the Urubamba lay 30 miles farther apart than previously thought, "opening" a 1,500-square mile region, a "veritable labyrinth of snow-clad peaks, unknown glaciers, and trackless canyons."[8]

But not unsettled, Mogrovejo reminded him. Below was a village of Indian and mestizo farmers and herders who had settled this far from Cuzco for a rea-son. The soldiers would have to hang back. "[I]f the Indians of Pampaconas caught sight of any brass buttons coming over the hills they would hide so effec-tively that it would be impossible to secure any carriers. Apparently this was due in part to that love of freedom which had led them to abandon the more com-fortable towns for a frontier village where landlords could not call on them for forced labor."[9] Which was just what the expedition needed.

At the bottom of the worst mule trail Bingham had ever seen, Condore and Mogrovejo, the two government officials, rode quietly in the rain from one "lone-some farm to another." They greeted the men of each house with a smile but then slipped a silver dollar into their palms when they shook hands. They informed the men that they were now obligated to be porters for the expedition. Because Indi-ans had learned never to accept work unless they had been paid in advance, offi-cials had learned to force pay upon them, threatening them with imprisonment or worse if they refused. The farmers pleaded that they had to tend their crops, that their families could not spare them, that they lacked the food for a week's march into the jungle. But the officials were implacable, and Bingham soon had half a dozen porters. "It seemed very hard," wrote Bingham, "but this was the only way in which it was possible to secure carriers."

Bingham slept easier after he met their paid guide for the march into the jungle—Isidoro Guzman, a bearded and stocky mestizo settler who had seen the Inca ruins firsthand. He was cheery and full of colorful stories, though the Americans weren't too charmed by the dinner he served them: steaming bowls of sheep intestine soup. "We were really in new country," Bingham wrote.

At noon the next day, they were off, following a trail leaving from behind Guzman's hut. The dragooned Indian laborers grumbled and pulled the mules along a steep, muddy path that rose and fell above the river. Sheets of rain hid the valley from them, and the vegetation edging the trail changed from grasses, to bushes, to full trees, dripping with water, vines, and strange, wispy bromeliads. Bingham was grateful when they stopped for the night at a settlement named San Fernando, a small plot of maize and two small huts where three or four Indian farmers lived. The farmers disappeared by morning; Bingham's expedition was as unwelcome as the Spaniards had been 350 years before.

The trip wore on the Americans. They had been traveling for a month now, and ghostly birdcalls, explosions of flowers, and massive trees were not enough to keep them going. Their tent leaked at night, leaving them exhausted and jumpy during the day. They had developed half-beards, and their skin picked up layers of grime. Although the elevation was dropping, the next day's route was a strain, full of constant climbs in and out of the tributary gulches that extended from the river like ribs from a snake's spine. The path was slimy with rotted leaves, and bugs landed on the men's bare skin, leaving strange bites and worrisome swells. When they weren't slipping into brooks, they were crossing lashed-log bridges, which were barely comforting—someone had been maintaining the trail. Bingham kept his rifle in his hand, watching the jungle for movement. As hard as the Americans had it, their Indian porters had it worse; they were unarmed, and each was burdened with more than fifty clumsy pounds of the expedition's gear.

At one that afternoon, they broke through a dense wall of trees and vines and emerged in a clearing. Guzman told them to stop and rest, as they "were now in the territory of *los salvajes,* the savage Indians who acknowledged only the rule of Saavedra and resented all intrusion." Guzman said they should send ahead a porter to tell the settler and his Indian neighbors they came as friends and were not seeking rubber gatherers. Without the warning, the Indians might attack or, worse yet, disappear into the jungle. Without their help, the expedition would never find the ruins.

The porter selected set down his pack and slunk reluctantly down the trail. After an hour of waiting, Bingham remembered, "Suddenly we were startled by a crackling of twigs and the sound of a man running. We were instinctively holding our rifles a little higher in readiness for whatever might befall—when there burst out of the woods a pleasant-faced young Peruvian mestizo, quite conventionally clad, who had come in haste from Saavedra, his father, to extend to us a most cordial welcome!"[10]

Heaving sighs of relief, the party shouldered their guns and followed Saavedra's son along the trail toward the river, where the woods grew taller, thicker, and darker before yielding to a bright green field of sugar cane. At its edge was a comfortable hut from which stepped a small, slight man wearing dusty pants, a soft poncho, and a wide hat to keep off the noonday glare. He looked up and the Americans saw quiet, sad eyes, a drooping moustache, and "the nicest smile I have seen in Peru," Foote wrote in his journal.[11] Bingham had never met a "more pleasant and peaceable little man."[12]

Juan Cancio Saavedra was no fearsome dictator.[13] He served the expedition members chicken, rice, and sweet cassava for dinner and explained that the land had the Spanish-Quechua name of Concevidayoc "because it was a lifesaver for him. The word means 'a spot where one may be preserved from harm.'" He lived there with his "good-natured Indian wife," three or four children, and a housekeeper. He grew bananas, coffee, sweet potato, tobacco, peanuts, and sugar cane, which he processed with a small, foot-powered mill, and then carried up to San Francisco de la Victoria de Vilcabamba once a year to pay his taxes.[14] Saavedra himself maintained the valley's trails and bridges, and two of his children were at school in Cuzco. Bingham was impressed. "In the bitter wilderness, far from any neighbours, surrounded by dense forests and a few savages, he had established his home. He was not an Indian potentate, but only a frontiersman, soft-spoken and energetic, an ingenious carpenter and mechanic, a modest Peruvian of the best type."[15]

Then why did landowners like Pancorbo fear Saavedra and men like him so much? What of Saavedra's supposed army of jungle Indians? Bingham grasped the truth that afternoon when a single "*salvaje*" emerged from the jungle. He was either a Machiguenga or an Asháninka—called a "Campa" by the Peruvians with Bingham—both peoples who had plagued the Spaniards to no end. In the seventeenth century, when missionaries leaned too hard on one headman to give up his wives, "such was the rain of arrows unleashed on them by the sacrilegious Indians," wrote one chronicler, "that in a brief moment the three looked like a hedgehog, so sewn together and pierced by darts were they."[16] In the eighteenth century, it had been the Asháninka that had rallied around the self-proclaimed Inca Juan Santos Atahualpa.

Yet the single, shy Campa who approached them hardly resembled the noble warrior Bingham expected. Instead, he was "by far the dirtiest and most wretched savage that [Bingham had] ever seen." He wore his people's unisex ankle-length tunic, the *cushma,* his long black hair was unkempt and matted, and his cheeks looked emaciated. He was his people's chief, and he had lost an eye. By evening, a young married man and his sister joined him, also looking poorly. "They all have colds," Bingham noted.[17]

They were not wild killers who needed punishment. Instead, they were running from "civilization." These Asháninka or Machiguenga had recently fled a rubber outfit owned by none other than Pancorbo, the landowner who had tried to keep Bingham at Vitcos.[18] Pancorbo had hooked them through debt peonage, perhaps even tortured them, and had certainly exposed them to European illnesses. They had rebelled, perhaps as part of the larger revolt in the region, and Pancorbo feared the revenge they might take. He was wary of Saavedra because the Campas now worked with him on much kinder terms—and, perhaps, because they had fled to Espiritu Pampa. Pancorbo may have thought Bingham was in danger, but he also feared what Bingham might say if he learned the truth.

Pancorbo needn't have worried. Bingham was not there to help the jungle Indians but to use them as guides. For some unexplained reason, one Hiram could not quite grasp, the Campa-Asháninka had sought refuge at the ruins of Espiritu Pampa—which they called Vilcapampa. They would take him there the next day.

Carrasco was ill when they awoke and had to stay at Concevidayoc. Bingham, Foote, and the rest followed Saavedra along the trail to Espiritu Pampa. They climbed up a final hill, and at noon they reached a promontory marked by a small, crumbling, rectangular platform nearly hidden by the underbrush. Saavedra pointed below them to an alluvial fan, and Bingham saw . . . nothing, save a clearing dotted with the Asháninka's steeply pitched huts and a valley covered by thick jungle canopy. The ruins were hidden beneath, Saavedra explained.

The group descended an unusually wide Inca stairway, over a third of a mile long. By the time they reached the Asháninka's houses, it had begun to rain, but no one was at home. Faced with a storm or outsiders, even ones vouched for by Saavedra, the Asháninka had chosen the storm. When the rain let up, Saavedra showed him a few ruined buildings near the clearing: approximately eighteen low, circular dwellings, some containing the remains of pottery. They didn't seem Inca to Bingham—but they did lead him to believe that people had lived there for centuries.

While they were exploring, a young male Asháninka with a "pleasant face" appeared, armed with a bow and long arrows. The young man had been hunting and showed them a bird he had caught. Perhaps remembering how he had established trust with the Indians of Colombia, Bingham gave him a dried apricot. Two of the Asháninka he had met the day before emerged from the jungle, followed by a friend. Prompted by Saavedra, the men pointed toward the woods. The true ruins, "Espiritu Pampa or Vilcapampa," lay in that direction.

It took half an hour to get there, the vegetation growing almost gothic in its intricacy, thicker and higher the farther they went—as if there was more to feed on. If there was a lost city in this forbidding jungle, it was the sort to be fled, not sought—the lost city that lurked in every explorer's feverish subconscious, whispering unspeakable loss, locked in choking plants and held together by the roots of massive ceiba trees. The air was thick with hot moisture, flies, and bees.

Finally, "behind a curtain of hanging vines and thickets so dense we could not see more than a few feet in any direction," the Asháninka showed Bingham fifteen to twenty small rectangular buildings. None were as impressive as those at Machu Picchu, but they were clearly Inca, tall with gable ends. There was Inca pottery in the ruins and a fine fountain with three spouts, much like those at classic imperial Inca sites. One building was rounded at one end—like the sun temples at Machu Picchu and in Cuzco. Had it served the same purpose? The Asháninka took Bingham to a second nearby group of buildings, among which was a huge structure 192 feet long, 24 feet wide, with twelve doors in front and twelve behind. In style, it was grand, the slightly smaller brother of the palace at Vitcos. But in construction, it was rough, nowhere near Vitcos or Machu Picchu in quality. Confused, Bingham asked the Asháninka to show him Vilcabamba. The Asháninka swept their arms at the jungle—it was all around them.

Bingham stumbled through the undergrowth after the lithe Asháninka, who never seemed to catch their tunics in the clawing thorns. The explorer was disconcerted. There was little way of knowing how many buildings lay underneath. "Ruins well scattered," he wrote in his journal. "Long hard job to clear all ruins. Hardly worthwhile." Other details baffled him. There was charcoal, suggesting there had once been a fire. There were also red tiles, like those that covered his house in New Haven—which to Bingham again seemed like evidence of European, not Inca, habitation.[19]

That night, back at the clearing, the Asháninka men did their best to make Bingham, Foote, and the rest feel unwelcome. While the nervous whites and their highland Indian porters tried to sleep, "our savage helpers determined to make the night hideous with cries, tom-toms, and drums, either to discourage the visits of hostile Indians or jaguars, or for the purpose of exorcising the demons brought by the white men, or else to cheer up their families, who were undoubtedly hiding in the jungle near by," Bingham wrote.[20] The women and children would stay hidden throughout Bingham's visit. The Asháninka were taking no chances with their visitors.

The group returned to Espíritu Pampa in the morning and were surprised by how much of the ruins they had missed the day before. After clearing away the vines and jungle to the west of the main ruins—"to our surprise, and apparently to that of the Indians"—they found two houses of superior construction filled with niches. They were houses fit for an emperor.

But when Bingham sent the Asháninka off to hunt for more ruins, all they could turn up were three small foundations and a bridge—or so they claimed. Given their nervousness, they might have thought it wise to limit the reasons for the strangers to stay. After measuring and sketching the buildings that had been revealed, Bingham agreed. "Damn the flies and bees," he wrote in his journal. It was August 18, and after six days straight of rain, hot jungle, and an ever-dwindling supply of food, he was exhausted. Bingham called off the search. One might surmise that the Asháninka watched the expedition go with no small relief.

At Saavedra's house they found that Carrasco's illness was more serious than they had thought; he had collapsed with fever. They said farewell to Saavedra the next morning and started the long haul out of the valley "in the midst of torrential downpour," perhaps leaving Carrasco to be carried by the porters.

Rain continued to fall as they climbed, making talking hard but thinking easy. Bingham's mind circled around a single question: What had he found down in Saavedra's realm? Was Espíritu Pampa the mysterious Vilcabamba of the chronicles, the place to which Manco and his sons retreated from the Spanish, worshipped the sun, and tried to survive?

Bingham wasn't sure. There was no doubt that the site fit the requirements of Vilcabamba, with a long palace-like structure where Manco's family might have entertained the local peoples. The ruins may have been rough, but that they were made from stone suggested that the Incas had especially carted the building material down from the highlands. On the other hand, the site was farther from Vitcos than the chronicles suggested, at least for Europeans: a full four to five days, rather than two or three. Most of all, Bingham had expected Vilcabamba to be a massive site, beautifully built and ornate, befitting the last of the Inca kings. Instead, Espiritu Pampa appeared sad and secluded, possessing inexplicable red tiles, as if Spaniards later lived there. It was nothing like Machu Picchu, which more perfectly matched his preconceived notion of a lost city. He allowed for the possibility that Espiritu Pampa was perhaps where Tupac Amaru fled, but suspected that it was not the true, magnificent last city of the Incas.

It was at that very moment that Hiram Bingham's thinking went astray. A later explorer would convincingly show that Espiritu Pampa *was* both Tupac Amaru's refuge as well as Vilcabamba the Old. In August 1911, however, Bingham couldn't see it, enchanted instead by the more immediate beauty of Machu Picchu.

As subsequent researchers have shown, all the evidence was in front of Bingham, or would be when he returned home. Vilcabamba's architecture was rough because it was built in a hurry, after the Inca empire's height. It was covered with red tiles not because Spaniards had lived there but because the Incas were not romantically static; they were pragmatists, adapting European technology for their future comfort and survival. The charcoal was possibly the remnants of the great fire that Tupac Amaru lit before fleeing to the jungle. Bingham and his men had gazed down at the alluvial plain from the same promontory as the Spanish. The explorers had left by the same Inca stairway on which Tupac Amaru had been led upwards by a golden chain, contemplating his fate.[21]

Most obvious of all was the presence of the Asháninka who called it Vilcapampa. Like other whites of his day, Bingham thought jungle people lacked a history, that they were savage, responding to the most base emotions and impulses. He seems not to have asked the most immediate question: Why had they made Espiritu Pampa, of all places, their point of refuge? It was haunting. Nearly four centuries since Manco fled to this secluded alluvial plain to pick up and start again, the Asháninka had done the same, this time fleeing the colonial violence of the rubber trade. As anthropologists would later find, the Asháninka also knew the *Inkarrí* myth, the story that had grown out of the execution of Tupac Amaru— only in their version, the Inca had lived in their midst, hidden in the jungle.[22]

When Bingham returned to the United States, he would lift Machu Picchu up as the true lost city of the Incas. In doing so, he framed the Incas' history as he wanted it to be: beautiful, soaring, imperial, pure—and eerily resembling the temples he had seen at Chicago's world's fair. Espiritu Pampa, however, was Inca history as it was and continued to be: damaged but alive, besieged but remembered, still a refuge for resistance. Nevertheless, Bingham was a man of his time—an early-twentieth-century white American who believed that Indians were either pure and dangerous or corrupted and timid. As such, Bingham may have viewed Espiritu Pampa as a degenerate hybrid. By visiting for only two to three days, he gave himself no time to challenge those conclusions.

Yet, Bingham had a chance to choose the right path. As he dried off and left Pampaconas for the drier climes of the upper Andes, Bingham knew that he had found three sites worth studying further—Machu Picchu, Vitcos, and Espiritu Pampa. One might yet prove to be Vilcabamba the Old. He decided that while he completed the further geographical objectives of that year's expedition, his topographers might clear, map, measure, and photograph the three key ruins. If the expedition conducted some light excavations, his men might even find artifacts that could tie Espiritu Pampa to Vilcabamba the Old, artifacts that he could then bring back to Yale.

Upon leaving the Vilcabamba valley, however, Hiram received a letter that complicated all his plans. Don Pedro Duque's son in Cuzco had investigated the strange telegram that forbade Yale from excavating. He wrote to say that just that very month, August 1911, the Peruvian government had issued a new *decreto*, one that would forever change how archaeology was conducted in Peru. As Duque explained to Bingham, the minister of Education had declared that all artifacts found through excavation belonged to the Peruvian state. Researchers could now only take photographs of unique objects. For every excavation, the Peruvian government would appoint a monitor. And until the Peruvian congress passed a full law protecting antiquities, the exportation of artifacts was "absolutely prohibited." Anyone who was caught exporting artifacts would be treated as a smuggler and subjected to a massive fine.[23]

The decree was the greatest leap forward in Peru's protection of monuments perhaps since independence, and its timing was no coincidence. Unsupervised excavation—looting, in other words—and uncontrolled exportation had been a problem for years, but Peruvian intellectuals had lacked a test case to force the government to take action. Hiram Bingham's claim that he was searching for the last, lost cities of the Inca provided just such an opportunity. Lima's Historical Society and a group of young intellectuals who called themselves the Society to Protect Monuments argued that Bingham's search for the lost Inca capital would lead to excavation, which would prevent Peru from excavating these sites—perhaps the most symbolic in Peruvian history—for themselves.[24] The minister of Education admitted that Yale had no official license to excavate, save President Leguía's verbal permission. The minister had felt compelled to issue the new decree.

Bingham's search had literally put the last cities of the Incas on the map—but, without fully realizing it, he had also changed how Peruvians protected those sites and talked about who could possess their remains. If Bingham wanted to return to the ruins of Machu Picchu, Vitcos, and Espiritu Pampa deep in the jungle, he would have to seek the Peruvian government's permission. And by doing so, he would have to grapple with a significant fact: these were not unoccupied ruins forgotten by the local peoples. They were the homes of Peru's modern Indians, who were using them to take refuge from modern Peruvian exploitation, to find a peace now disturbed by the arrival of Bingham's expeditions.

Bingham would no longer be exploring Peruvian history; he would be changing it, ever so subtly, and potentially at great risk to himself and the descendants of the people he studied. If he shifted his emphasis from discovery to possession, as so many explorers had in the past, he would have to contend with Peruvian understandings of whether Inca history could be owned, and by whom. Much like the story of what happened after Manco Inca founded Vilcabamba, Hiram Bingham's adventures were about to take a turn into the darkness.

Interlude: Titu Cusi

*A*fter his flight from Cuzco in 1536, Manco Inca had carved Vilcabamba from the jungle to create a final refuge of religious and political independence. Despite the rain and distance from Cuzco, Manco and his people lived well there, worshipping the sun in ways their relatives in Cuzco could only do in private. But as long as the Spaniards denied Vilcabamba's right to exist and Manco pursued his guerrilla war, the city was threatened by Spanish invasion.

In 1539, Cuzco saw the departure of 300 Spaniards led by Gonzalo Pizarro—who had once stolen Manco's wife, Cura Ocllo—and a column of Indian warriors led by Paullu, Manco's brother and rival for the title of Inca emperor. Manco's warriors ambushed the invasion with arrows and falling boulders, killing thirty-six Spaniards, but Pizarro's expedition pushed on to Vilcabamba. There, they found a family disaster unfolding.

Two brothers of Cura Ocllo had preceded the Spanish, claiming that they had come to join Manco. In person, however, they tried to convince Manco to abandon Vilcabamba and seek peace. Peace? After the betrayal by Paullu and others, Manco hated the word and feared that his own family members had led the Spaniards right to him. Ignoring Cura Ocllo's pleas, he beheaded them. "It is fairer for me to cut off their heads than for them to take mine," he told her.

His wife was heartbroken and refused to leave the scene of the cruelty, even as the Spaniards approached. Manco and his men tried to hold off the expedition with Spanish guns but then had to flee. He swam across the river, the Spaniards close behind. "I am Manco Inca!" he raged. "I am Manco Inca!"

The expedition burned Vilcabamba to the ground and kidnapped Cura Ocllo, who saved herself from being raped on the long march back to Cuzco by smearing feces on her body. Pizarro tried to use her as a bargaining chip until Manco killed his envoys, enraging the conquistador. She was sentenced to death. The Incas' great enemies, the Cañaris of modern-day Ecuador, stripped and beat her, but she never cried or moaned. She finally raged, "You lash out all your anger on a woman. Any other woman would do the same. Hurry up and finish me off so that you can satiate your appetite in everything."[1]

She bound her own eyes. The Cañaris filled her with arrows and sent her body back down the Urubamba as a message. The Incas found and brought her to Manco, who became "sad and desperate, and cried and made great lamentations over her, because he loved her much. With her body he retired to his seat at Vilcabamba."[2]

In his grief, Manco's thoughts turned to what family remained. He sent his messengers to Cuzco to recover his eldest son, Titu Cusi, who was being cared for by a kind Spaniard. They had a warm reunion, then, presumably with pleasure, followed the news of the drama unfolding in Spanish Peru. In 1541, a group of rival conquistadors stabbed Francisco Pizarro to death. The Spanish military pursued the assassins and conspirators, but seven escaped and sought refuge in Manco's kingdom. Seeing a friend in his enemy's enemy, Manco let them live at Vitcos, where they feasted together.

Assassins make poor friends. The seven Spaniards believed the crown would pardon them if they solved one of its problems. In 1544 during a game of horseshoes in the plaza of Vitcos, the Spaniards fell upon Manco with daggers and swords. Titu Cusi (now about fourteen), rushed to help, but the Spaniards turned on him as well. The Incas' jungle allies brought down the Spaniards, torturing and burning them alive but not before they slashed Titu Cusi with a spear, scarring his leg for life.

Manco lived for three days before he died. In that time he called his captains and priests to his side and asked them to train his three young sons, Titu Cusi, Sayri Tupac, and Tupac Amaru, as potential rulers and religious leaders. He told Titu Cusi not to weep, to care for the family, and "never to live with these [Spaniards] in peace so that what had befallen me may never befall you. Do not allow them to enter your land, no matter how inviting their words may be, for their honeyed words deceived me as they will deceive you if you believe them."[3]

But who was to be emperor? Although Titu Cusi was the eldest, Inca inheritance went not to the firstborn, but to the son whose mother had purer descent from the original Incas. Under this tradition, Manco's middle son, Sayri Tupac, had the greater claim. For twelve years, Inca priests and captains ruled the Vilcabamba in Sayri Tupac's place, guaranteeing peace by halting Vilcabamba's guerrilla raids against the Spanish. Their conservatism paid off. In 1549, Paullu, the collaborating "colonial Inca," died, and Spain's Philip II, soon-to-be king, wanted to try a new tactic to end Vilcabamba's threat to the Spaniards' claimed "just conquest" of Peru: reconciliation.

To make up for Manco's persecution, the crown offered generous terms to end his sons' exile. In 1557, Sayri Tupac emerged from Vilcabamba, converted to Christianity, and settled on his grandfather's estate in the sacred Yucay Valley. The crown's offer was a potentially transformative moment in colonial history, a near-apology for the conquistadors' treatment of the Incas who, though pagan, were nonetheless rulers in their own land.

The Incas did not see Sayri Tupac's settlement as a full reconciliation, however; it was a means to preserve Vilcabamba's independence while testing the Spaniards' word. When Sayri Tupac died suddenly less than four years later—some suspected he was poisoned—the Spaniards realized their mistake. Sayri Tupac had left the royal fringe, the *mascapaycha*, with his elder brother, Titu Cusi, who had been ruling Vilcabamba since Sayri Tupac's departure. Now about thirty, Titu Cusi was built like a tree trunk, the scar from the Spaniards' attack still visible. Saturnine in disposition, quick to both laughter and rage, he carried himself like a true lord. He dressed in beautiful tunics, masks of gold and silver, and presided over a strengthened sun religion. When a Spanish envoy came to negotiate his departure from the Vilcabamba, Titu Cusi at first refused. He fomented rebellion and raids among Indians throughout Peru. In temperament, he was his father's true heir.

Yet he had also seen some Spaniards' genuine remorse for his family's treatment. With the help of a *mestizo* translator named Martín Pando, he emotionally argued his father's case, playing upon King Philip's desire for peace. In 1567, Titu Cusi won an agreement that pardoned him, gave him land near Cuzco and a stipend, and guaranteed his son's marriage to Sayri Tupac's daughter, fortifying the imperial line. In exchange he renounced his claim to larger Peru, stopped raiding, and opened the possibility of leaving Vilcabamba—but not giving up the sanctuary's right to exist.

More fatefully, Titu Cusi allowed Catholic missionaries to minister to his people. Although he led Inca's sun-worshipping religion, by entertaining Christianity he might find a middle path to the future.

Instead, by ignoring his father's counsel, he gave the Spaniards the opening that they wanted.

The two Augustinian missionaries who came to Titu Cusi's kingdom were as different as night and day. Diego Ortíz, who arrived in September 1569, befriended Titu Cusi, despite the emperor's refusal to relinquish his multiple wives and sun worship. Titu Cusi grew to love Ortíz like a brother and bombarded him with food and gifts. The kindly friar earned the trust of his flock as a healer, not a sermonizer, and his church quickly grew.

It was Ortíz's counterpart who was the problem. Marcos García had made his church at the village of Puquiura the year before. He quickly wore out his welcome. García beat his young charges when he caught them "practicing idolatries" and railed against the Inca's own merry-making and polygamy. Worst of all, Puquiura was a stone's throw away from the temple of Chuquipalta and "the principle shrine of those mountains"—the massive white stone of Yurak Rumi, carved and hulking over dark waters.

García hated it. Yurak Rumi housed "the captain of a legion of devils," he preached to his flock: to worship the stone was idolatry.[4] García saw enemies everywhere. By late 1569, he believed locals were trying to poison him, and he attempted to escape to Cuzco. Titu Cusi was furious when he found out. No one left his kingdom against his wishes. His soldiers captured García, and Titu Cusi severely reprimanded the missionary. Ortíz rushed to García's side, however, and Titu Cusi softened, making an unprecedented show of faith: he would take them to Vilcabamba itself, a privilege denied to all Spaniards since the Pizarros murdered Cura Ocllo in 1539. The friars accepted on the spot, as Vilcabamba was where the Punchao sun idol resided and where Titu Cusi led the Incas' sun religion. The missionaries would fight the devil in his lair.

Titu Cusi denied them the pleasure, however. The rainy season had begun, and the trip from Puquiura to Vilcabamba took several days' journey up and down winding, muddy paths into the next valley. While the Inca traveled by litter, García and Ortíz shivered and slipped their way along the flooded track. "They held each other's hands while the sacrilegious Indians gave shouts of laughter," a fellow Augustinian later wrote.[5]

Once there, Titu Cusi gave them quarters outside the city. He sent beautiful women to tempt them nightly. The women wore long smocks, which the friars thought were blasphemous parodies of their dress but were likely just the dress of the jungle Indians.[6] Most humiliating of all, Titu Cusi denied them entry to the city proper and forbade them from watching the Incas' daily religious rites and from proselytizing to his people. While they were there, Titu Cusi dictated an emotional letter to Marcos García, numbering for the Spaniards the many indignities his family suffered and why he had maintained Vilcabamba's religious independence. Even he had his limits.

García and even good-natured Ortíz had reached theirs too, however. They walked back to Puquiura alone, arguing along the way. If they couldn't preach in Vilcabamba, they would make an even more audacious statement of their faith. They called together their converted and distributed firewood among them. They made a procession, with the friars at the lead. Behind a cross, wobbling in the sky, they sang their way across the river and wound their way up a thin, lush, and shady valley, soothed by trilling steams. When the friars arrived at the shrine of Chuquipalta, they began to chant the prayers for an exorcism. Here, with only the account of their fellow Augustinian Antonio de la Calancha to guide us, we have no idea whether they pushed away the Inca priests, whether Ortíz had doubts and grabbed García's sleeve, or whether the converts felt a brief pang of regret. All we know is the outcome: the friars and converts laid their wood at the base of the great white granite rock of Yurak Rumi and set it afire. "Now you all will see how treacherous is he who tricked you, and that there is no other God than that of the Christians," said the friars.[7]

The flames rose, licking the sides of the Inca shrine.

When Titu Cusi learned what the Spaniards had done, he rushed to Puquiura. His captains shook their spears and called for the friars' immediate execution. Instead, Titu Cusi was lenient. The Christian presence around Vitcos was strong, and the eyes of the Spanish empire were upon him. He banished hotheaded García from his kingdom, but he allowed Ortíz to continue on at his own church.

Yet the damage was done. Titu Cusi's captains and priests never forgave Ortíz for his blasphemy. More dangerously, García brought gold back to Cuzco. A Spanish miner got the scent and traveled to Vilcabamba to ask Titu Cusi if he could scout for silver and gold. Titu Cusi gave his permission, but when the miner returned a few days later with more treasure than the emperor expected, the Inca saw the impending danger. News of gold mining in the Vilcabamba "would only incite the greedy, and bring thousands of Spaniards" to the province.[8] Despite Friar Ortíz's pleas, Titu Cusi ordered his soldiers to kill the miner.

News of the death wouldn't reach the Spaniards until the following year, borne on the wings of an even greater tragedy. In 1571, Titu Cusi visited the palace and shrines of Vitcos on the anniversary of his father Manco Inca's death. He spent the day weeping and honoring his father with services to the sun. Late in the day, as if preparing himself for battle, he practiced fencing with Martín Pando, his mestizo aide. He sweated profusely and caught a chill. That evening he drank too much and went to bed. In the middle of the night, he woke, shouting with pain, vomiting, and bleeding from his nose and mouth. Friar Ortíz attended to him, and in the morning he watched Martín Pando and another of Titu Cusi's close friends give the emperor a concoction to halt the bleeding. At that moment Titu Cusi breathed his last breath.

The Inca's sudden death swept his wives, captains, and priests into passionate mourning. Searching for a culprit, they accused Ortíz, Pando, and Titu Cusi's friend of murder. They executed Pando and the friend on the spot, but bound Ortíz and left him naked overnight in the mountain cold.

In the morning, the Incas undid the missionary's ropes. They gave him a final chance to save himself. If your God is so holy, they said, then resurrect our Inca.

Part Three
The Resurrectionists

...confusion horrible of mangled bones and flesh dragged
in the mud And tatters soaked in gore, of hideous limbs
that dogs devouring fought for with eachother.

Jean Racine, Athalie, as quoted by George F. Eaton,
The Collection of Osteological Material from Machu Picchu, 1916.

Machu Picchu

. . . confusion horrible
Of mangled bones and flesh dragged in the mud,
And tatters soaked in gore, of hideous limbs,
For which dogs, devouring, fought each other.

—*Jean Racine,* Athalie, *quoted by George F. Eaton,*
The Collection of Osteological Material
from Machu Picchu, *1916*

Chapter Twelve

The Deal

*H*iram Bingham was sitting in the city of Arequipa—notable for the luminous white stones of its colonial buildings—when he had his first breakthrough concerning Machu Picchu's identity. After leaving Espiritu Pampa, Foote had convinced Bingham to spend a month writing up their experience, developing his pictures, and reading his books for ideas of what Machu Picchu and Espiritu Pampa might be. The work was frustrating at first, and Bingham procrastinated with pining letters to his wife. "I often wonder why under the sun I picked out a career that would force me to spend so much of my time away from my dear ones," he lamented. He mused that his six sons might eventually join him in research—a sort of family archaeological business.[1]

In Clements R. Markham's *The Incas of Peru*, published the previous year, he found an answer: Machu Picchu perhaps belonged to the story of the Incas' beginnings, not their end. According to one Inca origin story, during a time of great pestilence, a people named the Amautas retreated to a remote place named Tampu Tocco. The Amautas were brilliant builders and wise record-keepers, and at Tampu Tocco they "declared themselves to be children of the sun," founding the Inca line. In another story, Tampu Tocco was also a hill with three openings or windows, from which the great Inca founder, Manco Capac, emerged and then marched to the Huatanay Valley, where he plunged his golden staff deep into the earth and founded Cuzco.[2] In another version, Manco Capac then "ordered works to be executed at the place of his birth, *consisting of a masonry wall with three windows*" [emphasis Bingham's].[3]

One can imagine Bingham nearly dropping his book, remembering Machu Picchu's temple with three windows. Markham believed that Manco Capac's pilgrimage was based on an actual historical event, around 1100 AD, and that Tampu Tocco was located south of Cuzco. But what if it was to the north, toward the jungle? Was Machu Picchu Tampu Tocco? Had he gone in search of the Incas' final days only to find their point of origin? Quick to claim victory, Bingham chalked it up as yet another possible win in an already stellar year: Vitcos, the glacial bones, and now, Machu Picchu, possibly the cradle of something arguably far finer than gold: the Americas' pre-Columbian imperial history.

Alongside such achievements, his final two months on the 1911 expedition were anticlimactic. Lake Parinacochas proved shallow, and Mount Coropuna was not tall enough to be the "Apex of America," as Bingham had hopefully called it. In December, Bingham presented his archaeological findings to the Geographical Society of Lima: Carlos Romero may have cheered, seeing his archival clues put to good use. Max Uhle, the German archaeologist who ran Peru's National Museum, was far less happy, and he left Peru at the end of the year. Bingham left for the United States to reveal his findings to the public, intending to capitalize on the resulting sensation to prepare a new expedition. This one would be built around a more active engagement with Peruvian history: excavation, not exploration. To do so, however, he'd need help. He wired ahead.

On December 21, 1911, the fast-talking reporters of New York's best papers—the *Times,* the *Sun,* William Randolph Hearst's *American*—waited on a packed pier, each jockeying to be the first to get Bingham's attention when the United Fruit Company's *Metapan* arrived. It had been a big year for both anthropology and exploration, and Bingham's story promised a lot of both. The previous spring, the Norwegian explorer Roald Amundsen and the Briton Robert Falcon Scott began their race to the South Pole. In August, whites had captured the "last free survivor of the Red Man," a Yahi named Ishi, in the foothills of the Sierra Nevada mountains and given him a bed at the University of California's museum in San Francisco.[4] If Bingham's expedition managed to wrap both events into one package—the nationalist achievement of white exploration and romantic nostalgia for American Indians—it could be one of the year's most sensational stories.

The *Metapan* docked and down the gangplank walked a tall, tan explorer with his small, motherly wife on his arm and his second-eldest son, Alfred, following behind them. Hiram had met them in Panama, and Alfred later remembered his parents considering the "broad view of the Pacific . . . with their arms about each other in a more loving embrace than he had ever seen before or was to see again."[5] Wreathed in domestic bliss, Hiram now delivered headline-making news. Coropuna was a nice symbolic footnote—the flags of Yale and the United States fluttered 22,500 feet above Peru—and even Manco's rebel palace at Vitcos received short shrift, despite it being the one site whose identity Bingham had confirmed. The roughly built Espiritu Pampa got no mention, for the main event, now and forever, was Machu Picchu, which Bingham claimed was the magnificent citadel of Tampu Tocco, built by the "megalithic folk" from which the Incas supposedly sprang. Bingham made no reference to the clues he got from the Harvard anthropologist William C. Farabee, the help of Carlos Romero and his archives, or the fact that the ruins at Machu Picchu were common knowledge in the region. As for the Indian families already living in the ruins, Bingham dismissed them as "corngrowers [who] seemed to know little about the temples around which they had planted their crops. . . . They were of a different breed from the men who built the temples and had only dim traditions concerning them."[6] Thrilled, the press awarded the credit for discovering magnificent Machu Picchu to Bingham alone.

The reporters rushed back to their Underwood typewriters and pounded out the story that made Bingham a celebrity. "Explorers Find a City That Was," screamed one headline. If Ishi and Peru's "corngrowers" were what Americans wanted to see in the indigenous present—nearly "extinct" hunters or "degenerated" and "dim" farmers—then the Incas and pre-Incas embodied the glorious pre-European past, whose proper heirs, the newspapers hinted, were the Americans who recognized them. The *Christian Science Monitor* simply and forcefully declared that Bingham's revelation left "the theory that civilization was first brought to these shores in Spanish caravels in a ridiculous light."[7]

Readers likely scanned the page in search of the most important question in any hot-blooded dime novel of archaeological discovery: Had the expedition found Inca treasure? At that Bingham demurred. There was no gold, no silver, he explained. Machu Picchu's value lay in its buildings. "Nothing would have suited us better than to have brought specimens of the architecture home with us," he said. "This could not be done, however, as the Peruvian Government expressly forbids it. So we did the next best thing and filled up our notebooks with data and our minds with memories of what we saw."[8]

Technically, Bingham had told the truth. He had found no "treasure" at Machu Picchu, nor had he carted off any architecture. In order to get funding to return, however, he had brought back plenty of other specimens, natural and historical, to wave in front of his sponsors. Foote's collection was massive, for example. As Hiram's son later pointed out, Foote's insects produced "as many scientific papers in learned journals as resulted from the work of all the other members of the expedition combined."[9] Bingham had also ignored Peru's decree forbidding the exportation of artifacts. He had returned with a thin sheet of silver and some ceramic pots that he had bought from the pioneer Saavedra at Concevidayoc. At Espiritu Pampa, either he or someone in his expedition had found and pocketed bronze implements.[10]

Most important of all, there were the "glacial bones," whose existence Hiram revealed to U.S. President William Howard Taft and the other members of the Yale Corporation, the university's governing body, at their January 20, 1912, meeting. The bones were a bombshell, and the Associated Press spread the news countrywide.[11] But as Bingham made clear to the corporation, if Yale was to get "any lasting benefit" from his discoveries, the university would need to send out more expeditions to confirm his finds and place them in context. Moreover, Yale could break ground at Machu Picchu, which seemed pristine and promising in ways that Vitcos and Espiritu Pampa did not. Hiram Bingham wanted to go from exploration to large-scale excavation.[12]

The Yale Corporation loved the idea. It was new territory for the university. While Harvard's museum was a tomb for the culture of modern and pre-Columbian Native American man, Yale's Peabody was largely a church of natural history, filled with dinosaur bones, plant fossils, and meteors. In 1909, Bingham had been shocked to learn that Yale's Peabody had put the skulls he had collected from Choqquequirau directly into storage.[13] Bingham's new findings could revise human history in the Americas, but he also hoped to give Yale a collection of indigenous history that it would be proud to display in its museum: skulls, bones, ceramic vessels, and perhaps even precious metals. In exchange, Yale would put its own money behind its proud explorer for the very first time.

It would also be fresh territory for another potential funder: the National Geographic Society, which had matured since its founding in 1888 as a club of Washington, DC, intellectuals and military men to a popular monthly magazine with a countrywide membership of subscribers.[14] In all that time, however, the society had never funded an explorer interested in archaeology. To some, archaeology was still a speculative science prone to romanticism and fancy. *National Geographic Magazine*'s editor, Gilbert H. Grosvenor, felt otherwise. Hired by the inventor Alexander Graham Bell to reinvigorate the magazine with photos and more adventurous tales of discovery, Grosvenor worked late into the night as he pored over articles and boosted the magazine's circulation from 10,000 in 1905 to 84,000 in 1911. Grosvenor saw archaeology's importance and its potential appeal to readers, and in Bingham, he thought he had found its first great champion. The editor had passed on Bingham's articles in the past, but his victorious return in December convinced him that Hiram's explorations were worth his time. At Grosvenor's invitation, Hiram lectured to an audience of 1,200 at Washington's Masonic Temple and met with the Society's Research Committee.[15]

Afterward, Grosvenor wanted to make Bingham an informal offer to support another expedition, but his board was still unsure. In the meeting, Bingham had raised an issue that had similarly worried his Yale funders: while he was in Peru, the government had prohibited the unauthorized excavation of Peruvian ruins and flat out forbade the exportation of artifacts. In order to carry out the expedition that Hiram proposed, he needed to get the Peruvian government's permission to excavate, and he needed to find a loophole that would excuse Yale from Peru's increasingly strict antiquities laws. The National Geographic Society was uncomfortable venturing into politics, but Yale's funders wanted to make sure the university received benefits on the back end. As one of Bingham's chief funders explained, he would give Bingham $5,000 to excavate, but only if Bingham obtained a "concession" from the Peruvian president that would give Yale a valuable collection of artifacts to study and display.[16]

Luckily, Hiram had a friend in President Taft, who savored the challenge presented by Peruvian law. The protection of monuments and antiquities was hardly shocking to Taft. In the face of rampant looting of Indian burials and archaeological sites in the American West, America's Congress in 1906 passed the Antiquities Act, which allowed the president to set aside Native American ruins and other historic sites as national monuments to prevent the commercial looting of artifacts. "[P]ractically every civilized government in the world has enacted laws for the preservation of the remains of the historic past," the House of Representatives pointed out.[17] Individuals now had to be professionally sanctioned archaeologists to dig on public lands, shutting even Indians out from sites. Peru's laws were similar, only stronger.

Yet such protections could be used to Yale's advantage—if applied to their competitors. To make the planned expedition possible, Bingham cooked up a deal. Yale would ask Peru's president to make an exception of the law for Yale, giving them free reign to explore and excavate for ten to twenty years.[18] Yale would give half of whatever it uncovered to Peru's National Museum and then could export the rest to New Haven.[19] As a Yale man and diplomat, Taft enjoyed Bingham's idea thoroughly and directed the State Department unofficially to give Yale "all possible aid."[20]

America's diplomat in Lima reported that Peruvian President Leguía liked the idea, seeing it as another way to ingratiate himself with America's diplomats and businessmen. The "inhibitions imposed by existing laws" were tricky but could be side-stepped; if Bingham drafted an agreement, Leguía would not only ram it through Peru's congress, but he would also make the concession's privileges "exclusive"—making Yale Peru's sole authorized excavator. Leguía claimed that European universities and museums were eager to buy or secure similar rights, but he wanted a single, responsible American university like Yale to have the privilege and duty.[21] If Bingham agreed, Yale would have what amounted to a monopoly to excavate and export Peru's indigenous history for ten to twenty years.

The offer made Yale nervous. The exclusivity clause gave the deal a commercial bent, as if Leguía was signing away the country's antiquities as he had its mining interests. In Peru it might play as thinly veiled U.S. colonialism; in the United States it would seem like Hiram was actively preventing other reputable institutions from exploring in Peru—which was hardly good science.[22] Leguía won the day by assuring Bingham that it was the only way Yale's rights would ever be respected. While Leguía waited for Peru's congress to come back into session, Bingham and his expedition could begin its work, on the assumption that half of Machu Picchu's treasures would go to Yale at the end of the season and half would go to Peru. There was no reason to worry, Bingham may have thought, as recent Peruvian politics were aristocratic, not democratic, and Leguía's word was law.

The way clear, Bingham finalized the "Peruvian Expedition of 1912 under the Auspices of Yale University and the National Geographic Society." With $25,000—well over $500,000 in today's money—he built a new team to excavate at Machu Picchu and confirm the most controversial discovery of the previous year: the "glacial bones." *National Geographic* announced the expedition at the very moment when American and European enthusiasm for exploration reached its great prewar height. In March, the Norwegian Roald Amundsen announced that he had beaten the Englishman Robert Falcon Scott to the South Pole, and the world was on tenterhooks to learn what had befallen Scott. When Bingham set sail on May 16, the *New York Times* declared that by the end of the summer "over a hundred noteworthy expeditions from every important research centre in the United States and Europe" would be exploring, excavating, and hunting in South America, the Arctic, the Congo, and Egypt. With hindsight, the racial subtext inherent in the *Times*'s celebration is cringingly obvious—the newspaper declared that young, virile Harvard and Columbia men would be working "to erase all the black and dark spaces off the map."

Special praise was reserved for Yale, however: "The eyes of the entire scientific world are, perhaps, more directed to this particular field than to any other in the world, for it is in Peru that some of the mysteries enveloping the ancestry of man are expected to be revealed."[23]

It was in such celestial tones that Hiram Bingham himself thought about his return to Machu Picchu. But, as Gilbert Grosvenor reminded him, Hiram had a far earthier responsibility to his funders in New Haven: "We all hope that you will be able to excavate and bring back a shipload of antiquities for your museum at Yale."[24]

Chapter Thirteen

The Cemetery of the Incas

Yale's return to Machu Picchu in July 1912 meant one thing to American newspaper readers but something else entirely for the site's inhabitants.

The Indians likely could hear the expedition coming: the sound of axes, hacking up the trail from the Urubamba River below; swears as machetes missed their mark, sparked off an Inca terrace, and almost cut off a toe. Then, the terrifying sound of fire ripping through the underbrush, billows of smoke rising over their gardens in the ruins.

Anacleto Alvarez, Torvis Richarte, Tomas Fuentes, and their families had last seen the Americans the previous September, when expedition members Paul Lanius and Herman Tucker made a cordial visit to clear and photograph parts of the site. This time, the atmosphere had changed. The swaggering party that approached their huts one afternoon consisted of one of Bingham's new hires, a young engineer Kenneth Heald, a Peruvian soldier named Tomás Cobinas, and eleven Indians from the nearby town of Ollantaytambo, each carrying some combination of axes, machetes, shovels, and crowbars. The Ollantaytambo Indians were none too happy to be there; they were paid but otherwise "forced labor."[1] Heald had a letter from the prefect ordering local officials to find the expedition workers. Ollantaytambo's governor had rounded these Indians up and put them in jail "to see that they did not run away" before giving them to the expedition.[2]

The Indians' reluctance was obvious: beyond wanting to tend their crops, they were being forced into the abusive labor practices of the lower Urubamba, where tensions between Indians and whites ran high. They also did not relish the task ahead of them, tampering with Inca ruins. This would be dangerous work.

They likely had heard that the Urubamba had swept away a boy working for the white explorers the year before. When the Ollantaytambo Indians reached Mandor Pampa, they saw the body of an Indian who had been stabbed in the back the day before. Heald only regretted that he had not enlisted the man before he died. "He was a fine looking Indian," he wrote after viewing the corpse.

What Richarte and Alvarez thought of Yale's return, Heald never cared to record. We can only imagine their nervousness at the obvious conflict between the American and the Ollantaytambo Indians. The Indians had set a fire that they claimed got out of control, almost killing Heald and the Peruvian soldier. Heald suspected foul play. The Indian families at Machu Picchu must also have winced when Heald tried climbing Huayna Picchu, only to slip and nearly plummet to his death, dislocating his shoulder.

A few days later, the man who had started it all arrived: Hiram Bingham, the tall *yanqui* with the thin-lipped smile, accompanied by another Peruvian soldier, and an unctuous gentleman from Cuzco named Jara, who introduced himself as the "agent" of Mariano Ignacio Ferro, the owner of the land on which Machu Picchu rested. Ferro had been shocked to learn there was such a massive ruin on his property, or that there were Indians farming there, but Bingham already had struck a deal with him.[3] Bingham would give Ferro one third of what "treasures, monuments and whatever other riches that might be found" after subtracting the half promised to Peru.[4] Ferro's agent, Jara, would make sure Ferro got his share of whatever gold and silver the expedition might find, but would also ensure that Richarte, Alvarez, and Fuentes understood who owned the land on which they lived. Machu Picchu was still their home, but for the season, it was now an archaeological site, not a farm. Not that the men would have time to tend their crops—they worked for the expedition now.

With the Peruvian soldier watching the proceedings, Richarte and Alvarez could hardly protest. They may even have been excited to work for Yale at first— but likely not. They had come to Machu Picchu to work for themselves, a fact Bingham had once appreciated. Yale's arrival had pulled them right back into Peru's coercive labor system. To the Americans, this felt like exploration. To Richarte and Alvarez, the development was exploitative and upsetting—especially when they realized what Bingham wanted them to do next.

Looking out over the lost city of his dreams, still covered in vines, Hiram Bingham could hardly suppress his delight. "M.P. ruins as fine as ever," Bingham scrawled in his journal, "very impressive especially the Sacred Plaza and the view."

His return to Cuzco in late June had been rocky at first. In his 1911 book on South America, he had called Cuzco the "dirtiest city in the world." Upon arrival he had to make a silver-tongued retraction. Cuzco—or at least its intellectuals— forgave him and celebrated his achievements of the year before. News of Machu Picchu had reached the city in December 1911, and a group from the university in Cuzco rode out to see the ruins soon after. They named Bingham its "scientific discoverer," but noted that it had been visited many times before. Cuzco's *El Comercio* newspaper was more dramatic: "Few expeditions have been of such importance to the scientific world."

For the students at the university, Bingham's attention had been especially electrifying. For Luis E. Valcárcel, who had helped lead the strike a few years before, "the discovery of Machu Picchu" was a decisive moment in his life, helping to inspire him, "like so many other Cuzqueño youth," to deepen his study of Peruvian prehistory.[5] On June 2, the university made Bingham an honorary professor. Hiram repaid the favor by exhorting the student "sons of Cuzco, inheritors of the oldest civilization in all of America," to "heed the founders of Yale University, who took for their motto the phrase 'Light and Truth.'" The students applauded.[6] Had Valcárcel been there, he might have applauded as well. He was in Lima, however, on a mission that Bingham would soon be unable to ignore.

For the time being, Bingham's attention was focused on Machu Picchu. It was all well and good to talk about "Light and Truth" at Yale or the University of Cuzco, but now the expedition needed to get its hands dirty. The first order of business was claiming the ruins for science. Bingham charged every Indian but one with clearing the thick scrub that covered the buildings' walls. Trees "perched on the very tips of the gable ends of small and beautifully constructed houses." Bingham wanted the ruins looking as if the Incas pulled down their roofs days before. The expedition needed to make architectural plans, it was true, but he also wanted Machu Picchu looking wondrous for the photographs he would soon take.

As the ridge crackled with the sound of nearly 400 years of jungle growth burning away, Bingham set another worker to a special, daylong task: erasing "the crude charcoal autographs" of the previous Peruvian visitors—the now-deceased Agustín Lizarraga among them.[7] To Bingham, they were graffiti. They may also have been a galling reminder that he had not been Machu Picchu's "first."

On July 22, the expedition began to dig in earnest. Bingham took photos, leaving the grunt work to six Indians from Cuzco and a salty American engineer he had hired in Lima named Ellwood C. Erdis. They started with the sacred plaza—Bingham hoped that Machu Picchu hid a fine treasure or burial of some sort. With pickaxes and shovels they dug beneath the hewn altar of the northern, more mono-lithic temple, but revealed only a bed of boulders. "We [found] several exciting holes into which crowbar goes down full-length but all work is in vain," Bingham wrote in his journal. Beneath the temple of the three windows—Bingham's "evidence" thus far for Machu Picchu's being the site of the Incas' origin—they found a bottle-shaped grave, but it too was empty. Apparently, not even Machu Picchu had escaped looting.

It was time to widen the expedition's net. While Erdis and his men cleared ruins, Bingham would target the site's *machays,* or burial caves, as he had at Choqquequirau. To direct their opening, he had the osteologist Yale had released to confirm the glacial bones in Cuzco, George Eaton. To find the graves, however, he selected the Indians who knew the ridge best. The landowner's agent, Jara, explained to the farmers Alvarez, Richarte, and Fuentes that they were now—as Eaton later put it—the expedition's "grave diggers."[8]

This was asking too much of the three farmers. As Bingham later acknowledged, the three farmers believed that "a certain amount of bad luck might happen to their crops should they desecrate the bones of the ancient people buried in the vicinity."[9] Rather than help the expedition, they came back to Bingham's tent empty-handed two days in a row.

Bingham tried another incentive. He called over the Indian workers from Cuzco and told them he would give a Peruvian *sol* (fifty cents in U.S. dollars) "to anyone who would report the whereabouts of a cave containing a skull and who would leave the cave exactly as he found it, allowing us to see the skull actually in position." At the end of the day, the Cuzco Indians filed in, "tattered and torn by the thickets and jungles and baffled by the precipitous cliffs of Machu Picchu." Richarte, Alvarez, and Fuentes, however, announced that they had found eight burial caves and desired eight *soles*. Bingham was tickled pink, thinking that the Peruvians had merely been holding out for money above their wages. Perhaps, but equally likely is the possibility that Richarte, Alvarez, and Fuentes had made a simple choice: they could let these Indians from Cuzco make money by disturbing the graves and fouling *their* crops, or they could report the graves themselves, take the cash bonus, and hope for forgiveness.

On July 24, one year to the day after Richarte's son led Bingham into Machu Picchu, Richarte led Bingham and Eaton to the site's graves. The Indians hacked their way through the jungle slightly below the ruins to the northeast. The growth was thick, and they had to "wriggle snake-like through the jungle when the rank vegetation was not so dense as to require vigorous use of machetes."[10] The guides stopped and pointed to a large, irregular boulder, almost invisible in the underbrush. Beneath it was a small, wedge-shaped wall, four feet long and two feet high, made of small, rough stones. The Americans got down on their knees and began to pull the rocks away. Slowly, the interior came into view: a few broken pots and their first glimpse of Machu Picchu's old inhabitants—a skull and a few other bones—sitting upright with the knees pulled up to the chest in the manner of most Andean burials. Eaton would later declare that the remains belonged to a woman, about thirty-five years old. In a second cave, Bingham found the fragments of two human skulls. In a third, Eaton recovered a body with an oblong skull—an interesting example of pre-Columbian cranial modification. From another grave, Eaton pulled a small skeleton and a single, perfect, two-handled red ceramic pot. Yet another yielded six fragmentary skulls. Bingham opened one more burial cave, yielding two human skulls and a broken pot.

Bingham was disappointed. He knew that Inca archaeology would rarely yield tombs filled with gold and silver—the Incas carried their wealth with their mummies, and the Spaniards had taken both. He had hoped that Machu Picchu had somehow escaped the conquest, however, or that he might at least find bronzes and ceramics worth displaying. Instead, these first few graves contained "nothing," he wrote in his journal, speculating that "treasure hunters" got there first. Machu Picchu might yield surprises yet, but only through the detail-focused attention that he disliked.

On July 29, Bingham packed up his bags to continue the sort of work he was best at—riding between icy ridges and jungle-covered valleys, searching for further hints to the location of Vilcabamba the Old, the last refuge of Titu Cusi and Tupac Amaru.

He left Eaton in charge. Four years older than Bingham, Eaton was also a Yale man, but he took himself far less seriously. Prim and game, cultured and droll, Eaton found it amusing to slip references to French drama into his monographs. He called stale bread "Pre-Inca rolls" and mosquitoes "nocturnal entomological specimens." Beneath a thick-banded porkpie hat and a fashionably trimmed dark moustache, he would clamp down on his pipe and light it using a magnifying glass and the Andean sun. Unlike Bingham, he saw the Yale expedition, himself, and science in a slightly more ironic light: "Grave robbing is at best an unholy venture. The scientific collector of bones doubtless has better intentions than the mere treasure-hunter, but both follow, in part, the same course, and whichever one finds himself last in the race for the prize probably regards his competitor's work as unwarrantable desecration."[11] For Eaton, grave robbing and archaeology existed on the same spectrum, divided by a conveniently arbitrary line named science.

Eaton had a far more expansive definition of the word "treasure" than Bingham. Eaton was a scientist through and through, and in these simple "Indian graves," he saw much more than potsherds and broken bones. In them, he saw the humble remains of an entire people. As he examined skull after skull, he surmised that they belonged to the site's attendants. They were unlikely to be buried with many possessions but were still valuable as examples of humanity. He also struck on an explanation for the jumbled bones that went beyond grave-robbing—that they had been removed and venerated by the deceased's descendants. Duly inspired, Eaton continued opening graves. His interest in everything in them would make the collection invaluable, guiding Bingham to a dramatic conclusion regarding the site's identity.

Eaton would have accomplished little, however, without Richarte and Alvarez (Fuentes, who was older, would only occasionally show up for work). Over the course of the next month, they arrived each morning to escort Eaton to the graves they had found the day before. While Eaton took notes, they reached into dark holes to pull out the scorpions. They pointed out the bones that had grown ferns, the skulls that were attached to the mountain by roots, whose tendrils had wound through the eye sockets. From the slopes near Huayna Picchu they moved south along the eastern side of the ridge until they were high above the main part of the site. By late August, they had shown Eaton 52 burial caves—the beginning of a collection that would haunt Yale for nearly a century.

One morning, Richarte and Alvarez took Eaton 1,000 feet above the southernmost sector of the ruins to a finely built ceremonial terrace. It was approached by stairs on two sides and was sheltered from the sun by a massive rock. There, they dug into their twenty-sixth grave, yielding one of the year's most evocative funerary finds. There were two perfect bottle-shaped pots and one broken dish with a foot. There were several copper pins, a needle, and a curious copper disc with a handle. Eaton later imagined its owner using it as a mirror or to light fires. There were a pair of copper tweezers and the remains of a dog. And at the grave's center was a nearly complete human skeleton sitting upright with its knees pressed to its chest. It seemed to be female; across its shoulders was a coarse shawl, once held in place by a *tupu*, a shawl pin with a flat, round head. At her feet were delicate blackened curlicues of leather footwear, which the Indians maintained were very ancient. Eaton decided the woman was a "priestess," and that the terrace "must have offered an ideal resting place for the Inca and his royal consorts during their visits to Machu Picchu, or at other times for the resident Priests and Priestesses of the Sun and the Mother Superior of the Acclahuasi or House of the Virgins of the Sun."[12]

To Eaton, she was beautiful. The men who had to pack her into the expedition's food crates, however, seem to have been churning inside. A few days later, Richarte showed up for work without Alvarez. The younger Indian told Eaton that his neighbor was down by the river, experiencing some vague illness in his male organ. When Alvarez failed to return the following day, Eaton learned that the problem was "his testes, and that the other Indians say the trouble has been inflicted by the spirits of the dead Incas whose graves Alvarez has been robbing." The other Indians believed that Alvarez, Richarte, and the Yale expedition were cursed.

Eaton, however, was amused. "Richarte, less pious than the others, says that if the dead Incas send him any trouble with his private parts, he will tear open all the graves and smash every bone he can find," he wrote in his journal. "I hope Alvarez will not try to smash the fine skulls I have collected. If he tries to, he will have other troubles of his own to weep over!"[13]

Eaton stopped chuckling when Richarte also disappeared. After a week Eaton wondered where his "grave diggers" were. Without them, the excavation of burials ground to a halt, and Eaton spent his days packing and repacking bones in boxes. When they finally returned on August 14, Eaton conceded he had underestimated their distress. "Alvarez and Richarte reported for work this morning, but they seem not overanxious at the start to find graves. Perhaps they are really a bit afraid of the spirits."

Before the expedition arrived, the residents of Machu Picchu apparently believed that its bones should be respected. Their participation in the bones' removal cursed them—or worse, had broken whatever spiritual significance they once possessed. As Eaton's departure from Machu Picchu approached, the osteologist had an unnerving glimpse of what the expedition had done. One afternoon in late August, Richarte and Alvarez were digging out a boulder high above the ruins when they came to a grave with two bodies whose knee ligaments were still intact. They were so well preserved, Eaton thought, that they could have been interred twenty-five years before. Had the lure of Yale's money exhausted the supply of "ancient" graves and turned Richarte and Alvarez to the more recent? If so there was ample precedent—late-nineteenth-century anthropologists had made money by digging up recent Indian graves in the American west and sending their human remains to museums in the east.[14]

There were fewer precedents for the fact that Eaton's diggers were Indian themselves and were trying to square away their beliefs with the upsetting work they were forced to do.[15] When Eaton took the mummy from its cave, the Indians did something that unsettled him even more: they asked for shreds of the mummy's dried muscle fiber. They claimed they would add it to their pots to eat for good fortune. Eaton suggested to his later readers that it was a surviving "ancient savage superstition" bordering on cannibalism.[16] In his journal, he thought they might have been teasing him. But he let them take the ligament nonetheless.

A few days later in his journal, Eaton gave his native guides another nickname, one that alluded to a dodgier chapter in the history of science—one that no longer felt so distant: "my two reliable 'resurrectionists' Richarte and Alvarez."[17] Resurrectionists were those English and American men who in the eighteenth and nineteenth centuries stole into cemeteries at night to unearth the fresh corpses of the poor so that young doctors and scientists could illegally learn their trade through dissection and experimentation.

It was Eaton's attempt at humor, but it masked a larger truth about the Yale Peruvian Expeditions. Under Bingham's direction, the expedition had brought Machu Picchu to life, resurrecting Inca antiquity as no archaeologist had before. This resurrection came from something sordid, however—the coercion of Indians into what Eaton called an "unholy but profitable quest," one that culminated in actual consumption of the dead.[18] Treasure hunters had visited the ruins before and walked away with ceramics, but the Yale expedition was different. To Yale, everything at Machu Picchu, including the skulls and bones of the residents' ancestors, was a treasure to be paid for and possessed.

As Bingham was about to discover for himself, if there was a curse to Machu Picchu, then this was it: if something can be possessed, then it can be fought over. Yale was amassing one of the more scientifically important and spiritually evocative collections of Inca artifacts and human remains in history. But whose treasure was it?

Chapter Fourteen

The Debate

*W*hile Bingham and his men were excavating in Inca lands, Peru was going through an epoch-changing political crisis, one that turned the country's politics to the left and brought Bingham's expeditions to an epic confrontation with the sovereign nation of Peru over the ownership of pre-Columbian history.

In May, Peruvians had gone to the polls to vote for a new president. A member of President Augusto B. Leguía's foreigner-friendly Civilista Party was supposed to have won, but young progressives in the provinces—including Luis E. Valcárcel and many of Cuzco's students—started a grassroots campaign to get a more radical candidate on the ballot. Their choice was the mayor of Lima, a man named Guillermo E. Billinghurst. Despite being rich himself, Billinghurst was hailed as a candidate of the people, the representative of everyone who had been left behind by the previous thirty years of unchecked foreign development. The elites refused to put Billinghurst on the ticket, and on May 25, his supporters paralyzed the rigged election by blocking access to polling stations. It was a triumph of "popular will," declared one newspaper, and in Cuzco, it had raised local leaders up to the national level.[1] Prefect Nuñez turned the military on Valcárcel and his friends, arresting some and beating others. The authoritarian roots of Leguía's regime seemed entirely on display, and Valcárcel traveled to Lima to lobby for Billinghurst.[2]

Bingham had been worried about the disrupted election when he arrived in May, but his American and English business friends in Lima calmed his fears. Another election would be scheduled, and Billinghurst might win, but for the rest of the year at least, Leguía would continue as president. When Peru's congress convened in July, it would approve Yale's concession. Bingham had left the deal with the American minister and his friends at the Peruvian Corporation, the powerful British-owned company that profited from Peru's railroads, and gone exploring.[3]

The situation got worse. Billinghurst's supporters were tenacious. It was Valcárcel's first time in the capital, but it didn't stop him from rallying the students of Lima's most prestigious university with stories of the fight against Nuñez in Cuzco. He exhorted them to observe the words of Nietzsche: "I do not advise you to labor, but to fight. I do not advise you to make peace, but to conquer. Let your labor be fighting and your peace victory."[4] When it was rumored that Nuñez had paid crowds to kill Valcárcel upon his return to Cuzco, Leguía removed Nuñez from office.[5] Nuñez challenged Valcárcel to a duel, which the young intellectual only narrowly avoided, but the damage to Leguía's administration was done. On August 19, Valcárcel joined the opposition movement in cheering as Peru's congress selected Billinghurst, not Leguía, to take over the presidency in September.

Billinghurst's victory incited hopes of various reforms, including that of the nation's archaeology. While in Lima, Valcárcel befriended Juan Bautista de Lavalle, the young president of the Society to Protect Monuments, the organization that had prompted the previous year's ban on the exportation of artifacts.[6] Together they called upon the delegates to a Pan-American Student Congress to pass laws protecting monuments and against looting in their home countries.[7]

It was hardly a passion of youth alone. The elderly president of Lima's Historical Institute, Don Eugenio Larrabure y Unanúe, who had complained for years about of the loss of artifacts to foreign museums, and had sent his own law to congress in July. In his proposal, he called for the permanent ban on the exportation of objects of archaeological or antiquarian interest. Foreign museums had enough examples of Peruvian art already. Peruvians now needed to see their history as a sacred trust, to see that artifacts were worth more than money and that their commercialization was destroying the country's archaeological evidence.

Despite the gathering opposition, Leguía could have passed Yale's deal had Bingham been in Lima to help. When the American minister visited Leguía in mid-August, Leguía was astounded that he was there without Bingham. The concession had been sitting on his desk for weeks awaiting Bingham's signature.[8] Thinking quickly but not clearly, the U.S. diplomat signed his name in Bingham's place, which must have astounded Leguía even further. If Yale's concession was so important that the U.S. diplomat in Peru would attach his name to it, where was Hiram Bingham?

Just after midnight, Sunday, August 26, Hiram Bingham woke up in a long, dark house in Puquiura, the town where the Inca emperor Titu Cusi died. Feeling ill, he stumbled to the porch and vomited into the darkness.[9]

The weeks since leaving Machu Picchu had been hard. He had followed clues to a set of ruins named Llactapata, a few ridges away from Machu Picchu, and ridden into an incredible high-altitude valley, where he found ten "magnificent" glaciers, which he promptly named after Alfreda, Taft, Grosvenor, and his other benefactors. But afterward, his indigenous guides had abandoned him in an avalanche field of boulders and snow, showing him what they really thought about the expedition. He had come to Puquiura to revisit Vitcos and excavate, but he had been greeted by an epidemic of smallpox and typhoid that had already claimed twenty-seven of the town's one hundred fifty inhabitants. His attempts to excavate the beautiful white stone shrine of Yurak Rumi had only half succeeded: His team of Indian laborers rode horses—a privilege that Peruvian whites let few Indians claim. They "acknowledge[d] no overlord," and were decidedly unimpressed by Bingham. They only begrudgingly obeyed a local white's order to help the explorer drain the dark pool beneath the shrine. They revealed nine massive stone seats in the mud, but no artifacts. The next morning they were outright "insolent" to Bingham, feeling free to show their discontent in ways Indians closer to Cuzco did not. At the end of the day, the only treasure they handed him was the pedestal of a single ceramic pot.

That night, Bingham decided he was done. The next morning he rode over the mountains to the southeast, following the route given him by the old Indian the year before. Out of reach of mail and telegraph, he only heard the news that Leguía would not be president on September 4, two and a half weeks after the fact. He knew immediately what it meant: Yale's concession was in trouble.

He traveled to Lima "as fast as mules, slow trains and later steamers would carry [him]," cursing himself the entire way for exploring rather than minding the deal. When he arrived, he found that Yale's concession was indeed at the bottom of Leguía's list of last-minute favors. Bingham admitted his mistake to the American minister and set out to convince the next president, Billinghurst, of the importance of Yale's deal.[10]

The drama of the concession made Billinghurst less likely to listen. Leguía was rumored to have left debts of more than four million pounds sterling. Crowds chased his coach through the streets shouting "Thief! Thief!"[11] When Bingham and the American minister called on Billinghurst in his first day in office, the new president was correspondingly wary of touching one of his predecessor's sweetheart deals, rammed "through without regard for the letter of the law." Billinghurst said he wanted to "stand in" with the United States and would not oppose Yale's concession now that it was in the congress. Personally, however, he considered the project a "disgrace" to Peru. "He knows the country ought to do this kind of work itself, but is far too poor," Bingham explained to Yale's president, not quite grasping the seriousness of the situation: "this whole business is rather tiresome and not half so interesting as exploration."[12]

Bingham soon realized that Billinghurst's ambitions were bigger than just knocking down the policies of the previous president. Peruvian intellectuals were lobbying him to put a permanent stop to the practice of letting foreigners carry away the country's artifacts. Peru's minister of Education had signed a decree just the year before temporarily banning their exportation and the country's intellectuals wanted to see it enforced. When Bingham checked on the progress of the Yale concession in congress, he learned that it was under review by the president of Peru's Historical Institute, Don Eugenio Larrabure y Unanúe, the elderly gentleman who had proposed his own law banning the exportation of artifacts. Don Eugenio made it clear to Bingham that he was completely opposed to a concession that both allowed Yale to undercut the earlier decree and take artifacts back to New Haven and that was also exclusive, prohibiting Peruvians access to their own past. His response to the Yale concession, published in the country's newspapers, was direct: "Science does not advance through monopolies," he wrote.[13] His larger point was more subtle: the free flow of Peruvian art and artifacts had inspired greater study of the country, but it had also encouraged the widespread looting and destruction of archaeological finds by fueling a market of wealthy foreigners. Although the Yale team was not speculating in artifacts, its presence offered a space for discussion of that larger problem that fly-by-night looters did not.

The public tug of war between an American university and a sovereign country over the ownership of the indigenous past was a historic first. The question was not only whether Yale deserved artifacts and a say in the country's archaeological future, but also whether artifacts should leave Peru at all. The

In 1572, Spanish Captain Martín García de Loyola escorts a young Tupac Amaru to Cuzco, where the last Inca emperor would be executed. Tupac Amaru is led by a gold chain, and the Spaniard on the right carries the Punchao, the Inca's gold sun icon. The Inca chronicler Guaman Poma de Ayala drew and included the image in his manuscript (ca. 1600–1615) to prove the unjust nature of the Spanish conquest. The manuscript was lost until the early twentieth century. (The Royal Library, Denmark)

The Bingham family in Honolulu, ca. 1890s, on one of Hiram's visits back from Yale. From left to right, Hiram Bingham Jr., Clarissa Brewster Bingham, Hiram Bingham III, and his aunts, Elisabeth and Lydia. (The Bingham Family Papers, Manuscripts and Archives, Yale University Library) [By permission of Timothy Bingham]

(Below right) Hiram Bingham's wife, Alfreda Mitchell Bingham, heiress to the Tiffany & Co. fortune, with their second son, Hiram Bingham IV, in 1903. (The Bingham Family Papers, Manuscripts and Archives, Yale University Library) [By permission of Timothy Bingham]

(Below left) Hiram Bingham at 22, in 1898, returned to Hawaii to restart his missionary life, temporarily, before abandoning it for love on the mainland. (The Bingham Family Papers, Manuscripts and Archives, Yale University Library) [By permission of Timothy Bingham]

Gaunt and haggard, Hiram Bingham emerges from the jungle of Peru in August 1911 during his search for Vilcabamba, the last rebel city of the Inca. (Photographer: Harry Foote. The National Geographic Society)

(Above) Hiram and Alfreda and the first three of their seven sons: Woodbridge, Hiram IV, and Alfred, ca. 1905. The following year Hiram would break away to retrace the steps of Simon Bolívar through Venezuela and Colombia. (The Bingham Family Papers, Manuscripts and Archives, Yale University Library) [By permission of Bingham family]

(Below) On July 24, 1911, Bingham was led to Machu Picchu, an Inca ruin between Cuzco and the rebel kingdom of the Incas. He was accompanied by a Peruvian sergeant named Carrasco, on left, and, on right, a boy whose family lived at the ruins. They stand beside Machu Picchu's intihuatana, *used by the Incas to mark the passage of the sun. (Photographer: Hiram Bingham. The National Geographic Society)*

In July of 1912, Hiram Bingham and his expedition, now supported by both Yale and the National Geographic Society, returned to clear and excavate Machu Picchu. (Photographer: Hiram Bingham. The National Geographic Society) [Publication source: National Geographic Magazine, 1913]

In late 1569, early 1570, two Spanish missionaries performed an exorcism upon the great Inca sun shrine of Yurak Rumi, precipitating the fall of the Incas' independent kingdom. By locating the shrine in 1911, Hiram Bingham clinched his revelation of the adjacent Inca capital of Vitcos. (Photographer: Hiram Bingham. Yale Peruvian Papers, Manuscripts and Archives, Yale University Library) [Published in The Geographical Journal, 1911]

Hiram Bingham interviewing an Indian named Juan Quispicusi in the colonial town of San Francisco de la Victoria de Vilcabamba, 1911. Quispicusi accurately recounted the path that Manco Inca took while fleeing the Spaniards over three hundred and fifty years before. (Photographer: Harry Foote. The Yale Peruvian Expedition Papers, Manuscripts and Archives, Yale University Library) [Published in Harper's, 1914]

The ruins of Espiritu Pampa, as Hiram Bingham saw them in 1911, covered in jungle. Bingham failed to see the site's many buildings that would have confirmed its identity as Vilcabamba the Old. (Photographer: Hiram Bingham. The Yale Peruvian Expedition Papers, Manuscripts and Archives, Yale University Library) [Published in American Anthropologist, 1914]

Indian porter crossing the dangerous Concevidayoc River, August 1911, on Bingham's expedition to Espiritu Pampa, rumored to be the last city of the Incas. (Photographer: Hiram Bingham. The Yale Peruvian Expedition Papers, Manuscripts and Archives, Yale University Library) [Published in Incaland, 1922]

The Campa-Asháninka of Espiritu Pampa, as photographed by Bingham in August 1911. Like many jungle tribes on the eastern slopes of the Andes, the Asháninka fled rubber slavers downriver and took shelter at what may have been the Incas' final refuge. (The Yale Peruvian Expedition Papers, Manuscripts and Archives, Yale University Library) [Published in Harper's, *1914*]

Hiram Bingham and Isidoro Guzman, one of the expedition's many knowledgeable local guides at Espiritu Pampa, possibly Vilcabamba, August 1911. (Photographer: Harry Foote. The Yale Peruvian Expedition Papers, Manuscripts and Archives, Yale University Library) [Published in American Anthropologist, *1914]*

Young indigenous worker sitting in the Royal Mausoleum of Machu Picchu, alongside a niche in which the royal mummy of the Inca empire builder Pachacutec once may have rested, 1912. (Photographer: Hiram Bingham. The National Geographic Society) [Published in National Geographic, *1913]*

From left to right, Tomas Fuente, Torvis Richarte, Anacleto Alvatez, George F. Eaton, and a Peruvian soldier, excavating a tomb at Machu Picchu, 1912. Eaton called Richarte and Alvarez his "Resurrectionists" for their help digging up Machu Picchu's graves. (Photographer: Hiram Bingham. The National Geographic Society) [Published *in* National Geographic, *1913*]

Machu Picchu's Sacred Plaza, its heart of religious and imperial activity, after clearing, 1912. On right is the temple of the three windows, which for Bingham clinched the site's identity as Tampu Tocco, the mythical origin of the Incas. (Photographer: Hiram Bingham. The Yale Peruvian Expedition Papers, Manuscripts and Archives, Yale University Library) [Published *in* National Geographic, *1913*]

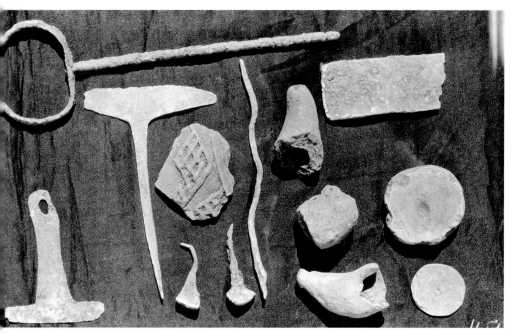

Colonial era artifacts excavated from Vitcos in 1915, loaned to Yale and possibly never sent back. In 2009, Peru sued Yale for their return. (The National Geographic Society)

Espiritu Pampa or Vilcabamba, the final refuge of Manco Inca and Tupac Amaru, 2008. (Photographer: Christopher Heaney)

country's newspapers led a vociferous debate over the matter. Most argued that foreign scientific parties like Yale should be able to invest their energies and come away with *some* artifacts, but that Peru should be the ultimate arbiter, protecting sites and monitoring all excavations. To fully sign away that privilege to Yale, sidestepping Peruvian law with the help of the U.S. State Department, smacked of dependency or, worse, colonialism. The drama went international. Peruvian intellectuals sent frantic telegrams to Harvard, the British Museum, and archaeologists in Berlin.

Bingham was shocked by the heat of the opposition. For the last three years, he had told his backers that Peru happily deferred to Americans in all matters. "I did not realize how greatly the favorable reception which I have always received in Peru was a reflection of [Leguía's] known good will to us," he claimed to Yale's president. He was surprised by the force of Peruvians' conviction: that they could excavate and protect the country's ruins and artifacts; that it mattered whether those artifacts rested in the United States or Peru. While Bingham made the valid point that Peru's energy might be better spent shutting down traders in illicit antiquities, at his core he had been guilty of a patronizing assumption: that Peruvians couldn't possibly care about their indigenous past.

Bingham was in over his head. He had embarrassed Yale, the U.S. State Department, and most of all himself. Fueled by equal parts self-regard and intellectual curiosity, he had attempted to anoint Yale as Peru's archaeological godfather as well as ensure a continuous northward flow of artifacts. The goals were naively overambitious, and his reputation was under attack. He had all but promised his backers a collection of artifacts for Yale's museum; to return empty-handed would be a disaster. Nervously, he assured Yale's president that he would secure "more than a hundred boxes for the museum."[14]

To do so, he accepted that he needed to make a tactical retreat on the matter of the concession—the newspaper *El Comercio* was running blazing editorials against the "monopoly [that threatened] national culture and the loss of the country's most valuable remains of past Peruvian civilizations."[15] With the American minister looking on, Bingham and Peru's President Billinghurst made a deal: Bingham withdrew the concession from Peru's congress, and Billinghurst said he would prepare a decree "which is to give us full permission to export everything we excavate before the first of December," Bingham wrote to Yale's president. After the public's opposition, it was a surprising victory. Yale would export *all* of its artifacts rather than the half it would have under the concession. There were "certain minor conditions which we shall be able to fulfill," but Bingham chose not to commit them to paper.[16]

Bingham wrote an open letter to the Peruvian public explaining that Yale had only asked for an exclusive concession on Leguía's recommendation. Yale's object had not been profit, he explained, but to shine a light on Peruvian scientific progress, to attract tourists and travelers to Peru, and "above all, to show the effectiveness of its motto, 'Light and Truth.'"[17] Thoroughly exhausted, he took a steamer south to Mollendo and boarded a train for Cuzco to have one final month of archaeological work.

The debate raging behind him, however, suggested that the trouble was not yet over. Peruvians were now more aware of the monetary, cultural, and intellectual value of their past. It would be hard for future foreign archaeologists to claim any great authority with the specter of Yale's concession hanging over them. Moreover, in an age when Latin Americans were increasingly nervous of U.S. intentions in the hemisphere, Bingham's attempt to push through a decree with the help of the U.S. State Department only proved their suspicions right: that North Americans wanted to run the entire region, from its mines down to its history. "We are worthy of our treasures, and he who wants to study them should come to our country, spend time in our country, leave his dollars in our country," one Peruvian wrote in to *El Comercio*. "It would be the final indignity if our government had to send Peruvians to North America to study what it now has in its own country. We're not sucking our thumbs anymore. Do you understand, North America?"[18]

It was in such a defiant spirit that Billinghurst's minister of Justice and Education finished and signed Yale's promised concession decree. He telegraphed Cuzco with the permission Yale needed to continue its explorations and export its collections. The expedition had until December 1, 1912, to finish its work under the watch of a Peruvian monitor, who would then inventory Yale's collection. When he was through, in the spirit of scientific collaboration, and only this once, the artifacts could leave the country for Yale.[19]

Such a decree hardly seemed like a win for Peru. The minister had not telegraphed *all* of its terms, however. The full decree and its revolutionary fine print would arrive in Cuzco by mail just before the Yale team's departure, when Bingham had the long trip home to contemplate the final victory Peru snatched from Yale's defeat.

Chapter Fifteen

The Prize

*T*he great irony of the month-and-a-half-long joust between Bingham and the Peruvian government was that it was over a collection of artifacts and specimens that neither party had seen.

As Bingham steamed south from Lima, Peru appointed a Cuzco history professor named José Gabriel Cosío to observe Yale's work at Machu Picchu. Cosío was an eager and well-meaning member of the generation of Cuzco intellectuals just older than Luis Valcárcel. He had a wide, clean-shaven face and large and unblinking eyes behind spectacles. Implicitly trusted within Cuzco and beyond, Cosío had been one of Albert Giesecke's first hires for the new University of Cuzco and a founding member of Cuzco's Geographic Society. In December 1911, when Cuzco learned of Hiram Bingham's visit to Machu Picchu, Cosío had assembled the Peruvian expedition group to investigate. Cosío recognized Bingham's contribution in promoting the site, and when the University of Cuzco made Bingham an honorary professor, it was Cosío who had read the articles of incorporation.

Yet, it was also Cosío who pointed out that because Agustín Lizarraga and others had known about Machu Picchu for years, Bingham deserved the modified title of "scientific" discoverer. Cosío was also the only individual to report the death of the boy who had carried the Yale expedition's equipment across the raging river.[1]

Cosío arrived at Machu Picchu on October 5 and was happy to see how thoroughly Yale had cleared the site.[2] As far as he could see, they had unearthed very little "treasure"—just potsherds and broken bones. Satisifed, Cosio returned to Cuzco and was there when Bingham returned from Lima with the news that the expedition could export its artifacts after Cosío made an inventory. On November 5, Cosío and Cuzco's subprefect watched osteologist George Eaton and engineer Kenneth Heald open eleven of the expedition's boxes, all filled with bones and potsherds. The next day Heald and Eaton opened more, and the Peruvians "then weighed the bunch, Cosío making list of weights and contents."[3] Cosío and the subprefect returned the next day to give the boxes the government seal necessary for customs in Mollendo. It is unclear whether Cosío and the subprefect reviewed every one of the boxes that Yale filled, but in the report he completed for the government in December, Cosío clearly stated that the expedition had not found untouched tombs, mummies, or precious metals. The tombs were half-looted, yielding only human skulls and bones, and "an immense quantity of stone objects, of potsherds, and *champi*"—Inca bronze—"although almost all broken and incomplete."[4]

Cosío's final inventory has never been found, so it is impossible to speculate as to how much greater detail he went into and whether he had seen more than he wrote about. But if his initial report was any marker, it seems that he was led to believe that Yale had found much of scientific value but little exceptional.

But Bingham had been fighting to carry back more than looted tombs, potsherds, and broken bronze pieces. Far more.[5]

To begin with, there were the 52 graves that Eaton, Richarte, and Alvarez uncovered from July through late August. Many were incomplete, but others were distinctly not, such as that of the "priestess" and all her earthly possessions.

In September, the discoveries piled on. Yale's success in the latter half of the season owed largely to the efforts of Ellwood Erdis, the American engineer whom Bingham had hired in Lima. At 45, Erdis knew how to find treasure and protect it. The son of an Irish cotton-mill worker, Erdis mined for gold in the Yukon before working for the railroads in South America. By laying track across the Andes, he had turned up burials. Erdis found he had a taste for excavation's hard work, attention to detail, and the patient wonder that kept a man digging. Thin but wiry, his face half-hidden beneath a large handlebar moustache and a comically large hat, Erdis gave Bingham's intellectual ambitions the elbow grease they needed.

He organized the remaining Indian workers like a mining camp and established a schedule of cash prizes. If an Indian found an entire skeleton, they received 80 cents. They received 20 for a skull, 20 for a whole pot, and 20 for a bronze. Erdis found that the citadel's builders had left offerings in the entryways of buildings and caves. They were soon pulling thin bronze medals from the soil, an obsidian knife, potsherds with carved faces, foot-long bronze pins with six-pointed stars at their ends, a broken silver bird's head and neck, engraved bronze bracelets, and the heads of Inca war clubs.

They found a bevy of complete or near-complete ceramic vessels, as well as the potsherds of 1,650 containers, ranging from tall liquid vessels to ornamented handles with the faces of animals and humans. Bingham would use them to create a typology of the region's ceramics—one still useful today. In the grave of one man, they found a pot filled with animal bones, grains, and other objects, which to Bingham suggested that its owner might have been a "medicine man," using a North American term for an Indian shaman.[6] They found caches of intriguing green serpentine counters and a finely grained stone box, about six inches wide, eight-and-a-half inches long, and two-and-a-half inches deep, covered with beautiful angles and spirals.

They built an excellent collection of metallic objects. There was no gold—the Incas carried around such finery, and little of it survived the conquest—but they found "about two hundred little bronzes and a few pieces of silver and tin." They found large bronze knives, a silver headdress, and a moon-shaped silver head-piece. In early September, Erdis pulled the expedition's most fabulous find from the northwest corner of one room: a "bronze knife, with handle decorated with figure of man with breech cloth, on stomach, feet in air, pulling on a rope, to which is attached a fish," he wrote in his journal.[7] It was a truly unique piece, and the figure was beautifully detailed, with an Inca nose, earflaps on his hat, and a look of "grim determination" on his face. William Holmes of the Smithsonian would call it "one of the finest examples ever found in America of the ancient art of working in bronze."[8]

The year's finest treasure, however, remained the tombs that Torvis Richarte and Anacleto Alvarez turned inside-out for the expedition, willingly or not. In early September, Richarte, who was younger, came back to work and quickly identified a new "cemetery" south of the site that yielded skulls, silver rings, and bronze pins. Richarte declared that Alvarez had "quit cave hunting definitely," but the money may have proved too tempting, and on September 19, Alvarez came back to work. That afternoon he and Richarte found a cave that yielded the ruin's second most delicate piece of metalwork: a small bronze pin with a tiny bronze hummingbird on top, a piece of string still threaded through its hole. They found a broken pot with a baby's skeleton at its bottom. A curious double burial would yield two skeletons, one with a stone and silver necklace still "at the neck of the dear departed," and, fascinatingly, a green glass bead—a European artifact, the first sign that the site was perhaps inhabited through the conquest. Bingham would have to ponder what that meant for his thesis that Machu Picchu was the Incas' birthplace.

When they were through, Richarte and Alvarez had opened 107 graves, yielding the remains of about 173 individuals. Bears or men had disturbed a few caves, but the majority felt surprisingly complete. Richarte and Alvarez "had small inducement to disturb any graves until the days of our arrival," Bingham would later acknowledge. There were no royal Inca mummies draped in gold, but as time went by, the Yale expedition realized they had found something even more important: a cross-section of the site's inhabitants, spanning the privileged "priestess" to the humble, malnourished worker. For those who knew how to read them, these bones were a treasure of a new sort, windows to their owner's past, gender, diet, and cause of death.

By collecting almost everything in the graves, no matter how modest, from humble metals to potsherds, Richarte and Alvarez let Yale make the first archaeological report in history on both the noble and common people of Inca society. Everything—from the skeletons to silver to stone carvings—went into 93 of the expedition's food boxes. Yale would ultimately list 5,415 lots of artifacts, but when counted in terms of individual bone fragments and potsherds, there were upwards of 46,000 pieces. It was a massive and invaluable array—priceless precisely because of its comprehensive nature. It was the only intact collection of human and artistic remains from an Inca royal estate that escaped the torches of the Spanish conquest. Put another way, Yale had now assumed the sacred trust of caring for Machu Picchu's tombs.

But if Yale had built such a wonderful collection, complete with beautiful objects of silver and bronze, then why didn't Cosío say so in his report?

Because the expedition, from the very beginning, thought that there would come a moment when it would have to take turns choosing pieces from the collection. According to Bingham's early plans, the expedition had to give half to Peru, then another third to Mariano Ignacio Ferro, who "owned" the ruins. If Bingham had asked around in the United States, he may have learned how contemporary archaeologists in Egypt dealt with similar divisions. To put it bluntly, excavators often hid or sold artifacts before the Egyptian Antiquities Service could make their inspection.[9] Likewise, Yale had made a practice of keeping their better finds quiet, both to protect them from being stolen and to have a little more control over the later selection process.

For example, the day that Cosío arrived to inspect the excavations at Machu Picchu, Erdis "[t]hank[ed] the lord that the bones and sherds that Richarte brought were rather burned." He wrote in his journal that evening, "[Cosío] was a little inquisitive about whether we had found any [pots], skulls, etc., but stood him off. . . . Wish to God he was not here, as he promises to be a greater nuisance than Jara"—the landowner's "spy."

Luckily for Erdis, Cosío's time at Machu Picchu overlapped with Richarte and Alvarez's least productive periods. Even then, Erdis noted which finds Cosío saw and which ones he didn't. For example, on October 10, a day that Cosío saw Richarte bring in a few rotted bones and potsherds, there was a second find that Cosío didn't see. This one included a much finer skull, a few green stone tokens, and the bronze hummingbird pin. Erdis took no chances. He left even the potsherds dirty, making sure that they not "look so attractive, and are not so likely to be chosen by other parties."[10]

This was the expedition's practice, if not its policy—one very different from Bingham's public calls for "Light and Truth." When the rainy season forced Erdis to end excavations on October 19, he packed up the last of the boxes and then sent them down to the river on porters' backs, where they were picked up by mules shuttling to Cuzco. The vast majority of these boxes were bones and potsherds, but a few were labeled "special 'scientific,'" which was the expedition's way of marking off the important pieces—the silver, bronze, bone, and stone rarities. When these boxes arrived in Cuzco, they were set aside. In late October, when Bingham feared that Peru would not let any of the expedition's artifacts leave, he telegraphed Eaton, and the osteologist spent a day unpacking and repacking their specimens to make an inventory. When he was done, he "took a small package of specials to Mr. Gregory"—Yale's geologist—"to care for until the weather cleared."[11]

There was no mention in Eaton's journal of whether he returned those specials to the main hoard for the inspection by Cosío and the subprefect, but from Cosío's published report, the answer seems to have been no. Cosío saw no silver pieces; he noted no whole ceramics; he made no mention of beautiful Inca bronzes, like the knife handle with the man fishing on it. When Yale retracted its concession, it no longer needed to worry that the Peruvian government would hold onto its finer pieces. But it kept up its veil of secrecy, perhaps out of fear that their hosts might be less likely to share if they knew that they had far more than bones and potsherds.

Given the year's final twist, it was the most strategic move the expedition could have made.

Hiram Bingham had never felt as disappointed as he did when he returned to Cuzco in November. The loss of the concession cut deeply. When he arrived in Peru that summer, he imagined that it would be just the beginning of a decade of leisurely, meticulous excavation of Inca ruins around Cuzco and beyond. The anger Peruvians had directed toward him in Lima changed all that. Instead of having decades to uncover the lost history of the Incas, he had to think in months. Bingham felt weary, he wrote to his wife: "My body has kept up its wandering, begun months before I was born—but my spirit has found rest . . . in your dear heart."[12]

So many of Bingham's ambitions that year had come to naught. He had hoped to excavate at Espiritu Pampa but had been diverted by Lima; he was no closer to discovering the true identity of Vilcabamba the Old. His other great hope for the year had been the confirmation of the "pre-glacial bones" from the Ayahuacco Quebrada. Bingham wanted to say that Yale had extended the human history of the Americas by tens of thousands of years. On that point he was also disappointed. Neither Yale's osteologist, George Eaton, nor its geologist, Herbert Gregory, would confirm the discovery, noting the bones and context could be recent. Bingham would have to retract his most groundbreaking claim—an embarrassing and possibly career-shattering turn of events. It would take until the 1920s for the Smithsonian's anthropologists to accept that indigenous peoples had been in the Americas since the Pleistocene era, if not before.[13]

Depressed and angry, Hiram Bingham rode out of Cuzco on November 5 to see the end result of the year's one undeniable achievement, the clearing and excavation of Machu Picchu, the lost city he loved. Braving thunderstorms and hail, his head swimming with the altitude, Hiram rode on, spotting the ruins, now naked and "very picturesque," from the road below on November 7. The rainy season had not yet pulled down Heald's bridge, but the tough climb up left him "winded after soft days in Lima."

When he saw Machu Picchu fully cleared for the very first time, the worries of the last two months faded to a dull roar. It was breathtaking. In anticipation of Hiram's arrival, Erdis had directed thirty to forty peasants in a thorough clearing of the ruins. Without the vegetation, Bingham could see it as the site's builders had: a vision of perfect temples, palatial complexes, fountains, and ceremonial stones, as pure an expression of imperial power as any in the Americas.

Erdis handed Bingham the ten-sheet map of the ruins they had made, and for the next week, between increasingly frequent rain showers, the engineer took the explorer through Machu Picchu building by building, showing him that the sites' complexes were organized by groups—linked houses with a single main entrance that could be "locked" through a combination of stone rings, bars, and long-decayed wooden doors. Bingham named one the "King's Group" and another the "Princess Group."

Bingham saw signs of defense everywhere: 1,000-foot precipices, a moat, two strong walls, signal stations. The narrow streets, stepped fountains, and more than a hundred stairways gave the impression of a bustling community fed by the hundreds of agricultural terraces that stretched down to the river, but able to turtle into its shell for protection if attacked by enemies coming from the jungle. "Here on a narrow ridge, flanked on all sides by precipitous or nearly precipitous slopes, highly civilized people—artistic, inventive, and capable of sustained endeavor—at some time in the remote past built themselves a city of refuge," Bingham would write. Yet its near-pristine walls suggested that their builders braced for an attack that never came.

To explain the site's seeming lack of conquest, Bingham had "tested" his theory that Machu Picchu was Tampu Tocco, the previously mythical cradle of Inca civilization. That fall, Bingham had sent Eaton south of Cuzco to visit the ruins of Pacariqctambo, the site that previous scholars had identified as the Incas' birthplace. Although Pacariqctambo would later be excavated and restored to show particularly fine ceremonial triple-jamb doors—a feature that Bingham never found at Machu Picchu—Eaton reported that it had neither caves nor windows, a detail that Bingham took as confirmation that it could not have been Tampu Tocco. Yet, there was a cave near Pacariqctambo: Eaton simply didn't see it.

Machu Picchu, however, had its temple with three obviously ceremonial and symbolic windows, the largest that had ever been found in any Peruvian site, Bingham thought. Bingham was now certain that Machu Picchu was the cradle of the Incas, where Cuzco's founder, Manco Capac, built a "masonry wall with three windows, which were emblems of the house of his father whence he descended."[14]

The blissful week's most important results were the 500 spectacular photos that Bingham took of the site, including details and panoramas that showed the place in all its glory: carved stones, perfectly fitted walls, temples that opened out upon the spiraling Urubamba valley, and tumbling fountains. Although it would take the Peruvian photographer Martín Chambi to capture the site's more reverential, natural side in the 1920s, Bingham's photos fully captured its civilization and majesty, and their publication in *National Geographic Magazine* would cement both Bingham's fame as an explorer as well as Machu Picchu's importance in the history of Peru and of the Americas entire. The indigenous achievement of that place bled through the viewfinder, immortalized in silky black and white, nourishing Bingham's ambitions at the moment they needed it most. No matter what had happened with the concession, Yale had done right by clearing the ruins and giving them their due.

It was an achievement, however, that would have been impossible without the help of the many Indian peasants who had cleared the ruins and now traveled back to Cuzco. Richarte, Alvarez, and Fuentes, who were already home, felt differently regarding Yale's impending departure. The expedition had disrupted their lives, and Alvarez and Fuentes were glad to move back to the homes at the site.

Richarte, however, tried to tap Yale for one last payment; he seemed thoroughly converted to seeing his home and its artifacts in monetary terms. On November 14, he led Bingham to the "Salon Grande," a carved cave—known today as the Temple of the Moon—that the peasant had discovered on the north slope of Huayna Picchu the month before. The route there was an old and disintegrating Inca road that went through a cave chute for two hundred feet, then straight up for seven or eight hundred feet to a series of connecting caves beneath a great cliff. The tall explorer followed Richarte on his hands and knees, then emerged half-blinking into an 86-foot-long and ten-foot-high cave, whose partly lined and partly shaped back wall bore a niche and several seats. Richarte had hoped to receive a special commission for finding the cave—which had yielded only small bronze tweezers and a brazier—but when Bingham was through with his photos, he disappointed the Indian. He had been paid enough, the explorer thought. Bingham appreciated his help in emptying the tombs of the Incas, of course, but the expedition had no future use of Richarte's services. Shortly after, Richarte moved to the river below.[15]

Hiram Bingham returned to Cuzco with a heavy heart to close up shop on the 1912 expedition and prepare for departure. The *arrieros* (muleteers) were paid, the mules were sold, and the 93 boxes of bones and artifacts were packed for travel.

Feeling resigned, Bingham said goodbye to all his contacts, thinking it unlikely that Yale would return to Peru.

His only crime, he thought, was that he had wanted to help Peru shoulder its archaeological load. But in the three and a half years since he found that purpose at Choqquequirau, Peruvian leadership and public opinion had decided that they would protect the country's history themselves. The country's bishops promised the minister of Education and Justice that they would prohibit the sale of religious relics and artwork. The government had already fined one Cuzco antiquarian two hundred pounds for trying to export forty cases of antiquities to a foreign buyer.[16] Proud of Cuzco, young Luis Valcárcel would soon found a historical institute to guard the region's ruins.[17]

Bingham's consolation was that Yale's boxes would leave the country unhindered, filled with artifacts that Eaton and Erdis had gathered for history and science, and that Richarte and Alvarez gathered for money and because they had little choice.

Before he could do so, however, the other shoe dropped. The full, finished version of the decree that allowed Yale to export its artifacts arrived in Cuzco on November 19, 1912, and was published the next day. It was everything that Bingham had expected, but it contained one very significant clause—one that Bingham either did not expect or did not detail to his benefactors: that the artifacts could leave the country but Peru reserved "the right to exact from the University of Yale . . . the return of the unique and duplicate objects it has extracted."[18]

In other words, the skulls, bones, and artifacts of Machu Picchu belonged to Peru, and when Peru asked Yale to send them back, Yale was required to do so.

It was historic. It was the very first time that Peru asserted ownership over antiquities leaving the country, backing that claim up with conditions that called for their return. It was a halt, however minor, in the outward flow of preColumbian art and culture that had started with the Spanish conquest.

"I had quite a time with the President and his Minister of [Education and] Justice in getting through the telegram to you," wrote the American minister, trying to get Bingham to look on the bright side. "Do you not think that under the construction given to your verbal concession, in view of the existing law, that you have practically won a victory, since your purposes are solely for scientific investigations?"[19]

Bingham did not agree. He had mounted this second full expedition to Peru to clarify the history of the Incas, it was true, but also to give Yale the beginning of a collection of South American antiquities, one that was supposed to grow over ten years of Yale directing Peru's archaeology. To not only have that achievement denied but also be the test case of Peru's new archaeological policy was the final humiliation. Never before had a country like Peru put such a condition on a foreign excavator. Though the grave contents of Machu Picchu could rest at Yale, Peru could someday demand their return, stripping the university museum of the core of its new South American collection, the prize that Bingham had promised Yale and his financial backers. Bingham was furious; Peru had won.

Or had it? Suddenly it mattered very much whether Erdis had kept José Gabriel Cosío, the Peruvian monitor, away from the expedition's finest finds. Without a complete inventory, Peru would not know what Yale had and didn't have—whether they had silver and beautiful bronzes, or potsherds and bone fragments and nothing more.

It was something like magic. Hiram Bingham had brought the 1912 expedition to Peru to solve the mystery of the last cities of the Incas and export half of what it found to Yale. Instead, the expedition had taken 93 wooden crates once filled with bacon, biscuits, and tea and turned them into miniature coffins, filling them with *all* they excavated—from skulls and bones to silver and bronze. If Peru ever called back the boxes, its officials wouldn't know what to expect. Yale controlled Machu Picchu's graves now.

Interlude: Tupac Amaru

*F*riar Ortíz shivered in the cold morning air below Vitcos, pulled on his vestments, and began to pray. He closed his eyes. He knew the Incas were watching him closely. He called out, asking God for a miracle. But when he stopped speaking and opened his eyes, he knew nothing had changed. It was the end of the rainy season, 1571, and lying before him, pale and lifeless, was the corpse of Vilcabamba's last chance for peace: the Inca emperor Titu Cusi, who had died horribly in Ortíz's care.

The Incas cursed Ortíz for his failure. Ortíz righteously declared that it must have been God's will that the emperor died. For that, the Incas thrashed him, pierced a hole in the flesh behind his jaw, threaded it with a rope, and dragged him over the mountains and down toward the religious refuge of Vilcabamba. They were afraid of killing a Spanish missionary outright, so they sought the advice of the new emperor, Titu Cusi's younger brother, Tupac Amaru.

If Ortíz had prayed for his survival, he was disappointed. In contrast to Titu Cusi, Tupac Amaru had been raised by Vilcabamba's priests, sheltered from diplomacy and exchange with the Spaniards. He was devout, intelligent, and well spoken, but reliant on his priests for counsel. When the Inca soldiers brought the missionary to the edge of the city of Vilcabamba, Tupac Amaru refused Ortíz an audience, sealing his fate. An Inca captain smashed open the Spaniard's skull with his club and laid his corpse on the road to be trampled. According to his fellow Spaniards, the Inca captains then buried Ortíz head first in a deep hole and drove a palm spear up his rectum.

With the friar's killing, Inca policy shifted from wary coexistence with the Spanish to hard-line isolation. They would never be able to send the Spaniards back to Europe on a raft, but they could cut all ties. Their military leaders destroyed the friars' abandoned churches, persecuted the remaining Christian converts, and stopped communication with the Spanish. The Inca captains kept the crisis in Vil-cabamba a secret until the following year, when they killed a Spanish envoy attempting to cross into the province.

For most residents of Cuzco, the envoy's death was a tragedy—a step backward to the days of Spanish-Inca war. For all the violence of the conquest, Incas and Spaniards had been able to work out a wary coexistence in Cuzco. The rights of the Inca nobility were respected, and a new class of *mestizo* children had been born, enjoying the nobility of both worlds. Some Spaniards genuinely recognized the injustice of Atahualpa's execution in 1533 and had hoped to draw out Manco's family to make a permanent peace. They had wanted to marry Titu Cusi's son to the daughter of his brother Sayri Tupac to shore up Inca power in a colonial setting. The murder ended those dreams and proved to both Spaniards and Incas that they had not come as far as they thought.

It became clear that the Spanish king's representative in Peru, the viceroy Francisco de Toledo, had been planning for, perhaps even encouraging, a crisis such as this one. Philip II had sent Toledo to Peru, in part, to resolve the Inca question peacefully. Toledo had other plans.[1] Early in 1572, before learning of any violence in Vilcabamba, Toledo called together Cuzco's Inca nobility to listen to a public reading of a history of the Incas that he had commissioned "with the express intention of demonstrating that the Inca empire had been an unmitigated tyranny, created but recently by force of arms and maintained through the merciless exploitation of its subjects."[2] In doing so, he hoped to deny the rights and property promised to Titu Cusi, whom the Spaniards still believed was alive. Following Toledo's lead, the chronicler argued that the Incas were corrupt and exploitative usurpers, not from Peru but from the lost island of Atlantis. The rebels in Vilcabamba were worse: Manco was a "traitor" and Titu Cusi was "a bastard and apostate."[3] Paullu, the Inca who had sided with the Spanish crown, was legitimate.

According to one Spanish priest in attendance, one of Manco's daughters, María Cusi Huarcay, saw that Toledo meant to demolish her family's ability to argue for their independence. She challenged Toledo, denouncing the fact that collaboration with the colonizers now determined legitimacy, rather than history and blood. Her father and brothers were the just "rulers of this kingdom," not usurpers.[4]

Perhaps more than any other moment in the Spanish conquest, Doña María and Toledo's exchange epitomized what was at stake when Manco fled to Vilcabamba: an argument over the unjust nature of the Spanish conquest and how Inca history would be told. Toledo was determined to make sure that Vilcabamba would be forgotten, its righteousness destroyed, its rebels made villains. He would legitimize Spanish rule by rewriting the Inca past and destroying its present symbols of independence.

For the moment, Toledo won. The forty or so Inca men in attendance understood that this new history was a test of their loyalty, and despite Doña María's protests, they attested to its truth. After sending the new history to Spain, Toledo sat back and waited for the Incas to make a misstep and give him a cause for war.[5] When he heard about the dead envoy, he had the justification he needed. On April 14, 1572, he declared "total war on the Inca as an apostate, prevaricator, homicide, rebel and tyrant"—the "war of fire and blood" that the captain of his guard, the young Martín García de Loyola, nephew of the Jesuits' founder, would prosecute so fiercely.[6]

Back in the jungle, Tupac Amaru raised his arms to the sky and led his people in worship, praying that the sun, their god, might keep the last city of the Incas safe from harm. Before him sat the mummies of his father, Manco, and his brother, Titu Cusi, who had fought the Spanish and negotiated for the Incas' independence as best they could. Sadly, their time had come. The bodies of all three would all be dismembered, scattered, burned, or lost before long, and Vilcabamba would disappear into the mountains.

In the end, however, it would be the Incas' version of history that would be championed. Toledo's execution of Tupac Amaru angered King Philip II, and when the viceroy returned to Spain he was jailed—ostensibly for failing to fix Peru's finances—and died in prison. Martín García de Loyola married the Inca heiress Beatriz, the daughter of Sayri Tupac—a moment immortalized in a painting that still hangs in the Jesuit church in Cuzco—but the king denied him permission to add Tupac Amaru's head to his coat of arms. García de Loyola died in Chile in 1598, when three hundred Araucanian Indians on horseback annihilated his camp. They used his skull as a drinking vessel.[7]

The injustice of Vilcabamba's destruction found one of its greatest champions in an indigenous scribe named Felipe Guaman Poma de Ayala. Born around 1550, Guaman Poma had been indigenous nobility, and he or a member of his family witnessed Tupac Amaru's execution. Spanish courts stripped Guaman Poma of his property in 1600, however, exiling him from his family lands. From then on he worked on a 1,200-page critique of colonial rule, his *Nueva corónica y buen gobierno,* and in 1615 sent it on the Spanish king. He filled it with his own incredible fine line drawings, depicting pre-Columbian burial customs and Inca culture. But it was most notable for how his images and arguments documented the Spanish mistreatment of their Indian charges and the Incas during Manco's rebellion and the execution of young Tupac Amaru.[8] The work was complex—pro-Andean, but Christian; but above all, it was a call for indigenous Andean rule and a rejection of the world that Toledo had established.

The treatise never reached the king's eyes; instead, it got lost in the Danish Royal Library, where it sat unstudied for centuries. In 1908, a German scholar brought it back to life—just a few years before Hiram Bingham's expeditions started a new debate over the meaning of the last Inca cities to Peru and the other countries of the hemisphere. Were Manco's cities evidence of a lost American empire of great cultural sophistication? Or were they a symbol of continued indigenous resistance to exterior domination? Did their contents belong to the world, or to Peru? Did their modern heirs live in Connecticut or Cuzco? Had Guaman Poma also come back to life himself in 1908, he would have understood the stakes of the debate between Yale and Peru immediately, as well as the bitter irony of its end.

Part Four

Bonesmen

Men's evil manners
live in brass

Their virtues
We write in water ✝

Henry VIII, William Shakespeare

Men's evil manners live in brass; their virtues
We write in water.

—*William Shakespeare*, Henry VIII

Chapter Sixteen

Between the Poles

*H*iram Bingham's trip back to the United States after the 1912 expedition was at first a bitter one. In returning to Peru, he had assured Yale that he would be able to excavate and export artifacts for decades to come. Instead, he had withdrawn the concession in the face of public condemnation. His claim that Yale had discovered pre-glacial bones would have to be retracted. And to top it off, he had won the exportation of Machu Picchu's artifacts only on the condition that they be returned when Peru asked.

Hiram was not about to fall on his sword, however. He felt wronged, not responsible. Upon his return to the United States, Bingham orchestrated a distracting media campaign. Capitalizing on the romance of Machu Picchu's revelation the previous year, he was able to whip the press into an indignant frenzy over Peru's mistreatment of American exploration. The headlines said it all: "Peru Hostile to Scientists Here After Hardships"; "Lost in Clouds After Digging in Lost City"; "Ministry of Peru Objects to American Exploration—Head of Yale Expedition Fears Government Neglect Will Destroy Work of Buried Inca City"; and, the most florid, "Braves Death to Dig Human Skulls 60,000 Years Old—Yale Archaeologist Brings 30 Skulls and 100 Heads from Inca City in Peru—Left to Die by Guides—Charges Latin Government Broke Faith and Tried to Confiscate Specimens."[1]

Bingham led his media campaign with Yale's excavation of the "fairy city" of Machu Picchu and the row over its artifacts. As the supposed cradle of Inca civilization, Machu Picchu was the "most important archaeological point on the South American continent," Bingham argued. He was vague as to what the expedition found beyond skulls and bones, but an unfazed *New York Times* speculated that the university had found several engraved bronze tablets that might shed light on the Americas' "original" inhabitants—an apparent reference to the foundational tale of Mormonism, Joseph Smith's announcement in the 1820s that he had discovered golden plates describing Jesus' visit to the native peoples of the Americas. Some Americans still associated Bingham with his family's religious legacy, it seems, and wanted to find Christian inspiration at the heart of the Americas' indigenous history.[2]

Religion was no longer a part of Bingham's narrative, however; Yale's investigations into the history of the hemisphere were a matter of selfless science, he explained. By contrast, Peru's attempt to prevent the exportation of its artifacts was downright uncivilized. "Never before have I known of a South American government to stop people from exploring," he declared.[3] Going into few details, he called the government's final decree "as insulting as it possibly could be." The expedition had prevailed, but it might never return to Peru. The press cheered. His story would make "an excellent thriller for 'the movies,'" with enough "material for at least 6,000 feet of whirling film."[4]

The story provoked a minor debate over the ownership of history. One Milwaukee newspaper dismissed Peru's objections, claiming that modern Peru's elite rulers were descended "not from the Aztecs" but from the conquistadors. "It is not as if pious descendants should say, 'You shall not disturb the graves of our ancestors!'" The *Christian Science Monitor,* which knew the difference between Peru and Mexico, disagreed. The *Monitor* sympathized with Peru's desire to protect and excavate its own treasures—as long as they actually did so.[5]

Bingham also had to defend Yale against the charge of monopoly. His enemies in Lima had telegraphed news of Bingham's actions to Harvard, the Smithsonian, and colleagues in Great Britain and Germany.[6] In public Bingham claimed that he had tried to swing the concession for all American institutions; that if he hadn't done so, a German institution might have worked out their own monopoly. In private, however, he admitted that the bigger "problem" was that Peruvians' increased awareness of "the extent of their treasures" made it harder for American museums to build collections.[7]

His colleagues, however, didn't buy his story. They believed Bingham had sensationalized archaeology and were shocked that Bingham had taken such steps that Yale might not return. "[I]t looks as if he had committed some crime," wrote Clements Markham, England's most distinguished historian of the Incas. The head of the Royal Geographic Society was less surprised, having talked to Hamilton Rice, Bingham's partner in Venezuela and Colombia: "Bingham is what we should call a little bit of a fraud. . . . [H]e himself is not qualified to do any real scientific exploring but takes the credit of the work done by his companions. The fact that he applied for such a law as you refer to shows what sort of man he is."[8]

It was even uncertain whether Yale would receive its consolation for Bingham's botched venture: the 136 boxes containing the skulls, bones, bronzes, and silver of Machu Picchu, one of the last such collections to legally leave Peru. On Christmas Day, eight months after the wreck of the *Titanic* killed 1,517 in the North Atlantic, the ship bearing the Machu Picchu collection, the *Turrialba,* ran aground on the Brigantine Shoals. Bingham felt sick when he heard the news. He had fought so hard to establish Yale as a safe and responsible home for Machu Picchu's dead, only to send them to a watery grave off the New Jersey shore. Fortunately, the United Fruit Company put him at ease. Although the crew had thrown the company's bananas into the ocean to save the passengers, Machu Picchu's treasure was safe.

In the midst of praying that nothing else would befall his boxes on the way to New Haven, Bingham was given a first bittersweet taste of his legacy. On January 11, 1913, he and his family took the train down to Washington, DC, for his greatest public honor as an explorer. That evening, the National Geographic Society threw one of the most notable banquets in the history of twentieth-century exploration. Billed as "The First Meeting of the Poles," it was the first encounter of the American Robert Edwin Peary, whom the National Geographic Society had championed as the discoverer of the North Pole, and Roald Amundsen, the Norwegian who won the race to the South Pole. Grosvenor invited Bingham to sit at the head table with Peary, Amundsen, and Grosvenor's father-in-law, Alexander Graham Bell. Bingham also gave the first speech of the evening. In white tie and tails, Bingham regaled 600 honored guests with stories of jungle, Inca ruins, and archaeological discovery. Feeling generous, he even thanked Peru's government for forcing the region's Indians to clear Machu Picchu. Bingham sat down to a round of applause, basking in adrenaline, flashbulbs, champagne, and happiness. In one night, he stood "between the discoverers of the ends of the earth" and raised his audience to the heights of once and future American civilization— a height he might never again achieve.

One point he would never admit in public, however, was the matter of who owned Machu Picchu's artifacts. He never revealed the crucial clause in the government decree that let Machu Picchu's artifacts travel to New Haven: that Yale would have to return them whenever Peru asked. On the Monday after Bingham's speech, his assistants unloaded his 136 "soiled and battered wooded cases" from a train and escorted them to Bingham's offices at Yale. The Peabody Museum's officials said there was so much that they would have difficultly displaying them alongside the dinosaurs. "Peruvian Trophies Here," read the *Yale Daily News*. Without irony, the newspaper cheered the arrival of what Peru thought was a loan and what Yale thought "the plunder of the ancient graves on the slopes of the Andes."[9] Bingham did not correct the mistake.

Perhaps it was because Bingham lost himself in writing. He spent the spring laboring over the *National Geographic* article that would fix Machu Picchu into the American imagination. Grosvenor declared that Bingham's first draft was "the most extraordinary narrative of discovery in South America that [he had ever] read."[10] Grosvenor postponed publication from March to June, devoted the entire April edition to Bingham's story, upped the number of photos to 250— including a beautiful foldout panorama of Machu Picchu—and printed 210,000 copies, 75,000 more than he had published the September before. In the end, Bingham's article, which Grosvenor titled, "In the Wonderland of Peru," reached one million readers. It was a fantasia of pristine ruins and storybook American adventure. Smoothing over the concession fiasco, Grosvenor declared to Yale's president that Bingham's revelations were "the most important made in South America since the discovery of America."[11] The way the magazine pitched it, an elite North American explorer had found the very start of indigenous America's greatest civilization.

The article created an international sensation, running in newspapers throughout the United States, Great Britain, and Germany. The fever dreams of the dime-store novels had come true. The *New York Times* devoted the whole first page of its Sunday magazine to the "Lost City in the Clouds," calling Bingham's revelation "the Greatest Archaeological Discovery of the Age." In a time when "there is nothing new under the sun," the *Times* declared that "one member of the daredevil explorers' craft has 'struck it rich,' struck it so dazzlingly rich, indeed, that all his confreres may be pardoned if they gnash their teeth in chagrin and turn green with envy." Bingham had "the superb good fortune to discover an entire city . . . a place of splendid palaces and temples and grim encircling walls. . . .

"He calls it Machu Picchu."[12]

The story challenged racist beliefs that the Americas' indigenous peoples were incapable of building empires and settlements. By the same token, it fueled all sorts of wild and covertly racist theories—that the Incas were inspired by Egyptians, that they were Atlanteans or Asians—all implying that native Americans could not possibly have built an empire without external help.[13] Inspired readers wrote poems about Machu Picchu's "Castle of the Three Windows" and began movie scripts on the "Romance of Inca days."[14] The "lost race" genre of popular fiction, full of lost cities and Incas, caught a brief second wind. In the following few years, the American boy hero Tom Swift would discover a lost world while digging a railroad tunnel through the Andes; the author of *The Phantom of the Opera*, Gaston Leroux, would send two Americans to Peru to save a Spanish heiress from being sacrificed to an Inca sun king; and in *The City in the Clouds,* an American explorer found a lost city named Apu in the Andes.[15]

It also led to at least one ironic recommendation. The *Boston Morning Herald* suggested that Peru not make the mistake that the United States had made with the spectacular Pueblo cliff dwellings of Mesa Verde, Colorado, as "we failed to lay a protecting hand over these prehistoric remains until the archaeologists of our own and other countries had pretty effectively raided the treasures, with the result that our guides have to explain in considerable part what 'used to be' there." Bingham may have winced at the reference. American locals had almost lynched Mesa Verde's excavator, Gustaf Nordenskiöld, for exporting its artifacts to Europe.[16]

Across the world, newspaper readers shook their heads at the wonder of it all. For Americans feeling regretful over the conquest of their own indigenous population, Machu Picchu offered a feeling of innocence and an almost imperial nostalgia for the pre-European past. It was easier to think of the noble, indigenous dead than the live Indians on and off reservations throughout the United States, fighting to protect native culture and treaty rights.[17]

Of equal interest was the debonair, driven, and now famous explorer who made it happen. Bingham signed with Houghton Mifflin to publish a book tentatively titled "Land of the Incas." Criticized at Yale for his frequent absences, he was in such demand that during one two-month period he declined forty invitations to speak, including one from the University of Illinois on the occasion of the birthday of another six-foot-four American icon, Abraham Lincoln. He made a name for himself in international relations as well. In an article for the *Atlantic Monthly,* he argued that the Monroe Doctrine, America's rationale for military intervention in the region, in fact threatened hemispheric peace. It provoked a major debate, including sharp words from Bingham's friend, former President Taft.[18] Taft needn't have worried. Bingham had not written it out of plain sympathy for Latin American countries; rather, he now had firsthand experience of how Americans looked to the rest of the hemisphere: "that the Yankees are selfish and are looking for national as well as personal advantage."[19]

Bingham remained best known, however, as a romantic explorer of Inca ruins. His lectures drew hundreds of students hoping to catch a glimpse of the distinguished, handsome historian.[20] After one lecture, a friend teased Bingham, "Did you know that you made a big hit here not only with the men, but also with the ladies?"[21] Not all attention was welcome. Bingham called the police on one crank who kept showing up to lectures; his pockets were full of bullets.[22] In the fall of 1913, he wrote to the editor of *Ladies' Home Journal* to complain about a potentially slanderous short story that featured a disagreeable, vain, and tall Yale graduate named Hiram Bingham.[23] Bingham received letters encouraging him to consider theosophy, which would ensnare another South American explorer, Percy Fawcett, with its teachings that modern humankind developed on Atlantis.[24] Hiram joined a clubbier and more secretive male society instead, the Freemasons. "How fast you are climbing the heights of fame!" marveled Bingham's aunt, who hoped that he would soon bear the title of "vice president, a stepping stone, perhaps, to that of President of U.S.!"[25] He was recognizable enough to readers that one weekly publication could quip, "You may murder your uncle and bury him in the cellar. But some day, two thousand years hence, a descendant of Professor Hiram Bingham of Yale will discover your uncle's skull."[26]

In December 1913, Bingham received the most surreal compliment of all: the part of Christopher Columbus in New Haven's holiday pageant.[27] Six-foot-four, dressed in fifteenth-century adventurer's gear, Hiram Bingham struck a heroic pose and "discovered" the New World and its indigenous inhabitants for his neighbors.

Bingham's declaration that he would not return to Peru proved poorly timed. Across the Atlantic, interest in South American exploration exploded in the mid-1910s. Pulpy fact and speculative fiction alike competed for the public's attention. In 1912, while Bingham excavated Machu Picchu, Sir Arthur Conan Doyle published *The Lost World*. When Curtis C. Farabee, the anthropologist who gave Bingham his map on ruins along the Urubamba, left for South America in early 1913, one newspaper speculated that he was searching for Conan Doyle's dinosaur-haunted plateau.[28] Bingham's revelation changed the life of British explorer Percy Fawcett, who turned from mapping Bolivia's borders to searching the Brazilian Amazon for a lost, monumental city that he called Z—a city that he would die trying to find a decade later.[29]

In a reversal of roles, Bingham's hero, former president Theodore Roosevelt, was waist deep in his own South American adventure. Having lost a third-party Progressive run for the presidency in 1912, in October 1913, Roosevelt departed for South America, his trip's only requirement being that he not be the "thousandth American to visit Cuzco."[30] Instead, Roosevelt plunged into the Brazilian Amazon with Colonel Cândido Mariano da Silva Rondon to map the path of the mysterious Rio da Dúvida, the River of Doubt. ". . . [I]f it is necessary for me to leave my bones in South America, I am quite ready to do so," Roosevelt explained.[31] When Roosevelt returned in May 1914, emaciated and half dead from the experience, the *New York Herald* and the *New York Sun* would turn to Bingham, "the foremost authority in this country on South America," to confirm the former president's claim that he had traced a new river nearly a thousand miles long. Honored, Bingham said that he saw no reason to question his hero's word.[32]

Bingham was far less generous when he heard about Captain J. Campbell Besley, a silver-haired British explorer who told the *New York Times* that he had discovered not one but "three wonderful cities of the Incas in jungle wilds where no white man had ever set foot before." He had also found the hip and thigh bones of two explorers supposedly "slain and eaten by cannibals." Flagrantly piggybacking off Yale, Besley said that he began his explorations where Bingham left off. One newspaper hinted that Machu Picchu "pale[d] into insignificance" alongside his own colossal city, Plateryoyoc.[33]

At that, Bingham knew he was a fraud—Plateryoyoc was Peru's El Dorado—but he felt threatened nonetheless.[34] Gilbert Grosvenor fueled his archaeological explorer's sense that he was in a South Pole sort of race to uncover the pre-Columbian history of the Americas. "Somebody is going to solve the mystery connected with these ancient peoples," he wrote. "Let us get there first."[35] The editor put *National Geographic*'s money on the table for an immediate return: $20,000—almost $450,000 in today's money—for not one but two years of continuous work in Peru. In exchange, Bingham promised two more sparkling articles and monthly dispatches that *National Geographic* could feed to the press. The only question was, did Peru want him back?

To address the problems of the previous year, Bingham designed a two-phase expedition. In 1914, a vanguard of six men led by the gold miner Ellwood C. Erdis would travel down to Peru that spring "to do reconnaissance work and mapping" of the region's ruins. In 1915, Bingham himself would return to Peru and announce a semipermanent "school or archaeological centre" near Cuzco where Peruvians and Americans could work together—and where Yale's finds would remain.[36] There was "no feeling against foreigners who wish to undertake first-hand anthropological work there, provided they will leave what they find in the country," he explained.[37]

Hearteningly, Bingham's plan met with the approval of Peru's national government. A conservative military coup had overthrown progressive President Billinghurst and said Yale could return as long as it sought the permissions it needed from the ministries in Lima. For Bingham—who had thought he would never return to Peru—this was a victory. It put him in so generous a mood that on April 14, four days before his men set sail, the explorer dictated an expansive letter to a member of Lima's Historical Institute. Bingham explained Yale's past actions and suggested that Peru interpret the clause prohibiting the exportation against artifacts "liberally, so as to encourage explorers to come and to spend money in the country and to do the kind of work which Peru would like to do but probably cannot afford to do for some years to come." The best solution would be that proposed in the concession of two years earlier: that Peru's museum and the foreign expedition take turns choosing artifacts.

"Personally I have no interest in building up a great museum here," Bingham wrote, "though I am very anxious to have archaeological material where it can be studied, and that was my chief object in bringing home material from Machu Picchu." To prove that his goals were scientific, Bingham made a noteworthy offer, one that showed his recognition of Peru's claim upon the Machu Picchu collection. "Now that we have about completed our studies on it I intend to send separate pieces to Peru."

Yet when Bingham had the letter translated into Spanish, he left out the references to the artifacts from Machu Picchu as well as the claim that Yale was uninterested in building a museum.[38]

Why had Bingham made the changes? Possibly because their studies would take longer than they thought. It was also likely that he feared that Peru, if reminded, might call back the entire Machu Picchu collection, shaming him in the eyes of Yale.

But the truth was that Bingham had just received a business opportunity—a way to secure his long-term reputation through a little short-term skullduggery. While the 1914–15 expedition's vanguard heroically explored Peru's geography, he would *buy* a world-class collection of South American antiquities and have it smuggled to New Haven. He would cut out the meddlesome Peruvian government and secure Yale a *permanent* collection—Peruvian law be damned.

Chapter Seventeen

Temptation

*B*ingham's decision to pay for smuggled artifacts was born of mild desperation, opportunity, and a growing disdain for Peruvian law—feelings shared by the Cuzco antiquarian who offered him the collection: Tomás Alvistur.

Bingham and Alvistur had met in July 1912 during the early days of Bingham's triumphant return to Cuzco. Alvistur was a dandyish dilettante who, like Bingham, had married rich—Bingham had stayed at his mother-in-law's hacienda, Huadquiña, in 1911—and had used the family money to feed his fascination with the Incas. Instead of exploring, Alvistur had built a "very fine" collection of about 366 pre-Columbian artifacts. Some he had pulled from Inca graves or ruins; others he bought from Indians or from dealers in the city.[1]

His taste was exquisite. Bingham had seen his museum in 1912 and had been impressed by the four massive Inca jugs that reached almost to his waist; a fifteen-inch-tall, green-black stone ceremonial chalice; an eight-inch-tall alpaca carved out of light brown stone; a brown stone bird, warm with pale concentric rings, so abstractly lifelike it seemed to tremble in one's hand. One particularly beautiful jug was even from Machu Picchu. It was 21.5 centimeters high, with a red handle and a red rim, and its front bore strange black and red trellis designs, diagonals and circles, all against a reddish-yellow background. Alvistur apparently had bought it in Cuzco from Agustín Lizarraga, the "other" discoverer of Machu Picchu, before he died.[2]

The controversy over Yale's concession, however, had focused scrutiny on the unlicensed excavation of monuments and sale of artifacts. In February 1913, the University of Cuzco's student association denounced the looting of the fortress of Sacsayhuaman.[3] That April, Peru's biggest newspaper thundered against an Englishman who was in London auctioning off a collection of 750 artifacts he had pulled from tombs in northern Peru.[4] And in November 1913, Luis Valcárcel founded the Historical Institute of Cuzco to monitor the region's archaeological monuments and artifacts. In this new climate, men like Alvistur, who had once identified themselves as harmless antiquarians, were cast as potential smugglers.

Alvistur felt persecuted. He claimed that the government was threatening to confiscate his collection. But he also saw an opportunity.[5] When the exportation of an item becomes illegal, prices go up. As Cuzco and Peru fell into a recession, Alvistur saw a way to cover the lavish lifestyle he had grown accustomed to: he would sell his collection to Hiram Bingham.[6]

His offers began in 1913, but it took until March 1914 for Alvistur to hit upon a price that Bingham could talk down: Alvistur's collection of 366 Inca antiquities in exchange for £2,200, or just over $240,000 today.[7] Alvistur claimed the price was a bargain, that Inca artifacts throughout Peru were disappearing, and that the collection would double in value soon. He was also clear about what it took to get the artifacts on a U.S.-bound ship. He would have to offer the customs officials a "great sum to allow the collection to leave, for, as you know, the exportation of ancient objects is prohibited."[8] In other words, in order to smuggle his collection to Bingham in New Haven, he would have to bribe Peruvian officials.

Bingham received Alvistur's letter on April 3, 1914, sliced it open, and smoothed it out upon his desk. On the one hand, the timing was terrible. He had gone through so much to return to Peru. If Peru's intellectuals learned that he bought smuggled artifacts, it would scuttle his plans for good. His wife was expecting their seventh child—it would be another son—and to press the incredibly opulent luck of their lives might tempt fate.

But it was tempting. Peru might still ask Yale to return the Machu Picchu collection. Alvistur's artifacts offered an ace in the hole: an untraceable collection of antiquities that Peru could never inventory and thus never recall. And in the turn of logic that has salved collectors' consciences down through the ages, Bingham truly believed that Yale was a safer place for artifacts than Peru. He may have believed that the very fact that Alvistur could offer to smuggle artifacts suggested that Peru was unable to prevent smuggling. And if that was the case, then Bingham perhaps thought it his chance—nay, higher calling—to pay Alvistur to smuggle them to Yale, where he could give the collection a good home. As for the legality of it all, we might guess his attitude from the year before, when he wrote to the U.S. minister in Peru with advice on how the Smithsonian's Aleš Hrdlička might get his artifacts out: "Legally I do not suppose the Director of Government has any authority to direct the Customs Department to permit Doctor Hrdlicka to take away the bones he may collect, but if the matter be kept quiet, I presume it will work out all right."[9] It was only a crime, therefore, if Peru's Ministry of Justice and Education found out.

Hiram Bingham made a counteroffer of £1,500, over $160,000 today. "I realize that the material is worth more than this, and I wish I could pay more," Hiram Bingham apologized, "but this is as much as I can possibly offer you."[10] The very next day, April 4, Bingham wrote, then rewrote his letter to the director of Peru's National Library, removing his claim that Yale had no interest in building up a great museum.

By late May the deal was done. Alvistur accepted Bingham's offer, packed the collection in seven large crates, and paid their way aboard the New York-bound steamer *Chimu*—named after a pre-Columbian Peruvian culture, ironically enough.[11] In mid-September the New England Navigation Company notified Bingham that it had received "7 Cases Inca Articles (Antiques)," consigned to Yale University.[12] The four large Inca jugs arrived soon after.

Bingham paid for the Alvistur collection entirely out of his family's deep pockets, but he soon folded them into the Machu Picchu collection.[13] When Bingham had unpacked and admired the artifacts—finer than anything they had found at Machu Picchu—Bingham thanked the shipping agent for his help making "Yale an *efficient* place in which to learn about Peru ancient and modern [emphasis added]."[14]

As long as no one in Peru learned about it, everything would be fine.

While Bingham haggled, his expedition's vanguard was navigating choppy waters of its own. They had left on April 18, 1914, with Ellwood C. Erdis in charge—the mustachioed engineer who had so successfully excavated Machu Picchu in 1912 and hid its finer artifacts from the authorities. Erdis was a "rough old western diamond," Bingham gushed, tough enough to take the lead during a difficult time in U.S.-Latin American relations.[15] The Mexican Revolution was expanding, and the hemisphere worried how the United States would react to its neighbor's struggle between elite and peasant factions. Sure enough, on April 21, while Erdis was navigating the Caribbean, 41 U.S. ships bombarded the Mexican port of Veracruz and began a six-month occupation. It brought the United States and Mexico to the brink of war and severely damaged America's reputation throughout the region. When Erdis arrived in foggy Lima on May 3, he learned that it was indeed the "worst possible time [he] could have come."[16] Anti-American sentiment was high, and the U.S. diplomat was demoralized. He doubted Erdis could get the usual government letter ordering local officials to help the Americans and permission to import the expedition's gear.

Erdis got it in a week. He owed his success to two factors, both mandated by Bingham. First, he represented the expedition's chief objective as geographical, not archaeological; there would be no large-scale excavation this year. Second, he brought a peace offering.[17] Shortly after his arrival, Erdis rode out to Peru's National Museum and sought out the director of archaeology and anthropology. He may have been expecting to find Bingham's friend in Lima's Historical Institute. Instead, he found himself looking down at a darker-skinned anthropologist with black, swept-back hair and impassively owlish spectacles. It was none other than Julio C. Tello, the indigenous Peruvian scholar who had sent Hiram Bingham Carlos Romero's article on Choqquequirau and Vitcos four years before.

Tello had come a long way since then. After earning his masters in anthropology at Harvard—likely the first Peruvian to do so—he toured the incredible Peruvian collections of Europe. It was a surprise to see how much had left his country in the last half-century. Tello returned to Peru in 1913. His timing was perfect. The country was still roiling over the Yale concession, and the government gave him the directorship of the country's new archaeological museum. It was, perhaps, the first time in Peruvian history that an indigenous Peruvian, not a European, was charged with collecting and reconstructing a national past.

Tello gave his directorship a political edge. He hoped the museum would help fight the illicit trade in antiquities, and he "joined" a Smithsonian expedition to collect ancient Peruvian skulls led by Aleš Hrdlička, the "skull czar" who argued that indigenous Americans had a short history in the hemisphere. Unsurprisingly, they clashed.[18] Hrdlička decided that Tello was a "Peruvian for the Peruvians." In 1915, he would warn Bingham against getting Tello appointed to the expedition as a "companion."[19]

In 1914, however, Bingham knew little about Tello's sympathies, and his own proxy, Erdis, proceeded on his mission of peace. After a mutually curious handshake, Erdis handed over the offering Bingham had sent in his care: a "box of Machu Picchu things," elsewhere referred to in Erdis's diary as "bronzes."

Appreciating the gesture, Tello offered to help Erdis get permission to bring Yale's equipment through customs.[20] For Yale, turning over some of the Machu Picchu brozes may have been a gesture of reconciliation—and possibly an attempt to nip in the bud any recalls of the Machu Picchu artifacts. To Tello, however, the package of bronzes suggested Yale's acknowledgment of the claim Peru had laid upon its material past. It could only have raised his expectations that Yale could be trusted and that the rest of Machu Picchu's artifacts would shortly follow.

Erdis and the rest of the vanguard reached Cuzco on May 19 with an "arsenal of modern apparatuses" in tow.[21] After fighting off the young street children who wanted to carry their luggage from the train station, the altitude-sick Americans collapsed into their beds at the Hotel Central. The next several days were spent in meetings with the University of Cuzco's rector and professors, the editors of the local newspapers, the prefect, and the mayor, who all warmed to the expedition's professed geographical plans.

While the topographers continued their "reconnaissance" of the 20,000-foot-high peaks around Cuzco, Erdis collected leads for Bingham. Joining him was the young Yale graduate Osgood Hardy, whose task that year was to learn Quechua in order to interpret the welter of Indian names and traditions that clung to the landscape. Intensely loyal to Bingham, Hardy was "For God, For Country, and For Yale" as the saying goes, and had resented the passengers on the ship down who had told him that the American occupation of Veracruz meant that the United States was "going to steal Mexico."[22]

Together, he and Erdis collected tales of ruins and trails surrounding Machu Picchu, solid gold rocks, tunnels that crossed under rivers, and other sundry rumors. No story was too lurid: stories of Inca cities, such as a "lake with an island in the center, which had an Inca palace on it, which the Indians never visited on account of fear"; mummies with sparkling emerald earrings; and walled caves filled with a dozen sitting skeletons.

While visiting the region's sites, however, the vanguard felt obliged to obey one of Bingham's other, less public mandates: to collect and buy human and cultural artifacts whenever they could.[23] The expedition would then study them in Cuzco.

The vanguard had managed to purchase a few artifacts—a broken ceramic pot "with twisted face, and monkey, on its back"—and to find a few graves, including a mummified mother and child. But in mid-July they made a discovery more spectacular than anything they had found at Machu Picchu. Ricardo Charaja, the expedition's most trusted Peruvian muleteer, stumbled upon a curious collection of artifacts scattered over a small hill beneath a glacier at 15,600 feet: a wooden club, a small animal skull, a carved wooden boat, and a broken silver "sun." Charaja called over the rest of the expedition, and together they found even more pieces of the silver sun, a bronze sun, a big-bladed bronze knife, a bronze shawl pin, seven bronze discs, a bronze breastplate "with holes around the edge and a face punched in the center by means of holes," and, last but not least, a three-quarter-inch "gold circle, marked and pierced"—the only gold the expedition ever found.[24] Bingham was delighted when he found out.[25]

What did the collection mean? The site's Quechua name gave a clue: Inca Churisca, or in English, Frozen Inca. Bingham later speculated that the find's location at the edge of a glacier seemed "to indicate that some Inca had been buried or lost on the ice" and had tumbled down onto the hill.[26] The supposition has strengthened over time. In the 1990s, the high-altitude archaeologist Johan Reinhard and his Peruvian collaborator Miguel Zarate made a thrilling series of discoveries on the peaks of Peru's highest glaciers: Inca subjects sacrificed to the mountain, wrapped up with finery and offerings. They caught the scent from a mummy bundle that, like Charaja's 1914 find, had tumbled down from a glacier.[27]

It was a "wonderful find," but one, like the special artifacts found at Machu Picchu, that Erdis kept from any Peruvian officials and academics. Because the last thing the expedition wanted was a Peruvian monitor, he kept the gold and silver under wraps. With the season's end fast approaching, however, the question remained: What to do with the artifacts? Erdis was afraid that the Peruvian government would confiscate the collection if they learned about it. For the same reason, Erdis would not send them back to Yale officially. They sat boxed up in a storeroom in Cuzco until September, when the expedition's surgeon, Dr. Edwin Meserve, left early for the United States. The expedition had learned of the assassination of Archduke Franz Ferdinand and the outbreak of World War I; Meserve was off to enlist for the Brits.

Bingham was furious—the doctor was breaking his contract—but Erdis saw an opportunity. He gave Meserve the artifacts in "17 envelopes and packages" to take back to Bingham in the surgeon's personal trunk.[28] Bingham had befriended the director of customs at Mollendo—even sending him copies of his famous article in the *National Geographic*—so Meserve's luggage was not likely to be inspected.[29] By defying the prohibition on exportation, the Yale expedition, like Alvistur, was now smuggling—on a small scale but smuggling nonetheless. Erdis would repeat the trick in November, when he sent the expedition's topographer back to Yale with two and a half skulls, a mummy, and the broken pottery idol in a "good steel trunk."[30]

Yet by smuggling the artifacts to New Haven, the expedition put them at risk. In mid-October, Meserve wrote to Bingham to say that everything in his luggage, including "several of the choice finds of the expedition which Mr. Erdis gave to me," had sunk with a ship in the New York harbor.[31] The day before, an 8,000-ton freighter emerged from the fog of the Ambrose Channel and ran aground Meserve's ship, the 5,000-ton *Metapan* of the United Fruit Company— the very same ship, curiously enough, that had carried Bingham back to New York in 1911 with the first news of Machu Picchu. The passengers were rescued, but its cargo—a snapshot of American consumption of Latin America at the time—remained in doubt: $500,000 in gold bars from Colombia, 60,000 sacks of coffee, 27,000 bunches of bananas, and not one but two sets of artifacts. One of Meserve's fellow passengers was none other than Bingham's imitator, Captain Besley, on his way back from Peru with his own collection.[32]

Besley stayed on the ship with his collection—and made sure the *New York Times* knew about it—but Meserve hadn't, outraging Bingham. "I hope very much that the trunk may be saved, both for your sake and ours, for the things which were entrusted to you by Mr. Erdis are naturally unable to be replaced," Bingham wrote to Meserve. Fortunately, Meserve learned that his trunk had also been recovered and mailed the artifacts to New Haven, apologetically. "I know how much they mean to you," he apologized to Bingham.[33]

With the artifacts before him, Bingham forgot his anger—or perhaps turned it back on himself. Here was an Inca sacrifice, a hint of the wealth and ancient ritual still hidden in Peru's mountains, and they had almost lost it at sea. Perhaps the Peruvians were right to keep their artifacts in the country, he may have thought. Bingham entered Inca Churisca's gold, silver, bronze, and bones into Yale's catalogues, alongside the Alvistur collection, but in late November, Bingham cabled Erdis not to send up any more cases of archaeological material.[34] When Bingham noted the glacial find of Inca Churisca find in *National Geographic* the following year, he only mentioned the "small wooden and bronze artifacts" and omitted the details of precious metals. Such a collection could not be admitted publicly without fear of their discovery by Peruvian collaborators.

This was the central irony of Bingham's and the Yale expedition's actions in 1914, from the Alvistur collection to the Inca Churisca artifacts: Bingham and the expedition had started collecting artifacts that they could never study, write about, or display publicly, having collected them by skirting Peruvian law. By taking them from their context, they were tainted and scientifically useless. Moreover, it meant that the expedition's men were looking over their shoulders, afraid that they might get caught building Yale's collection.

The expedition's youngest member, Bingham's assistant Osgood Hardy, especially felt the contradiction. Hardy spent the winter of 1914–15 studying Quechua in the former Inca town of Chincheros, one of the old seats of indigenous nobility. The town was high above Cuzco, where the land was green, lush, and beautiful. The old beliefs persisted. One local told Hardy that he "believed that the Sun should be worshipped."[35]

The town was so rich in history that Hardy was sorely tempted to walk away with more than the language. Hardy was staying with the local Indian magistrate, who had an "Indian drum" that he was willing to sell. But what Hardy really wanted was the town's *vara*—the silver-coated staff given by the Spanish to local Inca nobles as an emblem of their power, and which the magistrate was unlikely to sell. Hardy found the *vara*—and hid it under his bed.

"I hate to steal the blamed thing from the Gobernador for he has been pretty decent," he wrote in his journal letter to Bingham, but in "view of the difficulty of getting such things it would be a rather rare addition to the South American exhibit in Peabody."[36] As far as the archives go, Bingham never commented on Hardy's conundrum.

It was as frank as any expedition member got about Yale's temptations in Peru. But Hardy's journal also revealed that his intentions were being scrutinized in return. A week and a half before, a lesson on the word *viracocha*—a gentleman of European descent—took a curious turn. From his tutor Hardy learned that the Indians around Cuzco said Yale's expedition had been collecting Indian skulls in order to "[make] them talk."[37]

Hardy may have chuckled. In a way, getting the skulls to reveal their secrets was exactly Yale's goal. The Yale graduate's Quechua wasn't yet good enough to catch the story's full implication, however. After the execution of the first Tupac Amaru back in 1572, Peru's Indians began telling the story of how the Spaniards executed the *Inkarrí*, or Inca Rey, and then took his head to Lima where it kept talking. It was the Spaniards' possession of the Inca's head that gave them their wealth and control over the indigenous people of Peru. When that head was returned, Peru's Indians would rule once again.

In an incredible twist of history, Yale's study of the Inca past had made the expedition part of Inca legend. Bingham had been exploring the heart of Inca heritage and resistance for nearly six years, asking Indians for clues to the final refuges of Manco Inca, Titu Cusi, and Tupac Amaru, the last emperors. During those excursions he had been accompanied by soldiers and agents of the Peruvian state. The Indians made a logical connection: that Bingham and the Peruvian state were allies, and that they were collecting the Incas' bones for some larger political purpose.

But what that purpose was remained to be seen. The local Indians seemed undecided as to whether Yale's intentions were good or bad—an ambiguity that cut to the larger question of how Bingham's expeditions were understood in the countryside at the time. Did the Indians believe that the Americans were benevolent or that they were like the Spaniards, confiscating the skulls and bones of the Indian past to gain control of the present and future? Would the expedition return all it had taken? What would the Indians—and indeed, all Peruvians—do if they perceived the expedition as having broken that trust?

The young Yalie thought about the *vara* beneath his bed. "Will have to wrestle with the problem a little bit for I can't as yet make up my mind to steal it," Hardy wrote in his journal. He then dropped the dilemma for good, leaving future readers to wonder: did he or didn't he?[38]

Chapter Eighteen

Roads to Ruins

*L*ike the heroes of a boy's adventure novel, Hiram Bingham and his new dog, a handsome Airedale terrier named Checkers, bounded up the ruins of Ollantaytambo to stare out over the sacred Yucay Valley. It was April 1915, the sun was shining, and Bingham was back in the land of the Incas, on his third expedition dedicated to the secrets of Inca history.

In the modern town below was the expedition's new home base. After leaving Chincheros that winter, his assistant Osgood Hardy had rented a house in Ollantaytambo and refurbished it with workrooms, a dormitory, lavatories, a kitchen, a dining room, a storeroom, and a darkroom. This was Yale's new semipermanent archaeological institution, from which foreign expeditions could excavate Inca history. Any artifacts found would be left in either the institute or the National Museum in Lima. It was not quite an original idea—Harvard, Columbia, and the University of Pennsylvania had negotiated something similar with the Mexican government—but the plan suggested that Bingham acknowledged a future in which historical treasures stayed in Peru.[1] He had announced the plan in Lima, where it was welcomed as a victory for Peru. North American explorers had once tried to enrich their own museums, but "because they couldn't take their results from Peru, they now come to establish such a center in Peru's own territory," declared the newspaper *El Comercio*'s front page.[2] Such a center would be a site of exchange and collaboration, a place "where Peruvian and foreign students will always be welcome," Bingham wrote his contacts, who included the indigenous archaeologist Julio C. Tello.[3] Its name was Yanquihausi—House of the Yankees in gringo Quechua.

He had ridden that wave of praise to Cuzco, which had changed considerably in three years. It was now literally brighter than Bingham remembered—aglow with new electric lighting. A statue of an Indian stood in the Plaza de Armas— not an Inca, but a North American Indian that Albert Giesecke, the American head of the university, had bought from a Philadelphia ironworks.[4] The University of Cuzco invited the expedition to the formal opening of the school year. The expedition's new surgeon marveled at the ceremony the Peruvians put on. "The gold lace, swords, tall hats and canes! Great bluffers!"[5] Luis E. Valcárcel, the former student whose life had been changed by the revelation of Machu Picchu had further feted Bingham by making him an honorary member of Cuzco's Historical Institute.[6] Bingham shared the honor, however, with an individual who represented the other side of Peru's relationship to the United States: the Institute's other new honorary member was a famed ethnomusicologist named Daniel Alomía Robles, who had composed the score for the operetta *El Condor Pasa,* which depicted a struggle between Indian workers and North American owners of a mine.[7] He was a Peruvian cultural hero—and an opponent of perceived U.S. exploitation.

Bingham would learn more about Robles's sympathies soon enough. For the moment, however, he and Checkers stood atop Ollantaytambo, where Manco Inca had enjoyed his last great victory over the conquistadors nearly four hundred years before. Manco had then turned his back upon his father's lands in the sacred Yucay Valley to face his future downriver, where the straight and smooth Vilcanota became the twisting and powerful Urubamba. There, at the point where the Andes and the Amazon met, Manco founded Vilcabamba the Old. The Indians of the Vilcabamba River believed that Manco's final capital lay at Espiritu Pampa, the Plain of Ghosts.

Yet Bingham wasn't so sure. The previous fall he had developed a theory of his own, that Vilcabamba the Old was now known by yet another name: Machu Picchu.

After deciding that Machu Picchu was Tampu Tocco, the legendary cradle of Inca civilization, Bingham had struck upon a tentative chronology for the site. Predecessors of the Incas began construction in about 200 AD, he believed, and occupied the site for eight hundred years. From those predecessors emerged the "first real Inca," who then built the temple of three windows as a memorial to his origins. Nevertheless, Bingham had been puzzled by the presence of late Inca ceramics and the one European glass bead in the ruins. Had the Incas inhabited

Machu Picchu during the Spanish conquest or shortly thereafter? When had they left Machu Picchu?

The osteologist George Eaton then offered what Bingham thought was the key. After nearly two years studying Machu Picchu's ceramics and bones, Eaton declared that their origins lay throughout the Andes—reflecting the Inca practice of enlisting subjugated peoples as *yanaconas*, skilled servants of the nobility. Bingham was more fascinated by Eaton's second finding, however: that perhaps 150 of the 173 human remains from Machu Picchu were female—as if the city's final inhabitants were mostly women and a few high-born men.

Like a thunderbolt, Eaton's finding reminded Bingham of the story that drew him into Inca history back in 1909, at the Cradle of Gold—that the Inca's last city was the final resting place of the priests and the so-called Virgins of the Sun, the women who from an early age served the Inca religion and who supposedly slowly died out during the Spanish conquest. With unnerving eagerness, Bingham feverishly knit the clues together—the incredible preservation of Machu Picchu, the higher proportion of women. Had Manco Inca gone to Machu Picchu after the Spanish sack of Vitcos, expanding it to give refuge to his religious officiates? As he phrased it to readers of *National Geographic* that February, "Is it possible that at Machu Picchu we have the ruins of Tampu-tocco"—the legendary birthplace of the Incas—"and *also* the ruins of Vilcabamba-the-Old, the sacred city of one of the last Incas and the home of his women and priests?"[8]

The theory was a stretch—it made little sense for Manco to establish his final refuge even closer to Cuzco than Vitcos—but it was just the kind of imaginative and literary interpretation that Bingham loved. Machu Picchu was the beautiful Dulcinea to his Don Quixote, and he was enchanted by the poetic possibility that it was both the cradle and grave of the Incas. In this expedition, Hiram would search for the landmarks and roads that would prove his case. The vanguard had reported a few trails that might connect Ollantaytambo to Machu Picchu and Machu Picchu to Vitcos. The rest of the expedition would map and excavate—showing "just what was accomplished in the Western World for progress and civilization before our European ancestors called themselves in to take up the task," declared one enchanted Boston paper. Bingham would focus on retracing the path of Manco's final flight once and for all.[9]

Leaving Ollantaytambo, he and his team faced a choice: ride along the government trail on the right side of the Urubamba River, as they had so many times in the past, or cross a suspension bridge and take a trail that Bingham "had often looked at . . . longingly."[10] They chose the latter option, and a day's ride took them to Patallacta (City on the Hill), where Erdis and six Indian laborers were already hard at work.

While Bingham explored this year, his archaeological engineer would be clearing bush and mapping ruins near Machu Picchu, beginning with Patallacta. In contrast to the forced labor of past years, this year's workers were there by choice—or so Bingham saw it through his rose-colored glasses. "It is easier and pleasanter all around," Bingham wrote to his wife, adding that he now viewed the Indians as "really good citizens . . . patient and steady." With their help, Erdis would carry out light excavation to collect bones and potsherds that might clarify the region's chronology. What they had found thus far suggested that Patallacta was a late Inca agricultural site, whose terraces may have once fed Machu Picchu.

There were the usual artifacts—bronze, silver, and bone needles and pins—but their real interest was in human remains. From one cave, Erdis pulled 200 skulls and at least half a dozen mummies—one wrapped in brown and blue cloth, its arms clawing at its face, as if caught in midscream. They photographed Erdis standing in the midst of his haul, skulls piled at his feet, his arms full of bones. From another cave, Bingham got 20 skulls and the limbs of a dozen mummies. There had been more, but his Indian workers had burned the mummies' wrappings to kill the cave's bats before he arrived. Bingham tied a bandana around his mouth, crawled inside, and saved what he could, avoiding the dead, leathery wings on the floor. "It was dirty work but we got a fine haul," he wrote home, "enough to keep [George Eaton] busy some time—if he wants to come down here. Does he? The bones and mummies are now all here, resting comfortably in the archaeological room. Oh, if only we could have got there before the bonfire."[11]

Leaving Erdis on May 6, Bingham, Osgood Hardy, and Ricardo Charaja—the discoverer of the Inca Churisca artifacts—continued into the mountains, hoping that the path would take them to Machu Picchu. From above, Bingham could see just how many terraces lined the canyon's walls—evidence that the Urubamba had at one time supported a large population. They camped one night by a deafening stream and then hacked away at a path that had fallen into disuse. Trees and bushes whipped at their faces until they emerged from the woods onto an old Inca trail paved with smooth stones. Up and up it climbed, until they reached a 13,880-foot notch between two summits—later known as Warmiwañusca or Dead Woman's Pass.

The view beyond was rapturous. Waterfalls tumbled into a deep, quiet valley filled with rare gray deer, and two Inca trails climbed into the mountains beyond. They camped that night at a small but fascinating Inca ruin, "circular in form, with two large semi-circular houses, a narrow entrance passage from the hillside, lock-holes, and a little circular patio, balustraded by a low wall and overlooking the valley." This was Runcu Raccay, said the Indians, who knew these paths, having followed them for years. Bingham speculated that it was a fortified inn on the old highway to Machu Picchu. "We pitched our tent in the court, and enjoyed the lovely view, which the Incas had done before us."

The next day, the trail took them to "two pretty little lakes in the clouds" and a pass that framed the snowy mountains of the Vilcabamba. After a thousand-foot drop, the road forked yet again. The expedition took the path to the left, which climbed to another fortress-like set of ruins on a sharp ridge. Later called Sayacmarca, the ruins were defined by a curious horseshoe-shaped building with nine windows. A single staircase controlled access to the site and the trail beyond. Bingham imagined Incas pitching invaders onto the sharp rocks below. After a wet night, they continued on. The Indians again hacked away at the jungle-choked path ahead, putting in bridges when necessary. They shuffled through a tunnel the Incas had carved from the rock face. On the other side, Bingham caught a glimpse of the "grand canyon of the Urubamba . . . and in the distance the familiar outlines of Machu Picchu mountain—but oh so far below us!"

"We were on the right track," the jubilant explorer wrote to his wife. "Only follow the ridge—and we could see the line of the trail and we would eventually reach Machu Picchu. But what was this in the immediate foreground! First a flat round-topped hill fringed by a fine wall, and below it, in a green secluded dell, beautiful terraces and the ruins of a series of bath-houses—a fine cut stone gateway and houses under a dense jungle. We learned afterwards it is called Ccorihuayrachina or the place where gold is washed. It was a complete surprise." Beside the fountains was a massive boulder, slightly carved and surrounded by swamp—much like the white stone shrine of Yurak Rumi. Bingham was sure they were close. They followed the old Inca path along the ridge until Machu Picchu itself swung into heart-stopping view.

Bingham became the first foreigner to complete the now-famous Inca Trail to Machu Picchu and the first to document the beautiful ruins along its route. As later scholars have pointed out, there was something almost ritualistic about the trail's slow revelation of Machu Picchu—as if the four days of trekking over passes and secluded valleys gave the peace of mind and spiritual preparation that the Urubamba below denied and that Machu Picchu demanded.

The next day, May 13, 1915, he "climbed up to dear old Machu Picchu" and "nearly wept to see how it had gone back to jungle and brush. Even the Sacred Plaza was so dense we had to cut our way into it with a machete."[12] He hadn't seen it in two and a half years. It was a quieter place than it had been before: Fuentes, Alvarez, and their families remained at the ruins, but from the photographs Bingham took, it looked like no one was farming. Richarte and his family had moved to the river below.[13] The authorities had named Richarte the site's caretaker, and the money that came from the state had changed his life.[14] As Yale had shown him, archaeology was big business.

Having confirmed that Manco could have easily fled to Machu Picchu from Cuzco, Bingham set out to prove that the ruins were linked to Vitcos, Manco's white palace—and thus could be Vilcabamba the Old as well. He and Hardy left on May 27 and began the long, cold haul around the glacier-covered peak of Salcantay. They woke up in the mornings with ice in their water buckets, climbed in and out of valleys, and pushed through 16,000-foot-high forests. It was "wonderful new scenery," but it yielded no confirmation that Machu Picchu was also the grave of the Incas, as much as Bingham tried to force the evidence. At a lake named Yanaccocha, Bingham swore that the guide called it "Ungacacha"—the boggy place where the Spanish missionaries fell in the mud on their way to Vilcabamba the Old. Bingham so desperately wanted Machu Picchu to be Vilcabamba the Old that he decided that the friars had gotten the name wrong like him—that their bog was actually Yanaccocha.

When he arrived in the town of Puquiura on June 5, Bingham thus believed he had finally completed the task he set himself in 1911: to find Manco's last cities. He felt renewed. Unlike his last visit to Puquiura, there was no smallpox and the weather was good. He rode up to Vitcos, Manco's first palace in exile, where he had sent Erdis to excavate, hoping that past tomb raiders had left a little for Yale. Erdis found the usual assortment of Inca artifacts, bronze knives, and pins—19 boxes worth—but the great surprise was the discovery of Spanish artifacts alongside those of the Inca: iron nails, pieces of horseshoes, scissors, copper pins, iron hooks, a bronze button, a small stick of red sealing wax, a bowl of a rough brown pottery pipe, even three Jew's harps. "Who would ever have thought of such things?"

Erdis asked his journal.[15] Either Spaniards had inhabited the hill after the Incas' fall or these were the European goods that Manco's family or people enjoyed in exile, brought by the occasional Spanish visitor or achieved through trade. Had the Spaniard who stabbed Manco smoked this pipe? Had Titu Cusi's scribe used this wax to seal their messages to the viceroy?

Bingham felt a sense of victory. On June 9 he surprised his assistant, Hardy, with a birthday dinner in Vitcos's ruins. A few feet from where Manco was stabbed by the Spaniards and Titu Cusi fell ill and died, Bingham and his men feasted and drank cranberry juice spiked with cane liquor. Sitting in ruins, they toasted history, themselves, and their great shared adventure in Peru. Erdis recorded the moment: when darkness fell, a slightly drunk Bingham and Hardy made their way to their tent, Erdis recorded, "escorted by our faithful Benigno who kept their feet from straying from the crooked and narrow path by the aid of a one candle power lantern, they returned to their camp to dream of—who knows what?"[16]

Six days later, Bingham's larger dream—of exploration, Incas, and archaeology—was over for good.

Chapter Nineteen

The Trial of
Hiram Bingham

*W*hile the Yale expedition feasted at Vitcos, Hiram Bingham's future in Peruvian exploration began to fall apart. In 1912, Bingham had been accused of trying to "monopolize" Peruvian history, starting a new debate among Peruvians over the direction of the country's archaeology. In 1914, to get around Peruvian law, Bingham had paid an antiquarian to smuggle artifacts for him, and his vanguard had sneaked artifacts out of Peru in their luggage. This year, Bingham had set up his semipermanent institute in Ollantaytambo to make a fresh start. Yet while he was exploring, all of his transgressions, real and imagined, and all of Peru's fears, valid and not, came back to haunt him.

Rumors reached Cuzco that Yale had closed its Ollantaytambo institute to Peruvians and that it was abusing Indian laborers. Concerned Cuzco residents sent worried telegrams to Peru's president and the government in Lima. They whispered that Yale was excavating, that gold and silver idols had been found, and that hundreds of mules had smuggled that treasure out of the valley and to the United States. A public meeting on the subject was overwhelmed with "feverish accusations."[1] The minister of Justice and Education ordered the prefect of Cuzco to halt Bingham's work, but Bingham was in the field and could not be reached. The nation's top newspaper, *El Comercio*, went in for the kill: it wondered if Peru "would become the only country in the world without Peruvian antiquities."[2]

Luis Valcárcel decided to get to the bottom of the rumors. He had founded Cuzco's Historical Institute in 1913 for this very purpose: to protect the region's monuments from illicit excavation and smuggling. As the Institute's director, he had become a person of influence within Peru's developing archaeological community. Although Valcárcel had honored Bingham with membership in his society only two months before, he also edited *El Sol,* which had published many of the charges against the expedition. He was sympathetic to Bingham—Valcárcel had no problem identifying Bingham as Machu Picchu's "discoverer"—and seemed to have doubted the early rumors.[3] He was also a serious young man, however, and as ambitious as Bingham. If Yale was excavating, Peruvian law said they needed a monitor. If his Historical Institute investigated, he might get to work with Bingham, arbitrating between a prestigious North American institution and Cuzco's peasants, sifting through rumor and fact.

He departed on June 10 with three older members of the institute, including a Jesuit priest and Cuzco's elder statesman for indigenous rights, Dr. Angel Vega Enríquez, who hinted that he descended from Inca nobility.[4] In the towns of Urubamba and Ollantaytambo, the denunciations grew yet more sensational: that the expedition had smuggled out two hundred crates containing tunics woven with gold suns from Machu Picchu, gold rings, gold pitchers, and mummies filled with gold. But there were also flashes of truth: although the expedition paid its workers comparatively high salaries, their military escorts encouraged Indians to trade artifacts to the expedition for beads, mirrors, and whistles.

As Bingham found before them, Valcárcel and his colleagues learned why the coercive sale of artifacts may have upset the locals. One night, Valcárcel asked a local Indian farmer what he could tell them about the Incas. "Yes, of course, *señor,*" said the Indian. "They are our ancestors." He went on to tell the story of the last Incas of Cuzco, how they had fled through the Urubamba on the tops of the mountains, turning stone into bread as they went. "And where were they headed?" Valcárcel asked. "To the interior, *señor,* to the jungle," responded the Indian—an oral tradition, perhaps, of Manco Inca's flight to Vilcabamba.[5]

The Indians also told Valcárcel what they thought Yale was doing with mummies: reviving them to help Chile attack Peru, its long-time rival.[6] Intellectuals and peasants in the southern Andes were surging with pride in the Incas during the 1910s, mobilizing and rebelling around their memory; the idea that North Americans were resurrecting Inca ancestors as enemies of Peruvian people was thus particularly horrific.[7] In the eyes of Manco's former people—who had been forced to work for the North Americans, and perhaps remembered the boy who had died in the expedition's care—Bingham and his men had completed their transformation. As one American writer later unironically labeled Bingham, they were now "Conquistadors without Swords."[8]

Valcárcel did not know what to believe. At first, he dismissed the rumors of gold that swirled around almost any excavation. But on Monday, June 14, he saw Patallacta, the ruins from which Ellwood C. Erdis had pulled 200 skulls and at least half a dozen mummies. Valcárcel was shocked: it looked like Yale had been excavating without supervision on a massive scale, breaking Peruvian law. Erdis's rough test pits looked like "innumerable" holes to Valcárcel, poorly filled in and destabilizing the site's walls. Where vines and growth had been torn from the buildings, stones had already started to fall. It seemed less like a careful excavation than a brutal treasure hunt. "They've excavated so as not to leave a single potsherd," he scrawled angrily in his small yellow journal. "More than 200 excavations!"[9] Valcárcel shared Yale's definition of worth: everything was precious, to the humblest bone, and Yale had left nothing for the next generation of scholars. And if the tales of Yale's excavations were true, then what of the smuggling? What else had Yale done?

On June 15, Bingham and Hardy returned to Yanquihausi. They had barely settled in when a Cuzco soldier entered to announce that Valcárcel's commission had denounced Yale to Peru's superior court, charging that they had violated the decrees that forbade unauthorized excavation and prohibited the export of artifacts of any kind.

Bingham's journal entries that day were terse, but his reaction to the news is easy to imagine. Unlike the United States, which draws from English traditions of common law, Peruvian law draws from the civil traditions of the Napoleonic code. Under the Peruvian system, a case can begin with an accusation and not necessarily the observation of a crime. The accusation leads to an investigation by a public *fiscal* (prosecutor). The person under suspicion has great latitude in his or her defense, but the process can go on without a conclusive trial, during which time previously unsuspected crimes can emerge.

Bingham thus could hardly have been relieved to learn that Yale had been accused of smuggling gold artifacts from Patallacta and Machu Picchu. Upon questioning Erdis, he realized that Yale had indeed been excavating without a permit—that in 1914 Erdis visited every single government agency except the one whose approval he needed—the Ministry of Justice and Education. "[A]ccordingly we have actually been breaking the law by our digging at all, and if they want to they can make it very nasty for us," Hardy lamented.[10]

There was no room for guilt. Bingham refused to show the soldier the expedition's boxes. When Bingham learned that Valcárcel's commission was still in

Ollantaytambo, Bingham sent a soldier over to fetch them and then in a polite but tense conversation tried to explain himself. Bingham admitted they had excavated, but not at Machu Picchu or Ollantaytambo. They found no gold and only one silver shawl pin, he said, and had exported absolutely nothing.

Valcárcel's commission left on friendly terms, but the next morning Bingham learned that they had found four artifact-filled boxes left in the care of a local farmer and confiscated them as "evidence." Bingham exploded with rage. In all his years of exploration, no Latin American had ever laid hands on "his" collections without his permission. He set off for Cuzco immediately, unable to enjoy the view of the Sacred Valley behind him, disappearing in the clouds of an unusually wet dry season. As he rode, he perhaps tried not to think about what would happen if the Historical Institute expanded its investigations and discovered the artifacts that Alvistur and Erdis had taken out the year before. "Life: some call it luck," he scrawled in the front cover of his notebook, like a prayer.[11]

Rain battered the windows of the Hotel Central. Inside, Bingham scanned recent headlines, anxious at the gravity of the situation. *El Sol* alleged the Historical Institute had "proved" the charges against Yale.[12] The rumors in Cuzco were worse: Yale had supposedly used a steam shovel from the American construction of the Panama Canal to dig out between five hundred thousand and five million dollars worth of Inca gold from Machu Picchu and had then smuggled it out through Bolivia in more than 500 boxes.[13]

In public Bingham asserted that the charges represented a witch hunt and an attempt to embarrass the conservative government in Lima. He declared that the expedition's goal was purely scientific research; that Yale and *National Geographic* had spent far more than could ever be recouped by speculating in antiquities; that his articles on Machu Picchu had made Peru famous in 400,000 American households.[14] Suggesting that Peru's government hardly supported Yale as much as Bingham claimed, the president of the British-run Peruvian Corporation felt the need to tell Lima's officials "in the plainest kind of English, that what had occurred was a disgrace to any country pretending to be at all civilised [sic], and that if they did not wish to have the world look upon them as savages," they should appoint a monitor to clear Yale of the charges and let the expedition continue its work.[15]

Peru wasn't a colonial possession, however, and its government proved difficult to intimidate. The rumors even reached Vitcos, where Erdis was finishing his excavations. There was "much feeling against H.B." among the indigenous Peruvians who lived in the shadow of Manco's palace; even the expedition's friends believed the expedition was "taking out treasure, but [was] too smart to get caught."[16] Peru's Indian peasants were mobilizing against outsider landlords attempting to take their lands; the resistance to Bingham may have been part and parcel of their rising rage.[17]

Valcárcel refuted the charge that Yale had dug at Machu Picchu that year, but restated the fact that they had dug elsewhere without permission or oversight.[18] It was the test of everything he had been working for: whether he and his fellow Peruvians would take responsibility for their historical monuments and stop foreigners from excavating without oversight in the belief that elites in Lima would look the other way. He respected Bingham, but he also believed that Bingham was using his discoveries as a free pass to cover up all his errors, minor and major. As a resident of Cuzco, as a critic of North American influence upon Lima and Peru, and as a concerned academic who believed that Yale had broke Peru's trust, he would stand in Yale's way.

Bingham felt the reality of the situation sink in. Until the expedition's crates were opened and a monitor was appointed, he was "a semi-prisoner in Cuzco," neither able to explore nor clear his name.[19] He felt angry, self-righteous, and nervous. Although he thought himself innocent of true wrongdoing, the expedition had side-stepped and even broken Peruvian law. They had excavated without a permit, and if the Peruvians turned up evidence of his secret collecting the year before, his expeditions could be stopped for good. Bingham could be ejected from Peru—or worse.

Stuck in limbo, his mind may have reeled backward over his decade as an explorer. He had walked in the footsteps of Simón Bolívar, crossed the Andes two times over, and ridden Butch and Sundance's final mount. He had revealed Machu Picchu, which he had come to think was the cradle and grave of America's greatest indigenous empire. Despite all his successes, if word got back to the United States that he was nonetheless viewed as a smuggler in the field, his reputation would be ruined. The 1912 controversy over Yale's "monopoly" had damaged him enough, and this time around, he had no great discovery to distract his critics: the Inca trail to Machu Picchu was not enough, nor had he truly proved that Machu Picchu was Vilcabamba the Old. He began "suffering a considerable amount of mental depression," he wrote to a colleague. He spent days in bed, his guts in a knot.[20]

After two weeks of agony, Cuzco's prefect announced in the city's newspapers that there would be a hearing on July 1. Part inquest, part theater, the prefect and the *fiscal* would hear Valcárcel's accusations, Bingham's defense, and open the expedition's boxes to determine what it could of the truth. It was not a trial like in the United States, but it was as close as the expedition would get. Specifically, it would determine whether Yale had violated the executive orders governing excavation and prohibiting exportation. But at its heart were questions that went beyond the law: Had Yale conducted itself in good faith or in bad? Had it opened Inca history or hid it behind closed doors?

On the day of the inquest, just before three in the afternoon, Bingham and Hardy stepped out of the Hotel Central wearing their city best. They ducked their heads against the cold and walked past the home of the great Inca chronicler Garcilaso de la Vega without a sideways glance. When they reached the prefecture's arched promenade, they doffed their hats and stepped inside.

The wooden crates were lying in state in the prefecture's inner portico, and the participants in the inquest stood around them. In addition to Bingham, Hardy, and the prefect, there was Valcárcel, "the Inca" Vega Enríquez, the North American head of Cuzco's university, Albert Giesecke, Cuzco's mayor, and the *fiscal,* who was none other than Pancorbo—the cruel landowner who had failed to keep Bingham from seeing Espiritu Pampa and its Indian residents. When the reporters arrived, it was time to begin.

The prefect gave the signal, and two soldiers armed with screwdrivers took off the top of the first box. For a moment, everyone held their breath, then the soldier pulled away the packing paper, revealing a load of broken ceramics. Valcárcel let out "[a] gasp of delight" and fell upon the box, pulling out a potsherd to show to the crowd—proof that Yale had been excavating without government permission.[21]

Yet the Peruvian officials were little impressed. They grew up thinking of "treasure" as gold and silver. If Bingham thought he could get money for artifacts like these, then he was a fool. Bingham stepped in, pointed out that each potsherd was numbered, and made great pains to explain the scientific manner in which they would be studied. Pancorbo absent-mindedly nodded that the next box could be opened.

With a little less anticipation, the soldiers opened the second box, revealing a collection of bones—"and a poor assortment at that," scoffed Hardy. The newspaper reporters lost interest. Although it was clear that Yale was excavating, they too believed that smuggled treasure meant gold and silver. Peru was in a financial crisis and political unrest was rampant; perhaps there were better uses of their time than peering over a foreign explorer's shoulder.

"The third act, as in all good melodramas, produced the climax," wrote Hardy. The third box was labeled "specials." After the soldiers pried open its lid, Bingham reached inside and with a gentle flourish pulled away the packing to reveal a single unbroken pot, a bronze tool, and a bone shawl pin. Valcárcel emphasized their historical importance, "but was foiled by the Director's appeal to the jury which unanimously agreed on the first ballot that the pot would not bring fifty cents in Cuzco," Hardy crowed. Valcárcel did his best, holding up the artifacts to impress their great value upon his countrymen, but to little avail. He was talking as an idealistic and earnest scholar, but Bingham spoke to the egos of "civilized" men like Pancorbo, who made their fortunes on the backs of Indian labor and believed their potsherds and bones to be worthless.

They all filed into the prefect's salon, where Bingham gave his final defense. Far more was on the line than had ever been when he debated for Yale as an undergraduate. The moment for guilt and self-doubt had passed. He summarized his entire career as an explorer. He alluded to his experience in Venezuela when he was accused of espionage and declared that Peruvians also seemed to be unable to believe that anyone would spend money on exploration without hope of financial gain. He buried them in his affiliations, from the American Historical Association to London's Royal Geographic Society. Could such a man suddenly turn into a "criminal trader of Inca treasure"? He had excavated without a permit this year, it was true, but he had intended to leave everything in the country. If Peru wanted him to halt his work, he would. "I can assure you that you will never be bothered again by me or any of my boxes."[22] Inside, Hardy cheered.

It was Valcárcel's turn. He was shocked to see fellow Peruvians nod during Bingham's speech. Faced with the proof that Yale had defied Peru's prohibitions on excavation, they were swayed by Bingham's rhetoric and his claim—however false—that the Yale expedition was no longer interested in building a museum. Valcárcel had once cheered the Yale expedition's efforts. Now, he was disturbed by the ease with which Bingham acquitted himself by alluding to his own American largesse and by accusing him of opportunism. His Instituto Histórico was merely trying to hold Bingham to the letter of Peruvian law. He pointed out that Yale had not yet lived up to its 1912 agreement regarding the Machu Picchu artifacts. Why was the expedition back in Cuzco performing *more* research when Bingham had yet to publish an academic account of his first site? It was a sharp critique, but Valcárcel grew agitated and emotional, Hardy claimed, and his speech sputtered out. He sat down, exhausted.

At that very moment, a "suprise witness" got up to speak: Daniel Alomía Robles, the champion of Inca music. He shocked those gathered by revealing the impetus for the investigation. It started with the archaeologist Julio C. Tello, who had left Peru's National Museum earlier that year, having angered the capital's white intellectuals in a series of debates over the nature of Peruvian history.[23] In February, Tello got Hiram Bingham's letter announcing Yale's new semipermanent archaeological institute, "where Peruvian and foreign students will always be welcome."[24] Inspired or perhaps just curious, Tello tried to visit the Ollantaytambo institute. But when he arrived, whichever expedition members were there—it was likely Hardy—refused to let him in, perhaps doubting that a person of Tello's darker skin color could be an archaeologist. Either way, Yale's expedition was excluding Peruvians from their work. When Alomía Robles heard the story, along with the rumors of excavating and smuggling generated by the Indians around Ollantaytambo, he pushed the government into action. Alomía Robles had wanted to be the expedition's monitor, but he also believed he was following Peruvian law.

There was an awkward quiet. The Peruvians could only prove that the expedition had excavated without authorization; they would not be able to prove that Bingham and his men found gold and silver, bought Peruvian collections, or smuggled it all out of the country. Instead, what had brought the expedition to this crisis was far more symbolic: the expedition's likely racist exclusion of Tello, the indigenous future of Andean archaeology. Bingham's free fall was as much about prejudice as it was about broken rules.

The inquest was over, but without conclusion. Bingham was not cleared of the charges nor was any sort of judgment handed down. The *fiscal,* Pancorbo, explained that because Valcárcel's Historical Institute had started a legal procedure—one that had indeed shown that Yale excavated without a license—"justice would have to follow its regular course," and the investigation would continue. The government would still have to appoint a monitor who would observe the expedition's excavations and investigate the claims of smuggling at Peru's southern border.

Everyone shuffled out into the chilly Cuzco dusk. To cheer Bingham up, Hardy took him to the movies. Even that failed—the audience was full of Germans cheering their country's victories in Europe. The Americans slunk back to their hotel and went to sleep.

Bingham rode back to Ollantaytambo and canceled further excavation. He was so dejected that he observed the next day, July 4, by yanking up Old Glory and playing cards until midnight—a pastime he had avoided on all his expeditions until now. The next day, he tried to snap out of his funk by lighting out to Machu Picchu for one last visit. With his collar turned up against the unseasonable rain, he pondered the ruins, nearly invisible in the vines that now seemed to choke his dreams as well. He doubted he would ever return, wondering whether this was the closest he would come to solving the mystery of virgins, priests, conquistadors, and empires that had haunted his life these last six years.

The excavations never resumed. Although the Historical Institute chose Valcárcel and Vega Enríquez, "the Inca," as the monitors, Cuzco's prefect never paid them, and without payment they refused to work, effectively putting Yale's explorations in check. Exasperated, Bingham traveled to Cuzco and said his goodbyes. On his last night in the city, he watched a performance of Ollantay, a Quechua play about an Inca general who fell in love with the daughter of the Inca Pachacutec. The actors used U.S.-made machetes and headdresses that looked more Sioux than Inca, but those smaller ironies didn't prevent Bingham from keeping the program for his archives, a souvenir of the spectacle his life had become.

Before leaving the country, however, he got his chance to smile in the face of his accusers. Bingham, Hardy, and a few other members of the expedition left Cuzco, but not the Andes. They spent a week traveling south to Bolivia, and at Lake Titicaca they found that Valcárcel and Vega Enriquez had followed them to investigate the claims of smuggling. The duo had been unable to prove anything, and Valcárcel seemed to regret how intense the accusations had become.[25] Yet when they tried to join the expedition on a special boat tour of the Isla del Sol, covered with Inca ruins, the boat's captain forced them ashore along with the rest of the Peruvians. "They were a sheepish looking pair," the expedition's surgeon wrote home victoriously.[26] Valcárcel and Vega Enríquez watched the Americans steam away to enjoy the Inca past in ways they themselves were denied.

Bingham took the train to Mollendo, then a ship up to Lima, where he spent a week negotiating his departure. Because the expedition remained under investigation by the Peruvian government, it was too delicate a situation for the American consulate, which still smarted from the embarrassment of helping Bingham try to secure exclusive rights to Peru's archaeology in 1912. The explorer had to turn to his friends in the British business community to ensure his exit.

He would not go empty-handed, however. One irony of Bingham's notoriety that year was that antiquarians throughout the country had been writing to him to offer him sympathy—and their collections.[27] Peruvians were clearly of two minds when it came to these new prohibitions on excavation and exportation. Bingham chose not to respond to the letters, but in Lima he was angered enough by his treatment that he threw all caution to the wind and met with a collector who wanted to sell him a collection of ceramics from Nazca, on the southern Peruvian coast. "It proved to be very good stuff," wrote Hardy, ever Bingham's Boswell, "and the Director agreed to buy it if he could get it out all right, and the fellow, Ribeyro by name, promised that as his brother was in the customs house there would be no trouble at all."[28] Because Bingham's name was by now a red flag, Ribeyro consigned them to J. P. Simmons, New York. "It seems to me a strange thing to do," Bingham later wrote to a shipping agent once the pieces arrived in New York, apparently feeling little to no guilt, "—to consign the goods to a fictitious character like J. P. Simmons, but I suppose they thought it was necessary under the circumstances. The question is, how is Yale University to get hold of the shipment, when it has been consigned to J. P. Simmons?"

The shipping agent would oblige, and the artifacts would be sent by train to New Haven. Bingham had spent $25,000 (at least $480,000 today) on items for Yale's museum that Peru would never be able to trace. It would be his secret legacy, long after he had passed on.[29]

On August 19, 1915, Bingham and Hardy worked to get the expedition through customs. Hardy was nervous: "the Superintendent [threw] cold chills into me by wondering if he really should look at it all to see if we had some antiquities," he wrote.[30]

The ship left Peruvian waters that evening. As to whether Bingham looked back, Hardy's journal didn't say.

Chapter Twenty

Airborne

*I*t was October 2, 1915, and Yale's campus was noisy with undergraduates strolling to their third day of classes and boasting about their summers. Inside Room 2 of Lampson Hall, however, an awkward quiet reigned. Hiram Bingham shuffled his lecture notes and looked out over the half-filled seats of the classroom. He resigned himself to the fact that no additional students would be taking his hastily-planned course on South American history that fall. It was Bingham's first year as a full professor, but after the collapse of his exploring career in Peru, the achievement felt anticlimactic.

He believed he had done nothing wrong, but when word got out of his return to New Haven months ahead of schedule, his critics at Yale showed him little sympathy. One Peabody Museum board member told Bingham he sympathized with the Peruvians, "considering past education and the trying financial conditions under which the country now exists."[1]

Humiliated, Bingham tried to clear his name by providing New Haven's newspapers with copies of the *West Coast Leader,* an English-run Peruvian newspaper that had defended Yale. As reprinted in the *Yale Daily News,* the *Leader* ridiculed the "infamous lie" that Bingham was "shipping plate and 'pieces of eight' out of the country in ships freighted down like the golden galleons of Spain." Valcárcel was a "youthful nonentity" who had falsely accused an upstanding explorer, the *Leader* continued. "The authorities at Cuzco have succeeded handsomely in placing themselves on the same intellectual plane as the 'witch doctors' and 'medicine men' of the Congo, warning their people against 'white man's magic.'"[2]

No American newspapers reprinted Valcárcel's side of the argument, but Bingham considered raising his attempt to clear his name to a national level, fearing that rumors were already circling. Gilbert Grosvenor, his editor at *National Geographic*, talked him out of it, however. Grosvenor had recently spoken to another renowned South American explorer who had been shocked that Bingham had returned to Peru at all, given how he had bad-mouthed the country after the concession fiasco in 1912. "I realize all the facts are on your side, but you can't make the public realize the justice of your statements," Grosvenor wrote. "My advice is, don't do anything that will retract from the brilliance of your Machu Picchu discovery. [It] will loom larger every successive year."[3]

Bingham also kept quiet because he still had an iron in the fire in Peru. When he left in late August, it was without the bones and ceramics Yale had collected at Patallacta and Manco's palace at Vitcos: 74 boxes, filled with two tons of history. Bingham had originally intended to keep them at the semipermanent institute in Ollantaytambo, but now that his career in Peru was over, other arrangements had to be made. "As I do not expect to do any more work in Cuzco I want to get out everything that I possibly can," Bingham wrote to Ellwood Erdis, who was still in Peru.[4]

The problem was that Peru's Ministry of Education was enforcing controls upon excavation and exportation as strictly as it could. That fall, the government ordered two other archaeological excavators to turn over their finds to the National Museum.[5] From August on, Erdis waited for Bingham's business friends to get the Peruvian government to grant Yale permission to at least bring the collection to Lima for inspection by the National Museum's director. It took four and a half months to get it, during which time Erdis increasingly felt like Bingham had run away and left him holding the bag. It was "the hardest and most disagreeable job of my life," he later complained.[6]

When the artifacts arrived in Lima, however, the museum's director, Emilio Gutierrez de Quintanilla, understood the significance of what he saw. To start with, Yale seemed to have picked Cuzco clean. Like Luis Valcárcel, Gutierrez recognized the value of trepanned skulls and syphilitic bones, packets of mummy wrappings, stone weapons, tools, and colonial-era artifacts. They were the scientific treasure of the present. Yet Erdis was vague on the details that made such artifacts valuable, for example, at what level they were found and in what context. As a scholar, Gutierrez was horrified. In his final report, he blasted the Peruvian government for even considering letting the artifacts out of the country when Yale had yet to return the artifacts from Machu Picchu. He compared Bingham and his men to Pizarro and his conquistadors, traveling Peru in search of antiquities, looting the Inca past for Spain.[7]

The report appeared in Peru's largest newspaper, terrifying the government. Yale's corner responded by beginning a whisper campaign against Gutierrez, accusing him of selling off skulls that his rival, Julio C. Tello, had collected. The logjam finally broke when Erdis and the expedition's business friends threatened to shame Peru in the pages of *National Geographic*.[8] Erdis received a government decree, specially worded "so as to evade the law," that allowed the entire collection to go to Yale on the condition that they be returned to Peru at the expedition's expense in 18 months' time, with a full copy of the results of the study.[9] Valcárcel followed the affair from Cuzco and later registered his approval of the measure: like the artifacts from Machu Picchu, the artifacts from Vitcos belonged to Peru.[10] Erdis left on February 3, sick of the Andes. The two tons of bones and potsherds followed in his wake.

Bingham dismissed the entire display as "a sop to the multitude to show . . . how careful the politicians are of their archaeological treasures!"[11] But in truth, Gutierrez was more right than he knew. Although the potsherds and bones from the area around Patallacta had been carefully numbered, Erdis had botched the excavation at Vitcos. Unlike George Eaton, the osteologist who had made the graves of Machu Picchu so valuable, Erdis had failed to take detailed notes or diagrams of where he had dug, and he had let the artifacts get jumbled together. Thus, because of their haphazard collection, the artifacts from Vitcos—where both Manco and his son Titu Cusi faced their final hours—were rendered mute. Bingham never studied the artifacts from Vitcos, proving the Peruvians' worst suspicions correct. If the discovery of Vitcos was among Bingham's finest moments as an archaeological explorer, then its excavation may have been his worst. Entombed in Yale's basement, unlabelled, the artifacts of Vitcos would gather dust and lose all meaning. Manco's empire in exile died not once, but twice: this time by clumsy trowels, not swords.

Although Bingham blamed Peru, he also had second thoughts as to Yale's need for artifacts. "I cannot help wishing that we had never attempted to bring this stuff out, but had contented ourselves with leaving it peacefully in the mountains," Bingham wrote to his friend, the president of the English-run Peruvian Corporation, William Morkill.[12]

On March 25, 1916, Hiram delivered his final lecture on the Incas to National Geographic Society members in Washington.[13] He spoke of Manco, of Tupac Amaru, of the supposed Virgins of the Sun. The *Washington Times* covered it; the

Washington Post, more concerned with the war in Europe, didn't. It was the end of an era for public interest in the study of indigenous peoples in the Americas. Explorers across the globe shelved their efforts to decode languages and find lost cities and enlisted for Germany, France, and England. In Central America, Sylvanus Morley used his cover as an archaeologist to spy for the U.S. Office of Naval Intelligence, searching for German bases and anti-American sentiment. And on the very same day that Bingham gave his lecture, Ishi, the "last free survivor of the Red Man" who had emerged from the Sierra Nevada the same summer that Bingham had revealed Machu Picchu, died in a San Francisco hospital of tuberculosis. In an even more dramatic parallel to Machu Picchu's story, the doctors attending him ignored the protests of Ishi's friend, the anthropologist Alfred Kroeber, sawed off the top of Ishi's skull and removed his brain. Torn, Kroeber then sent it to the Smithsonian "skull czar" Aleš Hrdlička—the anthropologist who warned Bingham of Tello. Hrdlička placed Ishi's brain in a tank for future study.[14]

Bingham's charges were not so easily dispatched. He had built his career around Peruvian exploration, and his lasting obligations reminded him of Peru's "unjust" accusations—and perhaps his own hubris. Everywhere he turned there were reminders of Peru. When he fled the Andes that August, he "brought [with him] a Quechua Indian," Ricardo Charaja, the *arriero* who discovered the Inca Churisca artifacts and the Inca Trail. It seems to have been more as a reward for Charaja's allegiance—the only Peruvian ever to be listed as an expedition member—than an extension of Bingham's collector impulse, but it is hard to know. "Ricardo seems to be enjoying himself and is making progress with English," Hardy wrote soon after their return to New Haven. "He has already made himself fairly familiar with the town and will soon be quite at home." Charaja took a room on Crown Street, paying its $2-a-week rent by working for Bingham.[15] He started in the explorer's office, learning how to type, but soon was also working at Bingham's grand houses in New Haven and Salem. He lasted for a few years before returning to Cuzco, one of Bingham's sons remembered.[16]

While Charaja worked in the garden, Bingham labored at his desk. He owed *National Geographic* one final article, but his heart wasn't in it. "You can do such fine writing when you want to that I am at a loss to understand the present heterogeneous collection of scraps," Grosvenor wrote to Bingham when he turned in his rough draft. "Please remember that I have to think of the interests of our 500,000 members and subscribers. They would murder me if I gave them anything as irrational as this story."[17] The article was published to little fanfare. In January 1917, the National Geographic Society decided that it would fund no further expeditions to Peru for the foreseeable future.

Bingham was "relieved" to escape Peru's lost cities of the Incas—at least for the moment.[18] Like many in America, Bingham was swept up in the military preparedness movement brought on by the First World War and the Mexican Revolution to the south. When he had returned home the September before, he had watched his eldest sons act out a play in which a doughboy went off to war and a woman joined the Red Cross to follow him. Hiram applauded loudly. "Exploration promptly struck him as being about as trivial as making pin trays out of cigar bands," he later told a newspaper.[19]

The question was how he might contribute. America had not yet entered the war, and if it did, Bingham was a little too established—and tall—to fight. Searching for guidance, he turned to one of his oldest role models, Theodore Roosevelt. Two decades before, Hiram's uncle had dissuaded him from joining the Rough Riders during the Spanish-American War. Both he and Roosevelt were older now, and each had braved his own gauntlet of controversial exploration. In Roosevelt, Bingham also sought a mentor for his next possible avenue of effort: politics.

It was a subject also on Roosevelt's mind. In November, President Woodrow Wilson was up for reelection, and a wing within the Republican Party hoped to nominate Roosevelt as a candidate. On May 22, 1916, Bingham and twenty-three other Republicans had traveled to Roosevelt's home in Oyster Bay on Long Island to entreat him to run. Unable to go gently into retirement, Roosevelt—dressed in a khaki riding suit and framed by a pair of Abyssinian elephant tusks—read his acceptance from a roll of manuscript.

When the cheers subsided, the political theater continued on the lawn outside. While a *New York Times* reporter watched, Hiram Bingham pushed through the scrum to buttonhole the most famous man in America. "Colonel Roosevelt, I want to tell you how very frankly I stand," he declared. "When I was in Peru as a representative of the National Geographic Society I found much that didn't please me. I found that the claim to American citizenship won no respect. We were often accused of stealing gold there, and our statement that we were members of the National Geographic Society was no claim to consideration. They did not have a very high opinion of Americans there. So I decided that there were pleasanter occupations for an American citizen than exploring in Peru, and I came home. And when I read your speech about preparedness and Americanism, I decided that, despite my love for dear old Bill Taft, I was for you."

The Republicans cheered, and Roosevelt "clapped his hands vigorously," recognizing the historian whose hand he shook in the Oval Office eight years before. Bingham had aged much since then. He was only forty-one, but his hair was going silver.

"Good for you!" Roosevelt barked. "I can't tell you how much it pleases me to hear you talk like that. And it is exactly proof of what I was told by Edmund Heller"—who had been Yale's naturalist in Peru after hunting with Roosevelt in Africa. "He was in Peru, and he said that they believed there we were afraid to fight for our rights with Germany or Mexico, and that there was no respect for an American citizen."[20]

Bingham blustered back to New Haven, his mood unsinkable even when a Columbia anthropologist named Elsie Clews Parson sent a letter to the *Times* pointing out the strangeness of the exchange. She described her own visit to an Indian church in Santa Clara, New Mexico, where she was watched like a hawk; she learned that two Americans had stolen a crucifix five years before. She had a similar experience in Haiti, where she was identified with Americans who had bribed legislators for land concessions. Nevertheless, she had found that Latin Americans and Indians were willing to give North Americans the benefit of the doubt when they met them. "Of this liberal-mindedness it seems strange that Professor Bingham had in Peru no experience. It seems even more strange that Mr. Roosevelt, listening to Professor Bingham, could suggest that our military preparedness against any nation, whatever its manners or morals, could effect our own lack of manners or morals in the eyes of Latin Americans. Surely Mr. Roosevelt is not confusing respect for the Americano del Norte with fear of him? As a rule, carrying a gun brings no special conviction to others that you are either honest or polite."[21]

It was a close shot, but Bingham was by then sailing away. Roosevelt failed to receive the Republican nomination, but he became "Bingham's political patron saint from Oyster Bay."[22] Under Roosevelt's tutelage, Bingham's interest in Latin American history and the sympathy that accompanied it faded into the background. It was not a midlife crisis; it was a total transformation. Roosevelt swung Bingham a spot as a presidential elector for the Republican convention and encouraged him to enlist as a captain in the Yale battery, training Yale students to chase the Mexican revolutionary Pancho Villa south of the border.

The battery never got farther than Pennsylvania, but its aftermath suggested the curious legacy Bingham had already given Yale. One of the enlisted men was a rising senior and varsity player named Prescott Bush, a future senator whose son and grandson would become presidents. Bingham and Bush got along well, and that fall Bush and 117 other students took Bingham's course in South American history—the most Bingham ever had. The explorer regaled them with stories of archaeology, of excavating at Machu Picchu, showing them the skulls and artifacts his expeditions collected from Peru's last Inca cities. That fall as well, Bush was tapped to be a member of Skull and Bones—the secret society that rejected Bingham two decades before. The next year Bush and a few of his fellow Bonesmen were in artillery training at Fort Sill, Oklahoma. Fort Sill was the burial place of Geronimo, the great leader of the Chiricahua Apache who died in 1909 after fifteen years of imprisonment by the U.S. Army. One night, eager for trophies of their own, Bush and his fellow Bonesmen exhumed Geronimo's grave under the cover of darkness. "The skull of the worthy Geronimo the Terrible, exhumed from its tomb at Fort Sill by your club . . . is now safe inside the T— [Tomb] together with his well worn femurs[,] bit & saddle horn," one accomplice wrote to another society member in a letter recently unearthed in Yale's archives.[23]

Geronimo's actual grave was unmarked, but the possibility that they looted another Apache grave is no better. Bush and his fellow Bonesmen placed what may or may not have been the skull of the "last free Apache" in a glass case in the society's windowless New Haven "tomb," while less than a mile away, the human remains of the Incas' last cities gathered dust. It was Bingham's work taken to an extreme: a trophy of crushed indigenous resistance locked away in the Ivory Tower.

Hiram Bingham was trying to move on, however. In the winter of 1917, as United States' involvement in the war in Europe loomed, he traveled to Florida to enroll in aviation pioneer Glenn Curtiss's flying school. Planes had come a long way since the Wright brothers lifted off from Kitty Hawk fourteen years before, and in no time, Hiram was flying a JN–4 Jenny. He was channeling his pioneer spirit into a new frontier, partly out of patriotic preparedness but partly out of the same spirit of dissatisfaction that had turned him toward exploration back in 1905.

Even more than exploration, flight reflected the guiding premise of his life: to escape and soar above the crowd. When Congress declared war on Germany in April 1917, he had his pilot's license in hand. That May the Army hired him to organize the School of Military Aeronautics and a series of other schools across the country. In August 1918, now a lieutenant colonel, he traveled to France to run the Allies' largest air training base. Although he would only formally resign from Yale in the 1920s, World War I marked the end of his career as a practicing explorer and historian. He would finally complete a book about his excavation of Machu Picchu in 1930, and only after employing a former expedition member named Philip Means to create the first draft. As Bingham's own son details, the manuscript bore both their names: "Machu Picchu, a Citadel of the Incas, by Hiram Bingham and Philip Ainsworth Means." Bingham seems not to have liked Means's historical introduction, however, or its style. He kept Means's title, organization, and chapter headings, but dropped the Inca history and deleted Means's name from the title page, simply referring readers on to Means' own work on the book's final page. Even if Bingham now looked at writing as a chore, he demanded the full credit he believed he was due.[24]

There would still be moments, however, when the romance and failure of his time in Peru felt as fresh as ever. In 1916, while he was staggering through his final article for *National Geographic,* he dashed off a far breezier piece for *The Builder,* a magazine of Freemasonry, the secret society that was increasingly occupying Bingham's time. In the article—which his colleagues hopefully never read—Bingham hinted that the architects of Machu Picchu built suspiciously in line with the precepts of "the Craft" of the ancient eastern Masons. Far from Peru, perhaps watching Ricardo Charaja work in the back yard while he wrote, he even expressed the hope that the Indians "of the Central Andes should . . . in time enjoy some of the blessings of their glorious past. There is strength in the bone and sinew of this fallen race to enable it to be raised to that high level where it once worked."[25]

Yet when Bingham received his copy of that issue of *The Builder,* he saw that a clever editor had balanced his romanticism with a rich dose of reality: adjacent to his article was an old Rudyard Kipling poem named "The Palace." In the painful year after fleeing Peru, Bingham must have felt like his favorite poet had written the poem for him and him alone. In rolling Kipling verse, it described how a Masonic King's attempt to build a citadel was interrupted by the discovery of the ruins of a prior King's castle. "Taking and leaving at pleasure the gifts of the humble dead," the modern King cannibalized the former king's castle to build a palace of his own. But, like Bingham's career in Peru, it was not to be. "In the open noon of [his] pride," the King hears from the Darkness that he is done—that his "'palace shall stand as that other's—the spoil of a King who shall build.'" The King abandons the work and carves in a stone: "After me cometh a Builder. Tell him, I too have known!"

Bingham cut the poem out of the magazine and placed it in his personal scrapbook, likely seeing himself in its verse.[26] Never mind that Manco and the Incas weren't fellow Masons but conquered peoples. It was the poetry that counted.

Epilogue

Returns

$\mathcal{A}$fter World War I, Hiram rose through the ranks of the Connecticut Republican political machine. In 1922, he ran for lieutenant governor and won. In 1924, he ran for governor and won. Before he settled into the mansion in Hartford, however, one of Connecticut's senators in Congress committed suicide. The state's Republican Party boss had Bingham run for the vacant seat. Critics accused him of a "spirit of sport or flighty ambition," but Hiram's résumé and heroic charm proved unbeatable, and he won the special election.[1] At his swearing-in as governor in January, he delivered the longest inaugural address in Connecticut state history, hung an enormous portrait of himself in the governors' gallery, and threw a massive ball. He resigned the next morning and took the train to Washington, likely making him the only U.S. politician to ever be a lieutenant governor, governor, and senator in one 24-hour period.

He landed in Washington with a splash—a slim, handsome, silver-haired, fifty-year-old former explorer and pilot dressed in Tiffany-bought finery. "[T]he eyes of the ladies in the gallery popped" when he first took his seat on the Senate floor. "'Did you see the new Senator from Connecticut?' they bubbled. 'I tell you, he can put his clothes in *my* trunk!'"[2] He lined his mantelpiece with Peruvian artifacts and framed photos of celebrities. Within a month he was talking about his adventures on the radio. When asked how he was spending his time in the capital, he smiled and said, "I am still exploring."[3]

Bingham made commercial flight his great issue, and in the fall of 1925 he handily won reelection in Connecticut by campaigning as America's "Flying Senator." He hobnobbed with President Calvin Coolidge, Charles Lindbergh, and Amelia Earhart. He kept the press humming with fabulous photo ops. He raced a German zeppelin in a Navy airplane. He traveled by Autogiro to play golf. He arrived at a committee meeting by landing a blimp on the steps of the Capitol. "That's the way all Congressmen will arrive here soon," he told reporters.[4]

Bingham waded into international relations, arms akimbo. He visited his eldest son in China during the Chinese Civil War and made the papers at home when revolutionaries robbed him on a train. He helped negotiate more independent statuses for American Samoa and Guam, but fought to keep the Philippines under U.S. colonial guidance. Casting himself as Latin America's greatest friend in the Senate, he praised Simón Bolívar, fought for the right of Puerto Rican women to vote, and tried to keep the United States open to Latin American immigrants. His hemispheric sympathy only went so far, however. He supported the Marines' aerial bombing of Augusto Sandino's rebellion in Nicaragua and argued that U.S. citizens and their businesses needed military support abroad; he, of all people, had once been accused of spying and looting.

In the age of Lindbergh, Bingham was as powerfully symbolic as a politician could be—the cultured and aggressive Anglo-Saxon link between the Americas' indigenous past and its aerial future. Even a run for president seemed possible. "That man Bingham is at it again," marveled one Boston newspaper.[5]

But his fellow senators were less enthusiastic about the self-righteous performance of the "Professor." He broke the unwritten rule that newcomers keep quiet and took the floor thirty times in his first three days. He corrected his colleagues' pronunciations of foreign words and only socialized with Washington's wealthiest.

On October 29, 1929, while stock markets tumbled and pulled the country into the Great Depression, Hiram Bingham fell as well. During a hearing on lobbying, his fellow senators learned that Bingham had put a lobbyist on the congressional payroll and sneaked him into tariff negotiations as his aide. As with Yale's concession in Peru, Bingham admitted the facts but denied wrongdoing. His critics had him nonetheless. Tapping into a swelling resentment of the wealthy know-it-alls who had tanked the economy, "like lusty hawks" his critics leaped "upon their victim, the most gorgeous bird in the arena—the peacock of peacocks—and tore into his fine feathers until they were appeased."[6] His colleagues unleashed the most drastic of weapons: a vote of censure for acting contrary to "good morals and Senatorial ethics." Next in line for that dubious honor would be Wisconsin Senator Joseph McCarthy, censured in 1954 for his communist witch hunt.

Bingham's censure proved fatal. "The Senator's heart has always been in the Caribbean," scolded Memphis's *Commercial Press*.[7] In 1932, Bingham lost his office during the elections that gave Franklin Delano Roosevelt the presidency. He was forced to reinvent himself again, first as the president of the National Aeronautic Association, from whose pulpit he both praised and butted heads with Amelia Earhart before she disappeared while flying over his parents' missionary outpost, the Gilbert Islands. In 1937, Alfreda divorced Hiram for cruelty, "cold indifference," an "attitude of superiority," and for having a long-time mistress—Suzanne Carroll Hill, the wife of another former congressman. Alfreda married her accompanist, a kindly pianist, quiet like herself, and with him she finally visited Peru. Hiram married Suzanne, and they nested with shares of Tiffany & Company that Alfreda had signed over to Hiram.[8] He wrote a biography of Elihu Yale, Yale's controversial namesake. During World War II, he lectured to troops headed to the Pacific on the history and culture of the region. In 1951, he returned to the political spotlight one final time, to chair the communist-hunting Loyalty Review Board and investigate the loyalties of public servants who had worked and studied in China.

Despite his achievements—or perhaps because of his embarrassments—Hiram Bingham was sure that the one thing he would be remembered for was Machu Picchu.[9] He circled its memory like a condor, swooping down to it in moments of transition to rise again on its updraft. In 1922, when he was starting his career in politics, he published *Incaland*, the most rollicking version of his tale. In 1930, while he was recovering from his Senate censure, *National Geographic* published his lavish, expensive, scholarly—and actually co-written—account of the ruins, *Machu Picchu: A Citadel of the Incas*. The publication in 1948 of his final version, the runaway best seller *Lost City of the Incas*, coincided with the greatest honor of all, one Hiram thought he lost over thirty years before: an invitation to return to Peru.

After his departure from the Andes in 1915, Hiram had broken off contact with his Peruvian colleagues. But in the 1930s, one by one, they got back in touch. Peru by then had established a national commission to monitor the excavation of ruins. Julio C. Tello continued his climb to the top of Peru's archaeological community and sometimes sent Bingham books.[10] More importantly, Luis E. Valcárcel reached out to the explorer.

After Bingham's hurried departure, Valcárcel had continued his slow, steady rise through the ranks of Peru's historians, anthropologists, and intellectuals. He helped Albert Giesecke and the University of Cuzco start its own museum, to give artifacts a home in the region. In 1927, he electrified *indigenistas* throughout the Americas with his book, *Tempestad en los Andes,* in which he predicted that Peru's indigenous majority would one day rise up, creating a neo-Inca socialist state.[11] That same year, the authoritarian government of Augusto B. Leguía—the former Peruvian president had returned to power in 1919—temporarily imprisoned Valcárcel on a coastal island for writing articles critical of the government. In 1930, when Leguía was himself removed from power and imprisoned, the new government brought Valcárcel to Lima to run the national museum. Remembering his roots, Valcárcel took the opportunity to funnel funds back to Cuzco. He excavated at Sacsayhuaman, revealing the bases of the three great towers that were toppled after the great Inca rebellion of 1536. He also cleared Machu Picchu, perhaps for the first time since Bingham's 1912 expedition. The ruins would never be overgrown again.

Perhaps doing so warmed Valcárcel to his former adversary. He wrote to friends for a copy of Bingham's *Machu Picchu: A Citadel of the Incas.*[12] During a subsequent tour of the United States, he made an appointment to meet with Bingham in Washington, DC. They met on April 1, 1941, before the United States entered World War II, during a height of American popularity in the hemisphere owing to President Roosevelt's Good Neighbor Policy. Valcárcel's notebook from that trip was thin, but he made a point of noting that his talk with Bingham was "very friendly." They seem to have met in Bingham's home, where the explorer showed his old adversary a portrait of Simón Bolívar. The next day, Bingham took Valcárcel to the tony Metropolitan Club to have lunch with O. F. Cook, a botanist who had been on the 1914–15 expedition.[13] One wonders what they talked about—whether they broached the subject of that final expedition, so fatal to Bingham's plans, or whether they talked about Machu Picchu, their shared love. Perhaps it was just enough for Bingham and Valcárcel to sit down together, former adversaries but so alike in so many ways, and find that the past was not forgotten.

The visit affected them both. When Valcárcel returned to Peru, he wrote that Yale "had an important attitude towards South America."[14] A few years later, Bingham appreciated Valcárcel's "kind reference" to Bingham's expeditions in the *Handbook of South American Indians.*[15] When writing *Lost City of the Incas,* Bingham made sure to credit many of the Peruvians who had helped him on his way, including Carlos Romero, the crotchety archivist in Lima who pointed him toward Vitcos. Evidence that time had healed Peru's wounds—at least temporarily—came when Bingham's old friend, Albert A. Giesecke, the former head of the University of Cuzco, wangled the explorer and his wife, Suzanne, an invitation to an Inter-American Indigenista Congress in Cuzco in the fall of 1948. Hiram was ecstatic; he would get to see Machu Picchu once again. He was also "anxious to see what you have done at Sacsayhuaman, [Pisaac] and Ollantay-tambo," he wrote to Valcárcel.[16]

On the Binghams' way south, however, Peru's navy revolted. The president put down the unrest but also canceled Cuzco's congress. It would have been embarrassing—Hiram Bingham traveling all that way for nothing—but Giesecke convinced Cuzco's American-friendly Rotary Club to give Bingham something better. The club was about to cut the ribbon on a road up to Machu Picchu. Why not name it after the seventy-two-year-old explorer who made the ruins famous?

On October 12, Columbus Day, Bingham and his wife, Suzanne, arrived in Cuzco by a special car on the Southern Peruvian Railway train. They could have flown, but Bingham wanted to travel as he had in the past. He felt young again. The hills, grass, blue skies, and the clippings from *El Comercio* of Cuzco made him feel welcome. When the newspaper's reporter got on the train, Bingham's face lit up. "He shook hands with such grace," the reporter wrote. "He was of such a great height, and his absolutely white hair gave him the countenance of a great, venerable lord. He received us with a courtesy that filled us with emotion."[17]

The Binghams took the new train to Machu Picchu but rode mules to the top for old times' sake. The U.S. ambassador flew in from Lima and took a special train to join them. The road's engineer spoke, as did José Gabriel Cosio, who once monitored Bingham's expedition and was now Cuzco's mayor. Suzanne cut the ribbon that opened the Carretera Hiram Bingham, the Hiram Bingham Highway. Full of "intense emotion," the elegantly dressed explorer spoke over waves of applause. "This will remain one of the most grateful moments of my life," he explained. Hiram spent the afternoon roaming the ruins, branding them in his memory before he returned to the States.[18]

When he died eight years later, in 1956, Senator Prescott Bush reported his death in Congress, and newspapers across the United States remembered a legacy as monumental and damaged as the ruins he loved. Bingham was born beyond America's farthest frontier and came to rest eighty years later in its military heart, Arlington National Cemetery. *Time* magazine's obituary may have framed him best: "Senators I understand not at all," it quoted Bingham as saying. "I understand so much better the ethics and morals of explorers."[19]

Peruvians were a little more generous. In Cuzco, Jose Gabriel Cosío would lead a memorial for Bingham at the university, sharing "delicious anecdotes" about Bingham's early days in Cuzco before reaching Machu Picchu. One of the city's chief archaeologists would declare that Bingham had "done more for Cuzco than many Cusqueños."[20]

In Lima, Luis Valcárcel heard the news on the radio while sitting at the breakfast table with his son Frank. Valcárcel just shook his head, burying the past, perhaps forever. "He was a great man," he said.[21]

Sixty years later, Hiram Bingham remains the man who made Machu Picchu internationally famous, even if his title as "discoverer," "scientific discoverer," "rediscoverer," or "the first tourist" to the ruins is up for debate.[22] Machu Picchu has been the twentieth and twenty-first centuries' great engine of identity and prosperity for Cuzco, today bringing more than 800,000 visitors a year to the Inca citadel in the sky. Tourists can hike in, as Bingham did, or take a bus to the top. Where the family of Bingham's young guide once lived, there is now an $800-a-night hotel. Where his family once planted, pampered government llamas now manicure emerald grass. The most expensive train to the town below Machu Picchu costs $588 round trip; its name is "The Hiram Bingham."

Bingham is honored for being the foreigner who recognized the site's beauty and its future importance for Peru. Within a year of its revelation, Peru's intellectuals hailed the site as a symbol not only of the Peruvian nation, but also of what indigenous peoples accomplished before the arrival of Europeans. Machu Picchu has been hailed as the best of all Inca sites, the realization of their architectural and religious ideals—to worship the sun by building toward it, aligning altars along its path; to honor mountains by building out of them, quarrying stone from the site itself; to glorify water with *acequias,* canals of waters that fed burbling baths. In building Machu Picchu, it was as if the Incas and their workers reached into the Andes themselves, closed their fists, and pulled up the elemental temples waiting within—stone turned inside out, light and water tamed into structure but still fierce and flowing, like nature itself. Bingham's final work, *Lost City of the Incas,* captures that achievement and remains in print to this day.

Bingham's theory of what Machu Picchu actually was, however, has aged poorly. To his death the explorer remained convinced that it was Tampu Tocco, the cradle of Inca civilization, as well as Vilcabamba the Old, its grave.

It was neither, as his successors have shown. In 1915, Philip Means—the expedition member who would write Bingham's first draft of *Citadel of the Incas*—visited the site. The site was beautiful, he thought, but he was unconvinced by Bingham's claim that Machu Picchu was Tampu Tocco because of the Temple of the Three Windows—a doubt shared by the Inca expert Clements Markham.[23] They both pointed out that the chronicles suggested that the great Inca emperor Pachacutec would have built Machu Picchu as a frontier citadel during his mid-fifteenth-century push to expand his empire's eastern and northern borders.[24]

Time has largely proved that theory right. Anthropologists and archaeologists like Luis Valcárcel and Manuel Chavez Ballón studied Machu Picchu through the 1960s, yielding similar conclusions. Although Valcárcel incorrectly came to believe that the site was Pitcos or Vitcos, a theory that Bingham had long ago dismissed, he was sure that it was built by Pachacutec.[25] Historians, however, only began to reevaluate the site in the 1970s, perhaps wary of the way it had burned Bingham. In the early 1980s, Peruvian scholars Luis Miguel Glave and María Isabel Remy published a sixteenth-century document in which descendants of Pachacutec described a site named Picho.[26] A few years later, the great scholar of the Andes John Rowe confirmed Means's theory that Machu Picchu was a symbol of Pachacutec's conquest, while also recognizing the site's symbolic divinity.[27] Machu Picchu is now understood as a site of regional, spiritual authority as well as a royal estate whose upkeep was paid for by the familial cult that surrounded Pachacutec's mummy.[28] Tampu Tocco, the cave from which the first Inca emerged, remains associated with the site of Pacariqtambo, south of Cuzco.

So Machu Picchu was not the Incas' cradle; but was it their grave, Vilcabamba the Old? It was not. There too, time proved Bingham more romantic than scientific. In the 1960s, an American explorer named Gene Savoy scrutinized Bingham's geography and pointed out the obvious—that it made little sense for the last city of the Incas to be so close to Cuzco. Savoy was one of the last old-school explorers, relying on the Spanish chronicles, his own money, and a hunch that Bingham was wrong. Following in Bingham's footsteps, he traveled to the ruins of Espiritu Pampa, the site whose overgrown jungle and "savage" inhabitants had so intimidated Bingham. He cleared off the jungle with the help of Julio Cobos, a Peruvian who now owned the land. Uncovered, the site proved massive, suggesting that it well fit the description of Manco's capital in exile. Savoy announced that he had found Vilcabamba, the last city of the Incas that Bingham had seen but misunderstood.[29]

Bingham's own successors at Yale further shattered Bingham's theory. One foundation for Hiram's belief that Machu Picchu was the last refuge of the Incas' "sun virgins" was George Eaton's claim that the vast majority of the site's skeletons belonged to women. In the 1980s, however, Yale archaeologists Richard L. Burger and Lucy Salazar commissioned a new series of studies of Machu Picchu's material that proved Eaton wrong. Using modern technology, Tulane archaeologist John W. Verano showed that there was a relatively *even* ratio of women to men.[30] The graves belonged to lower-status servants, not pampered virgins. Their joints were worn and their backs were wrecked with lives of hard labor. During Manco's great rebellion around 1536, the Incas likely abandoned the site, taking their gold and silver with them.[31] As much as Bingham wanted it to be true, it would have been nearly impossible for Manco Inca to take refuge in Machu Picchu's heights, so close to Cuzco. He went into the jungle and built Espiritu Pampa, or Vilcabamba the Old, instead.

Bingham's error sprang from ignorance but was also somewhat charmingly rooted in his character. For him, it was entirely within reason that he could have found both the mythical origin and the romantic end of the Incas—and that they were the exact same site. Beyond that inspired 1911 expedition, when he used the archives and his boots to trace Manco's flight, he proved more dreamer than scholar. He heralded the start of large-scale excavation in Peru and established an extremely useful classification scheme of Inca pottery, but his academic reputation has seriously diminished compared to that of his contemporaries, like Max Uhle and Julio C. Tello.[32] Bingham's quixotic version of the site's story, however, is hard to shake. Some guides at Machu Picchu still tell tourists that Machu Picchu was the last resting place of the Virgins of the Sun.

Few archaeological theories hold up a century later. But if we judge Bingham on his paeans to Machu Picchu's technical beauty and symbolism for Inca history, his reputation is more secure. Machu Picchu is Inca architecture at its imperial height, filled with wonderful references to other Inca sites and stories. The Temple of the Three Windows indeed alludes to the Incas' origin stories. The Torreón, or Temple of the Sun, clearly "quotes" the Sun Temple in Cuzco. The site's Intihuatana is the largest ever found; scientists believe it was a sophisticated solar calendar for keeping track of equinoxes, solstices, and planting rhythms. High-altitude archaeologist Johann Reinhard calls Machu Picchu the "Sacred Center" of the region. An Italian researcher describes the ruins as the Inca historical cosmos in miniature.[33]

A Peruvian archaeologist named Luis Guillermo Lumbreras also finds cause for national celebration in Machu Picchu's most haunting feature: the Royal Mausoleum, the hourglass-shaped cave where Richarte's son brought Bingham on the very first day. Although attendants carried the mummies of Inca emperors and royalty from place to place as if alive, when they came to rest, they were housed in niches where they could be worshipped. Lumbreras believes that Pachacutec built this cave and perhaps the entire site as his mummy's home, much like the Egyptian pharaohs built their pyramids or the Chinese emperor Qin Shi Huang, who had himself buried surrounded by life-size terracotta warriors.[34]

Yet if Machu Picchu was one of Pachacutec's resting places, its occupant disappeared long ago. After the conquest, the Spaniards took Pachacutec's mummy from Cuzco to Lima, where it was buried, lost, or burnt. Machu Picchu is perhaps best understood as neither a cradle nor a grave, but a as cenotaph: a monument in honor of an individual whose remains are lost or lie elsewhere.

As the centenary of Hiram Bingham's first visit to Machu Picchu approaches, the ruins are currently more famous in Peru for their lack of another set of human remains: those of Pachacutec's attendants, who were uprooted from throughout the empire, were buried on Machu Picchu's slopes, and were exhumed nearly a half-millennium later by Hiram Bingham, who brought them to New Haven, where they have lain ever since.

For nearly a century, Peruvians have been seeking their return. Despite Luis E. Valcárcel and Bingham's later friendship, the effort began in 1916 when Valcárcel learned that Yale had indeed received a collection of artifacts that Tomás A. Alvistur had smuggled and shipped north through bribery. Although there was no way to prosecute Bingham from Peru, Valcárcel used the press to remind the government of the rights guaranteed by the decrees of 1912 and 1916: the return of the human remains and artifacts loaned to Yale.[35] To prevent the loss of further collections from the region, Albert Giesecke, the North American rector of the University of Cuzco, convinced one of the city's last great collectors to sell the university his artifacts, creating Cuzco's long-dreamed of museum, today the Museo Inka. Valcárcel was the museum's first director.[36]

On the international front, in late 1918, Peru's diplomat in the United States asked for the return of the collection exported in 1916. Yale won an extension because Bingham was engaged in the war, but the explorer seemed willing to honor his promises—at least in regard to the artifacts from Vitcos and Patallacta.[37] These artifacts exported in 1916, he wrote, "do not belong to us, but to the Peruvian government, who allowed us to take them out of the country on condition that they be returned in eighteen months." He considered letting the Peruvians "whistle for it," but knew better. "The matter has assumed a very large importance in the eyes of the Peruvians, who feel that we are trying to rob their country of its treasures," Bingham wrote.[38] *National Geographic*'s editor agreed: "I feel that we ought to abide by the letter of our agreement with the Peruvian Government and return all the material that we contracted to return, and I am glad that you share this view with me."[39]

But when Peru enlarged its request—whether it did so at Valcárcel's prompting is unclear—Bingham changed his tune. In 1920, Peru's consul in the United States asked again for the artifacts from Vitcos and Patallacta at Yale, but this time also cited the clause in the 1912 agreement that guaranteed the return of the artifacts that Yale had exported that year—to be precise, the skulls, bones, and artifacts from Machu Picchu, the centerpiece of Yale's collection.[40] According to Yale, Peru had passed a decree demanding that the unique artifacts be returned but allowing duplicate artifacts—potsherds and bones—to stay at Yale.[41]

It was a generous compromise, under the circumstances, but Bingham broke its terms, regardless: Peru would receive neither the unique nor the duplicate artifacts from Machu Picchu. Bingham well understood which pieces he extracted from Peru in 1912. Yet he claimed to his colleagues that the letter referred to the 1914–15 artifacts. At best, it was a mistake, perhaps due to the fact that he was still recovering from an illness after the war. At worst, he was covering up the obligation that Peru placed upon Yale nearly a decade before—perhaps out of resentment or embarrassment. The result was the same: Machu Picchu's artifacts stayed at Yale. In 1921, the Peabody Museum sent back 47 boxes of human skeletal remains and jumbled ceramic fragments from Patallacta. The other 27 boxes that left Peru in early 1915—including the artifacts from Vitcos—apparently stayed at Yale, alongside Machu Picchu's skulls, bones, silver, and bronze. In case the Peruvians complained, Bingham was already practicing his alibi. "When they see the material," he wrote *National Geographic*'s editor, "they will probably accuse us of having sent them a lot of rubbish. . . ."[42]

Perhaps believing himself liberated, the explorer-turned-politician finally handed over Machu Picchu's artifacts to the Peabody Museum in July 1923, nearly twenty-two years to the day since Bingham's first glimpse of the ruins. If they followed the protocol Bingham proposed, it would have been a casual affair: the

Peabody could choose what they wanted, putting to one side the "discards," from which Bingham might select a few choice pieces before they were "otherwise disposed of."[43] The Peabody was not nearly so lackadaisical, luckily, and took all the artifacts.[44] Bingham's documentation, however, proved elusive. In 1930, the museum's director asked whether Bingham had the catalogue cards that gave the collection sense and order: "As you know, the museum value of any specimen is in direct proportion to the information that is available concerning it."[45]

The Peruvians were similarly confounded. Bingham sent back so little documentation that the pieces from Patallacta were scientifically worthless.[46] Although individual Peruvians continued to call for the return of Machu Picchu's artifacts in the 1920s, some Peruvians began to think that the Patallacta artifacts *were* from Machu Picchu, fueling conflicting stories and wild speculation.[47] As the ruins became a symbol of a broader indigenous Latin American identity, the darker side of Bingham's tale of discovery grew, once again mirroring the United States' reputation in the region. Although pro-American sentiment was high in the late 1940s when Bingham visited, by the 1950s, the United States was supporting rightist political overthrow in Guatemala, and the rumors of Bingham's malfeasance merged with the story of U.S. imperialism in the Americas. From a less political perspective, Machu Picchu's legend had become as massive as a *ceiba* tree, and the Peruvians had come to resent the climbing vine—Hiramis Binghamensis, perhaps—that had benefited from the tree's growth.

In 1952, during his now-famous motorcycle pilgrimage up South America, a twenty-five-year-old Argentine named Ernesto Guevara, who would soon join Fidel Castro's struggle in Cuba and become the "Che" of legend, visited Machu Picchu. To him, it was a pure expression of a powerful indigenous America untouched by the conquistadors. He thought Machu Picchu was "an arm outstretched out to the future, a stony voice with continental reach that shouts 'Citizens of Indo-America, reconquer the past!'"

Che felt an equal measure of indignation at the site's recent history. "Here's the tragedy," Guevara lamented. "All the ruins were cleaned of underbrush, perfectly studied and described and . . . totally robbed of every object that fell into the hands of the researchers, who triumphantly brought back to their country more than two hundred boxes containing invaluable archaeological treasures. . . . Bingham is not the culprit, objectively speaking, nor are the North Americans guilty in general. . . . But where can we admire or study the treasures of the indigenous city? The answer is obvious: in the museums of North America."[48]

The sense that something was amiss was hardly limited to the site's Latin American visitors. In 1954, just two years after Che's visit, the actor Charlton Heston starred in a Paramount movie named *Secret of the Incas.* Inspired by a *National Geographic* article describing Bingham's theories, the film employed Bingham's friend Albert Giesecke as a technical advisor and was filmed on location in Machu Picchu. Heston played Harry Steele, a familiar-looking and unshaven explorer in a fedora and bomber jacket in search of the "golden sunburst" of the emperor Manco Inca.

When Steele enters Machu Picchu, the film resembles a dream version of Bingham's story. Steele trades barbs with a University of Cuzco graduate named Pachacutec and an Inca princess played by the Peruvian singer Yma Sumac. A representative of the Peruvian government is there to make sure no one "appropriate[s] any souvenirs." The movie's great conflict is whether Steele will get to Manco's treasure before a ne'er-do-well antiquities thief and a jodhpur-wearing American archaeologist. Steele wins, but his conscience weighs on him. He gives the idol to Pachacutec, who restores it to the Temple of the Sun. "I guess finding it meant more to me than keeping it," Steele says. But as the Indians celebrate, he hands his blonde companion a golden Inca shawl pin. "Must have fallen into my pocket while I was in the tomb," he drawls.

Secret of the Incas is hardly a classic, but its reach has been long. According to the costume designer for *Raiders of the Lost Ark,* the film's crew watched the film together several times, based Indiana Jones's costume on Heston's, and echoed a couple of plot points, like a scene in which Steele redirects a beam of light to reveal the true location of Manco's treasure.[49]

More importantly, in Peru, where *Secret of the Incas* was shown, the movie may have kept alive the idea of Machu Picchu's lost treasure. In 1961, Peru celebrated the fiftieth anniversary of Bingham's visit to Machu Picchu. After the newspaper *El Sol* revived the allegation that Bingham had looted Machu Picchu of gold and silver, Ricardo Charaja—the Yale expedition's sole Peruvian member, who had found the Inca Trail and the Inca Churisca artifacts—stepped forward in Bingham's defense. Long back from his foray to New Haven and now presumably well into his seventies, Charaja pointed out how much Bingham had been willing to spend, with no eye to financial gain.[50]

Seeking to get to the truth, archaeologists at the University of Cuzco sought to recover Machu Picchu's artifacts, which they believed Bingham had long ago returned to Lima. When they learned that Yale sent back only jumbled bones and ceramics from other sites, they asked the Ministry of Education to remind Yale of its obligations.[51]

If the ministry did remind Yale, they would have been as unsuccessful as Hiram's second eldest son, Hiram IV, known as Harry, who was simultaneously making his own attempt to redress the past. Harry had a strong conscience. As a vice-consul in France during World War II, he had helped 2,500 Jews escape the Germans. In 1961, Harry met with the director of the Peabody to plead Peru's case and see if Yale might return at least a few pieces. The museum's director, however, was firm: because a Yale archaeologist would be assigned to work on the skulls, bones, and artifacts in the "near future . . . it might be detrimental to research endeavors to break up the collection at this time."[52] Harry believed that "much of the collection of Inca pottery that is now carefully listed and stored at Yale could eventually be returned to Peru," but those hopes would bear no fruit.[53] The sympathy of Hiram's heirs was no longer relevant; Yale managed Machu Picchu's graves now. Harry traveled to Peru and attended the celebration at the ruins, but all he had to give the University of Cuzco was a box of his father's slides. In Cuzco, the day before the ceremony at Machu Picchu, Pablo Neruda's epic poem cycle, *Las Alturas de Macchu Picchu, The Heights of Macchu Picchu* [sic], was read.[54] "Return to me the slave that you entombed!" read one canto, undercutting the celebration.[55] Machu Picchu's workers remained in North America, however. Seven years later, another Bingham son, Alfred, presented Peru with a portrait of Hiram that as of 2006 still hung in an office at the ruins.

Which was not to say that Yale was unamenable to Peruvians studying the artifacts—as long as they came to New Haven. Luis Valcárcel made the trip in early 1962, a half-year after representing the Peruvian agency responsible for protecting ruins at the fiftieth anniversary. He spent two days and a night in New Haven, talking with Peabody scholars and students and—crucially—going through the Bingham collection of artifacts, perhaps the first Peruvian to enjoy that privilege.[56] In doing so, he was reminded of battles fought and lost, long ago. There, among the pieces flagged as being from Machu Picchu, he saw three artifacts that he knew came not from Machu Picchu, but from the collection of Tomás Alvistur: the green-black stone chalice, the light brown stone alpaca, and the abstractly beautiful brown stone bird.

Valcárcel made his discovery public, but discreetly. When Valcárcel returned to Peru, he wrote *Machu Picchu: El Mas Famoso Monumento Arqueológico del Perú.* In a chapter on "The Scientific Discovery," he credited Bingham for going past the chronicles, but let the residence of Machu Picchu's graves in New Haven pass by without comment. His next chapter, "Certain Enigmas . . . ," similarly made no mention to the legal status of the artifacts, focusing instead on how Machu Picchu seemed absent from the chronicles. Valcárcel closed the chapter with a curious paragraph, however. Presented without preamble, he noted the presence of Alvistur's chalice, alpaca, and stone bird in the Machu Picchu collection—objects that had never been published in any of Bingham's books. He noted that they came from Alvistur's collection but mused that they might have been sold to the antiquarian by the residents of Machu Picchu.[57] There was no reference to the legal status of the collection.

At seventy-seven, Valárcel had lost his taste for combat over Machu Picchu long ago. When Valcárcel dictated his memoirs in the late 1970s, he remembered his youth as a political provocateur and defender of the Indians in Cuzco. Yet when it came to the charges that Yale had looted and smuggled artifacts, he said that his commission had "not found a single testimony that could have proved the charges against the studious North Americans, headed by Bingham."[58] There was no mention of the inquest in which Bingham had humiliated him or of being left on the dock while the ship to the Island of the Sun floated away. Perhaps he no longer thought Yale had done much wrong, having made a sort of peace with Bingham long before. Perhaps some memories were still too embarrassing. Likely it was somewhere in between.

When Luis Valcárcel died in 1987, at ninety-six years old, he left no further comments on the strange history of Bingham and Machu Picchu save what his survivors remembered. His son, Frank, recalled that his father spoke with warmth of Bingham. One of Valcárcel's students, himself a historian, in 2005 offered that "Machu Picchu owes everything to Bingham, and Cuzco owes everything to Machu Picchu." Yet when it came to the question of Valcárcel's investigation of the Yale Expedition ninety years before, the student was surprised to be reminded that his teacher's memoirs cleared Yale of wrongdoing. He recalled Valcárcel saying otherwise—that Yale had smuggled artifacts after all.

Peru had to get through the 1980s, however, before it could sort out the ambiguities of Hiram Bingham's legacy. In the final decades of the twentieth century, Machu Picchu's artifacts were the least of Peru's worries. Agrarian reform led to bloody military repression, which led to guerrilla revolt and, ultimately, the horrific violence of the Shining Path Maoists, who made their first attack on the state on the hundred-ninety-ninth anniversary of the execution of Tupac Amaru II.[59] In the midst of that chaos, looting and smuggling exploded, fueled by improved transportation and a skyrocketing demand for artifacts by Western collectors and museums. Museums are a sacred trust, but they are also a business in which certain "products"—like a new gold Moché mask or a Greek urn—attract prestige and paying visitors.

The Peruvian government fought back. As Roger Atwood's *Stealing History* compellingly lays out, Peruvian and U.S. authorities worked together to pursue looters and smugglers, rekindling perceptions of state ownership of the indigenous past.[60] Authoritarian President Alberto Fujimori pacified the countryside but fled the country in 2000 on charges of corruption and extralegal violence—charges that would catch up with him in 2009, when he was convicted of human rights violations. His successor, Alejandro Toledo (2001–2006), however, took the politics of cultural patrimony to a new level. An indigenous Peruvian with a Ph.D. from Stanford, Toledo held a second inauguration at Machu Picchu, complete with a shaman's dedication to the local mountain gods. To some observers it was political theater and a bid to increase Peruvian tourism. To others it was deeply meaningful. For the first time since the Spanish Conquest, Peru's leader was proudly indigenous.

Toledo's administration put Peru back on a collision course with Yale. In New Haven, Yale archaeologists Richard Burger and Lucy Salazar were close to completing a blockbuster exhibit centered on Machu Picchu's remains. It would be the Peabody Museum's first show to tour the country, exposing a new generation to the Incas and generating accolades for all involved. When they asked Peru to cosponsor the show, however, they received a surprise. Toledo and his wife, a French anthropologist named Eliane Karp, had learned from a historian named Mariana Mould de Pease about the clause in the 1912 decree that gave Peru the right to bring back the artifacts. Peru called in its marker.[61]

The Peabody archaeologists were shocked. Archaeologically rich countries had asked for the return of long-gone artifacts in the past but with little success. For years, Greece had been calling for the British Museum to return the marble frieze that Lord Elgin lifted from the Parthenon in the early nineteenth century, when Greece was run by the Ottoman Empire—a story that bore some resemblance to Bingham's in that Elgin believed he was saving the sculptures and it was unclear whether he had license for study or export.

Unlike Elgin's story, however, Bingham's dated to a period when Peru existed as a nation and its laws affected foreigners' excavations. Moreover, the international atmosphere was changing. The boom in looting, anticolonial sentiment, new media, and international law had given countries like Greece, Italy, Egypt, China, and Peru platforms on which to pursue the return of their "cultural patrimony." Peru had already achieved the return of a number of recently looted artifacts with the help of the U.S. government. Over the next several years, premier museums all over the world would be forced to defend the acquisition of some of their finest antiquities. In 2003, the looting of the Iraqi Museum during the U.S. invasion reminded the world of the tragedy of lost culture—and how Western markets fueled looting and smuggling elsewhere. In 2007, the Metropolitan Museum of Art in New York agreed to return to Italy the famed Euphronius Krater, allegedly looted from an Etruscan tomb, and Greece won the return of artifacts from the J. Paul Getty Museum in Los Angeles. Archaeologists and museums began to pick sides. Although international conventions mandate the return of artifacts smuggled after 1970 only, many museums began treating source countries as if they wanted to empty the great "universal" museums of the world.[62]

At first glance, it is hard not to sympathize with Yale's archaeologists. Through their work and that of their colleagues, we know much about the site's more humble residents. To them, the 1912 executive order's appearance may have seemed suspect, as if produced for political convenience. Also frustrating was the fact that the Peruvians involved occasionally conflated the 1912 decree with the 1916 decree. Yale's archaeologists suggested that Peru's government was playing politics with the artifacts, whipping the press into a frenzy by hinting at the "treasures" of Machu Picchu. Although the collection contained some truly delicate bronzes, silver, ceramics, and stone pieces, it had nothing like the gold artifacts that had been looted from the Peruvian coast in the 1980s and 1990s. Yale also hinted that Peru's museums weren't safe, while the university had just committed to an expensive show, guaranteeing their continued display.[63] And then there was the matter of timeliness: as Yale and its lawyers would later portray it, Peru was holding Yale to an agreement after nearly a century of not doing so.

History, however, suggests otherwise. Peru had asked for Machu Picchu's skulls, bones, and artifacts before, and Bingham had failed to send them back. The explorer had indeed left skeletons in the Peabody's closet: the decree that mandated the Machu Picchu collection's return. Moreover, Yale's collection contained the artifacts that Bingham had paid Peruvians to smuggle for him. Peru's claim was more supported by history than the country's negotiators knew.

At first, Yale's modern curators refused to acknowledge the legitimacy of the executive decrees, but they did not close the door to making a deal to share the artifacts. Preparations for the traveling exhibit, meanwhile, continued as planned; it was a hard train to stop, given that the National Science Foundation gave the Peabody Museum a $300,000-plus grant to carry out the exhibition.[64] A compromise might have been reached had it not been for the Yale negotiators' denial that Peru ever owned the artifacts and its suggestion that Peru lacked the capacity or will to care for artifacts as Yale could.[65] For years, Peruvian archaeologists grimaced while North American colleagues shook their head at the country's struggle to protect its culture. It was a patronizing argument that ignored progress: Peru's cultural institutions had moved forward in leaps and bounds since Bingham's era. More importantly, the executive orders were proof that in the 1910s Peru did care about its history. The early negotiations over Machu Picchu's artifacts and Bingham's evasions were revelatory, and Peru was legitimately outraged that Yale denied their relevance.

Yale was surprised to learn that the third party in Bingham's later expeditions felt similarly. The National Geographic Society also wanted the artifacts' return. Its vice president, Terry Garcia, reviewed the society's documentation and felt there was "no question" that Machu Picchu's artifacts belonged to Peru.[66] National Geographic attempted to broker a deal, but the university was uninterested. The society was shocked. "It's so patronizing of them to suggest that you can't return these objects to Peru because they can't take care of them—that a country like Peru doesn't have competent archaeologists or museums," National Geographic's vice president told the *New York Times* in 2007. "Maybe if you were a colonial power in the [nineteenth] century you could rationalize that statement. I don't see how you could make it today. Why not acknowledge that the title belongs to the Peruvian people and work out an agreement with Peru? You get out from under this horrible controversy with Peru and you are still able to conduct scholarly work."[67]

Yale, however, seemed intent on rubbing salt in Peru's wounds. When the Peabody Museum's Machu Picchu exhibit opened in January 2003, a six-foot-four mannequin of Bingham photographing an indigenous worker greeted visitors when they walked in the door. The exhibition's text claimed that the collection became part of the Peabody "by agreement with the Peruvian government." With that, the levee broke. Peruvian diplomats publicly hinted that they were headed to a lawsuit. Yale's negotiators grew even more intransigent. In 2005, for the very first time, they offered a legal argument for why the artifacts belonged to Yale: an 1852 Civil Code that at one time governed what was discovered beneath the Peruvian soil.[68] The decrees passed in 1911 and 1912, prohibiting the exportation of artifacts and stipulating the Machu Picchu artifacts' return, rested upon an earlier decree, from 1893. It was Yale's opinion, after consulting with a Peruvian lawyer, that a set of laws passed in 1901 overturned the 1893 decree, invalidating the later 1911 and 1912 decrees and reverting ownership of buried "treasure" to the individual who finds it—read: Bingham—as laid out by the 1852 Civil Code.[69] Yale's claim was fascinating. If valid, Bingham needn't have negotiated with the government over the export of the artifacts from Machu Picchu and elsewhere.

In terms of history, however, it falls short as an explanation of what happened. The fact remains that Bingham and Peru behaved in 1912 as if Peru had control over its ruins and artifacts. His concession was his way of getting around the country's prohibition against unauthorized excavation and exportation. Public outcry at the concession forced him to withdraw it and recognize that the country was taking its decrees seriously. The 1912 decree was passed on the belief that the 1893 and 1911 decrees were in effect. Bingham's later dealings with Alvistur, the collector, were to get around the country's prohibitions. At no point do any references to the 1852 Civil Code or the modifications of 1901 appear in his archives.[70]

As tensions escalated, the issue took on spiritual import. As much as the university emphasizes the collection's archaeological importance to the world, many Peruvians saw the collection as what it first was: the burials of 174 human beings from throughout the Andes, whose ancestors now walk the streets of Cuzco and Lima. This is no mere sentimentalism; as harsh as the Spanish conquest was for indigenous people, colonial law protected Indian populations in a way that U.S. national policies did not. Today, Peru's president, no matter his heritage, represents a country of predominantly indigenous descent. And as historian Mariana Mould de Pease has noted, under U.S. law, the Native American Grave Repatriation Act (NAGPRA) orders museums to repatriate what human remains and spiritual artifacts they possess to their indigenous living heirs. In the United States in 2000, a Maidu named Art Angle and the anthropologist Orin Starn helped get the Smithsonian to return the brain of Ishi, the "last Yahi" who emerged from the Sierra Nevada in 1911 and died in 1916. The Redding Rancheria and Pit River Tribe, deemed by the Smithsonian to be Ishi's closest relatives, reunited the brain with Ishi's cremated remains and reburied them in an undisclosed California location.[71] While NAGPRA only applies to U.S. tribes, Mariana Mould de Pease has pointed out that institutions like the Smithsonian have set a precedent by returning mummy bundles to Cuzco.[72]

The symbolism in the Yale case is deepened by the fact that the human remains are from Machu Picchu, the royal estate of Pachacutec—either one of the great indigenous leaders of Andean history or one of its great imperialists. Pachacutec's mummy is long gone, but the fact that the bodies and artifacts of the men and women who attended him are at Yale remains deeply upsetting. In May 2006, 1,200 residents of the town beneath Machu Picchu rode the train to Cuzco to demonstrate and call for the return of the Machu Picchu artifacts to their "home."[73] "What if Peru had George Washington's things?" the director of the Instituto Nacional de Cultura in Cuzco asked the year before. "We would have to return them. They would mean something to the United States, not Peru."[74]

In the face of Peru's onslaught, Yale leaned back on its massive endowment and tried to ride out the storm. In the summer of 2006, Alejandro Toledo's term ended, and the presidency went to Alan García, who pledged himself to pro-U.S. policies. As Yale hoped, García's negotiators were friendly, allowing the university to cast the Toledo administration as political opportunists—most publicly through an article for the *New York Times* magazine.[75] In late September 2007, Yale's and Peru's negotiators announced that they had made a deal that would serve as a model for future negotiations between museums and archaeologically rich countries. At first blush, it seemed like Peru had won. If Peru let a "research collection" remain at Yale, the school would acknowledge Peru's title to the artifacts and return about 380 "museum-quality" pieces when Peru finished a museum to house them, hopefully by 2011, the hundredth anniversary of Bingham's visit to Machu Picchu. In addition, Yale would finance at least three years of academic exchange.

The agreement withered under Peruvian scrutiny, however. "How much longer will those pieces stay there? A century more?" the archaeologist Luis Lumbreras asked in the Peruvian newspaper *El Comercio.* Lumbreras turned out to be right. García's administration had revealed that all of Machu Picchu's graves would be returned eventually, but omitted a wrinkle that Yale shared with its own *Daily News:* that the "research collection"—chosen by Yale—would stay in New Haven for another 99 years.

On the one hand, the condition allowed Yale to keep researching Machu Pic-chu—a right it had perhaps earned. But on the other, it suggested that the com-promise truly was a breakthrough. Of the many countries waging campaigns to recover illegally or unethically held art, artifacts, and human remains, not one had let the institution under scrutiny so define the terms of their settlement as García's Peru had let Yale.

The compromise unraveled further when Peru's press learned that Peru's ne-gotiator, who was the minister of Housing, had agreed to divide the collection before Peruvian archaeologists could even inspect it. When Peru's archaeologists flew to New Haven to inventory the collection, they found that Yale's curation had not been as spotless as previously thought. Bingham and his successors' own publications contain references to moths eating mummy wrappings, the loss of certain animal remains, and "fires, floods, and frequent transfers."[76] In 1930, Bing-ham reported that the crown jewel of the Yale expedition—the ceremonial bronze knife with a boy fishing on its handle—had been stolen.[77] It has reappeared since, suggesting it was merely misplaced. When Peruvian archaeologist Sonia Guillén traveled to Yale in the 1990s, she found that the bones from Machu Picchu had de-teriorated and that students were using them in osteology classes.[78] The jumbled boxes that Bingham sent to Peru in the 1920s have suffered a similar fate, but that was in part due to Bingham's lack of documentation.

The Peruvians were most shocked, however, to find that the collection was bigger than they thought. They found upward of 46,000 pieces, compared to Yale's count of 5,415, plus 329 museum-quality artifacts. There certainly was a politics of counting going on here—Peru counted two teeth from one individ-ual as separate pieces, and Yale viewed the remains of a body as a single lot—but for the first time the Peruvian archaeologists understood what dividing the col-lection would mean.

Yet even then it was unclear what was from Machu Picchu, and thus up for negotiation, and what was not. Objects viewed one day were literally off the table the next. Until recently, Yale's online registry listed the gold and silver artifacts that Yale's expedition members took out in their luggage in 1914 as well as the artifacts from Vitcos and Patallacta, which should have gone back to Peru in the 1920s. When they were pointed out, the museum took down the online collection registry and claimed that the inventory was flawed—which, if true, was hardly comforting.[79] More pressingly, it was during this trip that Peru's officials under-stood what Valcárcel had alluded to: that when the Machu Picchu collection arrived at the Peabody in the early 1920s, it was mixed up with the 366 "very fine" ceramics and stone artifacts that Tomás Alvistur had smuggled out in 1914. The artifacts remained in Yale's collection, and the museum was vague as to which artifacts were which.

Although the revelation confirmed that Bingham was double-dealing, Peru believed that the poor documentation gave contemporary Yale an out. Because international conventions demand that only artifacts smuggled after 1970 be returned, Yale was not legally required to return anything that Alvistur sent to Bingham. Bingham's illicit acquisitions were thus an asset. Peru would later charge that Yale might use such a vague inventory to "move pieces between the collections from each expedition with little risk of its malfeasance being discovered."[80]

Peru was thoroughly disenchanted. In December 2008, the country sued Yale in U.S. District Court in the District of Columbia for damages and the return of *all* artifacts Bingham had taken from Peru. The lawsuit alleged that Yale's possession of these artifacts violated both the 1912 and 1916 decrees that let them leave the country as well as the spirit of modern international cultural property conventions. Peru accused Yale of breaking Peruvian law, of attempting to convert Peruvian property into their own, of committing fraud and conspiracy, and of exploiting the collection for profit. The suit raised the old charge that Bingham had smuggled gold artifacts through Bolivia, but its historical core was persuasive: in 1912 and 1916, Peru had told Yale that it could borrow its artifacts not own them. Coincidentally, two months later, the descendents of the Apache Geronimo sued both the secret society Skull and Bones and Yale for the return of Geronimo's skull, purportedly disinterred from Oklahoma and brought to New Haven in 1917.

After declaring a lack of involvement in the Geronimo case, Yale's lawyers called Peru's lawsuit "stale and meritless," suggesting they would argue that the statute of limitations allowing Peru to make its complaint had run out long ago. More immediately, Yale argued that Peru's lawyers ought to have filed suit in Connecticut, as the artifacts had been in New Haven for almost a century. The court's judge agreed and in August 2009 transferred the case to Connecticut's U.S. District Court instead. Shortly thereafter, Peru changed its lawyers without comment. In mid-October, Yale filed its memorandum in support of a motion to dismiss Peru's complaint. Sure enough, its general thrust was that the suit was time-barred, arguing that because of Connecticut's statute of limitations, Peru should have sued Yale earlier if it believed there was wrongdoing. Any witnesses from Bingham's time had died. Listing the many references to Yale's possession of the artifacts throughout the twentieth century, Yale's representation said that, at latest, Peru should have served Yale with papers in early December 2008. Peru's lawyers did so in early 2009. As for the overarching charge that Yale's possession of Machu Picchu's artifacts was illegitimate, Yale claimed it was "fully prepared to prove at trial that it has acted honorably throughout the long decades and that it is the lawful owner of the Incan materials kept at its Peabody Museum."[81] The memorandum offered no hint of what that proof would be.

As of this epilogue's writing, the lawsuit remains unsettled. Public attention in Peru has turned to more pressing issues, such as the failed reconstruction of southern Peruvian cities destroyed by an earthquake in 2007 and conflict over resource development between the government and the country's lowland indigenous peoples, like those whom Bingham met at Espiritu Pampa.

On Yale's campus, opinions have been mixed. On the one hand, the administration's stance has encouraged an ugly chauvinism. One *Yale Daily News* columnist laughably warned that returning the artifacts to Peru would put them at risk of terrorist attack.[82] Anonymous Internet message boards are no judge of a community's opinion, but the *Yale Daily News*'s website has liberated some contributors from demands of civility or even facts. "Whatever happened to the victor go the spoils?" asked one poster. "If a Peruvian explorer had found a bunch of American artifacts before we were a country and now refused to give them back, that would be fine by me as well. Yale found them, Yale took them, Yale has them. End of story."[83]

Other posters were far more sympathetic to Peru, suggesting that if cooler heads in the community prevail, Peru might see its artifacts by the hundredth anniversary of Bingham's visit. One anonymous Yale graduate who got to examine the artifacts in an archaeology class hoped "that Peru can see the serious, inspirational and culturally sensitive scholarship that Yale has been able to do with the artifacts." But, he or she went on: "That said, the artifacts belong to Peru. This is the bottom line, so hopefully a balance can be reached between Peru learning to appreciate Yale's work on their culture and history, and Yale returning everything to Peru as soon as possible."

I agree. In July 2009, I stopped by the Peabody Museum in New Haven, which my father first took me to when I was seven. The museum was undergoing renovation; the triceratops skulls were packed in cotton and gauze, as if they had toothaches. The dinosaur mural that I once had as a poster on my wall was being restored. Up on the third floor, I visited the Egyptian mummy that scared me when I was young. A group of teenage boys were there looking at it. "Two thousand years from now, they're going to be looking at me like that," said one, laughing.

I walked downstairs, where there are only two small rooms devoted to the Machu Picchu collection. One has a model of the ruins and a video, and it sees a healthy traffic of visitors. In the other room, no one lingers; it holds a few of the collection's smaller ceramics, painted with butterflies, birds, and geometric shapes. There are three not from Machu Picchu; bought in Cuzco, they hint. I wonder why the bronze knives, shawl pins, stone boxes, and silver rings are not on display. It's a room where absence makes a deep impression—patrons' lack of attention, the artifacts' lack of context, and the false impression that all Yale has are ceramics.

Leaving the Peabody, I feel torn. I do not believe the claims of major museums that if they send back one artifact, they will set a precedent by which all the world's art and artifacts will fly back to their creators' descendants. But I also believe there is some value in the international study and display of artifacts as examples of the world's diversity of art and culture. I grew up immersed in Peruvian, Oceanic, and African art and artifacts in the museums of New York. They filled me with wonder and sympathy. They made me want to travel. I want my future children to feel the same.

I draw the line, however, when a loaned collection becomes a trophy, and includes human remains. I believe that Yale University should return to Peru the skulls, bones, and artifacts that Hiram Bingham excavated and exported from Machu Picchu and other sites as soon as possible without conditions. Peru does not deny the importance of Yale's curatorship of the collection, nor how it has deepened interest in Peru. Instead, its representatives call for their return because they believe it is historically, ethically, and legally right. Before, during, and after Bingham's expeditions, Peru's intellectuals and indigenous people were prompting the government to regulate excavation and prevent the exportation of artifacts—legal safeguards that every archaeologist in Peru must follow today. The year that Bingham didn't seek Peruvian permission to excavate was the year his career in exploration ended. Nor could he legally export Peruvian artifacts without Peruvian permission—those artifacts left the country as loans. And when Bingham felt that those decrees prevented him from building the collection he thought Yale demanded, he paid for smuggled artifacts. Although it remains to be seen how Yale and Peru's modern legal confrontation will end, historical facts hardly favor Yale's possession of the Machu Picchu artifacts from the 1920s on. Bingham represented Yale in Peru, and the university should respect the decrees that were applied to his expedition.

The fact that these are not just artifacts, but the skulls, bones, and funerary remains of Peru's pre-Columbian dead, makes Yale's intransigence doubly incredible. It is indeed problematic when a country's government, like Peru's, claims to represent a historically marginalized indigenous group—but that should be a problem worked out between the government of Peru and its indigenous majority, not Peru and Yale.[84] These are not Greek sculptures on display in Yale's art gallery, planting the seeds of a hundred new artists—these are the skulls and bones and possessions of people who once struggled, danced, and buried family members of their own. Yale has contributed much by their study, but after the latest wave of work, it is hard to see what else might be gained by their examination by undergraduates in osteology classes. If, at their core, history and archaeology are our attempts to understand and respect the lives of the past on their own terms, then the respectful treatment of human remains is the litmus test of whether our practices are civilized or cruel. Yale's possession of Machu Picchu's dead not only lends an unattractive colonial tinge to the university but also shows how Yale refuses to recognize the expedition's place in the hemisphere's history of exploitation.

I also believe that the artifacts should go back because they prevent a mature appreciation of Hiram Bingham's legacy. There are few explorers in history who so fell in love with their subject. Bingham deserves credit for revealing Machu Picchu and for making it famous. With the help of Peruvian scholars like Carlos Romero and local informants like Juan Quispicusi, he went on to find Vitcos and Espiritu Pampa, scenes of the final moments of Manco Inca, Titu Cusi, and Tupac Amaru, three of the most important and tragic figures in Peruvian history. These were important rediscoveries: Machu Picchu represents the Inca empire at its height, and Vitcos and Espiritu Pampa embody Inca resistance to Spanish imperialism. Bingham did not understand all that he saw, and there were many Peruvians who had seen these ruins before him, but his desire to understand them within the story of Spanish and Inca struggle is one of the more compelling acts in the history of exploration. And in excavating, he started modern Inca archaeology—interested less in fabulous finds than in using chronicles, architecture, geography, and artifacts to understand how Inca legends matched up to the chronological reality. His expedition also paid attention to the lives of the humbler members of Inca society: the peons, the poor, and the transplanted. I study history because of Hiram Bingham.

In doing so, however, I have grappled with the less shining side of his legacy. Hiram Bingham was a man of his time, thoroughly bound by American piety, wealth, and colonialist attitudes toward the native peoples of the world. To explore and excavate, he took advantage of forced Indian labor. He was raised to believe himself the hero of his life, and at times obscured the help he received from the many Peruvians who preceded him in the archives and mountains. He loved his discoveries so much that he had to possess them, losing himself in the moral jungle of that decision. Bingham sought exceptions as a white American and representative of Yale, then bent and broke Peruvian law when he didn't get special treatment. When confronted by his Peruvian collaborators, he quit the work, kept Machu Picchu's artifacts at Yale, and went into politics, where his mistakes were less easily hidden.

Yet Hiram Bingham's trespasses also created a space for Peruvian debate. His high-profile expeditions were a lightning rod for Peruvian criticisms of foreign exploitation of history, unauthorized excavation, and the rampant exportation of artifacts. Peruvian intellectuals were able to convince the government, and perhaps the populace, that archaeology was a job better managed locally, that Peru was indeed indigenous, and that it did matter where its artifacts resided. By denouncing the expedition, indigenous Peruvians were able to take revenge, however slight, upon Yale for its use of forced labor. And in the vacuum created by Peruvian mistrust of foreign archaeologists, individuals like Julio C. Tello and Luis E. Valcárcel could thrive and develop as scholars.

When Bingham refused to return Machu Picchu's artifacts, he may have even pushed Peru toward stronger laws. In 1929, Peru's congress definitively declared that all ruins and the artifacts they contained were the property of the state, forbidding their exportation forever. It was by no means a perfect solution: the state can expropriate the lands of landowners and indigenous farmers alike if they contain ruins, and looting continues to be a major problem.[85] Nevertheless, it arguably marked how far the country's elites had come in valuing the protection of the indigenous past. Bingham may not have liked it, but he was part of that change.

Which is not to say that the story of Hiram Bingham and Machu Picchu can ever be made happy or resolved. Nowhere are the ambiguities of that legacy more evident than at Machu Picchu itself. Before entering the ruins, visitors pass four markers—three of bronze, one of stone, all inscribed in Spanish. The Rotary Club of Cuzco placed the first bronze plaque in 1948 to honor Bingham during his visit as the "Scientific Discoverer" of Machu Picchu. The second bronze marker dates to 1961, honoring Hiram Bingham on the fiftieth anniversary of the "discovery." Cuzco's department of industry and tourism placed the third bronze plaque on the seventy-fifth anniversary of the site's "scientific discovery"; it makes no reference to Bingham, instead "rendering homage to our sons of Inti"—the Sun—"who built Machupicchu, resplendent and signal monument of the culture of the Americas [*sic*]."[86] And on October 1993, 501 years after Europe's arrival to the New World, Peru's National Institute of Culture installed its stone marker, "rendering homage to Melchor Arteaga, Richarte and Alvarez, who lived in Machu Picchu before Hiram Bingham."

Below the ruins, by the Urubamba River, is an even more complex tribute to the ruins' past and present residents and visitors: the site museum of Machu Picchu, filled with explanations of native engineering, computer reenactments of sun worship, and more than 200 artifacts found at the site by Peruvian archaeologists. Far fewer tourists visit the museum of Machu Picchu than the ruins themselves, but those who do, perhaps on rainy days, learn much more about the Inca history of the site than from any guide—or from the exhibit at Yale. The museum credits Bingham for making Machu Picchu famous, but it also alludes to the controversy regarding the artifacts' export. Beyond two five-and-a-half-foot-tall mannequins of Incas building Machu Picchu, visitors can admire the only gold ever excavated from Machu Picchu: a single bracelet, found by Peruvian archaeologist Elva Torres as she collected soil samples for an American consulting firm.[87] The controversy over Machu Picchu's artifacts should not be misinterpreted as general antipathy against U.S. archaeologists and researchers. When foreign collaborators respect the laws of a country and engage in a spirit of open exchange, good work flourishes.

If the rain is still coming down, visitors can don their ponchos and inspect the brightly colored flowers trembling in the Orchid Garden behind the museum. If they've yet to visit Machu Picchu, they might return to the road and flag down one of the buses rumbling up the Hiram Bingham Highway—as good a monument imaginable to the explorer who made the ruins famous to the world. If they're feeling adventurous, however, they might ask one of the many local boys dressed in neo-Inca clothing to guide them up the two-mile footpath to the ruins instead. It is not the same path that Hiram Bingham took that July morning in 1911, and it is far less steep, but the way is no less breathtaking. In the shadow of Machu Picchu, the trail bridges the divide between the wild river below and the beautiful ruins above—that ambiguous path blazed by both Peruvians and Americans between reality and legend, loss and hope; from the cradle to the grave and back again.

Afterword

*T*here is a Peruvian saying that I often thought about during the research and writing of this book: "*Incas sí, Indios no.*" The phrase comments on the fact that it is easy to romanticize the pre-Columbian past while ignoring the indigenous present. Although the phrase has a long history in Perú, I heard it directed at foreign archaeologists, and I hoped it wasn't being said about me behind my back.[1] When a taxi driver told me that Hiram Bingham would have been shot had he come back to Peru, I winced. While I was in Peru, I grappled with Bingham's story in part to understand my own relationship to Yale and all the privileges and access that the university gave me. I tried to be aware of my own privileges and prejudices, trying not to fall into the same trap Bingham did by focusing on Machu Picchu—and now the controversy surrounding it—instead of studying more pressing issues in Peruvian history and modern life. I fear that I could have done better.

I never felt that fear as strongly as when one of my closest friends from Yale, James, came to visit me in Cuzco. The first person from his high school to go to Yale, James began college as a brilliant actor, charismatic, confident. We were sure that he would be the one to make it big. But then his plans changed. By the time we graduated, he had left his hunger for fame behind. He became aggressively earnest and openly struggled with privilege and personal pain—of himself and others—through music and action. He spent nights on the streets in New York bringing food to the homeless. He gave away all he had and then so much more that it could be painful to watch—and even more painful when he turned his standards on us. James, our other roommate, Adam, and I traveled together, but being with him grew harder and harder. James had less interest in arriving than searching for a moment. He had less interest in history than in saving everyone we met.

When he came to Peru, I was worried about how it would go, whether he would look at my life and smirk. At first, however, it was wonderful. We met in Lima, and I showed him the city. We got lost in its Chinatown, walking for hours. We flew to Cuzco, where Adam joined us, and we hiked up to Machu Picchu by moonlight. We hardly slept, we were so full of energy. Cuzco's storefront shamans rolled their eyes at us as we peppered them with questions. We talked about going down into the jungle to see Espiritu Pampa—Vilcabamba, the last refuge of Tupac Amaru—which I had yet to visit.

But we never would. We began to argue over who we were, whether I was hiding behind my fellowship and he was hiding behind political rhetoric. I wanted to do research, go to dinner, and talk; James filmed police harassing Indian market women. I grew defensive, fearing that because of my project I had missed an opportunity to explore like he had. He went walking for hours alone at night, sleeping very little. When I left, he stayed on. Despite not speaking much Spanish, he had made more friends in three months than I had in a year. When we hugged each other goodbye at Cuzco's airport, I felt like an estranged brother—like we were two magnets touching, identical but also opposed, flying in different directions. He seemed happy.

I would never see James again. He came back to the United States and worked for AmeriCorps in Atlanta. He made music, he helped build urban gardens, and he slept on the streets more and more often. James pushed and pushed at life, and then, in June 2007, he died, tragically and suddenly. For me, it was an angry loss; a sadness at losing one of the most complicated, closest friends I will ever have, but also a feeling that we were in an argument that could never be finished. He had been right; but he was also gone.

At James's memorial service, his sisters gave his close friends small canisters filled with his ashes. We were to spread them around the world. One friend swam them out into the Atlantic and another laid them in a Vermont forest. I held onto mine, and it weighed heavily on my bedside table. I did not know how to grieve or lay down my regrets. I could neither let James's remains float away nor really come to terms with what they meant.

A year later, in June 2008, I was tired of dreams in which I wept but awoke with a grimacing, dry face. I needed to say goodbye and to find the place where he and I could have met, even if it was fantasy—a place between remembering and possession. I had already made plans to travel to Peru, to recheck a few sources in the archives and nail down the last few pieces of this book. But perhaps I could do more. I already had the idea when I packed the canister that contained James's ashes in my backpack, said goodbye to my girlfriend, Hannah, and got on a plane to Cuzco. Once there, I met my sister, Jess, and my friends Shane and Gillian, already in Peru. We bought food, machetes, and duffel bags and took an eight-hour bus ride over the mountains beyond Machu Picchu and down to the bridge at Chaullay. We were headed to Espiritu Pampa to see the last city of the Incas—perhaps to say goodbye.

The Vilcabamba province is closer than it was when Bingham visited, but not by much. Roads, cars, and telephone wires connect it to Cuzco and the outside world, but the soaring cliffs make the place feel as timeless and protected as it did in 1911.

We take a taxi on a winding dirt road to Huancacalle, the town below the hill of Rosaspata. Our driver, a twenty-year-old, asks us whether we're looking for gold. We laugh, and I explain that we are here to see the ruins. He smiles and says that the Incas didn't build Vitcos; aliens did. I try to stand up for the Incas, but he has none of it. We are chuckling at each other—he might be playing a trick on the gringo—but it feels strange. A week-and-a-half before we left for Peru, *Indiana Jones and the Kingdom of the Crystal Skull* hit theaters. The blockbuster film propelled Harrison Ford's character to 1957 and the Cold War. Instead of Nazis and Holy Grails, he fought telepathic Soviet thugs and killer ants for a glowing crystal skull—one that needed to be *returned* to a city lost in the Peruvian jungle, not stolen from one. My sister pointed out the fact that the lost city turns out to have been built by aliens, not Indians—who are depicted as shrieking, spear-shaking savages—calling back to the racist theories that native peoples could never have built civilizations in the New World. I agreed, but I also appreciated how much our younger brother enjoyed the movie, even the scenes in which Indy's new-found son swings through the jungle like Tarzan. More personally, it was as if someone had taken all of my obsessions and shaken them into one bizarre atomic cocktail: the movie's early scenes were filmed at Yale, Indy ends up in Cuzco, and he returns an artifact to a lost city in the jungle. It felt like Spielberg and Lucas were giving a quiet nod back to Indy's distant ancestor, Hiram Bingham, but unrolling his story in reverse.

Now, talking to the driver, I worry that my sister and I were both right in a sad and upsetting way. What did it mean that he perhaps believed that the region's indigenous ancestors were incapable of building such beauty? Or that he thought I wanted to hear that? The conversation reminded me of how Bingham's identification of Machu Picchu as the last, lost city of the Incas sticks to the site, despite being disproved. I ask him whether he's heard of Indiana Jones. He shakes his head and beeps his horn at the children playing in the road. I begin to tell him about *Kingdom of the Crystal Skull,* but he interrupts me: "Yes," he says smiling. "That's it."

In Huancacalle, a village above Puquiura, we stay at the one hostel in town, the waggishly named 6pac Manco, run by the Cobos family. It was Julio Cobos who guided the explorer Gene Savoy to Espiritu Pampa in the 1960s. Julio has passed away, but his sons take turns running the hostel and contracting trips to Inca ruins for the foreign travelers who want to see more than Machu Picchu. This year, it's Vicente's turn. He hadn't heard that Savoy had died in September 2007—three days before Yale and Peru announced the compromise that would later be aborted—and before I realize it, I'm breaking the news.

He is shocked, and he walks us up the ridge of Rosaspata in silence. The hike is a steep one, but short, and by midmorning we're gazing at the wide plaza before Manco's massive, thirty-door palace, Vitcos. It was here that the renegade Spaniards stabbed the rebel Inca to death and here that his son Titu Cusi woke up bellowing.

It's quiet. Unlike Machu Picchu, which sees up to 2,500 visitors a day, there is only one other visitor on the ridge that morning. But it's not for lack of care. For more than two decades, local residents have gathered here every July 24 to celebrate Inti Raymi, an Inca sun ceremony, with traditional dress, dancing, and songs. Government archaeologists have also directed the ruins' reconstruction. Critics say they made some mistakes—Vicente taps his walking stick against one section and says, "Not as good as the Incas"—but the overall effect is stunning. It feels as though Manco himself could walk out from beneath the palace's massive white lintels at any moment.

That afternoon he takes us to Yurak Rumi, the great white stone shrine that the Spanish missionaries burned and whose pool Hiram Bingham drained to search for artifacts. It feels old, like a giant sleeping in a wonderful, lush, tree-lined valley. It's easy to imagine an Inca priest or the emperor himself, the royal fringe on his forehead, stepping atop the rock's crest and raising hands to the rising sun. Again, we are the only ones there, except for cattle and sheep on the hillsides around us.

Later that evening, I ask Vicente what he thought about the rumors of treasure that surrounded explorers like Bingham and Savoy. He shakes his head dismissively. His family has lived and worked with many explorers, and most had money already. They never excavated what they found—just cleared and mapped. "None of them have been interested in finding treasure, gold, silver. Just ruins. That was their treasure."

We leave at 7:30 the next morning, beginning the long march to Espiritu Pampa. We puff up the hill behind Huancacalle to the next valley, the Pampaconas, or Concevidayoc. We soon lag behind our *arriero* and his two mules. His name is Ivan, and though he is only twenty-one years old, he has been running cattle and gringos through the region for five years now. He's tall and healthy, with dark eyes, cropped black hair, and a handsome Inca nose. He's a little wary of us and rightly so. When I realize that he shares the same last name as the old man whom Bingham interviewed in the town of San Victoria de la Vilcabamba—which we pass through just before lunch—it's all I can do not to pump Ivan for his family history. We pass through the town of San Victoria de la Vilcabamba itself and meet a group of schoolgirls. When Gillian tells them where we're going, one of the girls hands her bag to a friend and jokes that she is going to Espiritu Pampa too. She and her friend burst into giggles, then bid us goodbye.

We climb over the pass, and the valley of the Pampaconas stretches out before us. In 1571, the terrain was muddy and harsh. This was where the Incas dragged the missionary Ortíz to his death. But in the midday sun of the dry season, it's stunning. We are surrounded by *nevados*—glacier-covered peaks—and as we descend into the next valley, the river snakes past the homes of small-scale cattle ranchers. Pale grass and stone fences give way to scrubby trees and underbrush. The river winds and drops into thicker vegetation and old walls held together by vines and moss. We camp that night at Ututu, a green alluvial plain. That night we see the clearest starscape we have ever seen. The sky is almost white with stars, so bright that even the dark spaces within the Milky Way are visible—strange shapes that held their own place in Inca cosmology. Darkness never seemed so alive and comforting.

Our second day takes us into the jungle. The air thickens, as does our sweat. We pass through ghostly clearings filled with trees hanging with moss and epiphytes, stolid cattle, and human-sized rocks that press from the grass like the stones Pachacutec supposedly brought to life to start his empire. Unseen birds send out sonarlike cries—pings and exhalations that make us feel quiet and alone.

The trail rises above the river, and we pass the houses of poorer, mostly indigenous families. Some are friendly, others suspicious. The region has seen its share of strife since Bingham passed through in 1911. In the 1950s and 1960s, farmers began resisting the power of wealthy landowners, invading the landowners' land and arming themselves. The movement fell apart under police pressure, but the national government enacted a series of agrarian reforms that redistributed land holdings to peasants. In the 1980s, the region was invaded by the Shining Path—mostly intellectuals from Lima claiming to fight for peasants yet summarily executing those unsympathetic to their cause. The Peruvian army was little better, massacring whole indigenous villages suspected of leftist sympathies. Although peasants elsewhere organized themselves into self-defense patrols, Ivan tells us that many in the Pampaconas simply fled and returned only in the late 1990s when it was safe.

We spend that night in Vista Allegre. When Bingham camped here, it was filled with massive cornstalks and loomed over by a giant, parasite-covered tree. Today it's a soccer field with a small school. The children from nearby households sit with us; my sister shares her colored pencils with them. The school's teacher and four fathers come by at nightfall to ask us to donate to their children's education. We happily oblige.

That night over dinner, Ivan's reticence lessens a little. He talks about foosball, his girlfriend, and the Inti Raymi sun festival held at Vitcos every year. He tells me that when he was younger, he took part in the festival's historical reenactments.

I'm puzzled: "Reenactments of what?"

"Of the Great Rebellion. When the Incas tried to throw out the Spaniards."

"Did some kids have to dress up like Spaniards?"

"Yes." Ivan grins. He knows what's coming.

"Were you ever a Spaniard?"

"No," he says. "I was always an Inca."

I'm up early the next morning to watch Venus disappear. An eleven-year-old named Felipe Poma Cabrera joins me. He says his half-Quechua, half-Spanish name with pride. He has been to Cuzco, but not Espiritu Pampa. He once saw a puma.

The hike that day is a hard one. Rather than descending, the trail takes us over the ridges and tributary streams that vein into the river below. After an hour, my heels are aching, and Shane has fallen into a brook. When Ivan announces we've reached a minor Inca ruin named Urpipata, we gladly stop to change our socks. The ruin's two buildings and wall don't look like much, but the modern explorer Vincent Lee, who has documented many of the secondary ruins of the Vilcabamba, believes that Urpipata was Machu Pucara, one of the last Inca fortifications to fall before the Spanish military expedition of 1572.[2]

The few residents we see are wary of us. A half-hour before we stop for the day, we pass a little boy and his older sister walking in the opposite direction. She takes a knife from her bag and holds it by her leg as we pass. We stop to look at a butterfly, and she stops, turns, and stares at us until we continue.

We arrive at Concevidayoc, where Bingham met the gentle frontiersman Saavedra. This too is a settlement, and we set up our tent on the soccer field, enjoying the view. An older resident with a cheekful of coca leaves tells me that there had been a Saavedra family here once, long, long ago, but they were gone now. When I asked about the jungle people whom Bingham met, he looks puzzled. "Maybe they were here, but not any more," he says. "They all ran away, into the mountains." In the schoolteacher's house behind us, a tinny radio whines like a flying saucer. Its owner is searching for love songs.

We reach Espiritu Pampa on our fourth day on the trail. Ivan gets us up early, and after only twenty minutes of hiking, we smell the smoke. I realize that a farmer somewhere is burning a field to prepare for planting, but for a moment history feels alive.

We pass fifty-yard streams of leaf-cutter ants. Suddenly, we're climbing Inca steps six feet wide. We reach the ridge and rest on a ceremonial *usnu*, the platform where the Incas made offerings before entering the city. If Bingham's successors are right, the Spanish invaders looked down from here four centuries ago and saw Vilcabamba, burning in the morning sun. Peru's archaeologists have restored the *usnu*, but trees have grown around it. To see the settlement below, we must take a few steps along the trail. Modern Espiritu Pampa finally spreads out before us—a few houses, a few fields, and a plain covered by jungle, hiding the old city from sight.

A massive Inca staircase takes us down. It has more than 300 steps and is wide enough for twin streams of llamas, coming and going. It is wide enough for the Inca to have been carried down on a litter. As we descend, I am caught up in emotion. What did it mean for the Incas to run here, so far from Cuzco, and lay down these stones, each one a prayer that the Spaniards could be outlasted? How did the

Spaniards feel descending them? Fearful? Victorious? How did it feel for Tupac Amaru to climb them for the last time, leaving his life behind?

There is a small town below, with a church where the villagers pray. We set up our tents on the grass platform below the church. I put James's ashes in my pocket. Ivan points us in the direction of a guide, but his wife tells us he's in Cuzco, leaving us to find the ruins ourselves. Without our packs we walk quickly, following a trail past orange trees, bananas, and coffee, new-looking farmhouses, a new soccer field.

After what seems like ages, the path turns, and before us are the ruins of Espiritu Pampa, or Vilcabamba the Old, the true lost city of the Incas. There is no one else there, and the quiet draws us in. A space about a quarter-mile square has been cleared. On our left are the remains of the fountain with three spouts. Steps take us into the main plaza. Half of the exposed ruins are restored, but many are not. There are many buildings still covered in the jungle. The main plaza is bounded on one side by a long many-doored palace or meeting hall, much like at Vitcos but completely collapsed. At the palace's corner is a large sacred boulder, like those at Machu Picchu. The main plaza drops down to a lower plaza where two more buildings sit. They are also unrestored, but their fine, white granite doorways mark them as homes of the royalty. There is the stone bridge atop which Bingham posed. Scattered in the ruins are the Spanish-style ceramic roofing tiles that Bingham misunderstood, but that for Gene Savoy helped clinch the site's identity as Vilcabamba.

The government keeps these exposed ruins clear of vines and undergrowth, but massive ceibalike trees remain in place, sheltering the site, keeping it cool and quiet. Their huge roots stretch out like tentacles, and their trunks reach up like great pillars that expand out into great long branches and full leaves. They are the jungle trees we dream of, draped with liana vines and mossy growth, and they make this place the very picture of a lost city, a sort of cathedral to human loss, preserved in green. The vines, the trees, and the stones all hang together.

It could hardly feel more different than Machu Picchu. Bingham wanted Machu Picchu to be the Inca's last refuge because what he loved about the Incas was their magnificence, their taste for beauty, their expansion and success. Bingham identified with the Incas as an idealized American empire whose greatest monument was Machu Picchu, celebrating and sanctifying power and authority. It was just the sort of lost city that Bingham could believe in—a people at their height, frozen in time.

Espíritu Pampa, by contrast, represents a people in flight, trying to recover and not disappear. It sits on a dropped plain between two mountains, nestled in trees. Although much of the ruins remain covered by jungle, what is exposed feels modest, a paler imitation of Inca architecture at its height, but desperately hopeful. Trees, never a big part of highland Inca cosmology, here feel crucial, protective. "This doesn't feel like a place you build when you think you might not make it," says Shane. "This is a place you build when you think you're going to survive."

But Manco and his family did not. Espíritu Pampa, more than any other Inca site I've been to, makes our celebration of Machu Picchu feel somewhat suspect. Do we think of the indigenous people of the Americas only at their precolonial apex, or for how they continue to face Europe's conquest of the larger Americas? Hiram Bingham failed to recognize that Espíritu Pampa was Vilcabamba the Old, the true last city of the Incas, because it looked nothing like the "pure" and peaceful site he had already seen at Machu Picchu. Espíritu Pampa's indigenous refugees presented a more complicated version of the Americas' history, one in which conquest and resistance was ongoing—a fact that may have made Bingham uncomfortable. Instead of grappling with that truth, he returned to the more beautiful site of Machu Picchu, where the expedition tied the ruins' residents back into the same systems of forced labor they had spent years avoiding. They were forced to dig up the remains of the Incas, a people they saw as their ancestors. Between Machu Picchu and Vilcabamba lie what is truly lost in any conquest: not greatness, but hope for a future; not treasure, but entire ways of human life.

I wish James could have seen it. I quietly leave my sister and friends and find a secluded area of the ruins, one of the few that the Campa Asháninka showed Bingham. Cleared from the jungle, there are unrestored, ruined houses here, held together by trees and roots. I hear running water a little ways away, and I clamber over the wall of the furthest house. I take a step and fall through four feet of underbrush. Miraculously, I'm not hurt and see that I've tumbled off a terrace that was hidden by leaves. I push through the vines and branches, scraping my face and forearms, and stumble onto the banks of a thin, clear stream. I begin to weep—the first time I have since James died. I pull the canister from my pocket and tip the ashes into the stream. They do not flow away as I expected, on to the Concevidayoc River, the San Miguel, the Urubamba, and finally the Amazon. They sink instead, staying where they are, James fighting me to the end. I begin laughing through my tears. There is more life in the dead than we can ever imagine, and it is so hard to let go. I reach into the water to pull out a single fragment of bone, to remember.

When I leave the clearing I see that we're no longer alone. There are five Peruvians visiting from Cuzco, where they study tourism. They tell me a government road will reach Espiritu Pampa in about a year. They are practical—Peru needs money, and its ruins are a way to get it. I tell them why I'm here, and they ask whether I've seen Machu Picchu's gold at Yale. They smirk when I say no, but they nod when I talk about how the graves got there. "You already know the true history, then," one says. "It's like this: You don't visit a friend's house and take a souvenir." He pauses. "I'm not calling Hiram Bingham a thief, but he said he would return what he found, and Yale hasn't."

It's a sentiment I agree with, but here, in Espiritu Pampa, it feels like arguing over a will at a funeral. We talk a little more, then I excuse myself, and my sister, friends, and I walk out of the ruins. On the way, we run into Ivan and another young muleteer friend of his, Uriel. Ivan has never seen the ruins before, and he's excited. "We're going to swing on the vines," Uriel says. "Like Tarzan." Ivan flashes us his most unselfconscious grin in four days. It's one of the nicest smiles I've ever seen.

The next morning, before we leave, Ivan points me to Espiritu Pampa's most established family. Their house is made of wooden planks, and through their cracks I can smell a low fire, breakfast. I announce myself, and a slight, elderly woman comes out, wiping her hands on her apron. Her name is Victoria, she's in her mid-60s, and she and her husband have lived in Espiritu Pampa for thirty years. I explain why I'm there, then I ask about ruins and explorers. "Gene Savoy?" I offer.

She wrinkles her forehead and shakes her head, then she offers the name of an explorer from Bingham's era instead—one whose name has mostly been lost to written histories. My pulse quickens a little.

She calls her husband out to continue the conversation. Cipriano is a lifelong farmer, sturdy and stolid, and he too shakes his head at the mention of Gene Savoy. It was Hiram Bingham who discovered Vilcabamba in 1911, he says. I push for more, but he gets bored. In a mix of Quechua and Spanish, he calls his nephew to the door to deal with the nosy gringo. Eloy is friendly, in his late 20s, and he's here to help his uncle tend the land. Leaning against the doorjamb, he gives a fascinatingly specific account of how Bingham reached the ruins, again leaving out Gene Savoy. He claims that Bingham left with perfect architectural plans of the site.

I find this interesting and say so. I ask about the state of the ruins since Bingham. Which is when he says it: "When Hiram Bingham came here the ruins were perfect."

"What?" I think I've misheard him. "Perfect? Perfect how?"

"They were perfect. The walls, the roofs, the stones, all perfect. Clear and uncovered. As if the Incas had just left." Eloy leans back in the house, asks his uncle something in Quechua. His uncle grunts in confirmation. "It was only when Bingham came, made his plans and then left that they fell apart," Eloy continues.

"They were taken by the jungle after Bingham left?" I ask.

"*Sí*," he says, as if it's the most obvious thing in the world. "The jungle."

My friends start calling me. It is time to leave, and Ivan is annoyed at how long I'm taking. I want to stay and ask more questions, but I can't. I fear I misunderstood, that there's been a breakdown in my Spanish. Did he mean to say that Vilcabamba stayed intact three hundred years after the Spaniards hauled Tupac Amaru off to Cuzco? That the ruins were waiting for the Incas' return? Or Bingham's arrival? That having served their purpose, they sunk back into the jungle? Or that by photographing, measuring, and mapping them, Bingham had pinned them to paper like a butterfly, killing them? The ambiguity of it enchants me for a moment: a lost city so perfect that it was beyond resurrection. It just was; it already gave refuge to the jungle's indigenous inhabitants. Only when the explorer came to study it did it fall apart, giving way to the jungle. Only when the explorer arrived was the last city of the Incas truly lost and ruined for good.

Or perhaps not. Bingham's story is romantic enough already, leaving little room for the residents who farm, grow, and think about all sorts of things that have nothing to do with the Incas. Who take refuge in history or exploit it as they see fit. Who hurry outsiders along so they can get on with their lives. Who "explore" us back, noting if we sit and talk about our own families with them, or ask prying questions and leave with a souvenir. Espiritu Pampa is a lesson on the history that can never be owned—all that thrives outside the archive, outside the museum, outside the classroom.

I consider taking off my backpack, being more like James. But Shane is calling. Ivan has his own girlfriend to get back to and has taken off angrily down the trail, annoyed at my delay. Jess and Gillian are following him. I realize it's time to go home even though I still don't want to. So I say my goodbyes, and Shane and I hustle down the trail. I kick myself for not asking more questions, for not listening more, for not being a better person, until we catch up with Gillian and Jess. They are whistling the theme from *Bridge Over the River Kwai* with a dozen children, who are all walking to school. The unbridled optimism of the moment is almost too much, too happy, too perfect.

Ivan waits for us. We do not get lost.

Acknowledgments

*A*book like this could not have happened without a great deal of help. First, there are the librarians and archivists who helped me navigate their collections. This project began in the Latin American Collection of the Manuscripts and Archives Department of Yale's Sterling Memorial Library; my thanks go to Cesar Rodriguez, Chris Weideman, Bill Massa, and everyone there who fielded six years' worth of questions and requests for copies. In the United States, I thank the staff of the National Archives and the National Geographic Society in Washington, DC, the Benson Library at the University of Texas at Austin, and Kylee Omo at the library of the Punahou School in Honolulu. In London, I thank the staff of the Royal Geographic Society. In Peru, I thank the librarians and archivists at the Archivo Regional del Cusco, the Centro de Estudios Regionales Andinos Bartolomé de las Casas, the newspaper *El Sol,* the Archivo Municipal of Cusco, the Museo Inka of Cusco, the Archivo General de la Nación, the Biblioteca Nacional, the Instituto Nacional de Cultura, and Ada Arrieta and the staff of the Instituto Riva-Agüero at the Pontificia Universidad Católica del Peru.

This book's errors and arguments are my own; for most everything else, I credit my mentors. From my time at Yale, I thank Rolena Adorno for teaching me about Guaman Poma de Ayala and the power of the written word, and Seth Fein for pointing me toward the Bingham collection. My deepest thanks go to Gilbert Joseph and Patricia Pessar, who challenged me when I needed it and supported me at all other times. At the University of Texas, I thank professors Erika Bsumek, Jorge Cañizares-Esguerra, and Seth Garfield for their edits and guidance; Jim Sidbury, Marilyn Lehman, and the staff of the History Department for their support; and the Donald D. Harrington Fellows Program for teaching me Texas hospitality.

In Peru, I had more guides than I can thank. First of all, thanks go to Henry Harman Guerra, Marcela Harth, and Lima's Fulbright Committee, and Xavier Ricard Lanard of the Centro de Estudios Regionales Andinos Bartolomé de las Casas (CBC) for bringing me to Peru. I thank José Cárdenas Bunsen and Keely Beth Maxwell for pointing me in the right direction as I hit the ground. For friendly reminders that I was "an Anglo-Saxon barbarian," I thank Pedro Guibovich. I thank Mariana Mould de Pease for provoking hours of research and debate; I hope we can continue the conversation. In Lima, I also thank Jose Tamayo Herrera, Federico Kaufmann Doig, and César Coloma Pocari. In Cuzco, I thank Donato Amado and Jorge Flores Ochoa for helping me understand the Cusqueño side of Bingham's explorations, and Dante Astete at Universidad Nacional de San Antonio Abad del Cusco. For helping me understand Peruvian archaeology and museums, I thank Fernando Astete at the Archaeological Park of Machu Picchu and my friend Veronika Tupayachi. I thank Blanca Alva Guerrero and Maria Elena Cordova of the Instituto Nacional de Cultura for explaining Peruvian cultural patrimony and the law. And lastly, I thank the children of Luis Valcárcel, especially Frank, who brought his father to life for me.

For sharing their thoughts on their grandfather, great-grandfather, and father-in-law, I thank David Bingham, June Bingham, Tiff Bingham, and all the members of the Bingham family I spoke to, however briefly. I especially thank Alfreda Bingham Shapere and Timothy Bingham for giving me permission to quote from their grandfather's papers.

For helping my work move from passion to publication, I must thank Lincoln Caplan of *Legal Affairs Magazine,* Kate Marsh and Peter Scoblic at *The New Republic,* and George Kalogerakis at the *New York Times.* I thank Emily Adams for creating the wonderful images that punctuate this book. A special thank you is owed to my agent Dan Conaway of Writers House, the most generous advisor imaginable, and his assistant, Stephan Barr. And finally, a big thank you goes to my patient editor, Luba Ostashevsky, and the rest of the wonderful Palgrave team: Laura Lancaster, Donna Cherry, and Roberta Scheer.

There are family members, fellow writers, friends, and other mentors who advised me, helped get me to Peru, kept me cheerful, and read my work at crucial times: Helen Aslanides, Roger Atwood, Wayne Barrett, Daniel Buck, Lambros Comitas, Ryan Floyd, Thomas Frampton, Paolo Greer, JL Chamberlain and Sons, Robert Jansen, James Jenkins, Ben Johnson, Brian Jones, Colleen Kinder, John Leivers, Brendan Lynaugh, Sandy Mayson, Annie Murphy, Gordon Radley, Michael Shifter, Johanna Silver, Cameron Strang, Rosa Sumar, Hugh Thomson, and Emily Weinstein. I thank my younger brother, Douglas, for his enthusiasm and sense of humor, and my stepparents, Vivian and Kevin, for their smiling patience. For being with me in Peru for that last trip, reading my work, and picking my brain throughout, I thank the high-altitude Shane Boris, Gillian Cassell-Stiga, and my sister, Jessica, whose heart is a bear. Adam Chanzit, Emily Guilmette, and Jared Leboff went beyond the call of duty for many reasons they know and will not hold over me. And for the best summer of my life, which was lucky enough to be the summer I finished this book, I thank my closest reader, Hannah Carney, who has enriched my life in so many ways.

The final thank you goes to Brigid and Bill, my mother and father, who met in Papua New Guinea, an Australian midwife and an American anthropologist trying to find their way. They gave their children compassion and curiosity, a sense of fair play, and a desire for adventure. This is their book too. For their unrelenting love and support, I cannot thank them enough.

A Note on Sources

O ne needs only scan the 1,140 entries of the Programa Machu Picchu's *Recopilación bibliográfica del Santuario Histórico de Machu Picchu* (Cusco: Programa Machu Picchu 2003) to get a sense of how many books touching upon Machu Picchu are out there.

Many shed light on its revelation and excavation, but the following publications proved crucial (their full bibliographical information is in the endnotes below). First and foremost are the writings that emerged from Bingham's expeditions. For the reader who wants the most exciting version of Machu Picchu's revelation, Hiram Bingham's *Lost City of the Incas* is a classic. The 2003 edition by Phoenix contains an excellent introduction by the explorer Hugh Thomson explaining why Bingham's account is at times unreliable. The following two accounts are hard to find outside of research libraries but are crucial for understanding what the excavations of Machu Picchu turned up: Bingham's *Machu Picchu: A Citadel of the Incas,* and George Eaton's *The Collection of Osteological Material from Machu Picchu.* For perspectives on Machu Picchu today, see Richard Burger and Lucy Salazar's edited companion to the 2003 Yale exhibition, *Machu Picchu: Unveiling the Mystery of the Incas* and the Instituto Nacional de Cultura's 2005 edited volume, *Machupicchu: Historia, Sacralidad E Identidad.*

To understand Bingham from a biographical standpoint, I most often turned to the work of his son Alfred Bingham, a lawyer who in his later years focused his keen mind on his family, producing two useful books: *Explorer of Machu Picchu* and *The Tiffany Fortune.* Alfred has since passed on, but both books are available in some libraries and online from his daughter Alfreda at the website http://www.machu piccuexplorer.com. Also useful—but more of a catalogue than a history—was his brother Woodbridge's *Hiram Bingham: A Personal History.* For some trenchant generational insights, I consulted historian Char Miller's *Fathers and Sons: The Bingham Family and the American Mission.*

To understand the world of South American exploration then and now, I've kept a few recent books close at hand: Candace Millard's *The River of Doubt,* Robert M. Poole's *Explorers House,* and Hugh Thomson's *The White Rock.* For the politics of American archaeology, I was inspired by Orin Starn's *Ishi's Brain,* David Hurst Thomas's *Skull Wars,* and Michael F. Brown's *Who Owns Native Culture?* For the history of Peru's jungle peoples, I looked to Michael F. Brown and Eduardo Fernández's *War of Shadows: The Struggle for Utopia in the Peruvian Amazon.* For trends in Andean history and archaeology, I've been influenced by the work of Brian Bauer, Catherine Julien, Peter Kaulicke, Brooke Larson, Sabine MacCormack, Gary Urton, and John H. Rowe. Lastly, there is the story in which this history is grounded—the sixteenth-century conquest of Peru. To capture that time, I relied heavily upon John Hemming's authoritative *The Conquest of the Incas,* still the benchmark account of Manco and his family's fall, and one of the best histories I know.

Most importantly, my work on the Yale expeditions' controversies and political contexts overlaps with and differs from four excellent publications that emerged while I was finishing my senior essay in 2003 or soon afterward. Marisol de la Cadena's *Indigenous Mestizo* omits the Yale expedition but treats the world of Luis E. Valcárcel and his fellow *indigenistas* in Cuzco from the early decades of the 1900s on; I believe that the international realm of the Machu Picchu story complicates, if only by a degree, de la Cadena's compelling argument that Cuzco's *indigenistas* were thoroughly bound by old Peruvian racial prejudices. Ricardo D. Salvatore's *Nepantla* article, "Local Versus Imperial Knowledge: Reflections on Hiram Bingham and the Yale Peruvian Expedition," laid out the Yale expeditions as a conflict between U.S. acquisitive imperialism and local, Incanist Cuzqueño politics. I clearly believe this is true, but I differ in that

I see the expedition's imperialism as far more frustrated than fulfilled; I also believe that Peruvian resistance to the expedition was not just about anti-imperial and anti-U.S. sentiment: it was very much a debate over how the law should treat pre-Columbian history, monuments, and artifacts, and what that meant for Peru's larger indigenous identity. Environmental anthropologist Keely Beth Maxwell was kind enough to forward me her dissertation, "Lost Cities and Exotic Cows: Constructing the Space of Nature and Culture in the Machu Picchu Historic Sanctuary. Peru," while I was starting my year in Peru. As with Salvatore, I appreciate the depth in which she traces the politics of cultural preservation and monument protection. I hope that my work goes further in plumbing the journals of the expedition members to more definitively pronounce upon the legality of the expedition's excavations and exportations. Lastly, I have taken seriously the call for dialogue in Mariana Mould de Pease's *Machu Picchu Y El Código De Ética De La Sociedad De Arqueología Americana: Una invitación al diálogo intercultural,* which sketched the outlines of the legal and political process by which Hiram Bingham supposedly "arbitrarily" exported the artifacts from Machu Picchu from Peru. The book also documents Mould de Pease's vigorous efforts to bring the story to Peruvians' attention. It does not, however, go into the biography of Bingham or the expeditions' closed-door negotiations and confrontrations with the Peruvian government and local intellectuals. These elements, I believe, make the story of Hiram Bingham and Machu Picchu far more tragic and the exportation of the ruins' artifacts far less arbitrary: it began in cooperation, genuine good will, and trust before coming apart in mutual recrimantions and perceived betrayals. I hope that *Cradle of Gold* enriches these authors' efforts with the archives in Peru and the United States that I have been able to access, telling the expeditions' story through narrative, with all the contradictions that entails.

By and large, however, this book is a work of primary research drawn from archives and publications in the United States and Peru, some of which were fruitful, others less so. All those I consulted are listed below. Those that most actively informed my argument are preceded by the abbreviations used in my endnotes. I have also abbreviated their box and folder numbers; for example, the Yale Peruvian Expedition Papers, Box 5, Folder 24 is listed as YPEP 5–24.

ARCHIVES:

Great Britain

RGS: Royal Geographic Society Archives, London, England

Peru

Archivo Regional del Cusco, Universidad San Antonio Abad del Cusco, Cusco

Biblioteca del Centro de Estudios Regionales Andinos Bartolomé de las Casas, Cusco

Archivo Municipal del Cusco

Archivo del Museo Inka, Cusco

Archivo General de la Nación, Lima

Biblioteca Nacional, Lima

INC: Archivo de Luis E. Valcárcel, Instituto Nacional de Cultura, Lima

IRA: Archivo Giesecke del Instituto Riva-Agüero, Lima

United States of America

Manuscripts and Archives Department, Yale University Library, New Haven, CT

    BFP: Bingham Family Papers

    YPEP: Yale Peruvian Expedition Papers

    ATH: Arthur Twining Hadley, President of Yale University, Records (RU 25)

    Secretary's Office, Yale University, Records (RU 52)

    Peabody Museum of Natural History, Yale University, Records (RU 471).

NA: National Archives, College Park, Maryland
NGS: National Geographic Society Archives, Washington, DC

PERIODICALS CONSULTED:

NYT: *New York Times,* New York
ECL: *El Comercio,* Lima, Peru
ECC: *El Comercio,* Cusco, Peru
ES: *El Sol,* Cusco, Peru
(For all other periodicals, see the scrapbooks in the YPEP and BFP)

OTHER KEY ABBREVIATIONS:

Hiram Bingham (HB)
Alfreda Mitchell Bingham (AMB)
Alfred Bingham (AB)
Woodbridge Bingham (WB)
José Gabriel Cosio (JGC)
Luis E. Valcárcel (LEV)
Lost City of the Incas (*LCI*)
Machu Picchu: Citadel of the Incas (*MPCI*)

Notes

PREFACE

1. See Mike French and Gilles Verschuere's 2005 interview with Deborah Nadoolman, costume designer for *Raiders of the Lost Ark,* on TheRaider.Net, http://www.theraider.net/features/interviews/deborah_nadoolman.php.

2. "Motion to Dismiss for Lack of Jurisdiction and Improper Venue by Yale University," Republic of Peru v. Yale University, Dockets.Justia.Com, Civil Action No. 1:08-cv–2109 (U.S. District Court for the District of Columbia, 4 March 2009), 4.

INTRODUCTION: THE LAST CITY OF THE INCAS

1. When the Spanish conquered the Inca empire, they imposed their spellings of Quechua, the common language of the Incas. IE, the city of Qosqo—as it sounds in Quechua—was written as Cusco (from the nineteenth century, it was written Cuzco). In recent years, however, Andeans and scholars have found spellings more appropriate to Quechua. I have tried to respect those re-spellings as much as possible in this manuscript. For the sake of clarity, however, for certain words I have chosen to defer to the spelling common in the early twentieth century, when Hiram Bingham was exploring: Cuzco, rather than Cusco or Qosqo; Inca, rather than Inka.

2. My account of the Inca's final days is indebted to John Hemming, *The Conquest of the Incas* (New York: Harcourt, Brace, 1970). For the description of Vilcabamba, I drew from Nicole Delia Legnani, "Introduction," in *Titu Cusi, a 16th-Century Account of the Conquest,* ed. Nicole Delia Legnani (Cambridge: Harvard University, David Rockefeller Center for Latin American Studies, 2005), 41. For the larger history of the Incas, see Michael Edward Moseley, *The Incas and Their Ancestors: The Archaeology of Peru* (New York: Thames & Hudson, 1992). For their achievements and sophistication in a hemispheric context, see Charles C. Mann, *1491: New Revelations of the Americas before Columbus* (New York: Knopf, 2005).

3. My description of the perils of the region draws from Michael Forbes Brown and Eduardo Fernández, *War of Shadows: The Struggle for Utopia in the Peruvian Amazon* (Berkeley: University of California Press, 1991), 24.

4. Martín de Murúa and Manuel Ballesteros Gaibrois, *Historia General Del Perú* (Madrid: Historia 16, 1987), 296.

5. For icons versus idolatry, see Kenneth Mills, *Idolatry and Its Enemies: Colonial Andean Religion and Extirpation, 1640–1750* (Princeton: Princeton University Press, 1997).

6. Murúa and Ballesteros, *Historia General Del Perú,* 298–99.

7. For more on Inca religion and the treatment of mummies, see Sabine MacCormack, *Religion in the Andes: Vision and Imagination in Early Colonial Peru* (Princeton: Princeton University Press, 1991).

8. Murúa and Ballesteros, *Historia General Del Perú,* 302.

9. Ibid., 307.

10. Hemming, *The Conquest of the Incas,* 448.

11. The anthropologist Henry F. Dobyns has argued that there were between 90 and 112 million people in the Americas before 1492, and that between 80 and 100 million died from the diseases that followed Columbus's arrival, a projection that has provoked much debate. Mann, *1491,* 94.

12. See Carolyn Dean, *Inka Bodies and the Body of Christ: Corpus Christi in Colonial Cuzco, Peru* (Durham: Duke University Press, 1999), and David T. Garrett, *Shadows of Empire: The Indian Nobility of Cusco, 1750–1825* (Cambridge, UK: Cambridge University Press, 2005).

13. See Alberto Flores Galindo, *Buscando Un Inca: Identidad Y Utopia En Los Andes* (Lima, Perú: Editorial Horizonte, 1994).

14. Alberto Flores Galindo, "The Rebellion of Túpac Amaru," in *The Peru Reader,* eds. Orin Starn, Carlos Iván Degregori, and Robin Kirk (Durham, NC: Duke University Press, 1995), 154.

15. For elite effacement of Inca and indigenous identities, see Mark Thurner, *From Two Republics to One Divided: Contradictions of Postcolonial Nationmaking in Andean Peru* (Durham, NC: Duke University Press, 1997), Ch. 1. For a longer duration of Inca identity in Cuzco, see Charles F. Walker, *Smoldering Ashes: Cuzco and the Creation of Republican Peru, 1780–1840* (Durham, NC: Duke University Press, 1999).

16. Alexander von Humboldt, *Views of Nature or Contemplations on the Sublime Phenomena of Creation; with Scientific Illustrations,* trans. from German by E. C. Otté and Henry G. Bohn (London: Henry G. Bohn, 1850), 411–15. For how Humboldt opened up non-Spanish scholars to studying the pre-Columbian peoples of the Spanish American world, see Jorge Cañizares-Esguerra, *How to Write the History of the New World: Histories Epistemologies, and Identities in the Eighteenth-Century Atlantic World* (Stanford: Stanford University Press, 2001), 55–59.

17. See Ward Stavig, "Túpac Amaru, the Body Politics, and the Embodiment of Hope: Inca Heritage and Social Justice in the Andes," in *Death, Dismemberment, and Memory: Body Politics in Latin America,* ed. Lyman L. Johnson (Albuquerque: University of New Mexico Press, 2004), 27–62.

18. Brown and Fernández, *War of Shadows,* 52–53. See also Eduardo Fernández, "La Muerte Del Inca: Dos Versiones De Un Mito Ashaninca," in *Anthropologica* (Lima: Pontificia Universidad Católica del Perú, 1984), 2; Gerald Weiss, "Elements of Inkarrí East of the Andes," in *Myth and the Imaginary in the New World,* ed. Edmundo Magaña and Peter Mason (Smithfield: Foris Publications, 1986).

19. Flores Galindo, *Buscando Un Inca,* 49.

20. Hemming, *The Conquest of the Incas,* 478.

CHAPTER ONE: THE BLACK TEMPLE

1. Hiram Bingham, *Across South America: An Account of a Journey from Buenos Aires to Lima* (Boston and New York: Houghton Mifflin, 1911), 294.

2. Hiram Bingham, *A Residence of Twenty-one Years in the Sandwich Islands* (Hartford: Hezekiah Huntington, 1948), 69.

3. Ibid., 84.

4. Quoted in AB, *The Tiffany Fortune and Other Chronicles of a Connecticut Family* (Chestnut Hill, Mass.: Abeel & Leet, 1996), 21.

5. Judith Ann Schiff, "Aloha blue," *Yale Alumni Magazine,* July/August 2004.

6. "The Hero of Micronesia," *The Congregationalist and Christian World,* 5 September 1908. Bingham Family Papers (BFP), 98–35.

7. "The Rev. Dr. Bingham Dead," *New York Sun,* Oct. 27, 1908.

8. Lillian Brown to Alfred Bingham (AB), Nov. 25, 1957, BFP, 98–30.

9. Quoted in AB, *The Tiffany Fortune and Other Chronicles of a Connecticut Family,* 32.

10. Woodbridge Bingham (WB), *Hiram Bingham: A Personal History* (Boulder, CO: Bin Lan Zhen Publishers, 1982), 10.

11. AB, *Explorer of Machu Picchu: Portrait of Hiram Bingham* (Greenwich, CT: Triune Books, 2000), 34.

12. Ibid., 35.

13. Ibid., 98.

14. Hiram Bingham III (HB) Scrapbook, circa 1880, BFP, 97–12.

15. As quoted in AB, *Explorer of Machu Picchu,* 37. See also Lee Meriwether, *The Tramp at Home* (New York: Harper & Brothers, 1889), 236.

16. WB, *Hiram Bingham: A Personal History,* 12. For natural history museum at Punahou, see *Catalogue of Oahu College and Punahou Preparatory School 1885* (Honolulu: Press Publishing Company Print), 13.

17. For more on the Chicago World's Fair, see Robert W. Rydell, *All the World's a Fair: Visions of Empire at American International Expositions* (Chicago: University of Chicago, 1987).
18. David Hurst Thomas, *Skull Wars: Kennewick Man, Archaeology, and the Battle for Native American Identity* (New York: Basic Books, 2000), 50.
19. See Noenoe K. Silva, *Aloha Betrayed: Native Resistance to American Colonialism* (Durham, NC: Duke University Press, 2004).
20. AB, *The Tiffany Fortune*, 36–40.

CHAPTER TWO: THE IVORY TOWER

1. My treatment of HB's doubts and transformation during college is indebted to Char Miller, *Fathers and Sons: The Bingham Family and the American Mission* (Philadelphia: Temple University Press, 1982), 74. I, however, see far more importance in the Spanish-American War to his change.
2. Ibid., 124.
3. HB, Feb. 1908 biographical draft for *Decennial Record* of the Yale class of 1898, BFP 97–16; WB, *Hiram Bingham: A Personal History*, 20.
4. Char Miller, *Fathers and Sons: The Bingham Family*, 122–24.
5. Woodbridge Bingham (WB), *Hiram Bingham: A Personal History* (Boulder, CO: Bin Lan Zhen Publishers, 1982), 20.
6. "A Demonstration at Yale," *New York Times (NYT)*, April 22, 1898.
7. HB III to HB Jr., May 9, 1898, BFP 14–14; Reuben Maury, "The Flying Senator," *Liberty*, June 29, 1929.
8. May 14, 1898, HB III to HB Jr., BFP 14–14.
9. David Hurst Thomas, *Skull Wars: Kennewick Man, Archaeology, and the Battle for Native American Identity* (New York: Basic Books, 2000), 124.
10. For more on Eben Horsford and his strange theory, see Gloria Polizzotti Greis, "Vikings on the Charles; or, The Strange Saga of Dighton Tock, Norumbega and Rumford Double-Acting Baking Powder," Needham Historical Society, 2004, http://www.greisnet.com/needhist.nsf/Vikingson-theCharles?OpenPage (accessed April 4, 2008).
11. See Nadia Khouri, "Lost Worlds and the Revenge of Realism (Les Mondes Perdus Et La Revanche Du Réalisme)," *Science Fiction Studies* 10:2 (1983): 170–90; and John Rieder, *Colonialism and the Emergence of Science Fiction* (Middletown, CT: Wesleyan University Press, 2008).
12. "Notes By Hi from Weston Hall, Massachusetts. July 5th, 1898," BFP 99–45.

CHAPTER THREE: THE COMPASS

1. HB to Alfreda Mitchell Bingham (AMB), July 10, 1912, BFP 15–40.
2. Alice Cooney Frelinghuysen, *Louis Comfort Tiffany at the Metropolitan Museum* (Metropolitan Museum of Art Publications, 2006), 109, 134.
3. AB, *The Tiffany Fortune and Other Chronicles of a Connecticut Family* (Chestnut Hill, Mass.: Abeel & Leet, 1996), 105.
4. AB, *Explorer of Machu Picchu: Portrait of Hiram Bingham* (Greenwich, CT: Triune Books, 2000), 52.
5. Ibid., 53.
6. HB to Carnegie Institution, Jan. 15, 1910, BFP Accession 87-M–89 5–108.
7. In many ways, Anglo-American scholarship replicated the stance of Northern European scholars since the colonial period, portraying Spanish-American history and peoples both indigenous and European as degenerate. See Jorge Cañizares-Esguerra, *How to Write the History of the New World: Histories Epistemologies, and Identities in the Eighteenth-Century Atlantic World* (Stanford: Stanford University Press, 2001).
8. Charles G. Reinhart, "If You Want to See a Man Who Has Done Something—LOOK AT that man BINGHAM!" (ca. 1925), BFP 97–13.
9. AB, *Explorer of Machu Picchu*, 58.
10. Mitchell Bingham, *Psychic Adventure* (New York: Vantage Press, 1978), 4–6.
11. For more on HB and the "strenuous life," see Char Miller, *Fathers and Sons: The Bingham Family and the American Mission* (Philadelphia: Temple University Press, 1982).

12. Edward Tenner, "Harvard, Bring Back Geography!" *Harvard Magazine*, May–June 1988; Neil Smith, "'Academic War Over the Field of Geography': The Elimination of Geography at Harvard, 1947–1951," *Annals of the Association of American Geographers*, 77:2 (June 1987), 155–72.
13. AB, *Explorer of Machu Picchu*, 74.
14. Ibid., 75.

CHAPTER FOUR: INTO THE ANDES

1. All quotes and descriptions in this chapter, unless otherwise specified, are from HB, *The Journal of an Expedition across Venezuela and Colombia, 1906–1907* (New Haven, CT: Yale Pub. Association, 1909).
2. Charles H. Harris and Louis R. Sadler, *The Archaeologist Was a Spy: Sylvanus G. Morley and the Office of Naval Intelligence* (Albuquerque: University of New Mexico Press, 2003).
3. Edmund Morris, *The Rise of Theodore Roosevelt* (New York: Modern Library, 2001), xxviii.
4. AB, *Explorer of Machu Picchu: Portrait of Hiram Bingham* (Greenwich, CT: Triune Books, 2000), 76.
5. "Explorers Fight Amazon Savages," *NYT*, May 12, 1920.
6. J. S. Keltie to Markham, Jan. 24, 1913, Royal Geographic Society (RGS), CB8.
7. Daniel Buck, "Treasuring the Andes," manuscript courtesy of author (Washington, DC: 2008).
8. John Hemming, *The Search for El Dorado* (London: Joseph, 1978), 195–98.
9. "Famous Sacred Lake of Guatavita Gives Up Treasure," *NYT*, Oct. 29, 1912.
10. Forbes Lindsay, "Wanderings in South America," *NYT Book Review*, Aug. 7, 1909.

CHAPTER FIVE: CUZCO, THE NAVEL OF THE WORLD

1. AB, *Explorer of Machu Picchu: Portrait of Hiram Bingham* (Greenwich, CT: Triune Books, 2000), 83.
2. Yale College Final Examination, June 1908, History C7, BFP 35–39.
3. W.B. Hay suggestion sheet, BFP 34–28.
4. AMB to HB, Oct. 26, 1908, BFP 14–6.
5. Bingham's journal from this expedition has been lost. Unless otherwise noted, all quotations in this chapter are from HB, *Across South America: An Account of a Journey from Buenos Aires to Lima* (Boston: Houghton Mifflin, 1911).
6. Daniel Buck, "The Aramayo Mule," *South American Explorer*, Feb. 1988; Anne Meadows, *Digging Up Butch and Sundance* (Lincoln: University of Nebraska Press, 2003), 130–34.
7. Julio Cotler, *Clases, Estado y la Nación en el Perú* (Lima: Instituto de Estudios Peruanos Ediciones, 2006), 95.
8. See Paul Gootenberg, *Between Silver and Guano: Commercial Policy and the State in Postindependence Peru* (Princeton: Princeton University Press, 1989).
9. Brooke Larson, *Trials of Nation Making: Liberalism, Race, and Ethnicity in the Andes, 1810–1910* (Cambridge: Cambridge University Press, 2004), 182–85.
10. Cotler, *Clases, Estado y la Nación en el Perú*, 128–30.
11. For estimated population figures, I drew from Marie Robinson Wright, *The Old and the New Peru* (Philadelphia: George Barrie & Sons, 1908), 280.
12. The translation "Navel of the World" perhaps originated with the *mestizo* Inca chronicler Garcilaso de la Vega in the seventeenth century. It has been disputed since then—"Placenta of the World" might be more accurate.
13. Bingham would have read Clements R. Markham, *The Incas of Peru* (London: Smith, Elder, 1910) for his version of the legend.
14. For the challenges of chronology and Inca history, see Catherine J. Julien, *Reading Inca History* (Iowa City: University of Iowa Press, 2000); Susan A. Niles, *The Shape of Inca History: Narrative and Architecture in an Andean Empire* (Iowa City: University of Iowa Press, 1999); Gary Urton, *The History of a Myth: Pacariqtambo and the Origin of the Inkas* (Austin: University of Texas Press, 1990); R. Tom Zuidema, *Inca Civilization in Cuzco* (Austin: University of Texas Press, 1990).
15. For accounts of imperial expansion, see Brian S. Bauer and R. Alan Covey, "Processes of State Formation in the Inca Heartland (Cuzco, Peru)," *American Anthropologist* 104:3 (2002); Brian S. Bauer, *Ancient Cuzco: Heartland of the Inca* (Austin: University of Texas Press, 2004); R. Alan Covey, *How*

the Incas Built Their Heartland: State Formation and the Innovation of Imperial Strategies in the Sacred Valley, Peru (Ann Arbor: University of Michigan Press, 2006).

16. Charles C. Mann, *1491: New Revelations of the Americas before Columbus* (New York: Knopf, 2005), 64.

17. John Hemming, *The Conquest of the Incas* (New York: Harcourt, Brace, 1970), 135.

18. Albert A. Giesecke, "Informe sobre el censo levantado en la provincia del Cuzco el 10 de setiembre de 1912," *Revista Universitaria* 2:4 (March 1913), 50.

19. Luis E. Valcárcel (LEV), *Memorias* (Lima: Instituto de Estudios Peruanos, 1981), 13.

20. Ibid., 50.

21. Willie Hiatt, "Flying 'Cholo': Incas, Airplanes, and the Construction of Andean Modernity in 1920s Cuzco, Peru," *The Americas* 63:3 (Jan. 2007), 338.

22. The literature on tourism and Cuzco and Peru's image of itself in the twentieth century is extensive, but see Marisol de la Cadena, *Indigenous Mestizos: The Politics of Race and Culture in Cuzco, Peru, 1919–1991* (Durham, NC: Duke University Press, 2000); Zoila Mendoza, *Creating our Own: Folklore, Performance, and Identity in Cuzco, Peru* (Durham, NC: Duke University Press, 2008); Helaine Silverman, "Touring Ancient Times: The Present and Presented Past in Contemporary Peru," *American Anthropologist* 104:3 (2002): 881–902. For the arrival of flight to Cuzco, see Willie Hiatt, "Flying 'Cholo.'"

23. Marisol de la Cadena, *Indigenous Mestizos: The Politics of Race and Culture in Cuzco, Peru, 1919–1991* (Durham, NC: Duke University Press, 2000), 72.

24. José Tamayo Herrera, *Historia Social Del Cuzco Republicano* (Lima: s.n., 1978), 130.

CHAPTER SIX: CHOQQUEQUIRAU, THE CRADLE OF GOLD

1. Unless otherwise noted, quotations in this chapter are from HB, *Across South America: An Account of a Journey from Buenos Aires to Lima* (Boston: Houghton Mifflin, 1911).

2. For monetary conversions here and throughout, I used Samuel H. Williamson, "Six Ways to Compute the Relative Value of a U.S. Dollar Amount, 1790 to Present," MeasuringWorth, 2009, URL http://www.measuringworth.com/uscompare.

3. Simone Waisbard, *The Mysteries of Machu Picchu* (New York: Avon Books, 1974), 6.

4. "Lost City Explored," from *New York Herald*, picked up by *Washington Post*, Apr. 23, 1909.

5. John Hemming, *The Conquest of the Incas* (New York: Harcourt, Brace, 1970), 481.

6. David Hurst Thomas, *Skull Wars: Kennewick Man, Archaeology, and the Battle for Native American Identity* (New York: Basic Books, 2000), 53.

7. Royal Geographical Society London and Douglas William Freshfield, *Hints to Travellers, Scientific and General* (London, 1893), 421.

8. HB to AMB, Feb.12, 1909, BFP 15–36.

INTERLUDE: MANCO INCA

1. For the effects of European disease, see Alfred W. Crosby, *The Columbian Exchange; Biological and Cultural Consequences of 1492* (Westport, CT: Greenwood Publishing, 1972).

2. Diego de Castro Yupangui and Nicole Delia Legnani, *Titu Cusi, a 16th-Century Account of the Conquest* (Cambridge: Harvard University, David Rockefeller Center for Latin American Studies, 2005), 136.

3. As quoted in Pedro de Cieza de León, Alexandra Parma Cook, and David Noble Cook, *The Discovery and Conquest of Peru: Chronicles of the New World Encounter* (Durham, NC: Duke University Press, 1998), 408.

4. Pedro Pizarro and Guillermo Lohmann Villena, *Relación Del Descubrimiento Y Conquista Del Perú* (Lima: Pontificia Universidad Católica del Perú, Fondo Editorial, 1978), 124.

5. As quoted in John Hemming, *The Conquest of the Incas* (New York: Harcourt, Brace, 1970), 214–15.

6. George Kubler, "A Peruvian Chief of State: Manco Inca (1515–1545)," *Hispanic American Historical Review,* 24:2 (1944); Liliana Regalado de Hurtado, *Religión Y Evangelización En Vilcabamba (1572–1602)* (Lima: Pontificia Universidad Católica del Perú, Fondo Editorial, 1992), 44.

7. Antonio de la Calancha and Ignacio Prado Pastor, *Crónica Moralizada,* vol. 5 (Lima: Universidad Nacional Mayor de San Marcos, 1978), 1800.

8. Yupangui and Legnani, *Titu Cusi, a 16th-Century Account of the Conquest,* 170–71.

CHAPTER SEVEN: BEST LAID PLANS

1. "Best laid plans . . . ," 1909 Nov-Dec Little Diary, BFP 96–3; Choqquequirau plans, June 15, 1909, BFP 18–85.
2. Quotes in John Hemming, *The Conquest of the Incas* (New York: Harcourt, Brace, 1970), 479; Antonio Raimondi, *El Perú,* Tomo II, Historia De La Geografía del Perú, Libro 1 (Lima: Imprenta del Estado, 1876), 160–62.
3. HB, *Across South America: An Account of a Journey from Buenos Aires to Lima* (Boston: Houghton Mifflin, 1911), 322.
4. HB, "In the Wonderland of Peru," *National Geographic Magazine,* April 1913, 511.
5. HB to Carnegie Institution, Jan. 15, 1910, BFP Accession 87-M–89; "Hopes to Find Lost Cities," *New York Sun,* March 16, 1911.
6. Richard E. Daggett, "Julio C. Tello: An Account of His Rise to Prominence in Peruvian Archaeology," in *The Life and Writings of Julio C. Tello: America's First Indigenous Archaeologist,* ed. Richard L. Burger (Iowa City: University of Iowa Press, 2009), 7.
7. HB to Tello, March 27, 1914, YPEP 10–129; Carlos Romero, "Informe sobre las Ruinas de Choqquequirau," *Revista Histórica* Tomo IV (Lima: Imprenta Nacional de Federico Barrionuevo, 1909), 99.
8. Description from AB, *The Tiffany Fortune and Other Chronicles of a Connecticut Family* (Chestnut Hill, Mass.: Abeel & Leet, 1996), 184; WB, *Hiram Bingham: A Personal History* (Boulder, CO: Bin Lan Zhen Publishers, 1982), 82.
9. José Tamayo Herrera, *Historia Social Del Cuzco Republicano* (Lima: s.n., 1978), 129.
10. "Reorganización de la Universidad del Cuzco," *El Comercio* [Cuzco] *(ECC),* March 10, 1910; "The Reminiscences of Albert A. Giesecke," Oral History Research Office, Columbia University, 1963, 119–28.
11. José Gabriel Cosío (JGC) to José de la Riva-Agüero, June 1, 1910, in *Obras Completas de José de la Riva-Agüero. XIV, Epistolario,* vol. II (Lima: Instituto Riva-Agüero, Pontificia Universidad Católica del Perú, 1997).
12. "Notas Sociales," April 5, 1910, *ECC.*
13. Tan marbled notebook from LEV's second year at the Universidad del Cuzco, 1910. Valcárcel Archives, Instituto Nacional de Cultura, Lima, Peru.
14. "Monumentos Históricos," Aug. 2, 1910, *ECC;* "Memoria presentado . . . ," Dec. 24, 1910, *ECC.*
15. For more on the relationship between Bingham and Giesecke, see Mariana Mould de Pease, "Apuntes interculturales para la historia inmediata de Machu Picchu: Las funciones de Hiram Bingham y Albert Giesecke," *Revista del Archivo Regional del Cusco* (Cuzco: June 2000), 133–147; Zoila Mendoza, *Creating our Own: Folklore, Performance, and Identity in Cuzco, Peru* (Durham, NC: Duke University Press, 2008), 67–69.
16. HB to Albert A. Giesecke, Nov. 25, 1910, archives of Albert A. Giesecke, Instituto Riva-Aguero, Lima, Peru (hereafter IRA), AG–0140.
17. HBIII to Carnegie Institution, Jan. 15, 1910, BFP Accession 87-M–89, 5–108.
18. Adolph F. Bandelier, *The Islands of Titicaca and Koati* (New York: Hispanic Society of America, 1910), 24. Alfred Bingham argued in *Explorer of Machu Picchu* that his father built the entire expedition around his desire to scale Coropuna, not his interest in the Incas, a goal only heightened by the realization that a feisty Rhode Island mountaineer named Annie Peck was also interested in the peak. Although Peck—who waggishly painted a moustache on her balaclava—and her cause of women's suffrage indeed galled Bingham, a closer examination of his correspondence suggests neither she nor the mountain was the true reason for his hurried return to the Andes that year. As Bingham wrote to his previous exploring partner, Clarence Hay, in a rare burst of humor committed to paper: "The only reason the mountain was mentioned at all [in expedition promotions] was that I thought there was one chance in a thousand that we ascend it, and if we had said nothing at all about it beforehand, it would be as though we had suddenly 'Cooked up a Peck of Pickled Peaks.'" HB to Clarence Hay, Mar. 21, 1911, BFP 18–90.
19. HB to Alfreda, Feb. 13, 1911, BFP 15–38.
20. Isaiah Bowman to W. M. Davis, April 17, 1909, RGS, CB7.
21. Bowman to HB, Aug. 1, 1911, YPEP, 5–27.

22. Quoted in Neil Smith, *American Empire; Roosevelt's Geographer and the Prelude to Globalization* (Berkeley: University of California Press, 2003), 80.

23. Ibid., 76.

24. Duff Gilfond, "A Superior Person," *American Mercury,* March 1930, 309.

25. For how these corporations' support helped tie Bingham's expeditions into the "Enterprise of Knowledge," a U.S. imperial and acquisitive project, see Ricardo D. Salvatore, "The Enterprise of Knowledge: Representational Machines of Informal Empire," *Close Encounters of Empire,* eds. Gilbert M. Joseph, Catherine C. LeGrand, and Ricardo D. Salvatore (Durham, NC: Duke University Press, 1998).

26. HB to Rev. H.H. Parker, Jan. 18, 1911, BFP 18–89.

27. HB to AMB, Feb 13, 1911, BFP 15–38.

28. "Lost Cities of the Incas," *Christian Science Monitor,* May 17,1911.

29. "Hopes to Find Lost Cities," *New York Sun,* March 16, 1911.

CHAPTER EIGHT: DEAD MAN'S GULCH

1. Decreto Supremo No. 89. Lima, April 2, 1822, republished in Rosalía Ávalos de Matos and Rogger Ravines, "Las Antiguedades Peruanas y su Protección Legal," *Revista del Museo Nacional* (Lima), vol. 40, 1974, 373.

2. Decreto Supreme, April 27, 1893; republished in Mariana Mould de Pease, *Machu Picchu Y El Código De Ética De La Sociedad De Arqueología Americana* (Lima: Consejo Nacional de Ciencia y Tecnologia; Pontificia Universidad Católica del Perú Fondo Editorial; Instituto Nacional de Cultura; Universidad Nacional San Antonio Abad del Cuzco, 2003), 136–37.

3. "Pertenencia de los monumentos arqueológicos," *ECC,* March 4, 1909.

4. Henry Stephens, *South American Travels* (New York: Knickerbocker Press, 1915), 22–23.

5. For more on "la Casa Grace," see Julio Cotler, *Clases, Estado y la Nación en el Perú* (Lima: Instituto de Estudios Peruanos Ediciones, 2006), 132, 141–42; Lawrence A. Clayton, *Grace: W.R. Grace & Co., the Formative Years, 1850–1930* (Ottawa, Ill.: Jameson Books, 1985).

6. My account of Bingham's movements in Lima (and all relevant quotes) are from HB to AMB, June 25, 1911, BFP 15–38; and HB Journal 1911, YPEP 18–1. For Leguía's political troubles, see Howard Laurence Karno, *Augusto B. Leguía: The Oligarchy and the Modernization of Peru, 1870–1930* (University of California, Los Angeles, PhD diss., 1970), 120.

7. "El Día/La reorganizacíon del Museo de Historia Nacional," *El Comercio* [Lima] (*ECL*), Sept. 22, 1915.

8. For more on Peruvian museum history, see Rogger Ravines, *Los Museos del Perú; Breve Historia y Guia* (Lima: Direccion General de Museos, Instituto Nacional de Cultura, 1989); Julio C. Tello and Toribio Mejia Xesspe, *Historia de los Museos Nacionales del Peru, 1822–1946* (Lima: Museo Nacional de Antropologia y Arqueologia E Instituto y Museo de Arqueologia de la Universidad de San Marcos, 1967).

9. Quoted in Ravines, *Los Museos del Perú; Breve Historia y Guia,* 39–40.

10. John H. Rowe, "Max Uhle y la Idea de Tiempo en la Arqueologia Americana," in *Max Uhle y El Peru Antiguo,* ed. Peter Kaulicke (Lima: Pontificia Universidad Católica del Peru, Fondo Editorial, 1998), 5; Teodoro Hampe Martínez, "Max Uhle y los Origenes del Museo de Historia Nacional (Lima, 1906–1911)," in *Max Uhle y El Peru Antiguo,* 131.

11. Max Uhle to Sir Clements R. Markham, 1912, in *Max Uhle y El Peru Antiguo,* 151.

12. Max Uhle claimed that Romero was a "zambo"—a person of mixed African and Indian heritage. HB to AMB, June 25, 1911, BFP 15–38.

13. J. G. Leguia, *Bio-Bibliografia de D. Carlos A. Romero* (Lima: Librería e Imprenta Gil, S.A.,1942), 5.

14. "Datos, Geog. Soc De Lima," June 23, 1911, YPEP 2–31.

15. Large book marked "Recipes" on cover, on inside, L.E.V. "Memoria" "1891." Valcárcel Archives, Instituto Nacional de Cultura, Lima, Peru.

16. HB Journal 1911, July 4, YPEP 18–3; HB to AMB, July 5, 1911, BFP 15–38.

17. "The Reminiscences of Albert A. Giesecke," Oral History Research Office, Columbia University, 1963, 229–30.

18. Personal conversation with Jorge Flores Ochoa, October 2005.

19. The belief, right or wrong, that an archaeological find might "rewrite the history of the Western Hemisphere" is an old rhetorical trope made no less charming by its repetition by scholars of all

backgrounds from at least the late eighteenth century on. For that exact phrase in reference to the Maya site of Palenque, see Jorge Cañizares-Esguera, *How to Write the History of the New World: Histories Epistemologies, and Identities in the Eighteenth-Century Atlantic World* (Stanford: Stanford University Press, 2001), 322.

20. HB to AMB, July 5, 1911, BFP 15–38.
21. HB to AMB, July 12, 1911, BFP 15–38.
22. David Hurst Thomas, *Skull Wars : Kennewick Man, Archaeology, and the Battle for Native American Identity* (New York: Basic Books, 2000), 135–36.
23. Ibid., 137–38.
24. Aleš Hrdlička, *Early Man in South America* (Washington: Government Printing Office, 1912), 287.
25. Ricardo D. Salvatore, "Local Versus Imperial Knowledge: Reflections on Hiram Bingham and the Yale Peruvian Expedition," *Nepantla: Views from South* 4:1 (2003), 69.
26. HB to AMB, July 15, 1911, BFP 15–38.
27. HB Journal 1911, July 14, YPEP 18–3.

CHAPTER NINE: THE DISCOVERERS OF MACHU PICCHU

1. "Hopes to Find Lost Cities," *New York Sun*, March 16, 1911.
2. Quotes and descriptions from Bingham in this chapter, unless otherwise noted, come from HB Journal 1911, YPEP 18–3; HB, "The Discovery of Machu Picchu," *Harper's Monthly*, April 1913, 710; HB, "In the Wonderland of Peru," *The National Geographic Magazine*, April 1913; HB, *Lost City of the Incas: The Story of Machu Picchu and Its Builders* [*LCI*] (New York: Duell, Sloan & Pearce, 1948; reprint: London: Weidenfeld & Nicolson, 2002). I have drawn mostly from the earliest version, the *Harper's* article.
3. Paul Baxter Lanius Journal, July 21, 1911, YPEP 18–10.
4. JGC, "Una Excursión a Machu Picchu," *Revista Universitaria*, 1:2 (Sept. 1912), 20–21.
5. AB, *Explorer of Machu Picchu: Portrait of Hiram Bingham* (Greenwich, CT: Triune Books, 2000), 156.
6. "Honors to Amundsen and Peary" (at which Bingham spoke), *National Geographic Magazine*, Jan. 1913, 23:1, 113–30.
7. See Charles Wiener, *Pérou Et Bolivie. Récit De Voyage Suivi D'études Archéologiques Et Ethnographiques Et De Notes Sur L'écriture Et Les Langues Des Populations Indiennes* (Paris: Hachette, 1880).
8. For a larger pattern of movement to the region, see E. J. E. Hobsbawm, "A Case of Neo-Feudalism: La Convención, Peru," *Journal of Latin American Studies* 1:1 (1969), 44. As for how long the Richartes lived there, Bingham says four years, but JGC, "Machupiccho / Ciudad preincaica en el valle del Vilcanota," *Boletín de la Sociedad Geográfica de Lima*, Tomo XXVIII—Año XXII, (Lima: 1912), 152, notes that Anacleto Alvarez had been living there for eight.
9. The boy's name takes a little sleuthing. Richard Burger and Lucy Salazar, *Machu Picchu: Unveiling the Mystery of the Incas* (New Haven, CT: Yale University Press, March 2004), names the boy who guided Bingham as Melquiades Alvarez. The source for that name, however, was photographs taken the following year, 1912, of a considerably older boy. Also, because the Richarte family lived closest to the Urubamba River and the trail up, it was their house that Bingham reached first, and more likely their son was sent with Bingham. For the location of the house, see George Eaton Journal, Aug. 22, 1912, YPEP 19–18). As for the first name being Pablito, "El Imperio del Sol," *ECC*, July 23, 2001, gave it this way.
10. Simone Waisbard, *The Mysteries of Machu Picchu* (New York: Avon Books, 1974), 143.
11. HB, *LCI* (2002 edition), 179.
12. For an excellent meditation on Bingham's importance and skill as a photographer, see Hugh Thomson, *Machu Picchu and the Camera* (Penchant Press, 2002). For useful critiques of the claiming power of Bingham's photography and writing, see Deborah Poole, "Landscape and the Imperial Subject: U.S. Images of the Andes, 1859–1930," *Close Encounters of Empire: Writing the Cultural History of U.S. Latin American Relations*, eds. Gilbert M. Joseph, Catherine C. LeGrand, and Ricardo D. Salvatore (Durham, NC: Duke University Press, 1998); Leila Gómez, *Iluminados y Tránsfugas: Relatos de viajeros y ficciones nacionales en Argentina, Paraguay y Perú* (Madrid and Frankfurt: IberoAmericana – Vervuert, 2009).
13. HB to AMB, July 25, 1911, BFP 15–38.

14. My portrayal of the debate over Machu Picchu's discovery draws from a number of works, including Daniel Buck, "Fights of Machu Picchu," *South American Explorer Magazine*, 1993; Hugh Thomson, *The White Rock: An Exploration of the Inca Heartland* (London: Weidenfeld & Nicolson, 2001); Thomson's "Introduction," in HB, *Lost City of the Incas;* Mariana Mould de Pease, *Machu Picchu Y El Código De Ética De La Sociedad De Arqueología Americana* (Lima: Consejo Nacional de Ciencia y Tecnologia; Pontificia Universidad Católica del Perú Fondo Editorial; Instituto Nacional de Cultura; Universidad Nacional San Antonio Abad del Cuzco, 2003); and Paolo Greer, "Machu Picchu before Bingham," *South American Explorer Magazine,* 2008.

15. Clements R. Markham, "The Land of the Incas," *Geographical Journal,* 36:4 (1910); Clements R. Markham, *The Incas of Peru* (London: Smith, Elder, 1910).

16. Wiener, *Pérou Et Bolivie,* 345.

17. Herman Göhring, *Informe Al Supremo Gobierno Del Perú Sobre La Expedición Á Los Valles De Paucartambo En 1873 Al Mando Del Coronel D. Baltazar La-Torre* (Lima: Imprenta del Estado, 1877), 106. My thanks go to Paolo Greer for this citation.

18. Paolo Greer, "Machu Picchu before Bingham," 40.

19. Mould de Pease, *Machu Picchu Y El Código De Ética De La Sociedad De Arqueología Americana,* 134–35.

20. Daniel Buck, "Machu Picchu: Polémica. El 'Hallazgo' De Un Farsante," *La Republica,* Aug. 31, 2008.

21. Carlos B. Cisneros, *Atlas Del Perú, Politico, Minero, Agrícola, Industrial Y Comercial* (Lima: Librería é imprenta Gil, 1904), 41. My thanks go to Daniel Buck for this citation.

22. Quoted in AB, *Explorer of Machu Picchu,* 26.

23. *discover:* v.8.d., Oxford English Dictionary, 2nd ed. 1989.

24. JGC, "Una Excursión a Machu Picchu," *Revista Universitaria,* 20–21.

25. Author interview with Romulo Lizarraga, Oct. 24, 2005.

26. J. P. Paz Soldán, "El Tesoro del Inca: Los Buscadores de Oro," *ECC,* July 27, 1911.

CHAPTER TEN: THE WHITE TEMPLE

1. John Hemming, *The Conquest of the Incas* (New York: Harcourt, Brace, 1970), 478.

2. "Datos, Geog. Soc De Lima," Jun. 23, 1911, YPEP 2–31.

3. HB to AMB, July 26, 1911, BFP 15–38.

4. HB, *Lost City of the Incas: The Story of Machu Picchu and Its Builders* [*LCI*] (New York: Duell, Sloan & Pearce, 1948; reprint: London: Weidenfeld & Nicolson, 2002), 127. For the search for Vitcos, see also HB, "Vitcos, the Last Inca Capital," *Proceedings of the American Antiquarian Society,* vol. 22, 1912.

5. HB to AMB, Aug. 3, 1911, BFP 15–39.

6. HB to Keltie, Aug. 3, 1911, RGS CB8.

7. HB Journal, Aug. 3, 1911, YPEP 18–3.

8. HB, "Along the Uncharted Pampaconas," *Harper's Magazine,* Aug. 1914, 452.

9. HB Journal, Aug. 5, 1911, YPEP 18–3.

10. HB to Iglehart, Aug. 4, 1911, YPEP 5–27.

11. HB Journal, Aug. 5, 1911, YPEP 18–3.

12. HB, *LCI* (2002 edition), 147.

13. HB to AMB, Aug. 7, 1911, BFP 15–39.

14. HB, *LCI* (2002 edition), 132.

15. As quoted in HB, *LCI* (2002 edition), 133.

16. HB Journal, August 8, 1911, YPEP 18–3.

17. HB, "A Search for the Last Inca Capital," *Harper's Magazine,* vol. 125 (1912), 704.

18. Brian S. Bauer, *Ancient Cuzco: Heartland of the Inca* (Austin: University of Texas Press, 2004), 9.

CHAPTER ELEVEN: THE PLAIN OF GHOSTS

1. Tradition from the Cofán Indians of southern Colombia, as relayed in Michael T. Taussig, *Shamanism, Colonialism, and the Wild Man: A Study in Terror and Healing* (Chicago: University of Chicago Press, 1986), 467.

2. For more on jungle Indians' struggles, particularly those of the Asháninka, see Michael Forbes Brown and Eduardo Fernández, *War of Shadows: The Struggle for Utopia in the Peruvian Amazon* (Berkeley:

University of California Press, 1991); Stefano Varese, *Salt of the Mountain: Campa Asháninka History and Resistance in the Peruvian Jungle* (Norman: University of Oklahoma Press, 2002).

3. See Adam Hochschild, *King Leopold's Ghost: A Story of Greed, Terror, and Heroism in Colonial Africa* (Boston: Houghton Mifflin, 1998).

4. Casement's numbers have been challenged as inflated. See Michael Edward Stanfield, *Red Rubber, Bleeding Trees: Violence, Slavery, and Empire in Northwest Amazonia, 1850–1933* (Albuquerque: University of New Mexico Press, 1998), 184.

5. HB Journal, Aug. 10, 1911, YPEP 18–3.

6. Ibid.

7. HB, *Lost City of the Incas: The Story of Machu Picchu and Its Builders* [*LCI*] (New York: Duell, Sloan & Pearce, 1948; reprint: London: Weidenfeld & Nicolson, 2002), 148–49.

8. HB, *Inca Land: Explorations in the Highlands of Peru* [*IL*] (Boston: Houghton Mifflin, 1922), 273.

9. HB, *LCI* (2002 edition), 149.

10. HB, *LCI* (2002 edition), 154–55.

11. As quoted in AB, *Explorer of Machu Picchu: Portrait of Hiram Bingham* (Greenwich, CT: Triune Books, 2000), 194.

12. HB, *IL*, 285.

13. For Saavedra's full name, which Bingham never provided, see Gene Savoy, *Vilcabamba: Last City of the Incas* (London: Hale, 1970), 78–79.

14. HB Journal, Aug. 16, 1911, YPEP 18–3.

15. HB, *LCI*, 155.

16. Quoted in Brown and Fernández, *War of Shadows*, 23.

17. HB, *IL*, 289; HB Journal (handwritten), Aug. 16, 1911, YPEP 18–1.

18. HB Journal, Aug. 16, 1911, YPEP 18–3.

19. HB Journal (handwritten), Aug. 16, 1911, YPEP 18–1. For his confusion, see also HB, "The Ruins of Espiritu Pampa, Peru," *American Anthropologist*, 16:2 (1914).

20. HB, *IL*, 296.

21. For works on the positive identification of Vilcabamba, see John Hemming, *The Conquest of the Incas* (New York: Harcourt, Brace, 1970); Vincent R. Lee, *Forgotten Vilcabamba: Final Stronghold of the Incas* (SixPac Manco Publications, 2000); Gene Savoy, *Antisuyo; the Search for the Lost Cities of the Amazon* (New York: Simon & Schuster, 1970).

22. See Eduardo Fernández, "La Muerte Del Inca: Dos Versiones De Un Mito Ashaninca," *Anthropologica* (Lima: Pontificia Universidad Católica del Perú, 1984), 2.

23. Alberto Duque, Cuzco, to HB, Aug. 14, 1911, YPEP 5–27.

24. "Sociedad Protectora de Monumentos Históricos," July 12, 1911, YPEP 35–52.

INTERLUDE: TITU CUSI

1. This quote and preceding from Diego de Castro Yupangui and Nicole Delia Legnani, *Titu Cusi, a 16th-Century Account of the Conquest* (Cambridge: Harvard University, David Rockefeller Center for Latin American Studies, 2005), 175.

2. Martín de Murúa and Manuel Ballesteros Gaibrois, *Historia General Del Perú* (Madrid: Historia 16, 1987), 251.

3. Yupangui and Legnani, *Titu Cusi, a 16th-Century Account of the Conquest*, 77.

4. Antonio de la Calancha and Ignacio Prado Pastor, *Crónica Moralizada*, vol. 5 (Lima: Universidad Nacional Mayor de San Marcos, 1978), 1800–1801.

5. Ibid., 1818.

6. John Hemming, *The Conquest of the Incas* (New York: Harcourt, Brace, 1970), 325.

7. Calancha and Prado Pastor, *Crónica Moralizada*, 1827.

8. Ibid., 1834.

CHAPTER TWELVE: THE DEAL

1. Quoted in AB, *Explorer of Machu Picchu: Portrait of Hiram Bingham* (Greenwich, Ct.: Triune Books, 2000), 231.

2. Clements Markham, *The Incas of Peru* (London: Smith, Elder), 45, 48–55.

3. HB, *Lost City of the Incas: The Story of Machu Picchu and Its Builders* [*LCI*] (New York: Duell, Sloan & Pearce, 1948; reprint: London: Weidenfeld & Nicolson, 2002), 59. For more on Tampu Tocco and the reconstruction of Inca origins, see Catherine J. Julien, *Reading Inca History* (Iowa City: University of Iowa Press, 2000); Gary Urton, *The History of a Myth: Pacariqtambo and the Origin of the Inkas*, 1st ed.

4. Orin Starn, *Ishi's Brain; In Search of America's Last "Wild" Indian* (New York: Norton, 2004), 36.

5. AB, *Explorer of Machu Picchu*, 271.

6. "Explorers Find a City That Was," *New York Sun*, Dec. 22, 1911, Bingham's Peruvian Expedition Scrapbook, YPEP 35–52.

7. "Pre-Inca City of Marble, *Christian Science Monitor*, Dec. 26, 1911, clipping in Bingham's Peruvian Expedition Scrapbook, PEYU 35–52. Again, see Jorge Cañizares-Esguera, *How to Write the History of the New World: Histories Epistemologies, and Identities in the Eighteenth-Century Atlantic World* (Stanford: Stanford University Press, 2001), 322.

8. "Explorers Find a City That Was," *New York Sun*, Dec. 22, 1911, BPES, YPEP 35–52.

9. AB, *Explorer of Machu Picchu*, 161.

10. Hiram Bingham, "The Yale Peruvian Expedition: Preliminary Report," *The Geographical Journal*, 39: 3 (Mar. 1912), 239.

11. "Finds Bones of Ancient Man," *NYT*, Jan.21, 1912.

12. HB to Arthur Twining Hadley, Jan.19, 1912, records of Arthur Twining Hadley, president Yale University RU 25, Manuscripts and Archives, Yale University Library (hereafter ATH), 8–008 0144.

13. HB to Anson Phelps Stokes, Oct. 7, 1909, Records of Sec. Office, Yale 1899–1953 Anson Phelps Stokes, YRG 4, RU 49, Manuscripts and Archives, Yale University Library, 10–0142.

14. For how National Geographic's support helped tie Bingham's expeditions into the "Enterprise of Knowledge," a U.S. imperial and acquisitive project, see Ricardo D. Salvatore, "The Enterprise of Knowledge: Representational Machines of Informal Empire," *Close Encounters of Empire*, eds. Gilbert M. Joseph, Catherine C. LeGrand, and Ricardo D. Salvatore (Durham, NC: Duke University Press, 1998), 76–77.

15. See Howard S. Abramson, *National Geographic: Behind America's Lens on the World* (New York: Crown Publishers, 1987); Robert H. Poole, *Explorers House: National Geographic and the World It Made* (New York: Penguin Press, 2004).

16. HB to Hadley, Feb. 23, 1912, quoting from letter from Ed Harkness, ATH 8–008 0144.

17. David Hurst Thomas, *Skull Wars: Kennewick Man, Archaeology, and the Battle for Native American Identity* (New York: Basic Books, 2000), 141.

18. For similar concessions in Egypt, then a de facto British colony, see Brian M. Fagan, *The Rape of the Nile: Tomb Robbers, Tourists, and Archaeologists in Egypt* (Boulder: Westview Press, 2004); Thomas Hoving, *Tutankhamun, the Untold Story* (New York: Simon & Schuster, 1978).

19. "Memorandum in Regard to Archaeological Exploration in Peru," by H. Bingham, ca. Feb. 12, 1912, National Archives (hereafter NA), M746, 823.927/30.

20. HB to Taft, Feb.12, 1912, YPEP 6–35; Huntington Wilson to H. Clay Howard, Feb. 26, 1912, NA, M746, 823.927/30. For more on U.S.-Peruvian relations, see Lawrence A. Clayton, *Peru and the United States: The Condor and the Eagle* (Athens: University of Georgia Press, 1999).

21. Howard to President Taft, April 1, 1912, NA M746, 823.927/30.

22. HB to Wilson, April 11, 1912, NA M746, 823.927/30.

23. "Young Americans Seek to Erase 'Black Spots' Off Map," *NYT*, June 2, 1912.

24. Gilbert H. Grosvenor to HB, May 2, 1912, YPEP 15–237.

CHAPTER THIRTEEN: THE CEMETERY OF THE INCAS

1. HB Journal Letter, May 5–6, 1915, YPEP 20–33.

2. Kenneth Heald Journal, July 6, 1912, YPEP 19–24. The rest of the account of Heald's clearing of the trail and Machu Picchu is taken from his journal, the April 1913 *National Geographic Magazine* article, and Bingham's *Lost City of the Incas*.

3. For Ferro's surprise at learning of the ruins on his land, see HB Journal, Sept. 8, 1911, YPEP 18–1.

4. Contract between HB and Jacinto Acuña, rep. of Mariano I. Ferro, Cuzco, July 9, 1912, YPEP 2.

5. Luis E. Valcárcel (LEV), *Memorias* (Lima: Instituto de Estudios Peruanos, 1981), 152–53.

6. HB, "Discurso Al Ser Incorporado Como Profesor Honorario De La Facultad De Letras," *Revista Universitaria*, 2 (1912); "El Dr. Hiram Bingham, Su Incorporación a la Facultad de Letras de esta Universidad," *ECC*, July 5, 1912.

7. HB, "In the Wonderland of Peru," *National Geographic Magazine* (April 1913), 452.

8. George F. Eaton Journal, Aug. 13, 1912, YPEP 19–18.

9. HB, *Machu Picchu, a Citadel of the Incas* [*MPCI*] (New Haven, London: Pub. for the National Geographic Society; H. Milford, Oxford University Press, 1930), 15.

10. George Francis Eaton, *The Collection of Osteological Material from Machu Picchu* (New Haven: Memoirs of the Connecticut Academy of Arts and Sciences, 1916), 4.

11. Ibid.,15.

12. Ibid., 24.

13. Eaton Journal, Aug. 7, 1912, YPEP 19–18.

14. See David Hurst Thomas, *Skull Wars: Kennewick Man, Archaeology, and the Battle for Native American Identity* (New York: Basic Books, 2000).

15. It should be noted that in northern Peru there is a tradition, dating back to the late sixteenth century, of Indians engaging in *huaquerismo*, or grave-robbing, alongside Europeans. See Jorge Zevallos Quiñones, *Huacas Y Huaqueros En Trujillo Durante El Virreinato, 1535–1835* (Trujillo, Perú: Editora Normas Legales, 1994).

16. Eaton, *The Collection of Osteological Material from Machu Picchu*, 41.

17. Eaton Journal, Aug. 20, 1912, YPEP 19–18.

18. Eaton, *The Collection of Osteological Material from Machu Picchu*, 49.

CHAPTER FOURTEEN: THE DEBATE

1. "A Populist Precursor: Guillermo Billinghurst," Peter Blanchard, *Journal of Latin American Studies*, 9:2 (Nov. 1977), 256.

2. Luis E. Valcárcel (LEV), *Memorias* (Lima: Instituto de Estudios Peruanos, 1981), 161–162.

3. For Bingham's negotiations, see HB to Hadley, June 8, July 11, Oct. 4, 1912, ATH 8–008 0145.

4. "En La Universidad," ECL, June 9, 1912.

5. "La situación en Cuzco," *ECL*, June 12, 1912.

6. Luis E. Valcárcel (LEV), *Memorias* (Lima: Instituto de Estudios Peruanos, 1981), 162.

7. Luis Valcárcel, black-cover notebook, 1912. Valcárcel Archives, Instituto Nacional de Cultura, Lima, Peru.

8. Howard to State Department, Aug. 31, 1912, M746 NA 823.927/20.

9. My narration comes from HB Journal, Aug. 24–25, 1912, YPEP 19–5.

10. Howard to State Department, Nov. 13, 1912, NA M746 823.927/29.

11. "La administración del Augusto B. Leguía," *ECL*, Sept. 25, 1912.

12. HB to Hadley, Oct. 4, 1912, ATH 8–008 0145.

13. "Nuestras riquezas arqueológicas," *ECL*, Oct. 25, 1912.

14. HB to Hadley, Oct. 4, 1912, ATH 8–008 0145.

15. "Nuestras riquezas arqueológicas," *ECL*, Oct. 25, 1912.

16. HB to Hadley, Oct. 26, 1912, ATH 8–008 0145.

17. "Nuestras Riquezas Arqueológicas; Una carta del Sr. Hiram Bingham," *ECC*, Nov. 14, 1912.

18. "Comunicados," *ECL*, Oct. 30, 1912.

19. "Comisión científica," *ECC*, Nov. 7, 1912.

CHAPTER FIFTEEN: THE PRIZE

1. JGC, "Una Excursión a Machu Picchu," *Revista Universitaria*, 1:2 (Sept. 1912), 20–21.

2. JGC to Riva-Agüero, October 11, 1912, in *Obras Completas de Jose de la Riva-Agüero. IIV, Epistolario.*

3. Heald Journal, Nov. 5–6, 1912, YPEP 19–24.

4. JGC, "Expedición Científica de la Universidad de Yale al Cuzco," *Boletín de la Sociedad Geográfica de Lima*, 29:3–4 (1914).

5. Mariana Mould de Pease has previously speculated that the Yale expeditions kept artifacts from view of the Peruvians. In what follows, I suggest there might be truth to that statement. Mariana Mould

de Pease, *Machu Picchu y El Código de Ética de La Sociedad de Arqueología Americana: Una invitación al diálogo intercultural* (Lima: Consejo Nacional de Ciencia y Tecnologia; Pontificia Universidad Católica del Perú Fondo Editorial; Instituto Nacional de Cultura; Universidad Nacional San Antonio Abad del Cuzco, 2003), 51.

6. HB, "The Story of Machu Picchu: The Peruvian Expeditions of the National Geographic Society and Yale University," *National Geographic Magazine* (February 1915), 215.

7. For quotes from Erdis in this section, see Erdis Journal, 1912. YPEP 19–20.

8. Quoted in HB, *Machu Picchu, a Citadel of the Incas* [*MPCI*] (New Haven, London: Pub. for the National Geographic Society; H. Milford, Oxford University Press, 1930), 192.

9. For more, see Brian M. Fagan, *The Rape of the Nile: Tomb Robbers, Tourists, and Archaeologists in Egypt* (Boulder: Westview Press, 2004); Thomas Hoving, *Tutankhamun, the Untold Story* (New York: Simon & Schuster, 1978).

10. Erdis Journal, Aug. 8, 1912, YPEP 19–20.

11. Ibid., Oct. 30, 1912.

12. HB to AMB, Nov. 20, 1912, HB 15–41.

13. David Hurst Thomas, *Skull Wars: Kennewick Man, Archaeology, and the Battle for Native American Identity* (New York: Basic Books, 2000),144–156.

14. Quoted in HB, *MPCI*, 229.

15. HB to Cook, May 16, 1915, YPEP 11–162.

16. "La industria de un anticuario," *ECC,* June 16, 1912; "Conservación de reliquias históricas," *ECL,* July 9, 1912.

17. Valcárcel speech in black-cover notebook (on inside cover is plan of Ccoricancha, 1912), Valcárcel Archives, Instituto Nacional de Cultura, Lima, Peru. For more on Cuzco's regional pride, see Donato Amado Gonzáles, "'El Serrano Esta Tan Terriblemente Exacerbado': La Lucha por un Regionalismo Autónomo (Cusco 1900–1930)," in *Genesis del Regionalismo y Localismo Cusqueño,* ed. Rosanno Calvo (Cusco: Municipalidad de Wanchaq, 1998).

18. Signed Oct. 31, 1912, published in Cuzco, "Exploración científica," *ECC,* Nov. 20, 1912.

19. Howard to HB, Nov. 13, 1912, YPEP 2–26.

INTERLUDE: TUPAC AMARU

1. Catherine J. Julien, "Francisco De Toledo and His Campaign against the Incas," *Colonial Latin American Review,* 16:2 (2007), 264.

2. D. A. Brading, "The Incas and the Renaissance: The Royal Commentaries of Inca Garcilaso De La Vega," *Journal of Latin American Studies,* 18:1 (1986), 1.

3. Pedro Sarmiento de Gamboa, Brian S. Bauer, and Vania Smith, *The History of the Incas* (Austin: University of Texas Press, 2007), 205.

4. John Hemming, *The Conquest of the Incas* (New York: Harcourt, Brace, 1970), 416.

5. Julien, "Francisco De Toledo and His Campaign against the Incas," 263–64.

6. Hemming, *The Conquest of the Incas,* 424; Martín de Murúa and Manuel Ballesteros Gaibrois, *Historia General Del Perú* (Madrid: Historia 16, 1987), 284.

7. Hemming, *The Conquest of the Incas,* 459, 461, 617.

8. For more on Guaman Poma, see Rolena Adorno, *Guáman Poma: Writing and Resistance in Colonial Peru* (Austin: University of Texas Press, 1986); Adorno, "Colonial Reform or Utopia? Guaman Poma's Empire of the Four Parts of the World," in *Amerindian Images and the Legacy of Columbus,* eds. René Jara and Nicholas Spadaccini (Minneapolis: University of Minnesota Press, 1992), 346–74; *Guaman Poma and His Illustrated Chronicle from Colonial Peru: From a Century of Scholarship to a New Era of Reading* (Copenhagen: Museum Tusculanum Press, University of Copenhagen & Royal Library, 2001); Adorno and Ivan Boserup, *New Studies of the Autograph Manuscript of Felipe Guaman Poma De Ayala's Nueva Corónica Y Buen Gobierno* (Copenhagen: Museum Tusculanum Press, 2003).

CHAPTER SIXTEEN: BETWEEN THE POLES

1. Bingham pasted more than 50 clippings about his return in his scrapbook. "Peru Hostile to Scientists Here After Hardships," *Evening Telegram,* Dec. 19, 1912; "Ministry of Peru Objects to American

Exploration," *Chicago Tribune,* Dec. 20, 1912; "Braves Death to Dig Human Skulls 60,000 Years Old," *Chicago Examiner,* Dec. 20, 1912. These and below in YPEP 35–52.

2. For eighteenth-century Spanish traditions of reading Amerindian sites as points of Christian origins, see Jorge Cañizares-Esguera, *How to Write the History of the New World: Histories Epistemologies, and Identities in the Eighteenth-Century Atlantic World* (Stanford: Stanford University Press, 2001), 323.

3. "At a Buried Inca City," *NY Evening Post,* Dec. 19, 1912.

4. "Hundred Skulls of People Who Lived in Peru 60,000 Years Ago are Brought to NY by Yale Professor," *Enquirer* (Cincinnati), Dec. 10, 1912; "Lost in Clouds After Digging in Lost City," *Evening Mail,* Dec. 19, 1912.

5. "Scholars and Peru," *Christian Science Monitor,* Jan. 10, 1913.

6. Thomas Barbour and Alfred W. Tozzer to State Department, Nov. 14, 1912, NA 823.927/23.

7. HB to Barbour, Jan. 17, 1914, BFP 19–95.

8. Clements Markham to John Scott Keltie, Jan. 18, 1913; J.S. Keltie to Markham, Jan. 24, 1913, RGS CB8.

9. "Peruvian Trophies Here," *Yale Daily News,* Jan. 13, 1913.

10. Grosvenor to HB, March 18, 1913, YPEP 15–241.

11. Grosvenor to Hadley, May 5, 1913, YPEP 15–243.

12. "Lost City in the Clouds Found After Centuries," *NYT,* June 15, 1913.

13. See "Important discoveries made in Peruvian tombs," *New Orleans,* June 24, 1913; "Cannibalism in South America," *Philadelphia Enquirer,* Feb. 21, 1914, YPEP 35–52.

14. Emma Mertins Thom to HB, Nov. 12, 1915, BFP 12–177; Isabel Inez de Guzman Garrison to HB, Feb. 8, 1915, YPEP 11–153.

15. Respectively, Victor Appleton (Howard Garis), *Tom Swift & his Big Tunnel, or, The Hidden City of the Andes* (New York: Grosset & Dunlap, 1916); Gaston Leroux, *The Bride of the Sun* (New York: McBride Nast, 1915); Coe Hayne, *The City in the Clouds,* or *A Tale of the Last Inca* (Elgin: David C. Cook, 1919). Citations courtesy of the wonderful website on "lost race" fiction, "Violet Books: Antiquarian Supernatural Fiction," http://www.violetbooks.com.

16. "The Lost City," *Boston Morning Herald,* June 16, 1913, YPEP 35–52.

17. The first formally chartered Indian organization in America, the Society of American Indians, was established in 1911. David Hurst Thomas, *Skull Wars: Kennewick Man, Archaeology, and the Battle for Native American Identity* (New York: Basic Books, 2000), 182. For the concept of imperial nostalgia, see Renato Rosaldo, *Culture and Truth: The Remaking of Social Analysis* (Boston: Beacon Press, 1993).

18. See Thomas L. Karnes, "Hiram Bingham and His Obsolete Shibboleth," *Diplomatic History,* 3 (1979), for more on Monroe Doctrine debate.

19. Albert Bushnell Hart, "Latin Americans Don't Trust Us," *Los Angeles Times,* Oct. 2, 1915.

20. HB to Henry W. Farnam, March 1, 1913, BFP.

21. George H. Blakeslee to HB, Nov. 25, 1913, BFP 21–114.

22. Farnam to HB, March 6, 1913, BFP 19–98.

23. HB to Charles H. Ludington, Sept. 26, 1913, BFP 20–110.

24. Augustus Knudsen to HB, Nov. 12, 1913, BFP 21–113.

25. Lydia Bingham to HB, Oct. 5, 1913, BFP 21–111.

26. *Every Week,* Sept. 11, 1916, BFP 97–13.

27. WB, *Hiram Bingham: A Personal History* (Boulder, CO: Bin Lan Zhen Publishers, 1982), 127.

28. Andrew McFarlane Davis to HB, March 19, 1913, BFP 19–99.

29. David Grann, *The Lost City of Z: A Tale of Deadly Obsession in the Amazon* (New York: Doubleday, 2009), 147.

30. Candice Millard, *River of Doubt: Theodore Roosevelt's Darkest Journey* (New York: Doubleday, 2005), 26.

31. Ibid., 52.

32. "Scientific World Is Already in Turmoil on Whether Mr. Roosevelt Found a River," *New York Herald,* May 8, 1914; "Experts Divided on Roosevelt Discovery," *NY Sun,* May 8, 1914, YPEP 35–52.

33. "Found Bones of Lost Explorers in Peruvian Jungle," *NYT,* Feb.18, 1914. See YPEP 35–52 for further coverage.

34. "New Haven, Conn.," *NYT,* Feb.18, 1914.

35. Grosvenor to HB, Jan. 16, 1914, YPEP 15–247.
36. See correspondence among Bingham, F.W. Shipley, and Aleš Hrdlička, March 1914, BFP 22–124.
37. HB to R.S. Woodward, Feb. 12, 1913, YPE 8–77.
38. Bingham to Ulloa, April 14, 1914, English/Spanish Versions, BFP 22–127.

CHAPTER SEVENTEEN: TEMPTATION

1. HB Journal July 4, 1912, YPEP 19–5.
2. Identification and description of pieces come from HB, *Machu Picchu, a Citadel of the Incas* [*MPCI*] (New Haven: published for the National Geographic Society; H. Milford, Oxford University Press, 1930), 161; LEV, *Machu Picchu, El Más Famoso Monumento Arqueológico Del Perú* (Buenos Aires: Editorial Universitaria de Buenos Aires, 1964), 81–82.
3. "Memoria del Presidente de la Sociedad," *Boletín de la Sociedad Geográfica de Lima,* 29:3–4 (1914), 12.
4. *El Siglo XX en el Peru a Traves de* El Comercio; Tomo II 1911/1912, 233–34.
5. See Eaton Journal, Oct. 5, 1912, YPEP 19–18.
6. For Cuzco's recession, see José Tamayo Herrera, *Historia Social Del Cuzco Republicano* (Lima, 1978), 108.
7. Calculations made using Lawrence H. Officer, "Dollar-Pound Exchange Rate From 1791," MeasuringWorth, 2008. URL: http://www.measuringworth.org/exchangepound/; Samuel H. Williamson, "Six Ways to Compute the Relative Value of a U.S. Dollar Amount, 1790 to Present," MeasuringWorth, 2009. URL http://www.measuringworth.com/uscompare/
8. T.A. Alvistur to HB, March 5, 1914, BFP 22–124.
9. HB to Howard, Feb. 14, 1913, BFP 19–96.
10. HB Memo to Hardy, April 3, 1914, BFP 22–127.
11. Alvistur to HB, May 28, 1914, BFP 22–131; HB to J. Louis Schaefer, June 1, 1914, BFP 23–132.
12. Receipt, June 3, 1914, Bingham cabled $2,425 (500 pounds) to Mollendo to pay Mr. Alvistur, New England Navigation Co. Railroad Company, Sept. 15, 1914, BFP 103–82.
13. Bingham later protested being asked to purchase any more artifacts for Yale's museum and refers to the last collection of Peruvian artifacts that he had to "swing" by himself; see HB to Stokes, June 7, 1917, YRG 4, RU 49, Records of Sec. Office, Yale U, Anson Phelps Stokes, Box 10, Folder 0144. For their inclusion with the Machu Picchu artifacts, see HB to Jeanne Kirkpatrick, May 19, 1915, YPEP 11–162.
14. HB to Schaefer, Nov. 19, 1914, BFP.
15. HB to Howell Cheney, Dec. 14 or 15, 1913, BFP 21–116.
16. Erdis Journal, April 22, 1914, YPEP 21–43.
17. For de-emphasis of archaeology, see "Memoria Correspondiente al Año 1914 que el Presidente de la Sociedad Geográfica Ingeniero José Balta presenta a la Junta General," *Boletín de la Sociedad Geográfica de Lima,* 30 (1915), xv; "La Expedición Científica de la Universidad de Yale," *ECC,* May 28, 1914.
18. Julio C. Tello, *Presente Y Futuro Del Museo Nacional* (Lima: Instituto Cultural "Julio C. Tello," 1952); César W. Astuhuamán Gonzáles and Richard E. Daggett, "Julio C. Tello, The Origin Seeker," *Chasqui,* Oct. 2005, 3.
19. Hrdlička to HB, Feb. 2, 1915, YPEP 11–152.
20. Erdis Journal, May 8, 1914, YPEP 21–43.
21. "Comisión Científica," *ECC,* May 9, 1914.
22. Hardy Journal, May 7, 1914, YPEP 22–46.
23. See Peruvian Expedition of 1914–15, Official Circulars, YPEP 20–36.
24. Hardy Journal, July 13, 1914, YPEP 22–46.
25. HB to Bumstead, Sept. 30, 1914, YPEP 10–142.
26. HB, "The Story of Machu Picchu; The Peruvian Expeditions of the National Geographic Society and Yale University," *National Geographic Magazine,* Feb. 1915, 209.
27. See Johan Reinhard, *The Ice Maiden: Inca Mummies, Mountain Gods, and Sacred Sites in the Andes* (Washington, DC: National Geographic Society, 2005).
28. Erdis Journal, Sept. 12, 1914, YPEP 21–43.

29. Manuel F. [Arispe] to HB, July 2, 1913, BFP 20–107.
30. Erdis Journal, Nov. 7, 1914, YPEP 21–43.
31. Edwin A, Meserve to HB, Oct. 16, 1914, YPEP 11–144.
32. "Liner Metapan Sunk in Harbor Crash; 168 Saved," *NYT*, Oct. 16, 1914.
33. HB to Meserve, Oct. 17, 1914; Meserve to HB, Oct. 21, 23, 1914, YPEP 11–144.
34. E. L. Anderson Journal, Nov. 26, 1914, YPEP 20–30.
35. Hardy Journal, Jan. 21, 1915, YPEP 22–46.
36. Ibid., Jan. 14, 1915.
37. Ibid., Jan. 3, 1915.
38. Ibid., Jan.14, 1914.

CHAPTER EIGHTEEN: ROADS TO RUINS

1. For the Mexico case, see Carmen Ruiz, "Insiders and Outsiders in Mexican Archaeology (1890–1930)" (University of Texas at Austin, Ph.D. diss., 2003).
2. "Por la arqueología nacional," *ECL*, April 5, 1915.
3. HB to Tello, Morkill, Bravo, Ballen, Llona, Schaefer, Blaisdell, et al., Jan. 23, 1915, YPEP 11–150.
4. Journal of Osgood Hardy, 1914–1915, March 1, 1915, YPEP; Journal of E. C. Erdis, Sept. 30, 1915, YPEP.
5. David Ford to mother, April 6, 1915, NGS.
6. "Una sesión del Instituto Histórico," *El Sol* [Cuzco] (ES), April 21, 1915.
7. "El Condor Pasa" was later adapted by Paul Simon and Art Garfunkel for their final album, *Bridge over Troubled Water*.
8. HB, "The Story of Machu Picchu: The National Geographic Society-Yale University Explorations in Peru," *National Geographic Magazine*, Feb. 1915, 184.
9. "Yale Party Off for Peru," *Boston Evening Transcript*, March 4, 1915, YPEP 35–52.
10. HB Journal Letter to AMB, April 18-May 20, 1915, YPEP 20–33.
11. Ibid.
12. Ibid.
13. HB to Cook, May 16, 1915, YPEP 11–162.
14. "Monumentos históricos," *ECC*, Nov. 29, 1912.
15. Erdis Journal, June 28, 1915, YPEP 21–44.
16. Ibid., June 9, 1915.

CHAPTER NINETEEN: THE TRIAL OF HIRAM BINGHAM

1. Luis E. Valcárcel (LEV), *Memorias* (Lima: Instituto de Estudios Peruanos, 1981), 186.
2. "Antiguedades peruanas," *ECL*, June 4, 1915; "El Instituto Histórico del Perú," *ECL*, June 16, 1915; "Las Investigaciones Arqueologicas," *ECL*, June 19, 1915.
3. Luis E. Valcárcel (LEV), *Memorias*, 186.
4. In late April, Vega Enríquez had tried and failed to show Bingham what were supposedly Spanish Viceroy don Francisco de Toledo's instructions for the capture of Tupac Amaru and the destruction of Vilcabamba in 1572. See Giesecke to HB, April 23, 1915, YPEP 11–160. For more on Vega Enríquez, see Rossano Calvo C., "Localismo, Tradicion y Proyectos Endogenos en el Cusco Aldeano (1900–1955)," in *Genesis del Regionalismo y Localismo Cusqueño*, ed. Rosanno Calvo (Cusco: Municipalidad de Wanchaq, 1998), 46–52.
5. Luis E. Valcárcel (LEV), *Memorias*, 186.
6. LEV Yellow notebook, 191[2?]—1915. Valcárcel Archives, Instituto Nacional de Cultura, Lima, Peru.
7. See Carlos Eduardo Arroyo Reyes, *Nuestros años diez: La Asociación Pro-Indigena, el levantamiento de Rumi Maqui, y el incaismo modernista* (LibrosEnRed, 2005).
8. Leo Deuel, *Conquistadors without Swords: Archaeologists in the Americas; an Account with Original Narratives* (New York: St. Martin's Press, 1967).
9. LEV Yellow notebook, 191[2?]—1915 Valcárcel Archives, Instituto Nacional de Cultura, Lima, Peru.
10. Hardy Journal, June 15, 1915, YPEP 22–46.

11. HB Journal, July–August, 1915, YPEP 20–35.
12. "La criminal excavacion en Machupiccho," *ES*, June 16, 1915.
13. HB to Grosvenor, June 22, 1915, YPEP 15–256.
14. "Una gran Sociedad Geográfica," *ECL*, July 14, 1915.
15. William Morkill to HB, June 19, 1915, YPEP 11–166.
16. David E. Ford Journal, June 11, 12, 18, 1915, YPEP 22–45.
17. Brooke Larson, *Trials of Nation Making: Liberalism, Race, and Ethnicity in the Andes, 1810–1910* (Cambridge: Cambridge University Press, 2004), 174.
18. Series of 7 questions for Luis E. Valcárcel with his answers, June 26, 1915, YPEP 2–25.
19. HB to Eaton, June 23, 1915, YPEP 11–166.
20. HB to Gregory, June 22, 1915, YPEP 11–166.
21. Description of scene and quotes that follow come from Hardy Journal, July 8, 1915, YPEP 22–46.
22. Draft of speech in HB's hand, YPEP 2–26.
23. Richard E. Daggett, "Julio C. Tello: An Account of His Rise to Prominence in Peruvian Archaeology," in *The Life and Writings of Julio C. Tello: America's First Indigenous Archaeologist*, ed. Richard L. Burger (Iowa City: University of Iowa Press, 2009), 17–18.
24. HB to Tello, Morkill, Bravo, Ballen, Llona, Schaefer, Blaisdell, et al., Jan. 23, 1915, YPEP 11–150.
25. Luis E. Valcárcel (LEV), *Memorias*, 187.
26. Ford to Mother, Aug. 5, 1915, NGS Archives.
27. P. Dieguez & R to HB, June 7, 1915; Jorge O. Young to Señor Presidente de la Comisión Cientifica Norte Américana de Objetos Incaicos, June 7, 1915; Belisario Rosas to HB, June 11, 1915; all YPEP 11–166.
28. Hardy Journal, Aug. 17, 1915, YPEP 22–46.
29. Bingham to Schaefer, Nov. 10, 1915, BFP; Bingham to Stokes, June 7, 1917, Records of Sec. Office, Yale 1899–1953 Anson Phelps Stokes, YRG 4, RU 49, Manuscripts and Archives, Yale University Library, 10–0142.
30. Hardy Journal, Aug. 19, 1915, YPEP 22–46.

CHAPTER TWENTY: AIRBORNE

1. E.S. Dana to HB, Sept. 30, 1915, YPEP 12–173.
2. "Peruvian Expedition Returns," *Yale Daily News*, Oct. 12, 1915; "Professor Bingham Had to Fight Weird Charges," *New Haven Register*, Oct. 11, 1915.
3. Grosvenor to HB, Dec. 29, 1915, YPEP 15–258.
4. HB to Erdis, Aug. 24, 1915, YPEP 12–171.
5. "El Dia / La reorganizacíon del Museo de Historia Nacional," *ECL*, Sept. 22, 1915; Erdis Journal, Dec. 3, 1915, YPEP 21–44.
6. Erdis to HB, Dec. 25, 1915, YPEP 12–179.
7. Emilio Gutiérrez de Quintanilla, *Memoria Del Director Del Museo De Historia Nacional; Esfuerzos I Resistencias 1919–1921*, 2 vols. (Lima: Taller Tipográfico del Museo, 1921), 282.
8. Erdis Journal, Jan 11, 1916, YPEP 21–44.
9. Ibid., Jan. 27, 1916.
10. Clipping—"Las excursiones en las ruinas de Ollantaitambo / Objetos arqueológicos," *La Prensa*, Dec. 22, 1915—found in Valcárcel notebook, small black, with only front cover, 1916. Valcárcel Archives, Instituto Nacional de Cultura, Lima, Peru. "Por la Historia Nacional," *El Sol*, Aug. 14, 1916.
11. HB to Grosvenor, Feb. 21, 1916, NGS.
12. HB to Morkill, Jan. [Date not given], 1916, YPEP 12–84.
13. "Land of the Incas His Lecture Theme," *Washington Herald*, March 25, 1916.
14. See Orin Starn, *Ishi's Brain; In Search of America's Last "Wild" Indian* (New York: Norton, 2004)
15. Hardy to HB, Sept. 7, 1915, YPEP 12–172.
16. WB, *Hiram Bingham: A Personal History* (Boulder, CO: Bin Lan Zhen Publishers, 1982), 172.
17. Grosvenor to HB, May 24, 1916, NGS.
18. HB to Grosvenor, Jan.10, 1917, NGS.
19. "Who's Who—And Why," *Saturday Evening Post*, May 17, 1925.

20. "Colonel Accepts Republicans' Plea to Make the Fight," *NYT,* May 23, 1916.
21. "Americans They Have Met," *NYT,* May 30, 1916.
22. "The Ananias Club," *Journal Courier,* Sept. 11, 1916, BFP 97–13.
23. Kathryn Day Lasila and Mark Alden Branch, "Whose Skull and Bones?" *Yale Alumni Magazine,* May/June 2006, 20.
24. AB, *Explorer of Machu Picchu: Portrait of Hiram Bingham* (Greenwich, CT: Triune Books, 2000), 325.
25. Hiram Bingham, "Evidences of Symbolism in the Land of the Incas," *The Builder,* 2:12 (1916), 365.
26. Rudyard Kipling, "The Palace," *The Builder,* 2:12 (1916), 365. Clipped and in Bingham scrapbook, BFP 97–13.

EPILOGUE: RETURNS

1. "Republicans Bolt Bingham for Holt," *NYT,* Nov. 27, 1924.
2. Duff Gilfond, "A Superior Person," *The American Mercury,* March 1930, 307.
3. "New Senators Are Making Good in Nation's Capitol," *Boston Transcript,* Feb. 16, 1925, BFP 74–37.
4. "Army Blimp Takes Senator to Capitol," *NYT,* July 27, 1929.
5. "A Defender of the Faith," *Boston Evening Transcript,* Jan. 26, 1927.
6. Gilfond, "A Superior Person," 308.
7. "Press Criticizes Bingham's Practices," *NYT,* Oct. 21, 1929.
8. AB, *The Tiffany Fortune and Other Chronicles of a Connecticut Family* (Chestnut Hill, MA: Abeel & Leet, 1996), 200–2. For more on Bingham's relationship with his family after the divorce, see WB, *Hiram Bingham: A Personal History* (Boulder, CO: Bin Lan Zhen Publishers, 1982). For the unflinching, moving perspective of one of Bingham's daughters-in-law, see June Rossbach Bingham Birge, *Braided Lives: A 20th-Century Pursuit of Happiness* (Smithtown, NY: Straus Historical Society, 2008).
9. Interview with WB, Aug. 1972, BFP Accession 87-M–89, 7–27.
10. HB to Giesecke, Aug. 9, 1941, IRA AG–0140.
11. Luis E. Valcárcel, *Tempestad en los Andes* (Lima: Editorial Minerva, 1927).
12. Philip Ainsworth Means to LEV, July 24, 1936. Valcárcel Archives, Instituto Nacional de Cultura, Lima, Peru (INC).
13. Red notebook belonging to Valcárcel labeled Estados Unidos, 1941, INC.
14. Luis E. Valcárcel, "De mi viaje a los Estados Unidos," *Revista Iberoamericana,* May 1943, 274.
15. HB to LEV, Aug. 31, 1948, Epistolario, INC.
16. HB to LEV, Aug. 31, 1948, Epistolario, INC.
17. "El Profesor Hiram Bingham en el Cuzco," *ECC,* Oct. 14, 1948.
18. "Las Ceremonias en la Historica Machu-Picchu," *ECC,* Oct. 18, 19, 22, 1948.
19. "Milestones," *Time,* June 18, 1956.
20. "Bingham ha Hecho por el Cuzco Mas Que Muchos Cuzqueños Dijo Chavez," *El Comercio,* Aug. 23, 1956.
21. Author interview with Frank Valcárcel, Jan. 2006.
22. Mariana Mould de Pease, *Machu Picchu y El Código de Ética de La Sociedad de Arqueología Americana: Una invitación al diálogo intercultural* (Lima: Consejo Nacional de Ciencia y Tecnologia; Pontificia Universidad Católica del Perú Fondo Editorial; Instituto Nacional de Cultura; Universidad Nacional San Antonio Abad del Cuzco, 2003), 44.
23. Philip Ainsworth Means, "Review: Inca Land, Exploration in the Highlands of Peru, by Hiram Bingham," *American Anthropologist,* 25:1 (1923), 100.
24. Philip Ainsworth Means, "Review: Machu Picchu, a Citadel of the Incas, by Hiram Bingham," *American Historical Review,* 35:4 (1930), 901.
25. Luis E. Valcárcel, *Machu Picchu: El Más Famoso Monumento Arqueológico del Perú* (Buenos Aires: Editorial Universitaria de Buenos Aires, 1964), 58–61, 88–91.
26. Luis Miguel and Maria Isabel Remy Glave, *Estructura Agraria Y Vida Rural En Una Región Andina/Ollantaytambo Entre Los Siglos Xvi-Xix* (Cusco: Centro de Estudios Rurales Andinos Bartolomé de las Casas/Archivos de Historia Andina, 1983).
27. John Howland Rowe, "Machu Picchu a La Luz De Documentos Del Siglo Xvi," *Histórica,* 14:1 (1990).

28. See Richard Burger and Lucy Salazar, *Machu Picchu: Unveiling the Mystery of the Incas* (New Haven, CT: Yale University Press, March 2004); Susan A. Niles, "The Nature of Inca Royal Estates," in *Machu Picchu: Unveiling the Mystery of the Incas;* Niles, *The Shape of Inca History: Narrative and Architecture in an Andean Empire* (Iowa City: University of Iowa Press, 1999).

29. For more on Savoy's story, see Gene Savoy, *Antisuy: the Search for the Lost Cities of the Amazon* (New York: Simon & Schuster, 1970); Savoy, *Vilcabamba: Last City of the Incas* (London: Hale, 1970).

30. John Verano, "Human Skeletal Remains from Machu Picchu: A Reexamination of the Peabody Museum's Collections from the Peruvian Expedition of 1912," in *The 1912 Yale Peruvian Scientific Expedition Collections from Machu Picchu: Human and Animal Remains,* eds. Richard L. Burger and Lucy C. Salazar (New Haven: Dept. of Anthropology Division of Anthropology, Peabody Museum of Natural History, 2003).

31. For more on modern research and conclusions on Machu Picchu, see Richard L. Burger et al., *The 1912 Yale Peruvian Scientific Expedition Collections from Machu Picchu: Human and Animal Remains;* Instituto Nacional de Cultura-Cusco, *Machupicchu: Historia, Sacralidad E Identidad* (Cusco, Perú: Instituto Nacional de Cultura, 2005); Federico Kauffmann Doig, *Machu Picchu: Tesoro Inca* (Lima: ICPNA, Instituto Cultural Peruano Norteamericano, 2005); Kenneth R. Wright and Alfredo Valencia Zegarra, *Machu Picchu: A Civil Engineering Marvel* (Reston, Va.: American Society of Civil Engineers, 2000).

32. Hiram Bingham, "Types of Machu Picchu Pottery," *American Anthropologist,* 17:2 (1915).

33. Johan Reinhard, *Machu Picchu: Exploring an Ancient Sacred Center* (Los Angeles: Cotsen Institute of Archaeology, University of California, 2007). For Italian Giulo Magli's theory, see Ker Than, "Machu Picchu Is Mini Re-creation of a Mythic Landscape, *National Geographic News,* June 15, 2009, http://news.nationalgeographic.com/news/2009/06/090615-machu-picchu.html

34. Luis Guillermo Lumbreras, "Machu Piqchu, El Mausoleo Del Emperador," in *Machupicchu: Historia, Sacralidad E Identidad,* ed. Instituto Nacional de Cultura-Cusco (Cusco, Perú: Instituto Nacional de Cultura, 2005), 14.

35. "Por la Historia Nacional," *El Sol,* Aug. 14, 1916.

36. For more on the purchase of José Lucas Caparó Muñiz's collection, see Luis E. Valcárcel (LEV), *Memorias* (Lima: Instituto de Estudios Peruanos, 1981), 214; "The Reminiscences of Albert A. Giesecke" (Oral History Research Office, Columbia University, 1963); Mould de Pease, *Machu Picchu y El Código de Ética de La Sociedad de Arqueología Americana,* 107.

37. Stokes to Hon. M. de Freyre, Nov. 25, 1918, APS 11–0144.

38. HB to Grosvenor, Nov. 28, 1916, YPEP 16–265.

39. Grosvenor to HB, Nov. 29, 1916, YPEP 16–265.

40. Eduardo Higginson to National Geographic Society, Oct. 29, 1920, NGS.

41. "Yale University's Memorandum in Support of Motion to Dismiss Peru's Amended Complaint for Failure to State a Claim," *Republic of Peru v. Yale University* (U.S. District Court for the District of Connecticut, Oct. 16, 2009), 5.

42. HB to Grosvenor, Nov. 1, 1920, NGS.

43. HB to Richard S. Lull, Director of Peabody Museum, Nov. 3, 1922; HB to Lull, July 14, 1923. Both in Peabody Museum of Natural History, Yale University, Records (RU 471). Manuscripts and Archives, Yale University Library, Box 3, Folder 18.

44. "Yale University's Memorandum in Support of Motion to Dismiss Peru's Amended Complaint for Failure to State a Claim," Republic of Peru v. Yale University (U.S. District Court for the District of Connecticut, Oct. 16, 2009), 26.

45. Lull to HB, Oct. 17, 1930. Peabody Museum of Natural History, Yale University, Records (RU 471). Manuscripts and Archives, Yale University Library, Box 3, Folder 18.

46. See Emilio Gutiérrez de Quintanilla, *Memoria Del Director Del Museo De Historia Nacional; Esfuerzos I Resistencias 1919–1921,* 2 vols. (Lima: Taller Tipográfico del Museo, 1921).

47. For Cusqueño distress over the lack of the artifacts, see "La Expedición a Machupichju," *El Sol,* July 19, 1928, as cited in Keely Beth Maxwell, "Lost Cities and Exotic Cows: Constructing the Space of Nature an d Culture in the Machu Picchu Historic Sanctuary, Peru" (Ph.D. diss., Yale University, 2004), 103. For evidence that Peruvians believed the Patallacta artifacts were from Machu Picchu through 1961, see "Para Establecer Museo de Sitio en las Ruinas," *ECC,* March 2, 1961.

48. Ernesto "Che" Guevara, "Machu-Picchu, Enigma de Piedra en America," *Siete* (Panama), December 1953, reprinted in *Casa de las Americas* (Havana) 28:163 (July-August 1987), 51. I thank Hugh Thomson for pointing me to this quotation.

49. See Mike French and Gilles Verschuere's 2005 interview with Deborah Nadoolman, costume designer for *Raiders of the Lot Ark*, on TheRaider.Net, http://www.theraider.net/features/interviews/deborah_nadoolman.php

50. For rumors of looted treasure, see O. Blanco G., "Machu Picchu: cincuentenario de un saqueo?" *El Sol*, 23 (March 1961), as cited in Keely Beth Maxwell, "Lost Cities and Exotic Cows: Constructing the Space of Nature an d Culture in the Machu Picchu Historic Sanctuary, Peru" (Ph.D. diss., Yale University, 2004), 103. For Charaja, see "Descubridor de Camino Real Incaico," *ECC*, May 12, 1961.

51. "Para Establecer Museo de Sitio en las Ruinas," *ECC*, March 2, 1961; "Universidad Pide Devolver Patrimonio Arqueologico," *ECC*, April 10, 1961; "Universidad Apoyara Gestiones de Patronato Arqueologico Para Devolucion de Ceramicas," *ECC*, June 15, 1961.

52. HB Jr. to Giesecke, May 2, 1961. Archivo Giesecke del Instituto Riva-Agüero (IRA), AG-D–033.

53. 1962 February 8, HB Jr. to Giesecke. IRA, AG–0141.

54. "Viaje al Cuzco—20 Julio 1961," in LEV Diarios de Viajes, INC.

55. My own inadequate translation of "Quién otra vez sepulta los adioses?" from Canto VIII and "Duvuélveme el esclavo que enterraste!" from Canto X. There is nothing like the poem in the original. Pablo Neruda, *Alturas de Macchu Picchu* (Santiago, Chile: Nacsimiento, 1954).

56. "En Nueva York, 1962," in LEV Diarios de Viajes, INC.

57. Luis E. Valcárcel, *Machu Picchu: El Más Famoso Monumento Arqueológico del Perú*, 81–82.

58. Luis E. Valcárcel (LEV), *Memorias*, 186.

59. Ward Stavig, "Túpac Amaru, the Body Politics, and the Embodiment of Hope: Inca Heritage and Social Justice in the Andes," in *Death, Dismemberment, and Memory: Body Politics in Latin America*, ed. Lyman L. Johnson (Albuquerque: University of New Mexico Press, 2004), 56–57.

60. Roger Atwood, *Stealing History: Tomb Raiders, Smugglers, and the Looting of the Ancient World* (New York: St. Martin's Press, 2004).

61. My timeline of Yale's and Peru's negotiations is drawn from Arthur Lubow, "The Possessed," *NYT Magazine*, June 24, 2007.

62. For various sides of the debate, see Ibid.; James B. Cuno, *Who Owns Antiquity? Museums and the Battle over Our Ancient Heritage* (Princeton: Princeton University Press, 2008); Peter Watson and Cecilia Todeschini, *The Medici Conspiracy: The Illicit Journey of Looted Antiquities, from Italy's Tomb Raiders to the World's Greatest Museums* (New York: BBS PublicAffairs, 2006); Sharon Waxman, *Loot: The Battle over the Stolen Treasures of the Ancient World* (New York: Times Books, 2008). The organization Saving Antiquities for Everyone keeps well abreast of the debate: http://www.savingantiquities.org/

63. My characterization comes from Lubow, "The Possessed," and various *Yale Daily News* articles, including Judy Wang, "Peru ends talks, will sue Univ.," *Yale Daily News*, March 2, 2006; Andrew Mangino, "Peru Dispute has long, murky past," *Yale Daily News*, April 14, 2006.

64. Mould de Pease, *Machu Picchu y El Código de Ética de La Sociedad de Arqueología Americana*, 72.

65. For example, see Judy Wang, "Peru ends talks, will sue Univ."; Andrew Mangino, "Peru Dispute has long, murky past."

66. Author's interview with Terry Garcia, NGS, Sept. 20, 2006.

67. As quoted in Lubow, "The Possessed," 68.

68. Christopher Heaney, "Bonesmen: Did Yale Plunder Peru?" *The New Republic*, October 23, 2006.

69. See Ricardo R. Rios, *Leyes y Resoluciones Sancionadas por los Congresos Ordinario y Extraordinario de 1901* (Lima: Imprenta de la Honorable Camara de Diputados, 1902), 112. I thank both Augusto Alvarez Calderón and Enrique Ghersi for spending so many hours explaining this argument and the intricacies of Peruvian patrimonial law to me.

70. For further evidence that Bingham believed the state had a claim on whatever treasure might be found at Machu Picchu, see the previously mentioned contract he signed with Mariano I. Ferro, who owned the lands upon which Machu Picchu rested. In it, Bingham promised him one third of what "treasures, monuments and whatever other riches that might be found" after subtracting the half promised to the Peru. Contract between HB and Jacinto Acuña, rep. of Mariano I. Ferro, Cuzco, July 9, 1912, YPEP 2.

71. See Orin Starn, *Ishi's Brain; In Search of America's Last "Wild" Indian* (New York: Norton, 2004).
72. Mould de Pease, *Machu Picchu y El Código de Ética de La Sociedad de Arqueología Americana*, 60.
73. "Movilización fue masiva," *ES*, May 10, 2006.
74. Author's Interview with David Ugarte Vega, then regional director of the National Institute of Culture, Dec. 9, 2005.
75. See Lubow, "The Possessed."
76. For disintegrating mummy wrappings, see Eaton to HB, June 24, 1915, YPEP 11–165; Richard L. Burger, "Preface," in *The 1912 Yale Peruvian Scientific Expedition Collections from Machu Picchu: Human and Animal Remains*.
77. HB, *Machu Picchu, a Citadel of the Incas* [*MPCI*] (New Haven, London: Pub. for the National Geographic Society; H. Milford, Oxford University Press, 1930), 192.
78. Thomson, *The White Rock: An Exploration of the Inca Heartland* (London: Weidenfeld & Nicolson, 2001), 97.
79. Yale Public Affairs Officer Helaine Klasky to Christopher Heaney, May 23, 2006, e-mail.
80. "First Amended Complaint against Yale University filed by Republic of Peru," Republic of Peru v. Yale University, Dockets.Justia.Com, Civil Action No. 1:08-cv–2109 (U.S. District Court for the District of Columbia, Apr. 20, 2009), 40.
81. "Yale University's Memorandum in Support of Motion to Dismiss Peru's Amended Complaint for Failure to State a Claim," Republic of Peru v. Yale University (U.S. District Court for the District of Connecticut, Oct. 16, 2009), 1.
82. Noah Mamis, "University, not Peru, is best place for cultural treasures," *Yale Daily News*, Sept. 19, 2007.
83. http://www.yaledailynews.com/articles/comments/26920.
84. See Michael F. Brown, *Who Owns Native Culture?* (Cambridge, MA: Harvard University Press, 2003) for other tugs of war over the possession of indigenous culture.
85. After listing all the measures "buyer" countries must take to combat the antiquities trade, journalist Roger Atwood recently suggested in his excellent *Stealing History: Tomb Raiders, Smugglers, and the Looting of the Ancient World* that "source" countries like Peru might also fight the problem with a legal antiquities market. By selling off some duplicate artifacts, Peru might fund further excavation, protection and community projects. It goes without saying that the idea does not extend to human remains. Roger Atwood, *Stealing History*, 247–248.
86. "monumento esplenderoso signo de la cultura Americana."
87. Kenneth R. Wright and Alfredo Valencia Zegarra, *Machu Picchu: A Civil Engineering Marvel* (Reston, VA: American Society of Civil Engineers, 2000), 43.

AFTERWORD

1. For use on foreign archaeologists, see, for example, Mariana Mould de Pease, *Machu Picchu y El Código de Ética de La Sociedad de Arqueología Americana: Una invitación al diálogo intercultural* (Lima: Consejo Nacional de Ciencia y Tecnologia; Pontificia Universidad Católica del Perú Fondo Editorial; Instituto Nacional de Cultura; Universidad Nacional San Antonio Abad del Cuzco, 2003), 75. For an excellent, challenging essay on the nineteenth-century historical context of the phrase, see Cecilia Méndez G., "Incas Sí, Indios No: Notes on Peruvian Creole Nationalism and its Contemporary Crisis," *Journal of Latin American Studies*, 28:1 (Feb. 1996), 197–225.
2. See Vincent R. Lee, *Forgotten Vilcabamba: Final Stronghold of the Incas* (SixPac Manco Publications, 2000).

Index